D1572233

Alien Neighbors, Foreign Friends

HISTORICAL STUDIES OF URBAN AMERICA

Edited by Kathleen N. Conzen, Timothy J. Gilfoyle, and James R. Grossman

ALSO IN THE SERIES

Alien Neighbors, Foreign Friends

ASIAN AMERICANS, HOUSING,
AND THE TRANSFORMATION
OF URBAN CALIFORNIA

Charlotte Brooks

The University of Chicago Press   CHICAGO & LONDON

CHARLOTTE BROOKS is assistant professor of history
at Baruch College, CUNY. Her work has appeared in the *Journal of
American History*, the *Pacific Historical Review, The Best
American History Essays 2006* (Palgrave Macmillan, 2006),
and *The Encyclopedia of Chicago* (University of Chicago
Press, 2004). This is her first book.

The University of Chicago Press, Chicago 60637
The University of Chicago Press, Ltd., London
© 2009 by The University of Chicago
All rights reserved. Published 2009
Printed in the United States of America

18 17 16 15 14 13 12 11 10 09   1 2 3 4 5

ISBN-13: 978-0-226-07597-6 (cloth)
ISBN-10: 0-226-07597-4 (cloth)

Library of Congress Cataloging-in-Publication Data

Brooks, Charlotte, 1971–
Alien neighbors, foreign friends : Asian Americans, housing, and the
transformation of urban California / Charlotte Brooks.
    p.   cm.
Includes bibliographical references and index.
ISBN-13: 978-0-226-07597-6 (cloth : alk. paper)
ISBN-10: 0-226-07597-4 (cloth : alk. paper)
1. Discrimination in housing—California—History—20th century.
2. Asian Americans—Housing—California—History—20th century.
3. Metropolitan areas—California—History—20th century.   4. Asian
Americans—Public opinion—California—History—20th century.
5. Political culture—United States—History—20th century.   I. Title.
        HD7788.76.U52B76   2009
    363.5′9950794—dc22   2008029629

For my father, Richard R. Brooks
And in memory of my mother, Peggy S. Brooks

CONTENTS

ACKNOWLEDGMENTS

I owe a deep debt of gratitude to the many institutions, colleagues, friends, and family members who have assisted and encouraged me over the past decade. Without them, I never could have completed this book.

A number of institutions supported my research and writing. Grants from The Graduate School at Northwestern University, the Historical Society of Southern California, the Harry S Truman Library Institute, the Northwestern University Department of History, the University at Albany Faculty Research Assistance Program, and the State of New York/United University Professions Joint Labor-Management Committee Individual Development Award Program helped fund research at archives throughout the country. Dissertation fellowships from The Graduate School at Northwestern University and from the International Migration Program of the Social Science Research Council, with funds provided by the Andrew W. Mellon Foundation, made possible both research and writing. Generous support from the State of New York/UUP Joint Labor-Management Committee's Dr. Nuala McGann Drescher program and the Dean's office of the Weissman School of Arts and Sciences, Baruch College, City University of New York, enabled me to complete the project.

Librarians and archivists made my research much easier than it would otherwise have been. I wish to express particular thanks to David Kessler and the rest of the archivists at the Bancroft Library, University of California, Berkeley, where I did much of my research. I am also grateful to the staff at the National Archives and Records Administration II facility; the National Archives regional office in San Bruno, California; the Hoover Institution;

the Stanford University Library Special Collections Department; the Young Library Special Collections Department at the University of California, Los Angeles; the California Historical Society North Baker Research Library; the Ethnic Studies Library and the Institute for Governmental Studies Library at UC Berkeley; the Harry S Truman Library Institute; the Franklin D. Roosevelt Presidential Library; the California State Library; the California State Archives; the University of Southern California Libraries Special Collections Department; the Huntington Library; the Los Angeles City Archives; the San Francisco Public Library's San Francisco History Room; the Los Angeles Public Library; and the New York Public Library's Schomberg Center for Research in Black Culture.

The Department of History at Northwestern University provided a vibrant and nurturing intellectual environment and one that encouraged me to think across disciplinary borders. Faculty members Joseph Barton, Henry Binford, Laura Hein, Melissa Macauley, and Michael Sherry offered assistance and valuable suggestions on various aspects of this project. Fellow graduate students, including Wallace Best, James Burkee, Marisa Chappell, Brett Gadsden, David Johnson, Karen Leroux, Michael McCoyer, and James Wolfinger, provided valuable feedback and comments on drafts of the original dissertation. I am particularly grateful to Nancy MacLean, who served as my advisor and has offered assistance from the earliest stages of this manuscript. I am very fortunate that, in her words, "advisors are forever."

While writing *Alien Neighbors, Foreign Friends*, I received much valuable input and support from a host of different sources. Dan and Candy Carlberg, Jill Brooks-Garnett and Paul Garnett, and Joy and Shigeko Nishime welcomed me into their homes as I traveled for research. Shana Bernstein, Wallace Best, Brett Gadsden, Pam Griffith, Maria Lizzi, Nancy MacLean, Gail Radford, Michael Sherry, and Amy Murrell Taylor read and commented on various chapters. Xiaojian Zhao both read and offered advice on a chapter and gave me an immensely helpful book of journalist Gilbert Woo's collected essays. Mary Dudziak, Kevin Leonard, Mae Ngai, Jeffrey Sammons, Robert Self, and Jeffrey Strickland made suggestions about different aspects of the project. Ellen Wu shared her dissertation with me, while Joel Weintraub offered assistance with the 1930 and 1940 U.S. census records. Richard Sheng generously provided copies of his family's collection of newspaper clippings and letters. Iris Berger and Dan White at the University at Albany gave me the time I needed to complete major revisions to the book. Cynthia Whittaker at Baruch College helped me secure the funding to put the final touches on the manuscript, and she and my other colleagues in Baruch's History Department have been unfailingly supportive. At the University of Chicago Press, Robert Devens and Becky Nicolaides were both incredibly patient and thoroughly professional, as was cartographer Harry D. Johnson of San Diego State University.

Finally, I wish to thank my family for their love and support over the past decade. Jim and Marlene Bentzien, Gus Brooks, Joy Brooks, Lisa Brooks, Jill Brooks-Garnett, Dara Griffith, and Jennifer Tucker all contributed in various ways to the completion of this book. My father, Richard Brooks, continually encouraged me in my work, and my mother, Peggy Brooks, never doubted that I would complete this project, even though she did not live to see it. Lastly, I am profoundly thankful for the love and support of my partner, Pam Griffith. Although I write about housing, she has shown me the true meaning of home.

ABBREVIATIONS

NSGW	Native Sons of the Golden West
OEM	Office for Emergency Management
PIC	Pacific Investment Company
PWA	Public Works Administration
SERA	State Emergency Relief Administration
SFHA	Housing Authority of the City and County of San Francisco
SSS	School of Social Studies
STDA	Sunset Transportation and Development Association
UCCRC	United Council for Civilian Relief in China
USHA	United States Housing Authority
WAHC	Western Addition Housing Council
WPA	Works Progress Administration
WPC	Workingmen's Party of California
WRA	War Relocation Authority

IN THE NOTES

ACLU-NC	American Civil Liberties Union Northern California Branch collection; California Historical Society North Baker Research Library, San Francisco
CFCU	California Federation for Civic Unity Papers; Bancroft Library, University of California, Berkeley
Fair Play Committee	Pacific Coast Committee on American Principles and Fair Play Records; Bancroft Library, University of California, Berkeley
Ford papers	John Anson Ford papers; Huntington Library, San Marino, California
JAERS	Japanese American Evacuation and Resettlement Study; Bancroft Library, University of California, Berkeley

JARP	Japanese American Research Project Collection of Material about Japanese in the United States, 1893–1985; Young Research Library, Special Collections, University of California, Los Angeles
LOWV-SF	League of Women Voters San Francisco Records; California Historical Society North Baker Research Library, San Francisco
NAACP-R1	National Association for the Advancement of Colored People, Region 1 records, Bancroft Library, University of California, Berkeley
NARA	National Archives; College Park, Maryland
Nash papers	Phileo Nash papers; Truman Library Institute, Independence, MO
SCCAOHP	Southern California Chinese American Oral History Project; Young Research Library Special Collections, University of California, Los Angeles
Sheng collection	Richard Sheng collection; in possession of the author
SRRPC	Survey of Race Relations on the Pacific Coast; Hoover Institution, Stanford, California

Introduction

At the end of World War II, *Nation* editor Carey McWilliams called the Pacific Coast America's "new racial frontier." At the heart of this frontier was California, where the population in 1940 already included whites, African Americans, Mexican Americans, Native Americans, and the largest number of Asian Americans in the continental United States. During the war years, more than one million migrants from across the nation poured into California, especially Los Angeles County and the San Francisco Bay Area. The new arrivals included Southern whites, Mexican Americans from across the Southwest, and a larger number of African Americans than lived in the entire state in 1940. California in 1945 was thus undergoing a profound racial transformation, but it was more than just a demographic shift. Before the war, Asian Americans outnumbered blacks in the state, and anti-Asian sentiment united California politicians, civic groups, and labor leaders in a way that few other issues could. The state's constitution singled out Chinese as a particular threat, California law prevented Asian immigrants from owning land and entering many professions, and white residents overwhelmingly supported the internment of Japanese Americans in 1942. But just three years later, a major change began to take place in California. Civic unity and "fair play" groups stood up to vigilantes and demanded decent treatment for returning Japanese Americans. Legislators began to dismantle old anti-Asian laws. And by the early 1960s, Chinese Americans and Japanese Americans were starting to experience unprecedented residential and social mobility throughout the state.[1]

This is the story of that startlingly rapid racial transformation, told through Asian American experiences in the housing markets of Los Angeles and San

Francisco.[2] At first glance, housing may seem a strange focus for a study of Asian Americans. Although housing was a major flashpoint of race relations in the urban North during the twentieth century, most scholars have cast housing conflicts as purely black/white struggles.[3] In addition, blacks today are the nation's most residentially segregated nonwhite group, while Asian Americans are among the least segregated people of color in the United States.[4] As a result, students of Asian American history rarely discuss housing, seeing it as secondary to other concerns, such as immigration restriction.

Yet much of the recent work on black-white relations in urban California confirms that housing was just as combustible a racial issue there as elsewhere, making its absence from Asian American scholarship both puzzling and problematic. Residential segregation plagued African Americans in many parts of urban California long before World War II.[5] During this period, Asian Americans outnumbered blacks in the Bay Area, and they comprised a substantial proportion of the nonwhite population of Los Angeles as well.[6] Furthermore, Asian Americans were *the* central focus of white supremacist activity in prewar California, where both major political parties and scores of civic organizations fought to exclude them from every facet of life. If residential segregation limited African American opportunities in prewar California, what effect did it have on the Asian Americans so frequently identified as a special menace to white society there?

This book contends that how and where Asian Americans found homes, or were denied them, is one of the best ways to understand California's racial dynamics and why they changed over the course of just a few decades. Housing did not play a causal role in this shift until the 1950s; still, as elsewhere in the nation, longtime conflicts over housing in the Golden State revealed the ways white residents understood their own racial identities, as well as where they drew racial boundaries. Furthermore, the racialization of California's urban (and, later, suburban) space reflected not only white residents' ideas about different groups, but also the ways nonwhites expressed their own identities and related to and understood each other.

In addition, housing reveals more extensive Asian American interactions with the emerging welfare state than most historians have recognized. Scholars tend to identify immigration and naturalization policy as the sole point of Asian American contact with the state.[7] Asian immigrants' unusual legal status— as racially ineligible for American citizenship for much of the period this book describes—did play a huge role in the relationship they and their American-born children maintained with various levels of government. However, this book demonstrates that Asian Americans also tried to use many New Deal–era social welfare programs, including the initiatives that remade the nation's housing markets in the years after 1933. The way they gained access to these initiatives suggests that widespread perceptions of all of them as "foreigners," regardless of formal citizenship status, became institutionalized in the domestic welfare state by the late 1930s.

Exploring Asian American experiences with federal housing programs also allows unusually precise comparisons with the other racial and ethnic groups that vied for the same resources. Under pressure from Southern legislators, Congress in 1935 prevented farm workers and domestic servants from participating in the most desirable of the new social welfare programs. Because so many blacks worked as sharecroppers or domestics, especially in the South, these occupational bars effectively excluded the majority of the nation's African Americans from old age and unemployment insurance programs. Yet occupational exclusion lacked finesse as a segregationist tool, for some African Americans worked in covered fields. In contrast, federal housing programs used unambiguous racial distinctions, rather than inexact occupational exclusions, to discriminate against nonwhites. Federal officials allowed and even encouraged local public housing authorities to segregate their projects; they also required local Home Owners Loan Corporation and Federal Housing Administration officials to collect comprehensive racial data on every urban neighborhood in the nation and to use this data in their mortgage decisions.[8] The operation of these programs in diverse urban California thus provides a remarkable view of the divergent ways federal and local authorities understood racial difference and desirability, and how various nonwhite communities, including Chinese Americans and Japanese Americans, responded to these understandings with their own political strategies.

Asian Americans' compromised citizenship status also limited their access to private housing during much of the period this book covers. Before 1913, Asian immigrants enjoyed the same property rights as other immigrants in California; that year, however, state legislators passed the Alien Land Act, which prohibited aliens ineligible for U.S. citizenship from owning land.[9] As revised in 1920, it also barred them from leasing land or profiting from land purchased in the names of citizen children. Most scholars have explored the law's impact on Japanese ownership of agricultural land, since legislators crafted the law to thwart the ambitions of Japanese immigrant farmers.[10] As this book shows, however, white real estate agents and residents used the statute's murky language to harass Japanese immigrants buying homes in urban areas. Land laws and other restrictions on ineligible aliens thus created a multitude of other problems for urban Asian Americans.

By the 1920s, the impact of Asian immigrants' ineligibility for citizenship effectively placed them at the bottom of a legal racial hierarchy of housing rights and privileges in urban California. African Americans and Mexican Americans certainly faced housing discrimination, much of it the result of racially restrictive covenants that, as "private contracts," were legally enforceable. Still, because Mexican Americans and blacks were either citizens or "eligible aliens," they enjoyed legal rights that Asian immigrants did not. In addition, federal and state laws ultimately affected the rights of all Asians, whether American citizen or alien. Because of the status of their parents, Asian American citizens were, in effect, "alien citizens," according to historian Mae Ngai, who contends that this "alien citizenship" was a "badge of foreignness that could not be shed" and a "concept [that] underwrote both formal and informal structures of racial discrimination and was at the core of major, official race policies."[11]

Housing clearly and spatially demonstrates how the meaning of "alien citizenship" changed dramatically in just a few decades. Even in this most domestic of areas, Asian Americans could never escape the burden of their "perpetual foreignness." Instead, international relations and foreign affairs dictated Asian American housing opportunities and rights for most of the twentieth century. California's postwar racial transformation did not result mainly from growing white acceptance of Asian American citizenship. Nor did it take place simply because of the repeal of prewar anti-Asian laws, although Asian Americans welcomed and benefited from such changes. Rather, it occurred largely because the meaning of Asian American "foreignness" itself shifted with changing American interests in Asia. As the cold war deepened, a growing number of white Californians saw Asian American housing integration as a necessary price to pay for victory in the struggle. And as thousands of Asian Americans began moving to neighborhoods where blacks could not follow, the racial geography of urban and suburban California in the late 1950s became the most obvious barometer of the state's racial transformation.

*

The diversity of twentieth-century urban California is a dizzyingly complex subject. In order to impose some discipline on the topic, this book concentrates on the Chinese Americans of San Francisco and the Japanese Americans of Los Angeles. Other Asian American communities existed in prewar California, but they were generally far smaller (Koreans and Punjabis) or more concentrated in rural areas and inland towns (Filipinos) than Chinese Americans and Japanese Americans. The groups on which this book focuses were the largest

Asian American ethnic populations in their respective cities. Their housing experiences and relationships with other urban dwellers thus reveal much about shifting perceptions of race and desirability in urban California.

The first six chapters of this book explore the way California's legal hierarchy operated in prewar and wartime Los Angeles and San Francisco, two unique cities with their own distinct racial traditions. The final two chapters compare the Bay Area and the Los Angeles metropolitan area in the years after World War II, when the old legal hierarchy fell apart and the cold war created a whole new basis for racial meaning across California. Through such comparisons, these final chapters draw larger conclusions about the sources and impact of the profound racial shift that is the central focus of this book.

San Francisco, the subject of chapter 1, was the birthplace during the mid-nineteenth century of a zealous anti-Chinese movement, which evolved into a blanket anti-Asian movement after 1900. The city was also the home of a robust, pan-European labor movement that was explicitly anti-Asian. In San Francisco, the legal hierarchy created by state legislators mirrored the way most white residents understood racial desirability. San Francisco's prewar housing market, in which the small black population enjoyed far more residential mobility than the larger Chinese American one, reflected this racial order, as did Chinatown's emergence by the 1870s as America's first racially segregated neighborhood.

As chapter 2 demonstrates, Los Angeles's racial traditions were far different but equally unique. Neither blacks nor Japanese Americans enjoyed much residential mobility in L.A., where middle-class white Angelenos drew a simple line between white and nonwhite in the housing market. This racial worldview, and the growing influence of eugenics and Nordic ideology in the southland, encouraged many European immigrants and white working-class people there to embrace residential segregation as well. In doing so, they did not hesitate to use whatever tools were available to them—especially the anti-Asian laws that were a product of San Francisco's racial traditions.

Federal conceptions of race further skewed California's housing market by the 1930s, as chapter 3 demonstrates. New housing programs, including public housing initiatives and the Federal Housing Administration's mortgage underwriting, worked largely through local administrators, whose understandings of race and place reflected regional biases. In L.A., federal programs gave local officials, businesses, and institutions a new ability to foster separate white and nonwhite private housing markets. For their part, public housing officials (with the blessing of the federal government) responded to demands from politically active African Americans but ignored people of Asian ancestry.

Chapter 4 examines the tensions that developed between California's legal racial hierarchy and changing conceptions of Chinese American and Japanese American "foreignness" before World War II. In San Francisco, Asian American access to federally subsidized housing depended not on need but on international relations. After Japan's brutal 1937 invasion of China, San Francisco's Chinese Americans parlayed white San Franciscans' growing sympathy for China into support for a segregated housing project in Chinatown. In contrast, a multiracial coalition from the diverse Western Addition neighborhood failed to gain an integrated housing project for that district. The group's challenge to segregation, and Chinese American accommodation of it, also set the stage for postwar battles about housing and minority activism in San Francisco.

Japanese Americans in Los Angeles found that the international situation increasingly limited their residential aims. Chapter 5 explores the way the deterioration of U.S.-Japanese relations in 1940 and 1941 affected Japanese Americans seeking private housing in L.A. In 1940, white Angelenos trying to prevent the construction of a housing development for Nisei (the American-born, U.S. citizen children of Japanese immigrants) equated it with Imperial Japanese "invasion." Once Japanese forces attacked Pearl Harbor, the federal government threw its weight behind the idea of Japanese Americans as a racial threat, and within a few months, authorities had interned the entire Japanese American population of Los Angeles.

In wartime San Francisco, the focus of chapter 6, the old anti-Chinese traditions became increasingly embarrassing because of America's new alliance with China. Congress's repeal of the Chinese Exclusion Act in 1943 further threatened the foundations of California's prewar legal hierarchy, which depended on Asian immigrants' ineligibility for citizenship. Yet prewar strategies, such as identifying with China, continued to shape Chinese American politics in San Francisco. And though thousands of black migrants arrived in the overcrowded wartime city, Chinese American leaders largely avoided interracial activism.

At war's end, Japanese Americans returned to a California whose demographics and racial politics were in flux. Massive wartime migration had left both San Francisco and Los Angeles even more diverse than they had been in 1941. As chapter 7 demonstrates, progressives throughout the state hoped to use the shifting situation to their advantage, creating multiracial coalitions for change in both San Francisco and Los Angeles. These alliances smoothed the return of Japanese Americans to California and successfully fought to end restrictive covenants in the state. Still, housing segregation persisted for all nonwhite Californians.

Chapter 8 examines the immense impact of the cold war on California housing and racial politics in the 1950s. Conservatives successfully Red-baited many racial progressives in California; even moderate civil rights organizations muted their demands and limited their activism to avoid criticism. At the same time, many cultural elites and policymakers grew deeply concerned about the way America's poor treatment of blacks affected international opinion, especially in the newly independent nonwhite nations of Asia. In response, numerous white Californians began to use national security arguments to question the residential segregation of Asian Americans, but not blacks, linking the former directly to the cold war in Asia. Asian American "foreignness," once used to write discrimination into law, now aided white acceptance in both the Los Angeles and San Francisco metropolitan areas.

*

In the broadest sense, this book attempts to understand the startlingly rapid racial transformation of mid-century California, the nation's "racial frontier." Housing was more often reflective of this change than the cause of it, yet it is uniquely suited to demonstrating the shift. Access to decent housing was often the key to better schools, jobs, services, and social mobility. Furthermore, people built their lives and identities around their homes; they saw their neighborhoods as the places where they and their children would enjoy the most intimate relationships of their lives, from friendship to courtship to marriage. The persistence of conflicts over race and housing in twentieth-century urban America vividly illustrates as much. Before World War II, Asian Americans lived in some of California's worst and most segregated housing, thanks both to the legal racial hierarchy and to the anti-Asian traditions that were especially strong in the Bay Area. But in the 1950s, Asian American housing opportunities expanded in Los Angeles and San Francisco even as white residents continued to resist black integration and all that they believed it meant.

By that point, Asian Americans were no longer the undesirable "aliens" that white residents had long rejected as neighbors. Within two decades, they had become "foreign friends" whom a growing number of white Californians felt obligated to welcome, if only for the good of the nation. What many of these residents could not comprehend was that Asian Americans were neither alien neighbors nor foreign friends. They were simply Americans looking for decent homes, just like anyone else.

* 1 *

Alien Neighbors

CHAPTER ONE

Chinatown, San Francisco: The First Segregated Neighborhood in America

During publisher Miriam Leslie's 1877 visit to San Francisco's Chinatown, her tour guide, a local police detective, claimed that the neighborhood's residents "reduce themselves generally to a condition of crowd, discomfort and clutter most repugnant to the American's habit of mind, but apparently the height of convenience to that of the Oriental." In the years after the Civil War, such assertions became racial "common sense" in San Francisco, where a ferociously anti-Chinese movement flourished and labeled all Chinese filthy, undesirable, and even subhuman. Anti-Chinese leaders contended that the presence of Chinese in the city and in California as a whole displaced "desirable citizens" and prevented "free immigrants who would become citizens" from coming to the state; worse yet, female workers were "degraded by association with Chinamen in the workshops during the hours of their labor."[1] Motivated by these beliefs, anti-Chinese mobs attacked Chinese residents, boycotted products made with Chinese labor, and forced white employers to fire Chinese workers. Hundreds and then thousands of Chinese who lived outside San Francisco's "Chinese quarter" began moving to the neighborhood out of concern for their own safety. Others followed under pressure from white residents and landlords who increasingly accepted the view that any white person, including a neighbor, was "degraded by association with Chinamen." Originally an ethnic enclave and a center of Chinese business, Chinatown by the 1870s had become a community whose rigid segregation white residents demanded.

San Francisco's Chinatown was America's first segregated neighborhood. Few scholars today call it that, however, because they associate residential segregation in the urban United States solely with African Americans. According to historian Arnold Hirsch, the "overwhelming application of explicitly racial restrictions that reflected the desires of the dominant white majority" was something "no other group had to face" in U.S. history.[2] Sociologists Douglas S. Massey and Nancy A. Denton agree, contending that white Americans subjected *only* African Americans to "a series of deliberate decisions to deny [them] access to urban housing markets and to reinforce their spatial segregation." Actually, Chinese Americans in San Francisco experienced these same types of restrictions for almost seventy-five years. By the 1870s—more than three decades before the residential segregation of African Americans became common in the urban North—the vast majority of Chinese in San Francisco lived in the compact Chinatown district north of downtown, not out of choice but because they lacked other options.[3]

Scholars rarely talk about such segregation because of the recent history of Asian American urbanization and the thrust of the new urban history itself. Much contemporary urban scholarship examines the public and private decisions and actions that produced and enforced the residential segregation of African Americans. In doing so, this literature appropriately questions white privilege and government complicity in the continued segregation and marginalization of urban blacks. It also seeks to understand the roots of the nation's "urban crisis," in which white flight and black isolation played such prominent roles.[4] Still, this sometimes teleological approach means that Asian Americans rarely appear in urban scholarship, because Asian Americans today experience lower levels of residential segregation than do blacks and Hispanics.[5] As a result, the new urban history often tacitly supports a "model minority" myth of Asian American success by ignoring earlier Asian American struggles with housing discrimination and segregation.

Further complicating the issue, San Francisco's Chinatown was in many ways the product of different circumstances than the black ghettos that emerged in the early-twentieth-century urban North. Before 1910, most African Americans in Northern cities lived in integrated neighborhoods, although often in spatial proximity to other black households. A combination of factors enabled white Northerners of all classes to segregate African American residents by the 1920s, however. These factors included turn of the century public transportation improvements; zoning and the creation of single-use districts in cities; the rise of eugenics and "race science"; and the proliferation of the automobile.[6] Chinatown emerged long before any of these developments.

Yet Chinatown was still segregated. In fact, no other racial or ethnic group in the city of San Francisco (or anywhere else in the country) experienced anything close to the kind of segregation the Chinese did by the 1880s. According to Massey and Denton, "the most 'ghettoized' city in 1890 was Indianapolis, where the average black person lived in a neighborhood that was 13% black." In San Francisco, the typical African American in 1890 lived in an area that was less than 2 percent black. In contrast, the average Chinese in San Francisco lived in a neighborhood that was more than 62 percent Chinese; more than 80 percent of San Francisco Chinese lived in a single assembly district. The unpublished census schedules for 1880, which included detailed descriptions of smaller enumeration districts, show a degree of isolation much higher than the official assembly district numbers suggest. Most Chinese outside Chinatown lived with other Chinese in just one or two boarding houses or laundries in an otherwise all-white neighborhood. Scores more Chinese were servants in white homes.[7]

Almost a half century later, the Chinese American population was actually more segregated than it had been in 1890. A 1939 housing survey reported that 4,787 of the 4,858 Chinese American–occupied dwellings in the city were in Chinatown, with the remaining 71 largely concentrated in a few low-rent areas south of Market Street. Almost all the isolated boarding houses and laundries in which Chinese outside of Chinatown had once lived were now gone, casualties of zoning ordinances and unrelenting anti-Chinese hostility. In 1940, Chinese Americans occupied 2,226 of the 2,246 total dwelling units (more than 99 percent) in census area A-14, the heart of Chinatown. In adjacent A-15, Chinese occupied 836 of the total 927 dwelling units, or more than 90 percent. Census tract A-13 combined Chinatown with part of North Beach, a white neighborhood with a large Italian American population. In 1940, Chinese lived in 1,016 of the tract's 1,589 dwellings, almost all of them in Chinatown proper. But in neighboring Nob Hill's census tracts (A-9 and A-10), Chinese occupied 33 of 2,079 dwellings (0.01 percent) and 18 of 1,981 dwellings (less than 0.01 percent), respectively. Census tracts A-3, A-4, and A-1, which consisted of North Beach proper and the waterfront, were almost as segregated: nonwhites (possibly but not necessarily Chinese) lived in only 47, or 1 percent, of the 3,858 dwelling units.[8]

While Chinese Americans in San Francisco were at least as segregated as blacks in the most restricted Northern cities of the era, they lived under even worse conditions.[9] In 1885, anti-Chinese members of the board of supervisors contended that Chinatown was "the filthiest spot inhabited by men, women, and children on the American continent." White supremacists made such statements in order to prove the supposed inferiority and baseness of the

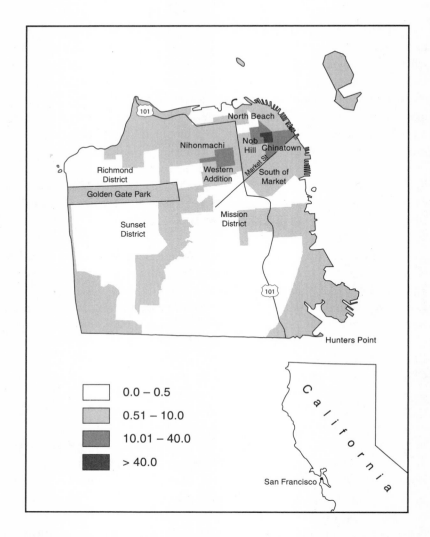

Asian American population by census tract (percent of total population), San Francisco, 1940. Almost all of the city's Chinese Americans lived within the borders of Chinatown. (Map by Harry D. Johnson, based on Minnesota Population Center, *National Historical Geographic Information System: Pre-release Version 0.1.* Minneapolis: University of Minnesota, 2004.)

Chinese, yet Chinatown was undoubtedly a very unpleasant place to live. Although certainly not the filthiest spot on the continent, it was eerily similar to the New York City slums Jacob Riis described in his 1890 book *How the Other Half Lives*. Lacking other options, five or six Chinese immigrants routinely crowded into a single tiny room, where they often ate and worked as well. Others slept packed into the basements of the quarter's buildings. Such conditions persisted for decades, prompting 1930s housing advocate Lim P. Lee to describe Chinatown's housing history as "sixty or seventy years of an abominable situation." In 1939, federal officials reported that almost 90 percent of Chinatown dwelling units were substandard; almost 80 percent lacked heat, and most also had no private bathing or cooking facilities.[10]

The segregation of Chinese Americans in San Francisco continued for so long because early in the city's history, Chinatown and its residents became crucial to ideas about whiteness there. Certainly, other factors contributed to the spatial (and economic and social) isolation of the Chinese American community. U.S. law prohibited Chinese immigrants from naturalizing, thus denying them the ability to participate in electoral politics the way so many other immigrant groups did. Like other immigrants, many Chinese also preferred to live among people who shared their language and cultural practices. By the early 1900s, Chinatown was even becoming a sort of tourist attraction, bringing needed dollars to its residents and enabling them to benefit in some ways from their spatial concentration. Still, few Chinese Americans wished to live crowded into just a few square blocks of the city's worst housing; white residents demanded it.

The specter of the Chinese played a crucial role for white San Francisco. The threat they allegedly posed to white labor helped bind together diverse native-born and European immigrant workers into multiethnic unions whose strength during this period was unusual. Political parties and numerous officials also embraced the Chinese issue, often using it to camouflage less appealing parts of their platforms. Many public health officials and middle-class reformers exploited anti-Chinese sentiment to gain legitimacy and respect in the city. Each of these groups cited the Chinese menace in order to justify the rigid segregation of Chinatown, and then used the poor conditions that hypersegregation created as evidence of the danger the Chinese posed.[11] In this circular process, beliefs about Chinese undesirability, filth, labor competition, and low living standards became so ingrained in the city's traditions and in the minds of its white residents that these ideas continued to shape San Francisco's racial geography long into the twentieth century.

THE ORIGINS OF NATIVISM IN SAN FRANCISCO

A onetime Spanish outpost and Mexican pueblo, San Francisco became a boomtown in 1849, when the California gold rush began. Gold fever made the city and the region the continent's most cosmopolitan; two-thirds of new arrivals came from outside the United States.[12] Europeans, white Americans, Chinese, free blacks, Chileans, and Sonoran Mexicans all streamed into California to hunt for gold. When gold was still relatively easy to find, white miners generally tolerated the presence of the Chinese. Governor John McDougal, who served from 1851 to 1852, called them "one of the most worthy of our newly adopted citizens." But as the supply of gold petered out, whites began forcing the Chinese off mining claims. The new California state legislature also created the infamous 1852 Foreign Miners' Tax, charging foreign miners a three dollar monthly fee and allowing tax collectors to confiscate mining plots for taxes owed. Although the tax supposedly applied to all non-American miners, officials enforced it mainly against the Chinese.[13]

Growing anti-Chinese sentiment also reflected the larger racial and economic issues of the time. In the 1850s, the question of slavery dominated national politics, especially whether states formed from newly-acquired Mexican territory would allow slavery within their borders. This nagging issue reflected the centrality of "free labor ideology" to the economy, culture, and society of the antebellum North. Free labor ideology stood in direct opposition to Southern slavery. Unlike a slave, a worker in a free labor system could sell his labor to the highest bidder, change employers at will, and, with hard work and frugality, perhaps become his own boss some day. Most Northerners agreed that black slavery in the South imperiled the free labor system in the North and in the West, since the "peculiar institution" required geographical expansion to survive and thrive.[14]

White Americans of this era frequently conflated blackness and slavery or servility as well. Northern white workers were losing much of their independence to factory bosses and industrial discipline; as historian David Roediger has contended, many embraced the idea that "Black oppression was the result of 'slavishness' rather than slavery," making the very presence of African Americans odious to vulnerable white workers. During the early nineteenth century, a number of Northern states that established universal white male suffrage simultaneously revoked many of the rights of black men, including the franchise. When northwestern territories, such as Illinois, Indiana, Ohio, and Michigan, became states, their constitutions barred free blacks from entering at all. To legislators in these new states, even free blacks threatened "real" free laborers, who were necessarily *white* workers.[15]

California entered the Union as a free state, but its embrace of "free labor" involved the kind of racial suppression and exclusion evident elsewhere in the nation. The white Americans who migrated to California and governed it believed the nation's Manifest Destiny was to conquer the continent for white civilization. The fluidity of Far West society also played a role in shaping white attitudes about nonwhites. Eric Foner contends that "where the social order was least stratified—as in the frontier states [like] California . . . legal discrimination was most severe," and not just against blacks. In his study of white supremacy in California, Tomás Almaguer describes the results: "White antipathy toward Mexicans, Native Americans, and Chinese and Japanese immigrants was typically couched within the rubric of this 'free white labor'/'unfree nonwhite labor' dichotomy." California's first constitution even denied African Americans and American Indians the right to vote or to testify against whites in court. An 1854 California State Supreme Court ruling extended these prohibitions to the Chinese and called them "a race of people whom nature has marked as inferior, and who are incapable of progress or intellectual development beyond a certain point."[16]

The Chinese kept coming to California despite the escalating violence there.[17] Some fled upheaval and unrest. In the 1850s and early 1860s, the Taiping Rebellion, a massive internal revolt, claimed twenty million lives and devastated the infrastructure and economy of central and southern China. A connected rebellion, the Red Turban uprising, convulsed Guangdong Province and created an impetus for emigration. Other Chinese, impressed by the Western wealth and power on display in Guangzhou, hoped to make a fortune at the "Gold Mountain." When the Central Pacific Railroad, desperate for labor, recruited Chinese both in California and China, the company found thousands of willing workers. After the completion of the railroad in 1869, many of the immigrants took other jobs that few whites wanted, such as cooking, washing clothes, mining, harvesting crops, and working in San Francisco factories.[18]

Despite the protests of white factory workers, employers exploited the new labor source until the national depression of the 1870s enabled the anti-Chinese movement to strike back. In the wake of severe job losses and wage cuts in the eastern United States, thousands of unemployed young white men came west by rail hoping for work. Compounding the problem, eastern manufacturers after the Civil War began to dump goods cheaply in western markets. Many

San Francisco factories closed, and those that remained in business some-
times fired whites and hired Chinese who were willing to work for less. The
Workingmen's Party of California (WPC) emerged from this volatile situation.
Party founder Dennis Kearney, an Irish immigrant turned demagogue, skill-
fully channeled the anger of the unemployed white men who gathered in San
Francisco's vacant lots to hear his harangues. Contending that the city's rich
capitalists used Chinese to drive white men's wages down to starvation levels,
Kearney urged his listeners to burn Chinatown to the ground. Under Kearney's leadership, the WPC remained a statewide political force until scandals,
schisms, and the end of the long depression finally destroyed it in 1881.[19]

Democrats and Republicans perpetuated the WPC's anti-Chinese rhetoric
but ignored its anticapitalist message.[20] In 1882, California legislators helped
convince their colleagues in Congress to pass the Chinese Exclusion Act,
which prohibited the entry of Chinese laborers into the United States for ten
years. In 1892, Congress extended the act—the first and only piece of legislation to bar by name a particular nationality from immigrating—for another ten
years. The exclusion legislation also declared Chinese immigrants already in
the country to be ineligible for American citizenship.

THE SOCIAL AND RACIAL GEOGRAPHY OF SAN FRANCISCO

Writing in 1946, 88-year-old San Franciscan Gertrude Atherton recalled "a
time, many years ago, when San Francisco halted far east of Van Ness Avenue,
and with the exception of the Presidio and the settlement around the old
Mission Dolores, there was nothing to be seen but miles of sand dunes."[21] By
1900, such dunes were just a memory. As its population grew, San Francisco
spread south and west from the first settled areas on the edge of the bay. Thousands of wood-frame and brick homes now dotted the fog-shrouded hills and
valleys of the growing city. Far from the wharves where fishing and industry
dominated, new middle-class areas, such as the Western Addition and Pacific
Heights, sheltered the city's wealthier families.[22] The catastrophic 1906 earthquake stopped growth for only a short period. Within a few years, builders
replaced the devastated Victorians of the older areas with more efficient two-
and three-flat homes and apartment buildings. Mediterranean stucco and Arts
and Crafts style bungalows sprouted in the newer and more fashionable areas.

Turn-of-the-century San Francisco remained a solidly working-class city
with a national reputation for union activism and power. In 1904, journalist Ray Stannard Baker called San Francisco the one American city where

"unionism reigns supreme." Union strength did not mean political dominance, however; employers frequently prevailed over striking laborers, and business leaders largely controlled city politics.[23] Still, the union-affiliated anti-Chinese movement continued to influence San Francisco politics at all levels well into the 1930s.

By 1900, the city had also grown more diverse, with thousands of Italians, Scandinavians, Russians, and other new European immigrants joining the predominately Irish, German, and Anglo population. Many of the newcomers, particularly single male laborers, worked in the factories south of Market Street and lived in the row houses and boardinghouses of that densely populated district. Others, especially the growing Italian population, fished or loaded boats at the city's piers and called North Beach home. Either way, the city generally welcomed them, even as immigration grew more controversial elsewhere. By 1910, many native-born white Protestants were complaining about the massive increase in southern and eastern European immigration that dated to the 1880s. Politicians, social scientists, and numerous other Americans of northern and western European ancestry questioned the whiteness of the newcomers, calling them unfit for American citizenship and arguing that they would weaken America's genetic stock. Critics also worried about admitting so many Catholics and Jews into the United States. These kinds of ideas, however, attracted relatively few followers in San Francisco. Many leading businessmen were immigrants or the children of immigrants, and scores were Catholic or Jewish.[24] During the 1890s alone, voters elected both a Catholic mayor (James D. Phelan) and a Jewish one (Adolph Sutro).

Even as sentiment against European immigrants reached a fever pitch elsewhere, then, most white San Franciscans stressed pan-white solidarity and focused their hatred on the Chinese. White San Franciscans of this era usually considered blacks to be inferior to whites, but in the Chinese and, later, in all Asians, they saw an active threat to white people, their institutions, their homes, and their families. In the classic study *Strangers in the Land*, historian John Higham defined nativism as "intense opposition to an internal minority on the ground of its foreign (i.e., 'un-American') connections." Higham excluded the anti-Chinese movement from this category, contending that it was "not . . . explicitly nationalist." Yet once the movement developed into a larger opposition to all Asian immigration after the turn of the century, it did become explicitly nationalist, casting Japan in particular as a threat to American sovereignty over California and the rest of the Pacific Coast states. At the same time, the anti-Chinese movement was always implicitly nationalist, construing the alleged decadence and decay of Chinese civilization as a special threat to white Americans and their national destiny to conquer and settle the West. Furthermore, as historian Mae Ngai points out, "nationalism's ultimate defense is sovereignty—the nation's self-proclaimed, absolute right to determine its own membership, a right believed to inhere in the nation-state's very existence."[25] Based on this definition, the Chinese Exclusion Act of 1882 marked the anti-Chinese movement as nativist in the extreme. It not only barred further Chinese immigration but also specified that Chinese aliens could never become naturalized citizens.[26]

No group or institution better exemplified San Francisco nativism than the Native Sons of the Golden West (NSGW), a San Francisco-based organiza- tion whose members included ordinary working men, as well as governors, congressmen, mayors, and much of California's legislature.[27] Alfred Winn, a Virginian who came to California during the gold rush, founded the Native Sons in San Francisco in 1875 to keep alive the history and pioneering spirit of the forty-niners. Commemorative and patriotic groups popular on the East Coast, such as the Sons and Daughters of the American Revolution, were usually "Anglo-Saxon" responses to the new immigration of the 1880s and 1890s.[28] However, any man born in California, as long as he was wholly of European ancestry, could join the Native Sons. The NSGW paid little atten- tion to the blacks and Latinos it barred from membership, but it remained an outspoken opponent of Chinese immigration and of Asians in general until long after World War II.[29]

In a period when native-born white Protestants often questioned southern and eastern European whiteness, the anti-Chinese thrust of San Francisco nativism automatically "whitened" European immigrants. The process took far longer east of the Mississippi; historians like John T. McGreevy, Matthew Frye Jacobson, and Russell Kazal have shown that southern and eastern European immigrants and their children used the Great Migration of African Americans to the urban North during the 1910s and 1920s to claim whiteness for themselves. By this point, San Francisco's immigrants already enjoyed a degree of acceptance uncommon elsewhere, in large part because of the presence of so many Chinese.[30] Nayan Shah has argued that at the turn of the century, "the Chinese as a scapegoat reconfirmed the boundaries of race and national difference that were crucial for union solidarity."[31] But as Shah notes, this was a reconfirmation, not an innovation.

The Chinese remained a potent symbol of unfair labor competition, low living standards, and racial difference long after many had left San Francisco for good. Lacking political power, Chinese immigrants had used the courts since the 1870s to fight immigration decisions as well as legislation meant to curtail their economic rights. However, Congress and judges increasingly limited the rights of Chinese to employ even these methods in their own defense. By the 1880s and 1890s, many Chinese tired of constant harassment and either returned to China or moved to less hostile areas of the country. The number of Chinese in San Francisco fell to 14,000 by 1900, far less than the estimated 30,000 in the city in 1875. Excluded from factory jobs and most other occupations, those who remained in San Francisco usually worked in Chinese restaurants and laundries, picked shrimp for the seafood industry, or took domestic service positions with white families. Still, they remained as essential to labor cohesion and white solidarity in San Francisco as they had been in 1877. In 1902, when Congress contemplated extending the ban on Chinese immigration another ten years, San Francisco unions and mayor Eugene Schmitz called for yet another boycott of "Chinese-made" products.[32] What those products might be was anyone's guess. Regardless, such tactics proved even more successful than they had in 1882 and 1892, for in 1904, Congress barred further Chinese labor immigration indefinitely.

The presence of the Chinese was thus crucial to shaping racial understandings in San Francisco long after the end of legal Chinese labor immigration in 1882. To the Native Sons and most white San Franciscans, California was solely for the white race. The threat to California, they believed, came not from the American South or the south and east of Europe, but from across the Pacific, where China waited to send its "coolie" hordes to overwhelm the state. The shared nativist desire to expel all Chinese from California set San Francisco's brand of white supremacy apart from anti-black racism elsewhere. After all, most white Americans at least grudgingly acknowledged the right of African Americans to live in the United States.[33]

SEGREGATING THE CHINESE QUARTER

The anti-Chinese thrust of San Francisco politics profoundly shaped the city's racial geography. In the early 1850s, a diverse and overwhelmingly male population lived to the west of Portsmouth Plaza, San Francisco's central square. Chinese made up a significant percentage of residents in the area that would later become Chinatown, but they by no means formed the majority at the time. Still, white residents began to refer to the area as "Little China" during the late 1850s and early 1860s because of the concentration of Chinese-run businesses there.[34]

The nativist movement of the late 1860s and 1870s quickly intensified this concentration by portraying the Chinese as filthy, perverse, and subhuman.

FIGURE 1.1. Dupont Street, the central thoroughfare of Chinatown, around the turn of the century. After the 1906 earthquake, Dupont was renamed Grant Avenue. (Courtesy of The Bancroft Library, University of California, Berkeley.)

Soon, few other San Franciscans were willing to live next to or be associated with such vilified people. "Any building adjacent to one occupied by Chinese is rendered undesirable to white folks," observed visitor B.E. Lloyd in 1875. White violence also played a major role in segregating the Chinese. In his 1871 book *Roughing It*, Mark Twain noted that "as I write, news comes that in broad daylight in San Francisco, some boys have stoned an inoffensive Chinaman to death, and that although a large crowd witnessed the shameful deed, no one interfered." Such violence continued in the 1880s, infuriating Chinese consul Zhang Yinhuan. White San Franciscans "have been burning, pillaging, robbing, and killing" the Chinese, he noted in 1886, and "their vicious cruelty is unbearable."[35] As conditions worsened, Chinese from other parts of the city moved to Chinatown, seeking safety in numbers.

Chinatown soon became hypersegregated, filled with Chinese barred from living elsewhere in the city and too scared to do so anyway. More than three-quarters of the city's Chinese crowded into a twelve-square-block area bounded by Broadway on the north, Sacramento Street on the south, Kearney Street to the east, and Stockton Street to the west. A white-authored 1882 map of the Chinese quarter shows a mere handful of white-owned businesses—mostly saloons, stables, and even a shooting gallery, all establishments of the type increasingly unwelcome in other areas. The few white-occupied homes in the neighborhood clung to the district's northeast border, forming a wall along Kearney, Montgomery, and Broadway. In several instances, vacant buildings or open space separated these houses from those occupied by Chinese tenants. According to the mapmakers, the district's other remaining whites were prostitutes, and even their brothels clustered together along Sacramento Street between Dupont and Stockton at the very southern edge of Chinatown.[36]

To "protect" the growing city, San Francisco authorities increasingly allowed brothels to thrive only in Chinatown and the neighboring Barbary Coast, reaffirming the existing negative stereotypes about the Chinese. Women of many different ethnic backgrounds worked in the brothels, but the Chinese bore the stigma. The majority of Chinese men left their wives in China, a practice American law encouraged by treating every Chinese woman immigrant as a potential prostitute. To many white San Franciscans, however, Chinatown's sex imbalance and prostitution business proved the moral perversion of the "heathen Chinese." Mark Twain observed that a Chinese was "a great convenience to everybody—even to the worst class of white men, for he bears the most of their sins." When Chinese men visited a brothel, they demonstrated their immorality; in contrast, prostitutes supposedly lured naive white boys into vice. Newspapers and magazines catered to such ideas, publishing lurid and sensationalized accounts of Chinatown opium use, gang warfare, and prostitution. Public health officials and turn-of-the-century reformers drew on such lore to label the area squalid and disease-ridden. Indeed, Chinatown itself became shorthand for the vices whites associated with the Chinese in general: filth, sexual and moral perversion, and opium use.[37]

Such stereotypes informed the city's forty-year campaign to get rid of Chinatown, which occupied prime real estate just north of downtown San Francisco. As historian Yong Chen notes, many white San Franciscans felt that "the politically disfranchised and increasingly socially marginalized Chinese . . . did not belong at the center of San Francisco." Moreover, city leaders and public health authorities contended that the filth and disease of the Chinese and their quarter posed a threat to the health and safety of the rest of city. In the 1870s, the board of supervisors forbade anyone from renting rooms with less than five hundred cubic feet of air per occupant—a law aimed at space-starved, segregated Chinatown. A few years later, the mayor drafted a resolution ordering all Chinese to leave San Francisco within thirty days, although the board of supervisors did not carry out the order. Still, an 1885 board of supervisors report declared the district "the rankest outgrowth of human degradation that can be found upon this continent" and blamed conditions on "the very nature of the [Chinese] race." In 1890, the supervisors passed the notorious Bingham Ordinance, the nation's first racial residential zoning law, which gave Chinatown's residents sixty days to leave their neighborhood. The Chinese Consolidated Benevolent Association, a group of merchants that defended the Chinese in such disputes, successfully challenged the legality of the most restrictive laws, including the Bingham Ordinance. However, Chinese could not litigate the racial nativism that restricted them to living in just a few square blocks of the city.[38]

After the devastating 1906 earthquake and fire destroyed Chinatown and the nearby downtown, city leaders tried to evict the Chinese yet again. This time, an unusual alliance of white slumlords and Chinese organizations with their own landholdings managed to thwart the city's plans.[39] Although city officials and civic leaders eventually relented, their decision did not reflect a deep change of heart about the Chinese themselves. The immigrants and their children remained as unwelcome outside their neighborhood as they had been before the catastrophe.

A GROWING POPULATION

By the mid-1920s, the number of Chinese Americans in San Francisco was growing rapidly after decades of decline. The city's Chinese population, which fell from about 14,000 in 1900 to 7,750 in 1920, shot up to more than 16,000 by 1930. Some of the growth stemmed from illegal immigration, which continued for decades after the passage of the Chinese Exclusion Act of 1882; the ratio of Chinese American men to women remained very high in Chinatown, in part because of such immigration. Still, in the 1910s and 1920s a growing number of Chinatown couples gave birth to children in San Francisco. Some of these parents were American-born laborers and businesspeople; others were Chinese-born men who immigrated to the United States as merchants rather than laborers.[40] Whatever the race or occupation of their parents, children born on U.S. soil were (and are) U.S. citizens. By the late 1920s, hundreds of these young citizens filled the streets and schools of Chinatown.

The growth of Chinatown's population strained the resources of the community, the boundaries of which scarcely budged after 1880. In the late 1900s and 1910s, Chinatown's white landlords rebuilt the earthquake-damaged community to maximize their profits, dividing most of the new structures into one-room cells for "bachelor" workers. These "bachelors"—many of whom had wives and families in China—disliked the tiny rooms, but they were relatively affordable, especially when several men chipped in to rent one together. Building owners also cut their own costs by offering only shared bathing, cooking, and toilet facilities. According to Chinatown resident Esther Wang, a typical post-1906 Chinatown apartment building contained "from thirty to sixty rooms on one floor with no bathing and laundry facilities and only one public kitchen." Landlords rarely—if ever—cleaned the shared areas.[41]

Although the anti-Chinese violence and rhetoric so routine before the earthquake ebbed in the years after the catastrophe, observers and civic leaders still claimed that the Chinese preferred living in dirty, cramped spaces. These arguments had always been a staple of campaigns to extend Chinese exclusion, unite white workers against "Asiatic" labor and living standards, and paint the Chinese as subhuman. In 1885, a special committee of the board of supervisors contended that "it is almost the universal custom among the Chinese to herd together as compactly as possible." A year later, Chinatown visitor Sue Sanders demonstrated how such stereotypes became "common sense" to whites in the city: "We [saw] . . . one house of ten rooms where seven hundred live and sleep, and this they say is very respectable living among Chinamen." This stereotype did not change much over forty years. As a Chinese American social worker lamented in the 1920s, "people say the Chinese live so crowded, but nobody will rent to us."[42] Such beliefs helped justify segregation and enabled city officials to ignore the district's increasingly desperate situation.

Compounding the problem, Chinatown was not a conventionally residential neighborhood. Businesses occupied the ground floors of almost every building, with some factories on the higher floors. Apartments for couples and families with children were usually the same cubicles that the "bachelor" men endured. Law Shee Low's family occupied a typical one-room flat in Chinatown. "We did everything in that one room: sleep, eat, and sit," she recalled. "We had a small three-ring burner for cooking. There was no ice box, and my husband had to shop for every meal." To make matters worse, the neighborhood had almost no parks or other recreational facilities.[43] Regardless, as the population of couples with children grew during the 1910s and 1920s, Chinese Americans who hoped to enlarge Chinatown or live outside it faced staunch resistance.

NATIONAL SEGREGATION, LOCAL ECHOES

During the 1910s and 1920s, the racial segregation of African Americans became as common in Northern cities as the restriction of Chinese Americans in
San Francisco. During and after World War I, as thousands of blacks migrated
to the nation's urban industrial centers, white residents began to demand and
enforce residential racial separation. Many recent immigrants even used segregation to stake a claim to whiteness.[44] Often these homeowners created private agreements, known as racial restrictive covenants, that barred residents
of certain areas from selling to anyone not wholly "of the Caucasian race."[45]
Others formed homeowners' associations to enforce imagined racial borders
and defend covenants, which courts sanctioned and enforced.

In San Francisco, whites in the neighborhoods bordering Chinatown also
formed homeowner and neighborhood associations that resembled the segregationist groups increasingly common elsewhere. To a certain degree, members responded to a resurgent anti-Asian movement then thriving in California: although largely anti-Japanese, its origins in the anti-Chinese movement
prompted white residents to reinforce the spatial boundaries that set them
apart from Chinese Americans. But in addition, few white neighbors could
ignore the stunning growth of Chinatown's population, especially the crowds
of children who now thronged the quarter's streets. In the mid-1920s, anxious Italian American parents in nearby North Beach even pushed the city to
build an "Oriental" secondary school in order to preserve the racial homogeneity of local junior high schools. Because San Francisco's Oriental School,
rechristened the Commodore Stockton School in 1924, offered only a primary
education, a growing number of Chinese American students now pushed to
attend North Beach's Francisco Junior High. After a year of contentious Board
of Education meetings, Chinese American students won the right to enroll in
Francisco largely because the city lacked the money to pay for a segregated
junior high school in Chinatown.[46] While frustrated by this setback, white
residents in neighborhoods such as Nob Hill and North Beach continued to
confine Chinese American residents to homes in Chinatown alone. As a white
resident concluded, in language straight out of the nineteenth century: "Let
the Chinese stay below Stockton. This is a white man's land."[47]

Indeed, nativism remained so pervasive in the 1920s that white San Franciscans, while they created segregationist neighborhood groups, largely ignored
restrictionist devices, including the covenants so popular in other cities. Their
reliance on racial tradition proved more than adequate: even Chinese Americans of means never managed to buy or rent homes in any of the newer outlying

residential districts, such as the Richmond or Twin Peaks. Chinese American newlyweds spent weeks searching the city for apartments to rent, only to come away disappointed. According to one observer, "the secretary of the Chinese Y.W.C.A. had circularized all the real estate agents of San Francisco to locate places which were opened to Chinese tenants," but "she received no favorable replies." As historian Albert Broussard has noted, if the San Francisco housing market was a ladder, "Chinese occupied the bottom rung."[48]

A NEW "THREAT"

For Chinatown residents, the home choices of Japanese newcomers reiterated the particular contempt with which white San Franciscans viewed both Chinese Americans and China itself. In the 1890s and early 1900s, tens of thousands of Japanese began immigrating to the Pacific Coast. Even as San Francisco nativists campaigned for permanent Chinese exclusion, they saw the Japanese as an even greater threat. "The struggle now is to exclude all Asiatic laborers," argued Jerome A. Hart in the *Grizzly Bear*, the magazine of the Native Sons. "If we, the sons of California, remain sluggish and inert at this crisis, our State in not many years will have become as Hawaii is—a Japanese colony with a small minority of white Americans." While most Japanese came to California to farm, union leaders called all of them "cheap" laborers who would undermine white wages. The newly formed Asiatic Exclusion League also dredged up familiar arguments about low Asian living and moral standards to make its case for exclusion. "Search the police records of Seattle, Portland, San Francisco, Los Angeles, New York, or any other Mongolian center and you will find—what? Bestiality, vileness, and filth," contended the League.[49]

Still, the Japanese commanded more respect than their predecessors. In 1905, Japan defeated Russia in the Russo-Japanese War, a victory that forced Western nations to take the rising empire seriously. In 1906, the San Francisco Board of Supervisors passed a resolution to segregate Japanese American children in public elementary schools, just as the city had long segregated Chinese American children. The ensuing controversy became an international incident, with President Theodore Roosevelt intervening to calm an angry Japanese government. The United States viewed with concern Japan's growing power in Asia, the product of rapid industrial and military modernization. The 1906 school affair ended with Japanese children returning to integrated schools and the United States and Japan concluding the 1907 Gentlemen's Agreement, under which the Japanese government halted further male labor emigration to the United States. White San Franciscans deplored the fact that Japanese children could attend "white" schools, but they understood that Japan's military standing forced the United States to treat Japanese citizens with some consideration. Even two decades later, during the Francisco Junior High debate, a school official privately attributed ongoing Chinese American school segregation to the fact that "Japan had a strong navy, and China had none."[50]

Federal pressure could not prevent nativist residents and homeowner organizations from keeping Japanese out of most San Francisco neighborhoods. Nativist spokesmen often described Japanese military progress in Asia and Japanese agricultural endeavors in California as parts of the same expansionist enterprise, and segregationist rhetoric in San Francisco frequently reflected these fears. Late in 1920, a Japanese American company tried to buy the Beck Apartments on Bush Street near the southern border of Chinatown. The Apartment House Owners' and Managers' Association and the San Francisco Real Estate Board charged that the purchase was part of a "well-laid plan to get control of apartment houses" and cited "other apartment house deals in which certain realty operators have been approached, and in which Japanese capital is interested." Opponents of the Japanese also used more familiar arguments about racial desirability and alleged Asian filth. When property owners along another section of Bush Street protested zoning alterations they perceived as Japanese-friendly, the president of the city's zoning board canceled the changes and declared that "to put Bush Street in the light industrial class is to turn it over to the Japanese . . . and a beautiful boulevard to the beach will have become a Japanese street." The Real Estate Board also instituted a boycott of all real estate agents doing business with Japanese.[51]

Japanese immigrants did not encounter quite the same extreme degree of segregation that Chinese Americans did, however. Neither federal nor local officials would tolerate the kind of violence that the Chinese routinely faced in nineteenth-century San Francisco. Regardless of their personal feelings about the Japanese, many of the city's leading businesspeople also sought to avoid embarrassing anti-Japanese incidents; trade with Asia, including Japan, was central to San Francisco's economic future.[52] Local politicians still fulminated against the Japanese, but none promoted the kind of vigilantism that prompted an earlier generation of Chinese to take refuge within Chinatown's borders.

Segregationist sentiments persevered in less violent ways, however. The large majority of Japanese immigrants found homes in an affordable neighborhood of rundown storefronts and old houses on the northeastern edge of the Western Addition. Once a fashionable area, it survived the great earthquake and fire of 1906 and then briefly boomed when displaced residents poured in, carving up the homes into apartments and establishing businesses. By the late 1910s, however, most of these refugees had long since left for newer and better areas. At that point, the district became popular with poorer laborers and families of almost every ethnic and racial background, including Japanese immigrants displaced by the quake. Most of the other residents paid little attention. Perhaps they agreed with nativist journalist Chester Rowell, who contended that while "sanitary conditions are unspeakable and sanitary regulations unenforceable" in Chinatown, the Japanese "build better and cleaner houses and admit some air to them." Either way, most of the area's tenants, many of them transients, expressed little interest in mobilizing to "defend" the neighborhood. When a handful of white homeowners and businessmen in the area tried to organize a segregationist association, it proved largely ineffective.[53]

Yet Japanese who sought homes in most other conventional family neighborhoods encountered genuine white hostility and vigilantism. While city leaders rallied to "save" Bush Street, arsonists torched the home of a Japanese who moved to a white, working-class area of Russian Hill. Facing such hostility, the vast majority of Japanese in the city stayed in the new Nihonmachi, which whites called "Japtown." Distance from its center indicated social status. As a Nisei, or second generation Japanese American, noted, "most of the richer Japanese businessmen and the Consulate people lived on the outskirts of Japanese town in a nicer district on Jackson Street." A few Japanese settled also in other rundown Western Addition and South of Market neighborhoods where African Americans and immigrant whites, but no Chinese, lived.[54]

UNIQUE MOBILITY

Unlike the Japanese, African Americans did not have to contend with the legacy of the anti-Chinese movement in San Francisco. Blacks in the city grappled with persistent economic discrimination; the craft and trade unions so important in the city traditionally excluded all nonwhites or only allowed blacks to join nonvoting auxiliaries (Asian Americans usually did not even have this option).[55] Yet in the prewar years, African Americans in San Francisco encountered far less segregation and hostility than black renters and homeowners elsewhere in the North.

In part, residential segregation was the product of technological and spatial changes, such as zoning, public transportation, single-use districts, and automobile transportation, but it also resulted from specific cultural and social factors. It reflected the racial aspirations of southern and eastern European immigrants and poorer native whites in the wake of World War I and the Great

Migration of blacks to the North. It also stemmed from the goals of African Americans themselves, especially businesspeople and leaders who responded to growing racial segregation and violence in the North by creating separate black cultural and economic spaces.[56] These factors were largely absent in San Francisco. Wartime anti-immigrant rhetoric and postwar Red-baiting of unions played poorly in the city, with its pro-labor and pro-European immigrant traditions. And the tiny trickle of African Americans who arrived in San Francisco in the 1910s could not sustain the kind of black institutions and business districts found in Northern cities with far larger African American populations. Indeed, the Great Migration barely changed the relationship between black and white San Franciscans, nor did it shake the anti-Asian foundations of white identity in the city; during this era, the Japanese came in far larger numbers.[57] It is ironic, then, that during the very period that the residential segregation of African Americans became commonplace throughout the North, white homeowners and landlords in San Francisco tolerated African Americans far more than other nonwhites.

Reflecting national trends, many California real estate agents saw black segregation as the wave of the future and vital to neighborhood desirability, yet they failed to convince most white San Franciscans of its value. In other Northern cities, whites began to demand residential segregation in response to the rapid and highly visible growth of the black population. This kind of growth simply did not occur in San Francisco. Historian Albert S. Broussard contends that "because San Francisco's black population remained small between 1900 and 1940, in contrast to its larger Chinese population, most whites never feared an 'invasion' of blacks into their neighborhood that would lower their property values and disrupt their way of life."[58]

Real estate agents and brokers who attempted to sow such fear repeatedly expressed frustration at their inability to do so. In 1925, the realty professionals who led white homeowner associations in the middle-class Sutro Heights and Sunset neighborhoods complained about African Americans moving into these areas. The president of the Central Council of Civic Clubs suggested that the city segregate all African Americans in a single section, but his idea stirred little public interest. Undaunted, the Sunset Transportation and Development Association (STDA) decided to undertake its own restrictive covenant campaign, organizing volunteers to canvass the district and collect fees for a covenant barring blacks. The movement, which began with great optimism, quickly floundered. Proponents used a variety of arguments to encourage residents to sign the covenant. They contended that district parents needed to protect their children, brought to public attention incidents involving African American homeowners, and described the covenant as "like a fire insurance policy . . . [for] protection against loss—loss in property value." By early 1928, however, the STDA secretary noted that "a wall of indifference seems to now impede further progress by the Association in this work."[59]

Lost among a much larger Asian American population in a region with unique racial traditions, African Americans enjoyed far more residential mobility in San Francisco than either Chinese Americans or Japanese Americans. Their relative mobility set San Francisco apart from other American cities of the early twentieth century. Black San Franciscans owned homes in Sutro Heights, the Richmond, the Sunset, and other white middle-class neighborhoods where Asian Americans dared not venture, except as domestic servants.[60]

A NEW INDUSTRY AND A BAD REPUTATION

In the late nineteenth century, white guides began taking visitors on "slumming" tours to see Chinatown's poverty and supposed perversity. Accounts of these visits appeared in many magazines and books of the era and made the neighborhood infamous, yet tour guides were often hard-pressed to fulfill visitors' expectations. Mary Wills, a Pennsylvanian, wrote in 1889 that "we had heard so much of these midnight horrors we expected to see what was really bad, or at least vicious. We expected vice, and were disappointed that we found only depravity." Many of the white guides understood vice well enough, since a number were patrons of the saloons and brothels of Chinatown and the neighboring Barbary Coast district.[61] Yet what they showed the tourists was largely a result of the city's own segregationist traditions. Opium and gambling dens were a favorite stop, and some were certainly authentic; as in China at the time, opium smoking and gambling remained fairly common in turn-of-the-century Chinatown. Still, most theaters, restaurants, saloons, and other leisure businesses outside Chinatown did not admit Chinese customers, while police and city officials purposely confined gambling and prostitution to Chinatown. Tongs, Chinese organizations with both legitimate and less savory functions, controlled much of the ensuing vice trade within the district. Still, even their legendary battles rarely involved white San Franciscans. Such details did not stop white guides from using tales of the tongs to make the tourists shiver, however.[62]

After the turn of the century, a number of Chinese American merchants who benefited from the money the slummers spent in the area organized to rid Chinatown of the very problems that white visitors came to see. Through these merchants' experiences with the slummers, many learned to identify other Chinatown attractions besides "depravity." They found that Chinese theaters, markets, and restaurants all had an exotic appeal to whites that drew both attention and cash. Many Chinese American merchants believed that if they could suppress gambling, tong wars, and prostitution, they could lure more timid tourists—even families—into the district to spend money. Greater familiarity with ordinary Chinese Americans would lead to better treatment of them. And by attracting a higher class of tourist, Chinatown leaders also hoped to discourage the drunken white revelers who harassed law-abiding Chinese Americans long past midnight.[63]

The merchants enjoyed uneven success, with white tour guides and some Chinese residents trying to undermine their efforts. In 1913, Chinatown leaders organized the Chinese Peace Society and succeeded in reining in the feuding tongs, although they did not manage to end the conflicts completely until the 1920s. Still, as Chinese American reformers worked to stamp out vice, some white guides simply fabricated it. A number led tour groups through poorly lit cellars that they called tong escape tunnels and hired Chinese men to pose as "opium fiends" for the visitors. Years later, a Chinese American man recalled with anger the way some Chinatown residents collaborated with the worst white guides. "I know there was a man on Jackson Street who lived in a dirty house with sand and mud floors and never took a bath in all his life," he said. "'The dirtier the better' was his motto for making money with the tourists."[64]

Still, Chinese American merchants began to make headway in part by cooperating with the least offensive guides and providing their own tours of Chinatown. In 1909, the Chinese Consolidated Benevolent Association published a guidebook that provided a list of less exploitative white guides by name and badge number whom the organization deemed acceptable. Another Chinese American guidebook issued a few years later assured tourists that "no part of San Francisco is so well policed and so safe for pedestrians as is San Francisco's Chinatown." At the same time, the author reminded visitors that her tour was "the only Chinatown trip starting from the Wong Sun Yue Tea Garden," hinting at the ongoing battle against the worst of the white guides. Chinese Americans struggled well into the 1920s to banish the most exploitative guides, whom they called "sensational fakers who maintained bogus opium dens, pointed out false lepers to wandering tourists, and described cuts of meat in Chinese butcher shops as carcasses of rats and other vermin." Even Chinese American children joined the battle, shouting "Liar!" at the most infamous guides as they took visitors through the area.[65]

The 1906 earthquake and fire, which destroyed most of Chinatown, actually helped Chinese American merchants further develop tourism. Although white investors owned most of the quarter's land, Chinese American businessmen used the clean slate they now had to build a new Chinatown facade that explicitly catered to exotic tourist ideas. Chinese shop owners embellished plain brick stores with curved roofs, green tile, and gilt trim. Several of the largest Chinese-owned tourist bazaars hired white architects to design "Chinese" buildings after the earthquake; after all, no one knew better how to express white fantasies of China than white people themselves.[66]

By the 1910s, then, more and more Chinese businesspeople actively courted white tourists as a way to survive and even prosper. Area businessmen, both immigrant and native born, formed the Chinese Chamber of Commerce in 1908 to improve the district's tourist economy, among other goals. Major firms, such as the Sing Chong bazaar on Grant Avenue, handed out colorful English-language postcards guaranteeing "one price" for tourists fearful of haggling with Chinese shopkeepers. Sing Chong also advertised in the English-language telephone directory.[67]

Innovative Chinese American restaurateurs soon joined the bazaar owners, catering explicitly to white tourists and trying to banish older stereotypes about Chinese eating rats and mice. By the 1920s, establishments on and near Grant Avenue offered bilingual menus with chop suey, chow mein, and other "Chinese" food described in reassuringly bland terms. The menu of the Grand View Garden Restaurant offered nine different varieties of chop suey (none containing rodents), as well as other foods that eventually became staples of Chinese-American cuisine: egg foo young, chow yuk, and pork fried rice. (On the back of the menu, in Chinese, the restaurant offered boiled squab, duck eggs, and other dishes that white tourists were unlikely to request—including plain white rice.) The Chinese Tea Garden, which did not even bother to translate its menu into Chinese, took top prize in the chop suey department, offering no fewer than thirty varieties (including "extra fine"). For those tourists who found chop suey too exotic, the restaurant also served peanut butter sandwiches.[68] By making Chinese food accessible (if unrecognizable to most Chinese people), these entrepreneurs created a thriving industry that became a mainstay of Chinatown. Indeed, they were the hope of the future, because white-owned power laundries were pushing Chinese laundries out of one of the few economic niches still open to Chinese Americans in the 1920s. As a sociologist reported, "the leaders of Chinatown seem to think that retail shops and cafes are likely to provide increasing employment for the younger generation."[69]

As tourism grew more important in the 1920s, numerous Chinese Americans invested their growing profits in Chinatown's lucrative but still segregated housing market.[70] Mrs. C. F. Low, a widow who made her fortune running a general store in Nevada, was one of the most high profile. In the mid-1920s, she moved to San Francisco and built the Low Apartments, a Western-style building near the North Beach border. The owner of what the *San Francisco Chronicle* called "America's first high class apartment house built exclusively for Chinese" had already leased more than half of its twenty-four apartments, the best in Chinatown, before they were even completed. By 1930, Chinese American entrepreneurs like Low owned the majority of Chinatown's land and buildings.[71]

Still, their takeover did not improve neighborhood housing in the increasingly overcrowded district, particularly for the working-class majority. Like their white predecessors, Chinese American owners charged their captive audience rents that were about 50 percent higher than what other San Franciscans paid for comparably miserable housing. One contemporary survey of the district noted that "there seems to be no noticeable difference between the two kinds of ownership [white and Chinese] since both resist changes and invent the happy philosophy that the Chinese population doesn't want first class living quarters."[72]

I CANNOT LIVE AS THEY DO

San Francisco's Chinatown tourism industry paralleled developments in New York, where white residents segregated and then exoticized the African American population. Author Langston Hughes lampooned the Jazz Age as the era "when the Negro was in vogue," a period when a growing number of white tourists visited Harlem's clubs and night spots. Some came away with a new respect for African Americans, but to others, the music and art they encountered simply confirmed their stereotypes about black sexuality and primitiveness. Harlem intellectuals, from Alaine Locke to W. E. B. Du Bois to Hughes himself, debated endlessly the way art and music portrayed African Americans to white America.[73] San Francisco's Chinese Americans faced a related dilemma. To draw middle-class white tourists with money to spend, Chinatown had to at least flirt with the kinds of exotic stereotypes that frustrated and stymied Chinese aliens and American citizens alike.

This flirtation ensured Chinatown's survival but trapped its residents in a handful of prescribed, acceptable roles. Mayors and political leaders no longer promised white constituents to erase Chinatown from the map and to rid the city of Chinese; instead, a growing number of white San Franciscans tolerated Chinatown's presence, and some actually recognized it as an asset. San Francisco's Chamber of Commerce even began calling it a must-see destination, "a foreign country of ten city squares, supposed to be a part of Canton, or a part of Tartary, as you please; living its own customs, rites and practices, modified by the white man's laws." In many ways, this attitude reflected a larger national shift in attitudes about China, now almost a semi-colonial state whose fall in Asia occurred as America grew more powerful there.[74] As long as San Francisco's Chinese Americans stayed within their district, nativist agitators left them alone, except to use stereotypes of them to warn against any residential integration or to mobilize whites against the new Japanese "threat." But if Chinese Americans sought something different—homes outside Chinatown's "ten city squares" or work in the mainstream economy—they faced insurmountable obstacles and intense hostility.

Furthermore, residential segregation did not politically benefit San Francisco's Chinese Americans the way it did African Americans elsewhere in the North. While intense housing segregation drove up rents in black areas of Northern cities, it also concentrated voters: by the 1920s, political machine bosses began to woo black newcomers with patronage, and African Americans started sending representatives to city councils, state legislatures, and even Congress.[75] In San Francisco, however, naturalization laws prevented the majority of Chinese American adults from voting, and the weakness of their homeland left them even less protected than the smaller Japanese American population of the city. Indeed, the only real role that residential segregation gave Chinese Americans in local politics was an unenviable and familiar one: they remained a conveniently visible symbol of racial threat for politicians and labor leaders alike.

The economic impact of segregation also set Chinatown apart. In much of the urban North, a new generation of African American businesspeople and leaders in the 1920s saw in black population concentration the key to economic self-sufficiency. Many sought to build a parallel black universe within increasingly hostile Northern cities. There, black-owned businesses and black-run social and cultural institutions would serve growing populations of African American residents without white interference.[76] Besides offering African Americans control of their own destiny, the vision of a separate black economic, social, and cultural sphere—although never wholly realized—materially benefited an array of African American merchants. In contrast, San Francisco

Chinatown's new tourism industry lacked the empowering potential of the Black Metropolis, for it depended explicitly on white outsiders and their perceptions of the area and tended to benefit mostly the wealthier and more established merchants on Grant Avenue. Aside from ending the tong wars, it provided fewer tangible benefits to the thousands of Chinese immigrants who dwelled in the streets and lanes west of Grant Avenue and did not speak enough English to work in tourist enterprises.

Furthermore, the growth of tourism in Chinatown and the move to embellish Grant Avenue with gilded eaves and tiled roofs occurred at a time when white celebrations of a mythicized and romanticized past were becoming increasingly common elsewhere in California. During this same era, regional boosters in Southern California helped create what later historians and observers have called the "Spanish fantasy heritage" of the southland. Among other things, promoters of Southern California sponsored events such as "La Fiesta de Los Angeles," a rose-colored paean to the Spanish past, and later the "Mission Play," a similarly themed theatrical production. However, "Anglo depictions of Spanish days . . . did not typically signal a willingness to embrace Mexican or Indian Californians as fellow citizens in the present," historian Phoebe Kropp has contended. "Anglo memories drew the region's temporal boundaries to place Anglos at the center of Southern California's future while exiling all others to its past."[77]

Although Chinese Americans led in developing Chinatown for tourism, the area's success essentially relied on the same dynamic that characterized the Spanish "fantasy past." White nostalgia was not just patronizing but also indicative of wider racial conflict and white Californians' overall racial concerns. In the agricultural districts where Japanese, Filipino, and Mexican American laborers predominated, white farmers praised the work ethic and supposed docility of the vanished Chinese. Urban dwellers fearful of Japanese American housing integration applauded the Chinese for their willingness to remain in their "place." These white Californians resembled the late-nineteenth-century white Southerners who romanticized "faithful" antebellum black slaves because they represented the older, more repressive, and more settled racial order of the antebellum period. White Californians' nostalgia for the Chinese had similar implications, as a sociologist's interview with a Central Valley farmer revealed. The farmer "is very favorable to the old type of Chinese laborer," noted the scholar, but "compares the younger Chinese with the American negro [*sic*], in that as each generation becomes more Americanized they become more independent and harder to handle." In reality, the first Chinese immigrants had been easier to "handle" because they lacked a strong homeland government to protect them. In the face of extreme violence, they dared not challenge racial mores the way the newer Japanese did.[78]

Many of the white tourists who flocked to Chinatown by the 1920s wanted to see a sanitized version of the "old type" Chinese, members of a supposedly ancient and backward race that posed no threat to white dominance. Not all visitors came for racial affirmation; some simply enjoyed the unusual, and like amusement park rides, Chinatown's "dangers" were titillating but never really menacing. Yet as Mexicans, Filipinos, and especially Japanese migrated to California cities, Chinatown's rigid borders and intense segregation comforted many whites. Its boundaries represented a racial and temporal hierarchy that confirmed white progress and Oriental backwardness. Of course, white expectations also forced Chinatown's younger, American-born generations to play roles increasingly distant from their own desires and identities. Dead-end jobs selling trinkets to white tourists appealed even less to these Chinese Americans, many of them graduates of American secondary schools and sometimes colleges, than to their parents. As a sympathetic 1927 *Literary Digest* article noted, "most of these people are making the discovery that for them the world grows constantly smaller instead of larger."[79]

These Chinese Americans also bristled at the enduring stereotypes of Chinatown that drew crowds of tourists. While the number of exploitative tour guides dwindled by the 1920s, portrayals of Chinese in popular pulp novels and the new motion picture industry perpetuated the same fantasies that had titillated the Victorian slummers.[80] As college student Chin Bock Choy complained, Chinatown to Jazz Age–era white Americans was still all about "the sensational discoveries of opium dens and gambling places, the tong wars and gunmen." Decades later, Victor and Brett de Bary Nee "discovered in Chinatown's old-timers a deep resentment of the curious and exotic picture of their lives which prevailed in white society" in these years. This anger strongly shaped their sense of identity and their relationship to the mainstream of American society. "Isolation and resentment developed a strong orientation to China, a pride in being Chinese, which is marked in all the old men of this generation," note Nee and Nee.[81]

Younger Chinese Americans dealt with their frustrations in various ways. Some began preparing for a future in China, where their education and skills might command respect and a salary and help build a new nation. Others, like Chin Bock Choy, sought comfort in the supposed spiritual superiority of Chinatown, and China. "If you infer that lack of [material] things accompanies the lack of culture, you are merely giving evidence of a gross materialism," he argued. "Chinese home life is orderly; it is based on filial love, courtesy, and mutual regard." But as Chinatown's population increased, and its apartments grew increasingly overcrowded, Choy's contemporaries searched for more tangible solutions. As one observer commented, a typical second-generation Chinese American "thinks, 'I do not want to live as my parents do. I *cannot* live as they do.' "[82]

CHAPTER TWO

Los Angeles: America's "White Spot"

On June 23, 1923, a newspaper called *Swat the Jap* appeared on the streets of Hollywood, cautioning white residents that "there is only one course open to all true blooded Americans, and that is . . . excluding and causing the expulsion of all Japanese, American-born or otherwise." Seemingly devoted to immigration issues, the paper actually emerged from a white homeowners' campaign to push Japanese residents from the Tamarind-Bronson district of Los Angeles. It also reflected a new demographic reality: Japanese from northern California were moving by the thousands to L.A., in part to escape the anti-Asian politics that were more prevalent in the northern part of the state.[1] Determined to keep the pressure on these immigrants, Northern nativist organizations began to exploit the issue of segregated housing, which promised to sway white Los Angeles far more than questions of labor or agriculture.

The fervor of the anti-Asian movement in the Los Angeles area never matched the zealotry of San Francisco. There, the local brand of nativism helped bind European immigrants and native-born whites, whether in labor unions or influential organizations such as the Native Sons of the Golden West. Whiteness often meant something quite different in 1920s Los Angeles. The Catholic lay journal *Commonweal* portrayed the city as "ruled entirely from top to bottom by the race known as the 'white Nordic Protestant.'" *Los Angeles Times* publisher Harry Chandler proudly called his home the nation's "white spot" because of its anti-union politics, but other Angelenos liked the phrase because they thought it referred to Southern California's "Nordic" racial composition. As anti-immigrant sentiment surged across the nation, many

L.A. residents boasted that their city contained a larger population of northern and western European descent than any other American metropolis.[2]

Indeed, Los Angeles was quite unique in comparison to other large northern cities of this period. To begin with, it lacked the kind of industrial base that provided jobs for southern and eastern European immigrants elsewhere. A large percentage of its newcomers were white Protestant Midwesterners who moved to Southern California for its warm climate and promise of a more relaxing lifestyle. Writing in the 1940s, Carey McWilliams claimed that as a result of such migration, "a glacial dullness engulfed the [L.A.] region" and made it "the most priggish community in America." Art critic Willard Huntington Wright lampooned the newcomers' "complacent and intransigent aversion to late dinners, malt liquors, grand opera, and hussies." Sarcasm aside, many of these new Angelenos distrusted immigrants, labor unions, Catholics, and Jews as much as they had back home and saw themselves as part of a superior "Anglo-Saxon" or "Nordic" branch of the "Caucasian race."[3]

Consistent with such beliefs, white Angelenos of various backgrounds demanded the residential segregation that other white Americans had come to value so highly by the 1920s. Anti-Asian activists from northern California soon seized on housing segregation to appeal to white Angelenos uninterested in or even hostile to the issues crucial to San Francisco nativism, including agriculture and labor unions. And to exploit the housing issue, these activists used the arsenal of legal weapons they had developed over more than half a century of agitation against Asians.

At the same time, however, they constantly grappled with the housing issue's limitations. Throughout the nation, the dynamics of race and housing differed from neighborhood to neighborhood, and Los Angeles in the 1910s and 1920s was one of the most racially diverse cities in the continental United States. In addition to native-born migrants and Japanese, tens of thousands of blacks and Mexicans and thousands of European immigrants streamed into Los Angeles.[4] Anti-Asian activists tried to use the threat of housing integration to convince white Angelenos that a larger Japanese "invasion" of California itself was underway, but in neighborhoods where African American rather than Japanese American integration was imminent, this message provoked little concern. Furthermore, housing's intensely local nature forced anti-Asian activists to invest significant time and resources in small areas that yielded only limited rewards.

In the end, anti-Asian activists likely deemed their L.A. campaign a failure, yet white residents of the neighborhoods they targeted would probably have disagreed. Like San Francisco nativists, Southern California's most fervent anti-Asian activists sought not just to segregate the Japanese in Los Angeles but to expel them from the state altogether. In contrast, the main priority of the white residents with whom the activists worked was always the expulsion of Japanese from L.A. neighborhoods, not the nation. They succeeded in this task to such a degree that their tactics influenced the home choices of thousands of Japanese residents, shaping residential patterns for the next two decades.

BUNGALOWS AND SELF-PROMOTION

Los Angeles, like San Francisco, was a Spanish and Mexican pueblo turned American frontier town, but the two cities shared little else in common. San Francisco's superb natural harbor and proximity to the gold fields helped it grow rapidly in the 1850s and 1860s to become California's uncontested social, economic, cultural, and industrial capital. Los Angeles remained a dusty backwater, torn by conflicts between its Mexican and Anglo residents. San Diego, a city with a superior harbor, seemed poised to dominate Southern California until Los Angeles outmaneuvered it to get a rail link to the East. With the city connected to the national railroad network, local officials began promoting Los Angeles throughout the country. Their boosterism attracted thousands of winter tourists but relatively few permanent settlers. Determined to change this, the Chamber of Commerce in the 1890s started emphasizing the city's sunshine and leisurely lifestyle rather than its agricultural opportunities. By the 1910s, thousands of prosperous Midwestern farmers, professionals, and businesspeople were migrating to Los Angeles for good.[5]

They arrived in a city whose physical layout reflected boosters' emphasis on subdivision, bungalows, and self-promotion. As the population increased, the city stretched out in almost every direction. A downtown business district dominated commerce until the 1920s, but after the 1890s its center moved steadily south and west, a reflection of the city's growth and sprawl. Small food and textile factories dotted the old East Side Industrial District near downtown, while the newer industries that emerged in the 1910s and 1920s were located both in the Central Manufacturing District to the southeast of downtown and farther out in the spreading suburbs.[6]

Los Angeles's population was also far less concentrated than cities of similar size. New immigrants to eastern and Midwestern cities usually sought inexpensive apartments or small, cheap "workers' cottages" close to manufacturing jobs. Most of the well-off, native-born newcomers to L.A. demanded modern single-family homes on large lots; poorer white migrants wanted ample space and the chance to build their own homes. In response, builders

threw up thousands of vaguely Spanish-style bungalows supposedly reminiscent of the city's pueblo past, while developers laid out more and more
home sites and tracts to the northeast (Pasadena and San Marino), northwest
(Hollywood, Glendale, and Van Nuys), south (South Gate, Bell, Lynwood,
Montebello, and Compton), and west (Beverly Hills) of central Los Angeles.[7]

After 1920, the automobile, which enabled developers to subdivide tracts
far beyond the reach of the city's streetcar network, helped further erode
downtown's standing. In the end, autos not only destroyed the streetcar system
but also encouraged the growth of suburban shopping and service districts
that rivaled and then eclipsed the central business district. The pattern that
emerged in Los Angeles by the 1920s foreshadowed the urban and suburban
development of much of the rest of the nation in the decades afterwards.[8]

NEXUS OF MIGRATION

White, Protestant, native-born, and prosperous Midwesterners were not the
only people migrating to Los Angeles in the early twentieth century. In the late
1910s and early 1920s, poorer whites from other regions, especially the South,
began arriving in L.A. in search of decent homes and jobs. As writer Mildred
Adams recalled, "they had rattletrap automobiles, their fenders tied with
string. . . . They camped on the outskirts of town, and their camps became
new suburbs." Many of these migrants settled in cheap tracts that developers
created for them in communities throughout Los Angeles County and built
homes for themselves on their free evenings and weekends with a few dollars'
worth of lumber at a time. They found jobs not in the offices of the central
business district but in new nearby factories such as Bell Foundry or Firestone
Tire. To make ends meet, many rented out rooms to boarders and planted
vegetable gardens in their back yards.[9]

If the Midwestern Babbitts looked down their noses at these fellow migrants, they certainly preferred them to the southern and eastern European
immigrants arriving simultaneously. Between 1920 and the early 1930s, the
number of Italian, "Jugo-Slav," Polish, Russian, Hungarian, and Greek immigrants almost doubled in the city of Los Angeles and the surrounding
county. Such populations remained tiny, compared to the cities of the East,
but native-born Protestant Angelenos still noticed their growth with dismay.
"The Spanish, French, Italians and the Greecians [*sic*] too are to my way of
thinking of most objectionable type," remarked W.H. Fitchmiller of Santa
Monica's Wilshire Development Association. "As a rule the families are large,
there [*sic*] culture is marked by it's [*sic*] absence, there is no such thing as the

finer qualities demanded by American citizenship apparent in them, dignity and character is lacking."[10]

This worldview reflected the small-town Midwestern origins of the middle-class migrants, but it also served the industrial dreams of the L.A. establishment. In the 1910s and 1920s, Harry Chandler and other city boosters staked L.A.'s future on its reputation as an anti-union city that embraced the "American Plan" of open-shop industry, welfare capitalism, and company control of workers. According to scholar Mike Davis, "as the premier American Plan metropolis, with the smallest percentage of European new immigrants, Los Angeles envisioned itself as the racial antipode to San Francisco, Chicago, Cleveland, and New York with their teeming Irish, Italian, Polish, and Jewish populations." Middle-class Anglos associated southern and eastern European immigrants with Bolshevism, labor activism, and biological undesirability—three traits they saw as mutually reinforcing. Not coincidentally, Los Angeles attracted some of the nation's leading proponents of eugenics, including physicist Robert Millikan, who supported "race science" groups like Pasadena's Human Betterment Foundation.[11] The findings of such organizations affirmed the economic, racial, and social views of both civic leaders and Los Angeles's white Protestant middle class.

THE OTHER MIGRANTS

In addition to southern and eastern Europeans, Los Angeles in the 1910s and 1920s attracted a host of migrants whose whiteness was even more contested, or flatly denied. Thousands of African Americans, part of the Great Migration, came to the city in the 1910s and 1920s both for jobs and to escape the brutal Jim Crow system of the South.[12] During the same years, numerous Mexicans fled the violent revolution in their country for greater security and opportunity in Southern California. As Alien Land Acts cut into the livelihood of the state's Japanese, many Issei also left hostile territory—in their case, northern California—for the booming southern metropolis. None of these groups enjoyed the wide choice of housing and jobs that their white Protestant migrant peers expected and demanded. Instead, residential segregation, employment discrimination, and general bigotry narrowed their horizons.

The structure of L.A.'s economy convinced white Angelenos of all backgrounds of their racial superiority even as it tied them to the city's nonwhite population. Middle-class and elite white residents virtually monopolized Los Angeles's professional and business sectors. By the 1920s, the poorer whites who settled in suburbs such as South Gate, Downey, and Watts, took jobs in the growing manufacturing sector, as did even the recent European immigrants whom civic leaders viewed with such suspicion. In contrast, most nonwhites found only low-wage positions in agriculture, domestic service, and day labor. Historian Josh Sides has noted that "white Angelenos who believed in the innate racial superiority of whites also found themselves unusually dependent on dark-skinned immigrant workers" to do most of the County's agricultural and service jobs.[13] This ironic dependence did not foster more sympathy, but merely disdain.

Different nonwhite Angelenos clustered in different sectors of the economy, largely as a result of white pressure. According to historian Mark Wild, white Angelenos consciously set out to separate each of the nonwhite groups "from Anglos (and each other) as discrete entities with specific symbiotic roles to fill in the social and economic life of the city." Anglo civic leaders and individual employers generally believed that different groups had different natural skills and abilities, a philosophy attractive to a white population that embraced eugenics, racial hierarchy, and Nordic superiority. The concentration of certain groups in certain professions suggests the way white Angelenos perpetuated shared stereotypes through hiring practices: most Mexicans worked as laborers, harvesters, railhands, and eventually low-level factory workers; blacks often took jobs as porters, waiters, and domestics; and many Japanese grew, transported, and marketed produce.[14]

Nonwhite Angelenos also made decisions about how and where to work, although discrimination always limited their choices. Mexicans frequently crossed back and forth over the border until the 1924 immigration legislation made this more difficult and expensive. By the 1910s, many of them also shunned migratory agricultural labor, settling permanently in Los Angeles County or the city itself and searching for local employment. African Americans, many of them migrants from Southern cities, avoided agriculture altogether.[15] As for Japanese workers, the majority eventually sought independence from white control through farming for themselves or working for other Issei.

THE JAPANESE IN LOS ANGELES

The success of the Japanese in agriculture angered many white Californians. Between 1885 and 1910, more than thirty thousand Japanese men immigrated to California, initially working as farm laborers or in canneries. However, by saving their wages and sometimes pooling them, many Japanese laborers purchased or leased land of their own in the years after 1900. The Japanese entered California agriculture at an opportune time, when rapid urbanization and the advent of refrigerated rail cars created both a growing demand for fresh fruits and vegetables in cities across the nation and a way to supply such produce. Through hard work and intensive cultivation methods, the Japanese grew profitable specialty crops, such as asparagus, strawberries, and lettuce, on their small plots. As early as the 1890s, however, San Francisco's anti-Chinese unions singled out the immigrants as a new "yellow peril," despite Japanese absence from the industrial sector. California's white small farmers, already an embattled group in a state where large landholders dominated agriculture, also saw the newcomers as unfair competitors. White farm laborers blamed cheap Japanese labor for thwarting their nascent efforts to unionize California's brutal agricultural industry as well.[16]

Still, many white Americans, including Californians, responded to Japan's rapid modernization and its growing influence and power in Asia with grudging respect. The era's race science cast blacks as inferior to whites, while influential eugenicists and many Angelenos derided Mexicans as examples of a degraded "mongrel race." The Japanese, however, provoked more complex sentiments. Racial theorist Lothrop Stoddard predicted a coming conflict between whites and "Asiatics" for reasons that political commentator Raymond Leslie Buell echoed. "The Japanese cannot be called an 'inferior' people as is done with the Indians and the negroes [*sic*]," he contended. "And they, alone of the color groups in this country, are represented by a sensitive and powerful government abroad."[17]

The Russo-Japanese War of 1905, in which Japan defeated the "white" empire of Russia, profoundly shook many American race theorists and other white supremacists. According to Stoddard, the Russo-Japanese War was "one of those landmarks in human history," and because of it, "the legend of white invincibility was shattered, the veil of prestige that draped white civilization was torn aside." While loathe to acknowledge Japanese successes, many California nativists shifted their rhetoric in the years after 1905. Although still relying on older themes, such as low "Asiatic" living standards and economic competition, the growing anti-Japanese movement also began warning of Japan's alleged desire to conquer and colonize California. The more genteel nativists, especially newspaper heir Valentine S. McClatchy, argued that the Japanese, while racial equals, were so different from whites that they were socially and biologically inassimilable.[18]

Grudging respect thus did not mean acceptance, as the Japanese learned when they tried to become naturalized citizens. The 1790 Naturalization Law allowed only "free white persons" to become U.S. citizens, although people of African ancestry gained naturalization rights after the Civil War. The 1882

Chinese Exclusion Act definitively declared Chinese immigrants ineligible for citizenship but left the status of other Asians uncertain. When Japanese tried to naturalize, however, lower courts generally declared them ineligible for citizenship because they were neither white nor African.[19] In its 1922 *Ozawa v. U.S.* ruling, the Supreme Court agreed.[20]

As ineligible aliens, Japanese immigrants occupied a very insecure legal position in California. Despite the 1907 Gentlemen's Agreement, which halted Japanese male labor immigration, anti-Japanese agitation continued into the 1910s and 1920s. Led by the Asiatic Exclusion League and the Native Sons of the Golden West, anti-Japanese forces in California protested the continued immigration of Japanese women, the growth of the Japanese American citizen population, and the success of Japanese farmers. In 1913, the California state legislature passed the first Alien Land Act, which made illegal the sale of agricultural property to aliens ineligible for citizenship but allowed them to lease plots for up to three years. The law emboldened organizations with nativist inclinations: after World War I, four such groups—the State Federation of Labor, the Native Sons of the Golden West, the Grange, and the American Legion—joined to form the California Joint Immigration Committee. The organization pushed for more stringent anti-Japanese and anti-Asian legislation, including a stronger Alien Land Act.[21]

This type of nativist legislation placed an increasingly heavy and sometimes intolerable burden on Japanese farmers. Passed by popular referendum in 1920, the second Alien Land Act eliminated the right of ineligible aliens even to lease land or to buy it in the names of citizen children, something many Japanese had done since 1913. When Japanese challenged the statute in court, they lost repeatedly. Laws discriminating against specific Asian groups violated the Fourteenth Amendment, but the Supreme Court ruled that the Alien Land Act, although based on explicitly discriminatory immigration policy, did not.[22] In the wake of failed court challenges, many Japanese continued leasing farmland illegally, but the new laws pushed others out of agriculture altogether. Sociologist Midori Nishi found that in the decade after 1920, the total acreage of Japanese-run farms in California fell from 361,276 to 191,427 acres. A substantial number of Japanese also returned to Japan for good.[23]

The land acts accelerated the movement of Japanese farmers to booming Southern California, where nativism did not dominate politics the way it did in the north. Anti-Asian sentiment was not unknown in the southland: in 1871, a white mob murdered nineteen Chinese residents in L.A. after a Chinese man accidentally shot a white man. Yet this vigilantism did not reflect the same depth of anti-Chinese sentiment as existed in San Francisco. Chinese and whites did not compete for factory jobs in Los Angeles, which also never developed the strong union movement that helped keep anti-Asian nativism alive in San Francisco.

The comparatively muted tradition of organized anti-Asian activism in Los Angeles boded well for Japanese migrants arriving in the early 1910s. Japanese farmers who owned no land needed a host of accomplices in order to make a living: sheriffs and district attorneys willing to tolerate their farming; white neighbors and voters uninterested in pushing officials on Alien Land Act enforcement; and most of all, white landowners willing to illegally lease plots to them. Southern California contained millions of acres of open land, much of it the property of large landholders who rented it to the highest bidder. By paying a premium to these owners, thousands of Japanese illegally farmed land throughout Orange and Ventura counties, which border Los Angeles County, by the 1920s. Closer in, many Japanese unlawfully leased Los Angeles County and city land, some of which developers had already slated for future housing tracts, including parts of Gardena, Canoga Park, San Fernando, Torrance, Hawthorne, Dominguez Hills, Palos Verdes Hills, and Venice.[24] Such arrangements proved advantageous to white builders, who made money from the Japanese but could evict them when development began.

Self-employment thus did not give the Japanese greater security than other nonwhite groups in Los Angeles. As historian Eiichiro Azuma has shown, after 1920 "interracial relations were uncontestable to the point of nearly total Japanese dependency on propertied whites, who could arbitrarily dictate the use of a few loopholes for their Issei tenants." Indeed, as late as 1940, Japanese Americans only *owned* 7 percent of the farms they ran in Los Angeles County, a number that revealed their vulnerability to white public opinion and the white accomplices upon whom they depended. And many Japanese who did not farm themselves still depended on agriculture in some way, delivering produce, wholesaling it, or selling it to the public at one of the fruit stands scattered across the metropolitan area. Regardless, some Angelenos resented the Japanese because of their apparent independence from the control of white employers.[25]

THE TOOLS OF NATIVISM

Anti-Japanese sentiment in California subsided during World War I—Japan was an ally—but it soon flared up again after the armistice. Anti-Asian groups collected signatures to put the more stringent Alien Land Act on the ballot, while the bruising 1920 U.S. Senate campaign became an exercise in anti-Japanese one-upmanship. Democratic incumbent James Phelan distributed campaign posters with a picture of a clawing yellow hand and the slogan "Stop the Silent Invasion"; Republican Samuel Shortridge won the election by promising "Protection for California."[26] Numerous other candidates on the ballot that year promoted the anti-Japanese cause with equal enthusiasm. Soon, the entire state, from the rural north coast to urban Los Angeles, was awash in anti-Japanese rhetoric.

Anti-Japanese homeowner movements in Los Angeles emerged from this atmosphere and flourished in two kinds of districts characteristic of the city's rapid growth. Pico Heights and Rose Hill exemplified the first type of area. By the 1920s, these two neighborhoods—close to the city center and already developed by the turn of the century—had lost whatever cachet they once enjoyed. The second kind of area was also typical of Los Angeles: an outlying, formerly rural tract newly subdivided for homes that working-class residents often built themselves. The Tamarind-Bronson district of Hollywood was just such an area. None of these neighborhoods were particularly fashionable, but each offered the kind of inexpensive housing that attracted both working-class whites and Japanese. And in each, Northern nativist groups recruited scores of residents who readily embraced anti-Asian language and laws in order to stake claims to whiteness and social desirability.

Builders subdivided Pico Heights, a modest neighborhood near the western edge of downtown, right after 1900. A number of Japanese arrived around the same time, initially settling on the low-lying and less expensive eastern side of the district. By 1920, continuing real estate development elsewhere made Pico Heights less desirable to middle-class residents than it once had been.[27] Laborers, clerks, laundrymen, and chauffeurs largely replaced the dentists, lawyers, bookkeepers, and small businessmen who originally purchased homes in the area. Builders started to erect multifamily dwellings for lower-income people, while growing numbers of residents took in lodgers to make ends meet. The percentage of area residents who owned their own homes plummeted between 1910 and 1920, and far more of the district's married women now worked. Growing numbers of southern and eastern Europeans and Mexicans, as well as additional Japanese, also began to trickle into the neighborhood. Finally, Loyola School, the city's oldest parochial school, relocated to Pico Heights in 1917, creating a magnet for Catholic Angelenos. The move was controversial among residents: the Jesuits actually purchased the land secretly through a Protestant intermediary because its original owner refused to sell to any Catholic.[28]

As anti-Japanese sentiment engulfed the state, Pico Heights residents who felt their own whiteness and Americanness under attack began to single out the Japanese as the least white and least American group in the district. Anti-Japanese sentiment was particularly intense on several blocks containing large numbers of first- and second-generation Germans and Austrians, people whose Americanism underwent deep scrutiny during World War I. In addition, a number of southern and eastern Europeans who moved to Pico Heights after 1910 became involved in the anti-Japanese movement there. Catholics also played prominent leadership roles in the new Electric Improvement Association, which residents organized in 1919 to rid the district of Japanese.[29] Members began by exerting pressure on white landlords to evict Japanese, but occasionally they bombed and burned Japanese-owned homes as well.[30]

When the local Methodist conference announced plans to build a church for Japanese in Pico Heights, San Francisco-based nativist groups quickly arrived to offer free advice and support to the working-class homeowners of the Electric Improvement Association.[31] Sociologist John Modell sees this kind of assistance as an attempt to build "the foundation for an anti-Japanese constituency of larger scope" in Southern California. Indeed, just a few months earlier, the Los Angeles County Anti-Asiatic Society had announced plans to recruit ten thousand new members. As Modell argues, the agricultural and labor issues that nativists used to attract members in northern areas of the state interested far fewer residents of urban, open-shop Los Angeles.[32] Neighborhood integration, on the other hand, frightened and angered race- and real estate–conscious white Angelenos and made them far more open to the anti-Asian message.

Anti-Asian groups attracted homeowners not only by offering segregationist expertise but also by speaking to the burning resentments of the working-class immigrants and Catholics whom middle-class Los Angeles "Nordics" scorned. Large numbers of Pico Heights Japanese worked as servants and gardeners for middle-class and wealthy Angelenos living elsewhere, such as the upscale Miracle Mile area of Wilshire Boulevard. A white Pico Heights resident claimed that the Methodist clergymen "all lived out in the Wilshire district where they knew there wasn't a chance in the world for them to have a Japanese living next door to them, or a Japanese church next door to them." In essence, she felt, the clergy viewed Pico Heights as their Japanese servants' quarters. Exploiting this anger, Clarence Hunt, the editor of the Native Sons' paper *Grizzly Bear*, labeled the Wilshire clergymen and their ilk "White Japs" for dumping "yellow trash . . . onto those districts of the city peopled by citizens who are thoroughly and always White themselves."[33] To Hunt, Pico Heights's agitators were whiter and more desirable than self-styled "Nordic" Angelenos.

The ideology of the anti-Asian outsiders also appealed to Pico Heights homeowners, because they could use it to justify the expulsion of longtime Japanese residents of the neighborhood. John Modell has ascribed the conflicts in Pico Heights and other areas to Japanese "residential invasion," but like many other area residents, Electric Improvement Association president Mr. Duffy and secretary Percy Jenkins both moved to Pico Heights *after* most of the Japanese they opposed.[34] San Francisco-style nativism, with its emphasis on expansive whiteness, Japanese inassimilability, and Asian exclusion, helped such men rationalize their attempts to push out those who had actually preceded them. San Francisco nativist groups and their Los Angeles subsidiaries supported what one activist described as "a state law that will dispossess Asiatics of every foot of California land they may have acquired title to." Scholars who interviewed local whites involved in the Pico Heights agitation discovered widespread support for such measures. As a leading nativist homeowner argued, "We don't want [the Japanese] in this country at all."[35]

L.A.'s city council responded to the Pico Heights campaign by forcing the Methodists to abandon their plans to build a church, but a similar conflict soon flared up in Rose Hill.[36] An older district northeast of downtown, Rose Hill had never been a fashionable part of Los Angeles.[37] The kinds of changes obvious in Pico Heights—a growing working-class population, a drop in owner occupancy, and an increased number of working wives—had also become evident in Rose Hill by 1920. The area resembled Pico Heights in other ways as well, for in the 1910s it attracted large numbers of southern and eastern European immigrant families and a significant German and Austrian population.[38]

San Francisco-based nativist organizations appear to have provoked and controlled the anti-Japanese campaign in Rose Hill from the very start, although they still chose to work through local residents. The ostensible leader of the anti-Japanese forces in the neighborhood was Thomas Coughlin, who in late 1921 formed the Rose Hill Civic Improvement Association and launched a full-scale campaign against the handful of Japanese families living in the area. Coughlin was a machinist who worked in the San Pedro shipyards during World War I, a time when labor unions enjoyed significant influence there.[39] What little evidence exists about Coughlin suggests that he was an ideal convert to San Francisco-style nativism: a union member and an Irish Catholic married to a Polish Catholic in an open-shop town dominated by Nordic Protestants.

But Coughlin almost certainly did not act alone, nor did he rely on his own resources. In the last months of 1921, white neighbors throughout the district put standardized, professionally printed anti-Japanese signs on their porches and lawns. The Civic Improvement Association also created a large banner with the words "Japs, Don't Let the Sun Set on You Here. Keep Moving" and strung it over Huntington Drive until police pulled it down for being on public land. To great fanfare, the association raised the banner again—this time on private land—during an evening ceremony and banquet at which a brass band performed. Representatives of the Native Sons of the Golden West and the American Legion then addressed the assembled crowds. A Japanese American student contended that after the meeting, a Japanese home in Rose Hill "was fired by an incendiary."[40]

Given the limited incomes of area residents and the large number of transients and renters in Rose Hill, funding for the brass band, the banner, and the banquet almost certainly came from organized anti-Japanese groups outside the district. By 1921, such groups struggled to keep the Japanese issue before a public they feared had become complacent after the passage of the 1920 Alien Land Act. To build more support for their cause, they depended on the Thomas Coughlins of Los Angeles—status-conscious, racially insecure residents of working-class areas where Japanese were beginning to look for homes. And apparently they delivered what they promised; the signs, the meeting, and especially the bombing stopped the trickle of Japanese into Rose Hill.[41]

Nativist forces soon found another area of L.A. eager for their expertise. Farms and ranches dominated the Tamarind-Bronson section of Hollywood before 1910; rather than single-family homes, most residents of the semi-rural area lived in boarding houses that sometimes mixed laborers of all ethnicities, including Americans, Europeans, Asians, and Mexicans. Those not employed in agriculture generally worked for the Pacific Electric Railway, which operated a nearby yard that employed people of all races as laborers and car washers.[42] In 1912, investors began purchasing land in the area and subdividing it, probably anticipating the future needs of employees in the new film industry. The subdividers did not have movie stars in mind; according to later assessors, the area's developers created it as a "low rental workingman's district." Some Japanese who already owned land in the area held on to their property after 1912, while large numbers of white families and a few more Japanese bought or rented in the district. In 1923, the city's Presbyterian hierarchy announced plans to build a new church on Tamarind Avenue for area Japanese.

Simultaneously, several of the long-standing Japanese residents applied for a permit to erect a large apartment building on their Bronson Street lots.[43]

While racial and religious insecurities initially fueled the anti-Japanese campaign in Pico Heights, class anxieties fed the movement in Hollywood from the start. Beatrice Poole, who with her husband Joseph moved to Tamarind Avenue after 1920, first organized area opposition to the church and then to the Japanese presence as a whole. As in Pico Heights, the decision of the Presbyterian hierarchy seemed to confirm to Poole and her neighbors that a middle-class, white-run organization had identified their area as a Japanese neighborhood. As one resident complained, "soon instead of Hollywood the Beautiful, it will be Hollywood the home of the Japs."[44] With Tamarind-Bronson now developing into a residential neighborhood, the Japanese presence in the area had suddenly become problematic.

Poole almost immediately reached out to the anti-Japanese organizations that by this point were gaining a reputation for their work with (and through) Los Angeles's segregationist white homeowner groups. Poole, the wife of a young carpenter, remained the public leader of the movement in Hollywood, but the Los Angeles Anti-Asiatic Society began calling the shots, as it had in Rose Hill. It almost certainly provided the money to print and distribute hundreds of anti-Japanese handbills throughout the area, send a wagon with anti-Japanese signs around the neighborhood, and hold at least two mass meetings at a hall owned by the American Legion.[45] Tellingly, none of the speakers at the first rally actually lived in the neighborhood itself. Instead, the crowd listened to outsiders, including representatives of the Los Angeles County Anti-Asiatic Society and the Native Sons of the Golden West, warn that residents of "the Pacific Coast are facing the greatest battle that has ever threatened the white man. It is to be the fight against the yellow man." Delegations from other neighborhoods that had experienced anti-Japanese agitation, including Rose Hill and Pico Heights, attended to offer support to the Hollywood residents.[46]

As in Rose Hill, Anti-Asiatic Society leaders apparently hoped that the Hollywood conflict would breathe new life into their L.A. recruitment efforts. Within weeks of the initial agitation, the group invited Beatrice Poole's new Hollywood Protective Association and other local anti-Japanese organizations to affiliate with it. Addressing the concerns of race-conscious white Angelenos, the group also pledged "to carry on an aggressive campaign against the Japanese whenever they may attempt to establish themselves in any community."[47] The message was consistent both with white Angelenos' growing demands for residential segregation and with northern California's

FIGURE 2.1. Mrs. B. G. Miller, a member of the Hollywood Protective Association, was among hundreds of white homeowners in eastern Hollywood who displayed anti–Japanese American signs on their homes in 1923. (Photo by staff photographer for the *Los Angeles Examiner*, May, 1923. Courtesy of the National Japanese American Historical Society.)

anti-Japanese nativism, which denied that Asian Americans had the right to live *anywhere* in California.

While the Northern nativists tried to use the Hollywood conflict, area real estate agents attempted to use the nativists. By the 1910s, white real estate professionals actively sought to "protect" white communities from unwanted residents of color and warned white homebuyers to avoid integrated neighborhoods as well. This drive for residential segregation occasionally involved pushing nonwhites out of places where they already lived or owned businesses, but usually it focused on keeping them from moving into certain neighborhoods. This was the pattern in Watts, another community that began as a

Pacific Electric Railway labor camp. White homeowners in neighboring areas both created race restrictions and relied on real estate agents to keep Watts's black and Mexican American areas from expanding.[48] In Hollywood, however, real estate agents backed the Anti-Asiatic Society's campaign not just to prevent construction of the church and to keep Japanese from moving to the area but also to expel those already there.

Area real estate agents barely hid their involvement in the anti-Japanese movement. The Hollywood Protective Association published a crudely racist newspaper called *Swat the Jap*, and while its main funding obviously came from the Anti-Asiatic Society, its publisher shared his telephone with the Hollywood Realty Company. That firm and other real estate brokers believed that forcing the Japanese out of Tamarind-Bronson would boost property values and profits in the area. As Oscar Ruff, a neighborhood anti-Japanese activist who operated his own real estate firm, maintained, "the Japanese hurt property values, no one wants to live near them." Japanese American resident J. Hirai understood the connection well. "Two or three years ago times were good and property sold everywhere," he recalled. "Now everything is dead, but here they say, 'We can't sell our property because the Japs live here.' When times are bad they blame us because they cannot sell their property."[49]

As in Pico Heights, the rhetoric of San Francisco-style nativism helped these real estate agents and many anti-Japanese activists justify their actions. Several leaders of the anti-Japanese agitation, including Joseph and Beatrice Poole and Oscar Ruff, moved to the district at least a decade after their Japanese foes. Regardless, they tried to frame the issue as one of Japanese "invasion" of a white neighborhood. In a letter to the *Hollywood Citizen*, Joseph Poole argued that anti-Japanese activists included "people who have worked for years to accumulate what little they have, and who have stood by helplessly with heavy hearts and watched this encroachment by the Japanese." Yet as one longtime white resident complained, no one had encroached on the Pooles and other agitators, most of whom "bought with the Japanese right beside them, of course they knew they were there." Even a few opponents of the Japanese had to admit that "some people don't investigate [the race of their neighbors] as much as they should," a difficult argument to make about residents such as real estate man Oscar Ruff.[50]

The Hollywood conflict revealed some of the same class tensions evident in Pico Heights. Neither religion nor ethnicity distinguished the white residents who supported the Japanese from those who opposed them, but wealth apparently played an important role. Those who spoke up in defense of the

Japanese included two physicians, an accountant, and a retiree wealthy enough to employ a live-in servant (not a Japanese, however). Few of the anti-Japanese agitators publicized their names, but the words of their leaders and their own actions suggested their deep resentment of their white opponents. "The whites on Hollywood Boulevard and north of the boulevard are feeling wronged that their Japanese friends are not wanted on Tamarind Avenue," charged Beatrice Poole. "Our only answer to them is, let them take the Japs up to the boulevard and allow them to colonize there."[51]

Indeed, middle-class and elite white Anglos, especially Protestants of northern and western European descent, appear to have expressed less overt hostility towards the Japanese than their poor and working-class peers. Middle- and upper-class Angelenos often hired Japanese as domestics and gardeners but rarely faced the possibility of Japanese neighbors.[52] Few Japanese could afford homes in newer, middle-class neighborhoods, and developers by the 1920s routinely covered such tracts with deed restrictions anyway. In older neighborhoods built before the advent of deed restrictions, however, poor and working-class white residents had to organize campaigns to cover their homes with racially restrictive covenants. As historian Thomas Lee Philpott has noted, a successful covenant campaign took "time, talent, and money"— often thousands of dollars, an astronomical sum for residents of these neighborhoods.[53] In Los Angeles, Japanese immigrants usually sought homes in just such areas, since they were affordable and lacked racial restrictions.

These kinds of class issues defined the conflicts in Pico Heights and Rose Hill, but in Hollywood, many of the anti-Japanese residents resented not just wealthier whites but wealthier Japanese. Describing the *white* residents of Tamarind-Bronson, a Hollywood real estate agent confessed: "That is the worst district in Hollywood just on account of those people." According to another observer, "the Japanese own all the nicest places on this street." Limited in where they could rent or purchase homes, Japanese residents with decent incomes often lived in neighborhoods where most of the white residents earned less than they did. Tamarind-Bronson's occupants included two pairs of Japanese brothers who owned eight lots on the street and two successful produce stores in the neighborhood. By 1923, they had begun to improve their residential properties in ways that many of their white neighbors could not afford to copy. Praising the brothers' new building as "attractive looking and entirely modern," a white neighbor sympathetic to them compared it to the home of a family prominent in the anti-Japanese movement: "It is an old shell of a house, nothing modern about it and an awful looking place."[54]

The perceived audacity of these Japanese residents grated on poorer whites in the area, for the brothers were visibly challenging the ideas of white racial supremacy so widely accepted in California and the rest of the nation.

This burning antipathy emboldened the Anti-Asiatic Society. In other neighborhoods, the organization helped residents report Japanese homes to local health authorities or the police, fight Japanese building permits, and even serve a Japanese family with forged court papers ordering them to move. But in Hollywood, anti-Japanese leaders took the campaign one step further. Proclaiming that Japanese had no right even to live in California, the nativist-backed Hollywood Protective Association petitioned the city council in the summer of 1923 to condemn Tamarind-Bronson's Japanese-owned lots and turn them into a park.[55]

FIGHTING BACK?

Japanese homeowners and residents responded to these growing protests in ways that revealed the deep fissures within their own community. Tensions between old-timers and newcomers characterized many migrant and immigrant populations in the urban North, including Jewish and African American communities. Japanese Americans, on the other hand, tended to split along somewhat different lines. The more highly educated and wealthier Japanese immigrants, regardless of when they arrived, disdained the majority of the Issei as backward peasants who were an embarrassment to Japan. Many elites even compared the mass of Japanese immigrants to the Chinese whom both they and the white population despised.[56]

As anti-Japanese sentiment mounted, Japanese community leaders accepted widespread white allegations that most Issei were filthy and maintained poor living standards. Certainly, some of Los Angeles's Japanese residents lived in substandard conditions, a situation that state law actually promoted. By denying ineligible aliens the right to own or even lease land, the Alien Land Acts discouraged many Issei farmers from investing in decent homes. At the same time, Japanese residents were likely no more or less dirty than their non-Japanese neighbors; white resentment of Japanese home improvements in Tamarind-Bronson suggested as much. Still, the prominent Japanese Angelenos who implored Issei gardeners and truck farmers to clean their homes and yards and make themselves more presentable apparently took white complaints seriously. In response to the Hollywood conflict, Sei Fujii of the Los Angeles Japanese Association cautioned fellow immigrants: "if there is anything in our daily conduct which is repugnant to the good customs and manners of America and otherwise objectionable, we must be good enough to change it right away." Japanese-language newspapers, which usually expressed the views of more elite Issei, also exhorted Japanese immigrants to adopt American standards of behavior and attire.[57] Even the small Japanese American professional class chastised poorer Japanese for their troublesome behavior. Los Angeles's only Japanese American attorney argued that "there is prejudice against the Japanese, but I realize full well that there is some just reason for some of it because of the behavior of some members of the group."[58]

Leading Japanese had few options other than to embrace this approach, which resembled the "racial uplift" ideology of their black middle-class contemporaries. The strength of white supremacist sentiment, a lack of other choices, and elites' feelings of superiority made the tactic attractive to both groups. As historian Victoria Wolcott notes, African American racial uplift, which emphasized "individual hard work . . . and stressed a bourgeois moral code of appropriate behavioral norms," flowered in the "dark period of disenfranchisement, segregation, and violence" at and after the turn of the century. At the height of anti-Japanese nativism in California, the strength of the Japanese government arguably gave Japanese immigrants more leverage than African Americans living under Jim Crow. Still, Tokyo usually ignored housing strife and similarly local matters, focusing instead on larger issues such as pending immigration legislation. Left to their own devices, officers of the Los Angeles Japanese Association offered legal advice to Japanese home seekers but understood far too well that the immigrants enjoyed very few rights in the first place.[59] Already predisposed to assume the worst about other Issei, they readily turned to behavioral prescriptions for problems they could not really solve.

Many Japanese leaders themselves remained confused about the extent of immigrant rights, a reflection of legal gray areas and the misinformation that white nativists circulated. In 1920, the San Francisco Real Estate Board and the Apartment House Owners' and Managers' Association wanted to stop Japanese from buying residential property, especially apartment buildings. The state's ferociously nativist attorney general, Ulysses S. Webb, offered to help by investigating possible violations of the Alien Land Act in San Francisco. The Alien Land Act supposedly applied only to agricultural property, but its ambiguous use of the term "real property" gave Webb grounds for harassment, if not actual confiscation. Such tactics led to great bewilderment among the Japanese. Sociology student Koyoshi Uono claimed with certainty that in cases involving Japanese immigrants, "ownership of land for

residential purposes is obviously restricted by the California Alien Land Law."
In 1948, Justice Hugo Black agreed. Because of the use of the term "real property" in the law, he wrote, "it would therefore appear to be a crime for
an alien of Japanese ancestry to own a home in California, at least if the land
around it is suitable for cultivation."[60] Neither Japanese nor nativists ever fully
litigated the issue, since both sides likely feared losing.[61] Still, numerous Issei
throughout the state believed that they did not have the right to own residential
property, and many bought homes in the names of their citizen children.[62]
Others avoided purchasing homes altogether or did so only in neighborhoods
where there was no white opposition to their presence.

Since nativist organizations successfully recruited local officials and politicians, Japanese home seekers faced many challenges in protecting the few
rights they had. Local law enforcement officials took their cues from men such
as Los Angeles County Sheriff William Traeger, who served as chairman of
the Anti-Asiatic Society. In one incident, a deputy sheriff and homeowner
named George Perdue used his authority to push a Japanese family out of his
own neighborhood, making the dubious claim that "a law [was] passed 50
years ago forbidding colored races to settle here."[63] Law enforcement officials
in a different suburb looked the other way as white residents burned one
Japanese-owned home and stoned another. Under these circumstances, even
Japanese consular officers in Los Angeles struggled to find decent homes in
which to live.[64]

THE VALUE OF WHITENESS

The Japanese were not the only immigrants who contended with American
racial nationalism, but the Immigration Act of 1924 at least allowed limited immigration from Europe. In doing so, it hinted at the potential whiteness of such
immigrants—compared with the absolute nonwhiteness of Asians, who could
no longer enter at all. Wealthier and better educated Issei resented American
laws and attitudes that lumped them together with Japanese peasants and the
Chinese whose racial fitness many Japanese thinkers questioned. For their
part, less privileged Japanese immigrants, the majority of whom possessed
at least an eighth-grade education, expressed bewilderment at the way white
Americans favored uneducated European immigrants over Japanese.[65]

During the 1920s, a portion of Los Angeles's southern and eastern European immigrants scrambled to claim and embrace "whiteness" by separating
themselves from the Japanese, especially in areas away from central city neigh-

borhoods. Events in Pico Heights hinted at this type of activity; the anti-Japanese movement in Belvedere, an unincorporated east-side suburb with a mix of newly developed lower-income housing tracts and open land, confirmed it. Belvedere's residents included Mexicans, Italians, Russian Jews, and numerous other European immigrants. By 1920, a handful of Japanese families had also moved to the district, but they soon faced grassroots opposition in which European-born families played a leading role. Fire destroyed at least one Japanese-owned home in Belvedere, while vigilantes visited other families to pressure them to leave. In one case, white residents even beat a Japanese neighbor, whom the police then pushed to drop charges against his attackers.[66]

Frustrated Japanese homeowners such as J. Sato, who was threatened by a largely foreign-born residents' group, understood to at least some extent the racial "transformation" underway. "White people! I suppose white people were Jewish, Italians, Russians, and low class Europeans," declared Sato, whose views on the subject many self-described Nordics shared. Another Japanese resident told an interviewer that the European immigrants of the area "try to make us think they are rich and well educated Americans, but we laugh at them for we know better." Dr. Keitoku Watanabe expressed the feelings of many Japanese about the laws that rendered all of them ineligible aliens. "A man with a fine character, why shouldn't he be a citizen?" wondered Watanabe. "The people come from all those countries in southern Europe and they can be citizens."[67]

As the Japanese increasingly understood, citizenship conferred precious rights, the lack of which left them unable to defend their property rights effectively in crucial local forums. When nativist organizations banded together with homeowner organizations in Los Angeles, they exploited this weakness. Urged on by the Hollywood Protective Association, the Los Angeles City Council eventually condemned two of the controversial Japanese-owned lots in Tamarind-Bronson. A frustrated Issei neighbor remarked that "the Japanese are helpless, there is nothing they can do until a price is set upon their property and then they may object to the price." At the request of the same white residents, city officials also revoked building permits for the Japanese church. In the process, Los Angeles Issei learned a very grim lesson about power and politics that would shape their home and neighborhood choices in the years that followed. By the late 1920s and early 1930s, most no longer tried to move to white, working-class areas. Rather, as one scholar concluded, "the Japanese seem to follow Negro invasions and are, in a sense, part of these invasions."[68]

LOS ANGELES COSMOPOLITANISM

The unequal status of different nonwhite groups in Los Angeles created a legal racial hierarchy of housing opportunity in the city. In the face of nativist-influenced resistance, a large number of Japanese Angelenos settled in the racially unrestricted neighborhoods straddling Central Avenue, a hub of black business that stretched southward from downtown and housed most of the city's African Americans. In Los Angeles, the segregation of African Americans took place in a manner similar to that in eastern and Midwestern cities; although blacks had lived in L.A. in small numbers since the mid-nineteenth century, white residents after 1910 responded to the Great Migration by restricting property and moving out of integrated central city neighborhoods. As the city spread, the proportion of housing open to blacks shrank.[69]

The size, relative spatial concentration, and citizenship rights of the black population placed African Americans at the vanguard of the Central Avenue district's slow movement southward into hostile all-white territory. African Americans could and did push the area's borders, albeit carefully, because their citizenship status gave them a level of protection that Japanese did not enjoy. White homeowners who used nativist laws and techniques against Japanese homebuyers had fewer options when African Americans arrived, especially if they were unwilling to employ violence. Some white residents vandalized and attacked the homes of African Americans who dared move to their neighborhoods. Most other whites simply fled, tacitly conceding space to African Americans even as they denied it to Japanese.[70] Contemporary reports suggest that white residents of "invaded" areas did not necessarily prefer one group to the other. Regardless, no anti-black organizations comparable to California's well-developed anti-Asian organizations existed to advise and assist homeowners determined to stop African American integration. Even the activity of the second Ku Klux Klan in California targeted a host of other groups, from Catholics to Jews to Mexicans, in addition to blacks.[71]

Los Angeles blacks also wielded a small amount of political power, which discouraged city authorities from completely disregarding their rights. By the late 1920s, the population of black Los Angeles had grown to about 35,000. Largely confined to the multiracial Central Avenue district, blacks often voted as a bloc the way they did in most Northern cities. Unlike much of the urban North, however, African Americans' tendency to vote Republican worked in their favor in heavily Republican Los Angeles, where they sometimes became a decisive swing vote in close local races.[72] Black political influence, however limited, combined with African American citizenship to force city authorities to temper their most racist proclivities. Indeed, the worst instances of anti-black violence and vandalism occurred outside city limits. African Americans comprised such a small proportion of the overall L.A. County population that they enjoyed few protections once they left Los Angeles proper. City officials quietly made zoning changes that turned parts of integrated neighborhoods such as Central Avenue into industrial zones, shrinking the amount of housing available to all nonwhites; however, they could not respond to white segregationist activity by cavalierly condemning black-owned property the way they had with Japanese lots in Hollywood.[73]

White residents often came to fear black integration, because it was harder to thwart than Japanese "infiltration." Whites in areas where anti-Asian groups were not active may or may not have grasped the exact way Japanese aliens' ineligibility for citizenship shaped their responses to segregation, but they certainly understood the results. As one white homeowner commented, "personally, I really prefer the Japs. . . . [They] won't buy a house if there is a feeling of antagonism among the neighbors." Blacks, however, used the quiet expiration of covenants to enter many neighborhoods where whites opposed their presence. African American lawyers understood that lower-income whites in districts close to the city center often lacked the money to cover their properties with new covenants, renew expiring ones, or enforce existing ones in court. Anti-Asian laws cost white residents no money, but when pressing lawsuits, they faced citywide African American networks that pledged funds to defend black homeowners. On the one hand, African Americans were somewhat more likely than Japanese Americans to live in segregated areas, because so many of the latter lived on and farmed plots of land officially within city limits but in relatively undeveloped areas. However, the slightly greater "integration" of Japanese Americans did not equal better housing. The average value of nonwhite-owned homes and the nonwhite rate of homeownership were both well below those of the white population. However, because African Americans had a much greater ability to confront white segregationists, they were far more likely to occupy decent rather than substandard homes in Los Angeles, and their homes were, on average, far more valuable than those of Asian Americans.[74]

The growing population of Mexican Americans in the 1910s and 1920s also perturbed many Anglos, who rejected Hispanic neighbors but relied on Mexican labor and romanticized the region's pueblo past. A few thousand Mexican Americans inhabited rundown house courts and shacks in the Plaza district, the center of the old Mexican pueblo and an eyesore in the opinion of many Anglos. More troubling to most Anglos, a growing number of Mexican

Americans lived scattered throughout the city and county in *colonias*, agricultural camps, and modest working-class housing. Anglos dependent on Mexican labor but intent on undertaking what William Deverell calls a project of "turning the Los Angeles [Mexican] adobe past into something literally and figuratively whiter," tried to push out these Mexican neighbors or confine them to marginal "dogtowns" away from nicer blocks.[75]

Still, Mexicans, although mostly noncitizen immigrants, enjoyed certain advantages over Japanese in the city's housing market. Anti-Japanese organizations portrayed the Issei as aggressive and a racial threat to white California. In contrast, the widely shared stereotype until the 1920s was that Mexicans were necessary and docile laborers who would eventually "fade away" as modern Los Angeles grew. Throughout this period, the racial status of Mexicans also remained unclear. The majority of white, native-born, middle-class Protestants in Los Angeles did not consider Mexican Americans "white," but southern and eastern European immigrants, whose own whiteness was contested, often did. Federal government census takers counted Mexicans and Mexican Americans separately from "whites," yet Washington, D.C., still deemed Mexicans racially eligible for citizenship. As a result, the Alien Land Act did not apply to them. State and local authorities vacillated on the racial status of Mexicans as well. As historian Natalia Molina has shown, local "Americanizers" and public health authorities targeted Mexicans both as a peculiar problem and as potential American citizens. In contrast, such officials generally ignored Asian immigrants and their citizen children altogether, considering them all beyond the boundaries of citizenship.[76]

The uncertainty of Mexicans' racial status affected their housing choices. Vigilante groups of southern and eastern Europeans in Belvedere visited Japanese families to force them out, but hundreds of Mexicans purchasing or renting homes in the same east-side neighborhoods encountered little resistance. Considerable numbers of Mexicans lived in Pico Heights, but white homeowners directed their fury at the Japanese alone. Historian Scott Kurashige contends that in L.A., "one 'successful' effort by an all-white neighborhood to drive out a minority 'invader' sent a message to all other prospective buyers." Actually, such efforts did not always send those types of "messages," because racial definitions varied so greatly from neighborhood to neighborhood. Class, national origin, employment, and religion all affected the kind of white identity residents assumed. Mexicans shared the Catholic religion with many eastern and southern Europeans; they sometimes labored together in factories, although the Mexicans faced greater discrimination and usually earned less money. Southern and eastern Europeans may also have responded more vehemently to the Japanese because their differences were greater and less ambiguous; indeed, the Japanese represented the antithesis of citizenship, given their legal status. The fact that nativists gave all "white" residents tools effective against only Asians likely helped channel white immigrant activism as well.[77]

In addition, many Anglos considered some lighter-skinned, middle-class people of Mexican ancestry "white." These Mexican Americans usually called themselves "Spanish" and lived in Anglo neighborhoods. Significantly, local real estate agents, assessors, and developers also acknowledged such distinctions, dividing Mexican Americans into "peon Mexicans" and more respectable "Spanish" residents.[78] Few Mexican Americans could exploit this racial loophole, either because of their skin color or their income. Yet Japanese had no such loophole, the result of northern California nativism and Southern California's infatuation with Nordic ideology and racial segregation.

Slippery local racial definitions and the cult of the Nordic combined to give some L.A. neighborhoods, such as the Central Avenue district and, eventually, Boyle Heights, a diversity found nowhere else in the continental United States at the time. Such neighborhoods mixed white immigrants with African Americans, Asian Americans, Mexican Americans, and native- and foreign-born Jews. Blacks, Asians, and, to a certain extent, Mexicans, moved to these areas because they had few other choices. Some white immigrants and their children earned too little to live elsewhere, while others worked nearby and ranked convenience over racial concerns. Yet the citizenship status of many "white" residents hints at other motives. While conservative "Americanizers" coerced thousands of European immigrants to become citizens during and after World War I, a fairly high percentage of the white immigrants of Los Angeles's integrated neighborhoods remained unnaturalized. Their citizenship and residential choices suggest at least some rejection of the kind of racial Americanness that so many other white Angelenos—including Belvedere's European immigrants—embraced. Indeed, the suspicion and concern with which elite whites viewed mixed neighborhoods of any type highlights the significance of such choices.[79]

These integrated neighborhoods were not a multicultural paradise. Rundown and overcrowded, they contained much of the city's worst housing stock. Residents of different backgrounds sometimes viewed one another as competitors for scarce resources, including jobs. African Americans sometimes exhorted whites not to "put American-born black people on the same basis as Asiatics and all other foreign races. . . . The black people helped make this country." Area residents occasionally accepted prevalent stereotypes or looked down on each other. Japanese American Kazuo Kawai, describing his childhood in L.A., echoed J. Sato's scorn for certain groups. "I started going to Ninth Street School, one of those east-side schools which is infested by a horde of poor and dirty little Mexican, Negro, Italian, Greek, and Jewish children," he recalled.[80]

Still, individuals of different backgrounds who lived side by side or attended the integrated schools together formed friendships that often lasted for years or even a lifetime. As Mark Wild has argued, "much of the tension in central Los Angeles before World War II emanated from Anglo residents, resentful of the growing number of Asian, Mexican, African American, and sometimes European newcomers."[81] Such Anglos fought the expansion of the integrated districts, sometimes with lawsuits and in other cases with vandalism and violence.

SURFACE CALM

After the upswing of anti-Japanese agitation and violence in the mid-1920s, overt, organized campaigns against the Japanese waned in L.A. In some areas, white homeowners achieved their immediate goal of keeping Japanese out of their neighborhoods; in others, black home buyers came instead, breaking the pattern of segregation and enabling the Japanese to follow.[82] In Hollywood, stinginess (or poverty) killed the restrictionist movement: when the city demanded that white property owners pay $10,000 to convert the condemned Japanese lots into parkland, residents balked. Still, a 1939 survey showed that more than a decade later, the anti-Japanese conflicts of the early 1920s continued to shape residential patterns. Whites who used nativist laws generally halted Japanese movement into the neighborhoods this chapter describes—unless African Americans, or, sometimes, Mexican Americans, entered such areas. Furthermore, numerous Issei decided against buying homes, afraid of violating the vague Alien Land Act. As late as 1940, the home ownership rate in predominately Japanese American areas hovered around just 12 percent, almost 40 percent below the overall city rate; the home ownership rate among blacks in largely African American areas was much higher, around 30 percent.[83] In other words, the anti-Japanese movement succeeded in restricting Japanese American housing opportunities in Los Angeles until World War II.

At the same time, though, the diversity of Los Angeles and the popularity of Nordic ideology protected Japanese Americans from the extreme isolation that Chinese Americans endured in San Francisco. Both groups sought better housing during these years, but only the Japanese achieved any semblance

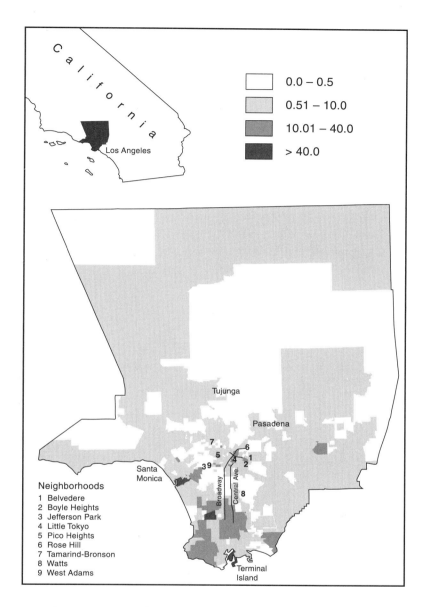

Asian American population by census tract (percent of total population), Los Angeles County, 1940. The seemingly high percentage of Asian Americans in tracts on the county's edges did not reflect an unusual degree of racial integration, but rather, the presence of Japanese American farmers in sparsely populated agricultural areas. (Map by Harry D. Johnson, based on Minnesota Population Center, *National Historical Geographic Information System: Prerelease Version 0.1*. Minneapolis: University of Minnesota, 2004.)

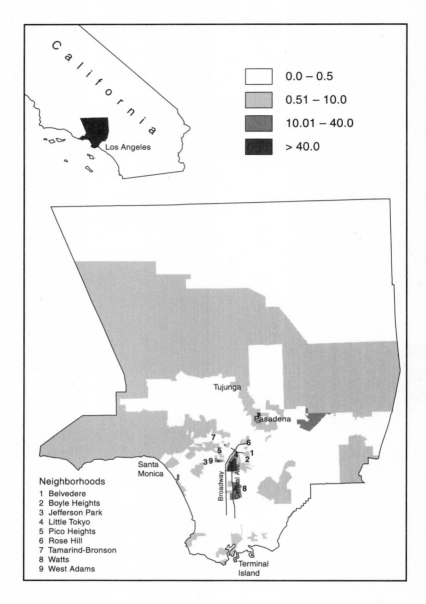

African American population by census tract (percent of total population), Los Angeles County, 1940. (Map by Harry D. Johnson, based on Minnesota Population Center, *National Historical Geographic Information System: Prerelease Version 0.1.* Minneapolis: University of Minnesota, 2004.)

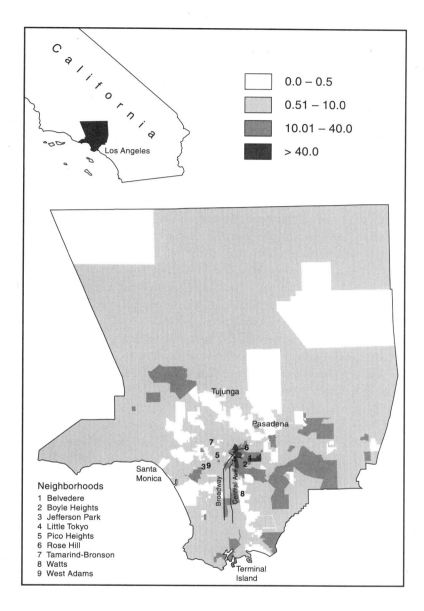

Estimated Mexican American population by census tract (percent of total population), Los Angeles County, 1940. (Map by Harry D. Johnson, based on Minnesota Population Center, *National Historical Geographic Information System: Pre-release Version 0.1.* Minneapolis: University of Minnesota, 2004.)

of it. San Francisco Chinatown's population occupied a unique and unen-viable place in the city's imagination: the epitome of inassimilability and nonwhiteness. The Japanese Americans of Los Angeles were luckier, for the racial diversity of the southern part of the state shielded them from this sin-gular status. Indeed, nativist organizations based in northern California never managed to appeal to the thousands of white Angelenos who saw African Americans or Mexican Americans as a greater threat than Japanese.

However, anti-Japanese hostility remained just below the surface through-out much of metropolitan Los Angeles. "So long as Japanese do nothing to improve their status, no opposition appears," clergyman Sidney Gulick noted. "Where, however, they seek to buy property and build, fierce opposition is promptly expressed by property owners in the vicinity." In Pico Heights, where some Japanese families hung on despite white hostility, the Electric Improvement Association, with the help of nativist organizations, continued a low-level campaign against them. More than a decade after its formation, the group, working with the Native Sons of the Golden West, easily persuaded the city council to reject building permits for two Japanese-owned lots. Anti-Asian officials also continued to use the Alien Land Act to harass Asian Americans who they knew had not broken the law. On the city's fringes and in the semirural areas of L.A. County, white residents more often turned a blind eye to Japanese truck farmers and gardeners, who constituted only temporary "nuisances" because of their inability to purchase land. If, however, these Issei placed their children in the public school system, white resistance mounted; after all, Nisei might prove a "detrimental influence" to white youths, as a real estate appraiser later contended. If the Nisei school-age population grew too large in such areas, white parents knew to invoke the state constitution, which allowed the segregation of Asian American students in separate classrooms or separate schools.[84]

Northern nativists failed to recruit many white Angelenos to their larger cause, yet they still succeeded in circumscribing Japanese American oppor-tunities. Housing, an intensely local issue, likely consumed far more nativist resources and manpower than it ever produced. It did not create lasting con-stituencies for anti-Asian groups either, given the degree of neighborhood turnover in rootless Los Angeles. But while white residents and officials dis-criminated to varying degrees against blacks and Mexican Americans, they generally conceded the right of such people to exist in the state of Califor-nia and to exercise certain limited rights. In contrast, anti-Japanese activists helped convince a significant number of white Angelenos, both citizens and officials, that Japanese had no rights whatsoever. If blacks and Mexicans were marginal, Japanese and other Asians existed completely outside the boundaries of American citizenship, society, and law.[85] This conception of Japanese Americans, together with the citizenship status of the Issei, greatly limited their ability to seek better housing and fairer treatment. It also helped guarantee their exclusion from the New Deal housing programs that began to reshape Los Angeles by the mid-1930s.

The New Deal's Third Track: Asian American Citizenship and Public Housing in Depression-Era Los Angeles

In 1934, architect and Public Works Administration (PWA) official Arthur Gallion reported that in Los Angeles, "the housing problem involves many races: native White, Negro, Mexican, Russian, Chinese, and . . . Japanese." Gallion's description captured both Los Angeles's diversity and the way housing officials approached it. The New Deal helped create a social welfare state in America, but people of color encountered discrimination in most of the new federal programs, including those dedicated to housing. Indeed, the New Deal only intensified the residential racial segregation that white Americans had tried to create during the 1910s and 1920s.[1] Still, Los Angeles's diversity baffled authorities who attempted to inject race into the new housing initiatives. Faced with dividing scarce resources among different groups, local and federal housing officials bickered about entitlement, whiteness, and racial categories in general. In the end, both federal and local authorities chose to keep Asian Americans, alone among all L.A.'s minority groups, from participating in new housing programs. This decision blocked Asian American access to much of the housing created during the Depression and at the same time helped place them largely outside the emerging social welfare state.

The Depression exposed the fragility of the entire Southern California economy and devastated an already faltering real estate market. Land subdivided for homes remained empty, tenants sought cheaper apartments, and landlords and homeowners throughout the city delayed repairs and upkeep. In the old, diverse central areas, houses built in the 1880s and 1890s slowly crumbled. In the working-class suburbs, new residents, mostly Dust Bowl refugees, built unpainted shacks without running water, electricity, or sewer access.[2]

The steady influx of these migrants and mounting relief costs angered many civic leaders. In Los Angeles, "the undesirable citizen," Erskine Caldwell sardonically commented, "is one who does not report an income in the higher brackets." City and county leaders lobbied the state to institute residency requirements meant to exclude newcomers from relief programs. The Los Angeles Police Department at one point even posted officers at the state border to stop Okies and Arkies from entering Southern California. Los Angeles County officials also blamed Mexican Americans for their "abuse" of relief funds and coaxed—and then coerced—thousands of supposedly indigent Mexicans and their citizen children to leave the country.[3]

Still, when Republican Frank Shaw became mayor in 1933, he welcomed New Deal programs, including housing initiatives. These programs marked the first major federal government intervention in the housing market. Before the 1930s, housing policy was largely local, instituted through city councils, zoning boards, and court rulings. However, local officials throughout the nation could not cope with the Depression's impact on the housing market, a major economic pillar in many areas. By the time Franklin Roosevelt took office in 1933, residential construction had dropped 95 percent since 1928, while banks foreclosed on the mortgages of thousands of Americans.[4] To address these problems, President Roosevelt convinced Congress to pass a grab bag of housing programs that included funds for experimental greenbelt towns, limited-dividend low-income housing, and rural cooperatives. Like local officials throughout America, Mayor Shaw and officials in his administration hoped to win for Los Angeles some of the money and benefits of these new programs.

However, the diversity of Los Angeles County confounded federal program officials' pat biracial formulations The PWA Housing Division and, later, the United States Housing Authority (USHA), both struggled with the racial ambiguities and complexities of Southern California. So did the Federal Housing Administration (FHA) and the Home Owners' Loan Corporation (HOLC).[5] In the end, all these programs not only helped foster greater residential racial segregation in Southern California but also undermined the meaning of Asian American citizenship there.

THE PWA PROGRAM IN LOS ANGELES

Rather than open-site, outlying land development, the PWA Housing Division emphasized central district slum clearance in Los Angeles and other cities. As historian Gail Radford notes, "influential local business leaders liked slum clearance programs, because they rebuilt, at public expense, run-down parts of cities that often threatened their own property investments." Public housing would replace demolished housing units but not create additional ones, another major selling point for real estate interests and landlords worried about competition. For these reasons, Mayor Shaw and the elite Angelenos who owned most of the land downtown initially welcomed the PWA program. Shortly after the agency launched its slum clearance and housing initiative, the supportive mayor appointed a fifteen-member Los Angeles Municipal Housing Commission (LAMHC) to oversee the program in the city.[6]

The composition of the commission reflected the interests involved. Rather than actual slum dwellers, the mayor chose leading real estate agents, bankers, lawyers, university officials, and businessmen, as well as two prominent women involved in charitable work. Acknowledging—barely—Los Angeles's racial diversity, Shaw also selected Paul Revere Williams, an African American architect and Republican loyalist whose clients included some of Hollywood's biggest white stars. Mexican Americans were the city's biggest minority group and one of its worst housed, but Shaw ignored the Latin American Protective League's request for a seat on the commission. Largely poor and unnaturalized, Mexicans did not vote, nor could most of the Japanese whose living conditions were often similar, and who also received no representation on the commission.[7]

Unsurprisingly, Commission members planned slum clearance and housing projects that reflected the interests of white business elites. The introduction to one area initiative frankly stated that "it is the intention of the plan presented, to redeem this attractive close-in site. . . . The poorer class shall receive better housing in the present good Old houses," not in new housing on the slum clearance site. In addition to "redeeming" valuable central city land by moving the poor away from it, the PWA program also gave commissioners an opportunity to tinker with Los Angeles's cosmopolitan areas. As in the 1920s, many white Angelenos saw the racial and ethnic integration of such districts as suspicious and even dangerous. Erle Fiske Young, an LAMHC advisor and sociology professor at the University of Southern California, expressed such views in his proposal for one clearance area. "This factor of population mixture probably has more bearing in determining the ultimate character of such a slum from the sociological and economic point of view than any other one thing," he claimed. Empowered to stop interracial mixing of all types, commissioners sketched out a plan for slum clearance that segregated nonwhite groups from each other, as well as from whites. The commission eventually proposed separate housing for whites, African Americans, Chinese Americans, and Japanese Americans.[8]

The PWA had its own distinct racial agenda. Racial liberals and Northern Democrats, whether out of personal conviction or a determination to increase the Democratic share of the black vote in 1936, hoped to give African Americans a stake in the New Deal. Harold Ickes, who oversaw the PWA and its housing program, insisted that African Americans receive jobs building public housing, as well as units in completed projects. Still, neither Ickes nor his subordinates challenged the residential racial segregation of blacks that had so recently become part of the nation's urban landscape. Instead, they supported building "colored projects" in existing black neighborhoods.[9]

Mayor Shaw also wanted to provide projects for African Americans, whose support proved important to his 1933 election, but he too had no intention of challenging residential segregation. PWA officials directed local authorities to maintain existing residential patterns but also granted great discretion to define what those were. The LAMHC took full advantage of this loophole. Rather than a multiracial project for one of the city's multiracial neighborhoods, it planned a "colored project" for an almost wholly African American area far from downtown L.A. This approach had two advantages. First, it would enable Mayor Shaw to show that he had improved housing specifically for African Americans. Second, it would allow the commission to isolate and anchor a largely black community far from the business district, where the proximity of African Americans allegedly harmed property values. Paul R. Williams hated race restrictions but accepted the LAMHC's limited vision in the hopes of improving housing for blacks in Los Angeles. He eventually located an almost completely African American block in an area miles from the business district. Williams promised that "the rehabilitation of this section would re-house the same group of people, only under modern and sanitary conditions."[10] In a program aimed at "redeeming" near-downtown districts by forcing poor tenants to move out of them, this East Adams Colored Project was an aberration. The project's goal was to prevent population movement rather than prompt it.

The commission's approach to other groups also reflected local elite whites' understanding of race. The LAMHC selected for its first proposal the "Utah Street site" on the northeastern edge of Boyle Heights, a multiracial east-side neighborhood. Residents of the immediate area included a sprinkling of Jewish immigrants, as well as a large number of Mexican Americans and Molokans, members of a Russian Protestant sect. The LAMHC envisioned a Utah Street Project with a mixture of Mexican American and Molokan tenants, tacitly acknowledging the potential whiteness of the former and suspect whiteness of the latter. While fairly fluid, this understanding of whiteness did not extend to the Asian Americans who shared blocks and neighborhoods with Mexican and European immigrants. Commissioners did not consider putting Asians in its "white" projects, nor did they see a place for Chinese or Japanese in "colored" housing. And while officials initially listed Chinese and Japanese among the needy groups who might receive housing, the LAMHC showed little interest in developing projects for either community.[11]

Chinese Americans finally requested a project of their own. At face value, the request seemed reasonable: the city planned to expand Union Station, razing much of old Chinatown to accommodate it. Still, most Chinese Americans had moved out of old Chinatown by the early 1930s, leaving behind a few rundown, faded blocks of shops, restaurants, and Chinese associations. To protect member interests, the Chinese Chamber of Commerce and former L.A. Chamber of Commerce president George Eastman drafted a plan in 1933 for a new, merchant-oriented Chinatown. With private funding scarce, C. Lyle Powell, the Chinese chamber's architect, retooled the group's plan to include housing and framed it to appeal to the racial sensibilities of LAMHC members. "A new, attractive and segregated Chinese Colony for Los Angeles [would] be accessible to the tourists," Powell argued. "The reputation of Los Angeles . . . can be greatly benefited by the advertising possibilities of a Chinese section to be known the world over."[12] San Francisco's Chinatown had become one of the city's biggest tourist draws; if L.A. built a new Chinatown, perhaps Southern California, too, could profit.

The Chinese Chamber of Commerce and Powell understood their audience. A Chinatown thus conceived would raise the property values of the areas on its borders—namely, parts of the central business district—achieving a major objective of slum clearance. In addition, such a project would supposedly prevent Chinese Americans from trying to move into other districts, especially all-white areas. According to Powell, in other cities "where such scattering has taken place, the result has been very detrimental not only to real estate values but in many other ways." Through using the language of segregation, Powell persuaded the initially dubious LAMHC to add the chamber's plan to the other projects already under consideration.[13]

THE END OF PWA HOUSING IN LOS ANGELES

By this point, however, the PWA was grappling with problems that threatened to undermine most of its housing initiatives throughout the nation. In July 1935, a Cincinnati circuit court declared the federal slum clearance program largely unconstitutional because of its use of eminent domain. The decision made almost every L.A. submission untenable. Only those projects sited on single-owner vacant land and requiring no condemnation could proceed.[14]

Desperate to create any housing at all, the embattled PWA increasingly imposed its will on local housing groups such as the LAMHC. PWA land appraiser Homer Phillips quickly took control of all Los Angeles initiatives and imposed limits on which nonwhites would qualify for projects. Local authorities in San Pedro, the port area of Los Angeles, had proposed Terminal Island as a possible site for vacant land housing. Hundreds of Japanese fishing families made their homes there, living, as a local police officer said, in a "slum district" of "weather beaten shacks crowded together" that he called "a firetrap of the worst kind." Interested in the possibility of open land, Phillips drove out to San Pedro and inspected the area. While the harbor site was far from downtown employment, Phillips saw potential in it. But he did not feel the same about the Japanese residents of the area. "These people, of course, we could not house," he noted, not even bothering to explain something so self-evident. Instead, he suggested building a project for use by white Navy families when the fleet was in, although he did not "personally believe a permanent tenancy could be maintained in this project" because of the transience of the sailors.[15]

Phillips's rejection of housing for Japanese Americans did not indicate any kind of federal policy shift. From the outset, Washington discouraged Asian American projects—even the Chinatown initiative, which enjoyed powerful backers. George Eastman first suggested a Chinese project directly to federal authorities, but Robert Kohn, then head of the PWA, rejected it out of hand. The influential former Chamber of Commerce president then pressed the LAMHC to demand the development despite federal demurrals. He even persuaded Mayor Shaw to raise the idea with Washington. Federal officials played along but never took the idea seriously, and Phillips quietly axed the Chinese project after his arrival in California.[16]

Federal public housing policy essentially mandated this approach. Throughout Los Angeles, ineligible alien Issei-headed households included American-born citizen children. In the PWA's view, however, these citizen children essentially acquired the status of their alien parents, because only families with American citizen *heads* qualified for public housing units. This rule barred most of the Asian American families in Los Angeles from receiving benefits. No evidence exists to establish whether federal authorities crafted this rule purposely to exclude Asian American citizens or simply did so unthinkingly; either way, it worked to deny the validity of young Asian Americans' citizenship, since more than half the Japanese Americans in Los Angeles were American citizens.[17]

These New Deal racial biases fit well with state law and local tradition and explain the LAMHC's unwillingness to push for Asian American housing, except when it involved a Chinatown tourist trap. Officials had crafted land laws and other statutes with the express goal of driving Japanese from the state, and federally subsidized housing for the Japanese American population of Los Angeles thus contradicted state policy. Legislators who opposed allowing Asian immigrants even to lease land were highly unlikely to allow them to lease government-owned apartments. Local social welfare traditions similarly discouraged Asian American participation. Historian Natalia Molina has shown that Los Angeles County's "public health programs directed towards the Japanese were not about extending social membership but about policing boundaries," in contrast to initiatives that benefited Mexicans or considered them potential Americans (and whites).[18] New Deal housing initiatives in Los Angeles merely extended this local practice of excluding Asians altogether while including Mexicans and blacks, albeit on a segregated basis.

By the fall of 1935, with time and money growing scarce, federal housing officials tightened racial definitions to exclude some of these other groups as well. In 1934, federal officials had described the Mexican Americans and Russian immigrants of the planned Utah Street Project as distinct "racial groups"; still, the PWA initially deferred to the LAMHC, which labeled both communities "white." Now, federal officials began to impose their own definitions. In August 1935, Homer Phillips scoured the city and found an open land site in Boyle Heights. Racial restrictions kept blacks and Japanese Americans out of the immediate neighborhood; most residents were Mexican Americans and European immigrants—exactly the groups the LAMHC proposed housing together at Utah Street. But back in Washington, officials initially balked, because "photographs indicate Mexicans in [the] surrounding area" of the project. Phillips quickly reassured them that local ideas had not swayed him: "It is true that there are Mexican families to the east of this site, but we do not propose to suggest that they be mixed with the White families who would live in our proposed project."[19] With federal officials firmly in charge of a controversial and shrinking program, Mexicans, regardless of citizenship, no longer qualified as white.

In the end, neither the LAMHC's initial proposals nor the PWA's later selections won final approval. Still struggling to show some progress after more than a year of work, PWA leaders in October 1935 rejected all projects not in the advanced stages. After almost two years of work, the LAMHC came away empty-handed. Charles Linder, an LAMHC staff member, pointed out that every advanced project receiving funds was located east of the Mississippi

River. "This is so manifestly unfair to the western half of the country that we are surprised that such a program would even be considered," he complained.[20] Nevertheless, the PWA Housing Division was likely quite happy to be freed from the complex racial dynamics of the urban west.

THE HOUSING ACT OF 1937

In 1937, Congress passed the Wagner-Steagall Act, which President Roosevelt signed into law as the Housing Act of 1937. The act replaced the old PWA Housing Division with the USHA, which enjoyed an advantage over its predecessor: in 1937, the Supreme Court changed its stance on eminent domain. Increasing numbers of urban California residents came to support programs such as public housing, a reflection of how profoundly the Depression was affecting the state. Brutal disputes over agricultural labor organizing tore the Central Valley apart, a general strike divided San Francisco, and Okies and Arkies starved on California roadsides. Desperate citizens embraced utopian initiatives for ending the Depression, including the Townsend Plan and the Ham 'n' Eggs pension scheme. Growing support for programs such as public housing eventually compelled then governor Frank Merriam to sign enabling legislation that he earlier vetoed; in 1938, liberal Democrat and new governor Culbert L. Olson embraced New Deal programs far more enthusiastically. Responding to this shift, L.A. officials restarted the old housing program, creating the separate Housing Authority of the City of Los Angeles (HACLA) and the Housing Authority of the County of Los Angeles.[21]

The resolution of racial issues in the city housing program also reflected political shifts in Los Angeles. Like their peers elsewhere, many African Americans in the city switched party affiliations after 1932 and took a keen interest in New Deal housing programs. New Republican mayor Fletcher Bowron reached out to them and to other Democrats as he formed his administration, a reform coalition that opposed the city's Republican establishment. In addition, Bowron appointed progressives, including local black Democratic activist Jessie L. Terry, to the new HACLA board. Mexican American citizens in Los Angeles also began to organize politically in the late 1930s, especially within labor unions and some groups aligned with the Communist Party. While Bowron selected no Mexican Americans for the HACLA board, its new members included them in a large and diverse tenant selection committee chosen to determine who would live in the first project, a Boyle Heights development dubbed Ramona Gardens. In addition to Ramon Welch of the Spanish American Congress, representatives from the National Association for the Advancement of Colored People (NAACP), the Urban League, labor organizations, liberal Jewish groups, and similar organizations sat on the selection committee.[22]

Residents of Los Angeles's diverse central areas closely followed the HACLA program. The new, interracial Citizens' Housing Council (CHC), composed of progressive church and civic organizations, formed to monitor the HACLA. Group members included representatives of nonwhite organizations and numerous white liberals, such as Helen Gahagan Douglas, at that time a member of the Democratic Party's National Committee. Although some black and Mexican American homeowners sued when officials condemned their property for housing projects, most community leaders supported what the Mexican American newspaper *La Opinión* termed an "important project."[23]

The tenant selection group and the CHC persuaded city housing officials to reconsider the rigid "colored/white" approach of their predecessors. A 1937 WPA study had already refuted Erle Fiske Young's thesis linking diversity to slum formation and juvenile delinquency in Los Angeles.[24] Now, the Advisory Committee on Tenant Selection, which met with city authority representatives during the autumn of 1940, pushed the board to create integrated projects. Black assemblyman Augustus Hawkins recalled white board members' initial reluctance to embrace this approach. "We had a showdown with the Authority there on the matter of admitting Negroes," he recalled, and praised Jessie Terry, who "led in the fight." On December 26, board members unanimously determined that "the racial composition of the neighborhood in which the [Ramona Gardens] housing development is located is to be used as a guide for determining the racial composition of the families living in the development." In doing this, the HACLA created one of the very few interracial public housing developments in the entire nation. California's only other such project was in Oakland, a community with a similar tradition of black political activism.[25]

In contrast, the county public housing program followed a segregationist agenda similar to the earlier LAMHC initiatives. Although county jurisdiction included the city of Los Angeles, board members ignored L.A.'s black population, which wielded no influence outside city limits. In fact, Lillian Jones and other members of the National Negro Congress pressured the Los Angeles City Council to create a separate city authority for just this reason. Ceding all power to the County "would mean that nothing would ever get done," at least for black citizens, she argued. Jones was right. In 1938, the Housing Authority of the County of Los Angeles applied for federal funding for its first three housing projects, all of which it planned for sites outside city limits. Officials designated one of these projects in the Belvedere district for "persons of the Mexican race," while the other two would serve only white residents.[26] The County Authority's approach was not surprising, given the agency's origins. Although the County Authority was an official county agency, the contemporary journal *Housing Yearbook* credited its initial creation "to the initiative of the Los Angeles Chamber of Commerce." Like the chamber, and L.A.'s elite in general, the board contained no members of color. It also did not create a tenant selection committee.[27]

County officials' decision to divide Mexicans from whites reflected ongoing local debates about the place of Mexican workers and families in Los Angeles. Evidence suggests that L.A. County authorities saw racial difference in far starker terms than their city counterparts, even before the Depression.[28] Segregated in separate schools, Mexican Americans outside city limits also faced greater residential isolation than those within L.A. Still, Mexican and Mexican American laborers remained vital to county agribusiness. The Depression changed the situation, however, and white officials soon targeted Mexican Americans as a problem race. Even after the end of mass deportation, such racial distinctions remained embedded in county policy and practice.[29]

In contrast to the old LAMHC, county housing officials by the late 1930s drew the racial line boldly in their projects. Arguably the HACLA also rejected Mexican "whiteness," creating separate quotas for whites and Mexican Americans in Ramona Gardens, but the County Authority took this "logic" much further with its completely segregated project. County officials claimed that the development, called Maravilla, should not only be separate, but also "built in accordance with the habits and customs of these people." This vision of Mexicanness profoundly shaped the county housing program. "Because this Project was planned for Mexican families," county officials maintained, "a great deal of study was given to the arrangement of buildings so as to provide ample space and facilities for neighbor groups to assemble." The apparently peculiar characteristics of the "Mexican race" guided many of the other decisions planners made about the Maravilla Project. Architects laid out "adequate space for children to play either on smooth pavement or on plain dirt." In contrast, both white projects received superior concrete play areas, reflecting planners' assumptions about Mexican children's play habits—and perhaps their cleanliness. The authority applied similar beliefs to the adult tenants, creating paved horseshoe, badminton, and shuffleboard courts for white residents. Mexican Americans received an unpaved dirt area for "such community activities as barbecues and the like." County housing officials also expressed regret when the outbreak of war in late 1941 forced them to simplify their design for Maravilla; they had initially planned "buildings . . . designed to simulate the early California adobe houses. . . . The concrete blocks approximated the size of adobe blocks used by the Mexicans during the pioneer days."[30] The white projects, on the other hand, reflected modern building styles.

The two housing programs that emerged from diverse Los Angeles before the war thus reflected larger struggles over racial definitions, power, and place in Los Angeles. In the city, where minorities and their white allies had some say, housing officials established a project that mixed groups based on a strict neighborhood quota system. The County Authority, on the other hand, continued the LAMHC's segregationist practices but with harder racial lines and a less inclusive definition of whiteness. Because the County Authority's jurisdiction included the city (but not vice versa), the HACLA's relatively progressive policies remained in tension with county directives intended to institute and reinforce segregation everywhere.

ASIAN AMERICANS AND THE NEW HOUSING PROGRAM

In its adobe paean to mission Mexicans, the County Authority followed a trend of ethnic essentializing popular in 1930s Los Angeles. A decade earlier, businesswoman Christine Sterling formed a corporation to renovate Olvera Street, a short lane in the old Mexican Plaza area of downtown. She and her partners remade the lane into their fantasy of old Mexican California, or what historian William Deverell describes as a "shops-and-stores invention complete with picturesque Mexican troubadours and pushcarts." Olvera Street idealized a sanitized racial past over a messier present, entertaining tourists even as Los Angeles County officials deported thousands of Mexicans and their citizen children.[31]

Like white landowners throughout Los Angeles County, Christine Sterling and her partners also profited from Asian American residents' marginal status, now reaffirmed by both federal and local housing officials. Sterling owned much of the old Chinatown section of Los Angeles, which she sold to the city when officials expanded Union Station.[32] Once the PWA rejected a Chinese project, she saw another way to cash in. First, she purchased the proposed Chinatown project site that federal housing officials rejected in 1935. Using Olvera Street as her model, she and her partners then created "China City," an exoticized block of Chinese shops, restaurants, and winding alleys.

A few displaced Chinese American entrepreneurs leased space in China City, but most balked at renting from Sterling again. Some even described

FIGURE 3.1. After Los Angeles's Old Chinatown was razed in the mid-1930s to make room for an expanding Union Station, businesswoman Christine Sterling purchased the land that the PWA Housing Division had once considered for a Chinese American housing project and built the tourist-oriented "China City" shopping development. Many Chinese American merchants who previously owned businesses in Old Chinatown avoided China City, which a number condemned as cheap and tacky. (Photo by Harry Quillen, ca. 1937. Security Pacific Collection / Los Angeles Public Library.)

China City as "undignified" and "cheap." On the one hand, builders incorporated motifs from the recent movie *The Good Earth*, based on Pearl Buck's novel about China, which was a relatively respectful portrayal of Chinese and one that benefited Chinese American merchants of the era. But China City, backed by the white-run Chinese Culture Society, promoted less flattering ideas about China as well. The development featured rickshaw pullers, who ferried visitors around for a quarter per ride. Only the poorest classes in the

cities of China pulled rickshaws for a living; indeed, historian Emily Honig
has noted that Shanghai residents of this period considered rickshaw pullers
and their work as "bestial," "inhuman," and "almost animal-like."[33]

Chinese American merchants depended on white Americans' exotic ideas
about China, but a large number rejected the demeaning aspects of China City.
Eventually, Chinese American Peter Soo Hoo organized a group of Chinese
American investors to create their own space. In the late 1930s, the Chinatown
Corporation bought a parcel of old Santa Fe Railroad land in the northeast
corner of downtown. Their New Chinatown used the same blend of exoticized
shops and restaurants as China City and competed with Sterling's venture
for tourist revenue. But while New Chinatown investors added some of the
architectural touches that attracted tourists to China City, their Chinatown
also reflected a striving, modernizing China that demanded the respect of
the West. According to a contemporary observer, "New Chinatown has the
grandeur of a modern city in China," while "China City has the atmosphere of
a small Chinese village."[34] Still, neither development offered any new housing.

Although L.A. public housing served a diverse group of Angelenos by the
early 1940s, it remained off limits to Chinese Americans and to the far larger
Japanese American population. More than thirty thousand Japanese Americans lived within the County Authority's jurisdiction, many of them in substandard homes, yet county officials made no allowances for them. The Housing
Authority of the City of Los Angeles, though relatively progressive, proved
only slightly more inclusive. Representatives of every other sizable minority
community in Los Angeles sat on the city's tenant selection committee, including Mexican Americans, blacks, and Jews; but no Japanese Americans were
included. Similarly, the HACLA drew up rigid quotas for whites, Mexican
Americans, and blacks, but did not include Asian Americans in its calculations—even though they were more likely than African Americans to live in
substandard homes.[35]

In the end, only two Japanese Americans applied to live in Ramona Gardens. This apparent lack of interest simply reinforced the assumptions of
social service workers, who tended to praise both Chinese and Japanese Angelenos as taking care of their own and staying out of trouble.[36] Concerned
about community image, many Japanese American leaders sought to preserve
this belief and to discourage Nisei from applying for any social welfare programs. The need for such assistance certainly existed: an official survey of Los
Angeles showed that over one hundred Japanese American families on the
east side alone qualified for Ramona Gardens because of their low incomes
and poor housing. Unlike African American and Mexican American groups,

however, Japanese American organizations largely avoided involvement in the struggle for public housing in L.A. In early 1941, the Japanese American Citizens League (JACL) inquired about representation on the tenant selection committee but did not press the matter when the HACLA failed to act. As historian Brian Masaru Hayashi has contended, the Nisei "leadership group . . . was, in the words of an observer, 'a perpetual committee excluding the average man.'" Nisei elites enjoyed more economic security than most of their peers and had little need for public housing. Nor did they want white Angelenos to associate social welfare use of any kind with their community. Indeed, the Japanese American newspaper *Rafu Shimpo* implied that Ramona Gardens failed to meet Japanese American housing standards.[37]

Discrimination based on citizenship status discouraged even those Japanese Americans willing to flout community pressure. City Authority head Howard Holtzendorff claimed that "the Orientals have not displayed much interest in our public housing program," but he did not mention the way the HACLA's own regulations created this apathy. The majority of Nisei still lived in family units headed by alien parents, whose citizenship status rendered all members of the household ineligible for public housing. Holtzendorff knew this because the HACLA had rejected just such a family. Issei citizenship status also had a more pernicious effect. As Robert K. Carr of President Truman's Committee on Civil Rights observed in 1947, "Japanese were conspicuously absent from the relief rolls before the war, partly because the Issei feared deportation as indigent aliens if they applied." The Japanese American families who qualified for Ramona Gardens lived in heavily Mexican east-side neighborhoods. In the early and mid-1930s, they watched white officials deport many of their Mexican American neighbors—including alien parents and citizen children—for using county assistance and public hospitals. Mass deportation of Japanese aliens was probably unlikely, given the high cost of travel to Japan in comparison to Mexico.[38] Still, Los Angeles Issei had no way of knowing how county officials would act, and the Mexican deportation, together with the array of state and local laws that targeted Japanese in particular, discouraged Issei parents and Nisei children from using social welfare programs, including the housing now available to other nonwhite groups.

ASIAN AMERICANS AND NEW DEAL CITIZENSHIP

Nationally, gender traditions and the Southern Jim Crow system played a vital role in molding the New Deal social welfare state. Congress passed legislation that in effect created a "two-track" social welfare system in which white male wage earners enjoyed the benefits of generous initiatives with no shame attached (including Old Age Insurance and Unemployment Insurance), while women and blacks had access only to stigmatized programs (such as Aid to Dependent Children).[39] New Deal housing programs mirrored this split: generally, white, male-headed families alone could use FHA underwriting to purchase new, single-family homes. In contrast, the less prestigious public housing program served both white and black citizens, but often on a segregated basis (and generally restricted to male citizen–headed families). In addition, Congress built substantial local control into all the stigmatized initiatives, knowingly giving officials on the ground additional opportunities to discriminate against people of color.

Local control gained even more importance in diverse places like Los Angeles, where agency officials and city and county authorities negotiated the access of groups other than whites and blacks to the emerging social welfare state. Because federal officials did not make specific provisions for such people, the fit between local tradition and federal policy priorities in such places became crucial. In Los Angeles, the wrangling between area housing advocates and Washington resulted in the inclusion of Mexican Americans and the complete exclusion of Asian Americans from the public housing program. Mexican American access to some public housing developments reflected membership—however compromised—in the emerging social welfare state. In contrast, the exclusion of Asian Americans both hardened L.A.'s existing legal racial hierarchy in housing and fixed the place of Asians as outside the new, entitlement-based citizenship.

In essence, the Los Angeles experience reflected the channeling of Asian Americans onto a "third track" in the U.S. social welfare system. Ineligible aliens, whether aging Issei or Chinese, enjoyed almost no right to any social welfare programs; even the use of county relief could result in their deportation for indigence. Their American-born children already faced many of the same hurdles as other nonwhites: racial discrimination usually confined them to agricultural or domestic work, effectively shutting them out of the "top track" programs of the Social Security Act. But as the dependent children of Asian aliens, they bore an additional burden. Head-of-household provisions effectively passed their parents' ineligibility for public housing and other social welfare benefits on to them.

Written out of much of the welfare state at its very inception, Asian Americans could not assume that the passage of time would improve their access to the new benefits of citizenship. The death of the older generations would eventually remove formal legal barriers, yet the cavalier attitude of federal and local officials toward Asian American citizenship in 1930s Los Angeles did not bode well for future inclusion. Most L.A. Nisei did not know in 1938 and 1939 just how little their citizenship meant; unorganized and politically naive, they were shocked by their 1942 internment. But the attitude of federal and local officials even in the mid to late 1930s hinted at the difficulties Nisei would face in trying to claim their citizenship rights. So did the experience of San Francisco's Chinese Americans with the same housing program, albeit in an entirely different manner. Ironically, federal and local perceptions of Asian Americans as fundamentally foreign eventually paved the way for Chinese American access to public housing.

CHAPTER FOUR

"Housing Seems to Be *the* Problem": Asian Americans and New Deal Housing Programs in San Francisco

By the mid-1930s, Japanese Americans owned a majority of the art goods and trinket stores on Grant Avenue, San Francisco Chinatown's major tourist thoroughfare. Struggling with the Depression, Chinese Americans disliked the business competition, but they resented their rivals' ethnicity far more. In 1931, Japan annexed the far northern Chinese province of Manchuria. Six years later, it invaded China proper. During the 1930s, most Americans paid far more attention to the Depression than to this war, but the worsening conflict in Asia slowly influenced American public opinion about China and Japan.[1] By 1939, many white San Franciscans and tourists alike began siding with China and treating Chinatown as a surrogate, in spite of the long nativist tradition in the city. Chinese Americans used the ensuing sympathy and goodwill to raise money for China relief and compete more effectively again Japanese American businesses on Grant Avenue, as well as to press for a Chinatown housing project.

The Depression devastated San Francisco. Average annual wages in the city fell from $1,500 in 1929 to $1,080 in 1933, while relief loads increased at a rate of 250 percent per year. For the first time, city officials pledged money to the Community Chest for distribution to the unemployed, and eventually they created a work program and put public relief bonds on the ballot. According to historian William H. Mullins, "the government of San Francisco consistently seemed more alert than the city or county of Los Angeles to the needs of its citizens. . . . The responses of public officials demonstrated a greater willingness to face the problems of the depression [*sic*]." In contrast, Los Angeles mayor John Porter blithely observed that "we do not find it

FIGURE 4.1. By the mid-1930s, Grant Avenue in San Francisco's Chinatown had become a nationally known tourist destination. Before World War II, both Chinese American and Japanese American merchants owned businesses there, as this late 1930s photograph of the 700 block of Grant Avenue demonstrates: the Japanese American–owned Iwata Trading Company sat directly across the street from the Chinese American–owned Kuo Wah Company, and just down the block from the famous Chinese American Hang Far Low restaurant. When Japan invaded China in 1937, this interethnic business competition became increasingly tense. (California Historical Society, FN-31285.)

necessary to feed our unemployed men here. In San Francisco I saw free soup kitchens. There are none here."[2]

During the early years of the Depression, Chinese Americans suffered less severely than other racial minorities in the city. According to historian Judy Yung, "given their low socioeconomic status, Chinese Americans had less to lose by the economic catastrophe," especially since few owned stocks, bonds, or property, or competed with white workers for employment. Still, the length of the crisis and the growing scope of need eventually overwhelmed the resources of Chinatown community groups. By 1931, some 3,500 Chinese Americans in San Francisco were unemployed, about one-third of the entire working-age population.[3]

City officials initially ignored this growing need, both because of San Francisco's racial traditions and because of the attitudes of conservative Chinese American leaders. As Chinatown's mutual aid and family associations struggled to feed the poor, the Chinese Consolidated Benevolent Association (CCBA)—an elite, merchant-dominated group that city officials recognized as Chinatown's unofficial government—refused to appeal to San Francisco leaders for help, likely fearing the impact outside aid would have on CCBA power. But in 1932, Chinese American Marxists confronted the CCBA and also joined other city radicals in mass demonstrations for city aid. Such challenges put Chinese American elites on the spot and forced city leaders to take action, especially because of Chinatown's growing importance to San Francisco tourism. Later that year, officials started distributing groceries to the area's American citizens. Rather than threatening unemployed Chinese "bachelors" with deportation—a threat that would have been far too costly to carry out—city leaders also cooperated with the CCBA to open a shelter for such men. In the mid-1930s, the State Emergency Relief Administration (SERA) stepped in to provide unemployment assistance to 2,300 Chinese American families in the district. New Deal programs eventually supported Chinatown's unemployed and hungry as well—but only if they were American citizens.[4]

That very distinction created an ironic predicament for Chinese Americans in Depression-era San Francisco. By the late 1930s, the war overseas was reshaping nativism in the city; anti-Asian groups increasingly focused their vitriol on the Japanese American population, and some white residents and tourists even boycotted Japanese American–owned stores in favor of their Chinese American competitors, whom they identified with China. While encouraging such connections, a growing number of Chinese Americans also struggled to gain inclusion in the new, entitlement-based citizenship of the New Deal era. The small measure of access they achieved, however, simply highlighted continuing white perceptions of all Asian Americans as foreigners.

CHINATOWN TOURISM

Intent on reviving the local economy, San Francisco businesspeople, including Chinese Americans, used the end of Prohibition in 1933 to develop the city's nightlife and promote it to tourists. In 1936, Charley Low built Chinatown's first cocktail lounge, a venture so successful that he launched the Forbidden

City nightclub two years later. The club and its imitators initially catered to white Americans but eventually drew Chinese American patrons to their floor shows. Other Chinese American businesspeople soon got into the act, buying neon signs for their restaurants and stores and refurbishing their exteriors.[5]

The resulting "modernization" worried numerous young Chinese Americans. Historian Nayan Shah has shown that many of them sought to "replace nineteenth-century images of the Chinese as inscrutable aliens living in mysterious clan networks of single men with images of assimilating, Americanized nuclear families," even though such families were still a minority of Chinatown's population. But this goal existed in tension with Chinatown's need to preserve the mystique that drew tourists to the district in the first place. In a letter to the new English-language *Chinese Digest*, resident D. L. Chinn described how Chinese Americans had once "bemoaned the uncleanliness and backwardness of our grocers" but now "bemoan the fact that Chinatown is indeed taking on a Western aspect." After admitting that he was not sure where to take friends or tourists any longer, Chinn expressed the underlying dilemma: "Do we know what we want? I don't!"[6]

Young Chinese Americans sensed that the very misconceptions of Chinese difference and backwardness they sought to dispel actually drew white Americans to Chinatown in the first place. According to the *Chinese Digest*, white visitors came to the district to see "a bit of Old Cathay in a foreign setting . . . the glamour, the mysticism, the exotic lure of the Far East." Describing Chinatown's thriving nightlife, reporter Jim Marshall claimed that "at first, only tourists patronized Chinese night clubs, expecting to whiff opium smoke and maybe see a hatchet or two flying." Local writer Sidney Herschel Small described what he thought Chinatown tourists wanted: "an opium den full of smokers. Tunnels. Tongs. Slave girls."[7] Obviously, a difficult task confronted young Chinese Americans seeking to change their image and promote "exotic" tourism at the same time.

Complicating matters, white civic leaders who hoped to further develop Chinatown's tourist potential rarely consulted its residents. By the mid-1930s, Grant Avenue began to gain national renown as a safe tourist destination and a necessary stop on any San Francisco trip. To heighten the district's allure, the Downtown Association, a group of prominent white businessmen, convinced city officials to install special "Chinese" streetlights along Grant Avenue. The organization also launched a project to transform St. Mary's Park on Chinatown's southern border into a "Chinese garden." The park initiative angered some Chinatown residents, who saw it as an imposition from outsiders. The *Chinese Digest*, more acquiescent, gently chided the project's opponents, reminding them that "although [the garden] may benefit others, it will also, and undoubtedly mainly, benefit the Chinese merchants." Yet *Digest* staff members and other Chinese Americans struggled to control Chinatown's development and image, contending that "we must make haste to inform our city officials that we do not contemplate having outsiders represent us." The valuable tourist trap was also their home, and with this in mind, younger Chinese Americans, especially the American-educated segment of the community, set out to make tourism a learning opportunity, rather than a slumming one. As historian Gloria Heyung Chun has noted, in their view, "tourism would no longer be a thrill show, but an educational experience. The tourist would learn about China and Chinese culture by being exposed to genuine expressions of things Chinese."[8]

For these younger Chinese Americans, however, defining "Chineseness" proved elusive, and earning a living from it frustrating. White employers rejected Chinese Americans, white landlords refused them, and the Depression further narrowed their horizons. Eventually, some of them contemplated a future in China itself, despite the fact that few had ever been there. The time seemed right: the Kuomintang (Nationalist Party) reunified much of China in 1927 and was struggling to modernize the nation's infrastructure and economy. American-educated Chinatown youths began to think about China as a place where their training and ideals could serve a larger purpose—and where racism would not limit them. Still, when a Chinese American organization in New York called for essays on the topic "Does My Future Lie in China or America?" the ensuing discussion revealed that even those who favored going to China could not agree on how to define "Chinese." Was it ancient? Modern? In opposition to the West and its values, or not? During this era, leaders, reformers, and intellectuals in China constantly debated the meaning of Chineseness as they sought legitimacy in the face of Japanese and Western encroachment.[9] If they could not agree on what being Chinese meant, the sons and daughters of San Francisco's Chinatown were at an even greater disadvantage.

By the late 1930s, American popular culture began to provide some clues. In 1931, Pearl Buck published *The Good Earth*, a novel about a Chinese peasant family's struggle for survival. Buck's book extolled Chinese endurance and the peasantry's deep love of the land, two themes that touched a deep nerve in an America where so many small farmers now faced destitution. The book sold hundreds of thousands of copies in the United States, won the Pulitzer Prize for fiction, and in 1937 became a popular film. While not the only factor changing American ideas about the Chinese, it proved incredibly influential.

According to journalist Harold Isaacs, it "almost singlehandedly replaced the fantasy images of China and the Chinese held by most Americans with . . . a new, more intimate, and more appealing picture of the Chinese themselves." So did the work of Lin Yutang, a Western-educated Chinese émigré who tried to explain China and its culture to the West. His books *My Country and My People* (1935) and *The Importance of Living* (1938) largely reinforced the image elucidated by Pearl Buck of persevering, agrarian China (Lin and Buck were friends). Older Chinese stereotypes even met their match in pulp fiction and "B" movies: Charlie Chan, a benign, Confucius-quoting Chinese Hawaiian detective, eventually challenged the maniacal Fu Manchu.[10]

The uncomfortable reality of Japanese imperialism likely helped popularize the *Good Earth* image of China as well. Japan's growing military presence in Asia potentially threatened American interests there. Equally significant, the emergence of a modern, industrialized, and powerful Japan challenged deep-seated ideas of Asian backwardness and inferiority. This threat to many Americans' equation of whiteness with modernity and racial superiority helps explain in part why Buck and Lin were so popular in the 1930s. Their work did not contest the link between white and modern; to them, the real China was an ancient, passive, agrarian civilization, fundamentally unchanging and unthreatening.

Regardless of this undercurrent, many Chinatown activists and leaders embraced *Good Earth* Chineseness. The Chinatown Beautification Committee, formed in preparation for San Francisco's 1939 World's Fair, encouraged merchants to change the appearance of the more Western storefronts to be "all-Chinese." Committee leaders also called on shop employees to "wear native costumes, especially during the Exposition." Such clothing had fallen out of vogue in Chinatown after the 1911 Revolution; indeed, a growing number of Chinese in Shanghai, Hong Kong, and other urban areas in China eschewed such garments as well. Still, as the *Chinese Digest* reminded the Exposition's Chinese American group, "stunts and shows should be 'slanted' to please western [*sic*] eyes." And Western eyes wanted *The Good Earth*, complete with traditional garments. The Chinese American–run Chinese Factors group even built a Chinese village at the Exposition grounds and dubbed it the Good Earth Settlement.[11]

CITIZENSHIP AND ENTITLEMENT

Community activists discovered the limits of *The Good Earth* when dealing with city government, however. In May 1936, Chinese American Citizens Alliance

(CACA) leader Dr. Theodore Lee asked the board of supervisors to install night lighting at the Chinese Playground. Although Chinatown had little play space and a growing population of children, the board rejected the modest request. An annoyed *Chinese Digest* editor complained that "Chinatown has given more in taxes and demanded less in public improvement than almost any other district, and the scales are heavily one-sided—in the city's favor."[12] But with so few eligible voters, Chinatown had no way to push the Board to take any action.

The city's response frustrated Chinese American residents, but by the mid-1930s, some had found another place to turn: the federal government. When WPA jobs became available in late 1935, hundreds of Chinese American citizens applied. WPA officials did not treat Chinese Americans and whites equally. Rather, they placed the majority of Chinese American applicants and other nonwhites in unskilled labor positions. Still, WPA jobs made a real difference for many Chinatown families struggling to survive. The WPA also provided unanticipated opportunities for a handful of college-educated Chinese Americans who worked in the agency's Chinatown office.[13]

Some of these WPA workers worried about the impact of federal assistance on the moral fiber of their community. Ethel Lum, one of San Francisco's dozen Chinese American WPA social workers, described what she saw as the "definite change of mental attitude toward dependence upon public support" in Chinatown. According to Lum, many Chinese Americans now believed that "it is the duty of the 'public government,' the great '*wong gar*,' to provide for every one's needs." Lum called these changing ideas about public assistance "foreign to the Chinese mind," tacitly accepting the argument white social workers long used to justify their neglect of Chinatown.[14]

Not all Chinese American social workers agreed, however. Contact with federal and local welfare programs convinced some that government could play a positive role in their community. Like members of other ethnic groups at this time, a number of these young Chinese Americans began expressing what historian Lizabeth Cohen has described as "new expectations of the state." As WPA social worker Lim P. Lee contended years later, Chinese Americans never expected outside assistance before the New Deal, because "there was no one who had paid attention to them." During his time with the WPA, however, he began to think about the different ways government assistance could help Chinese Americans. So did Samuel Lee, an SERA supervisor. Frustrated at watching so much government relief go to Chinatown's slumlords, he helped convince other young Chinatown residents to focus on the district's housing problems; after all, almost every young Chinese American had experienced them firsthand.

Convinced of Samuel Lee's strategy, the editors of the *Chinese Digest* printed a series of articles and editorials on the housing problem in mid-1937. Timed to coincide with Congress's debate about the Wagner-Steagall Act, these articles supported the legislation and called on "progressive elements of the community" to address housing ahead of any other issue. *Digest* editors contended that "as things are today, we have to take the most crucial problem and tackle that. And housing seems to be *the* problem." Chinese American housing activists then circulated a petition in Chinatown urging passage of Wagner-Steagall and sent the signatures to local congressmen.[15]

Such activism revealed the way the New Deal inspired even those Americans whom it largely excluded. Writing more than a decade later, Lim P. Lee recalled that until Wagner-Steagall, "we advocates all were dreamers, having no firm grasp of future prospects. There wasn't one person who knew how to take real action to reform sixty or seventy years of an abominable situation."[16] Wagner-Steagall changed that. Chinese Americans rallied around the proposed legislation, which seemed to offer them their only chance at better housing.

But when Warner-Steagall finally passed, Chinatown did not benefit. The new law gave local housing authorities discretion over site and tenant selection, exposing once again the political weakness of the Chinese American district. Although anti-Chinese sentiment had softened during the 1930s, anti-Asian nativism still reigned in San Francisco politics and housing. It had already thwarted earlier housing programs: in the early 1930s, neither city officials nor PWA authorities explored the possibility of improving San Francisco's worst slum. A 1937 WPA study of San Francisco housing conditions omitted Chinatown as well. The new San Francisco Housing Authority (SFHA) also paid little attention to the Chinese American district. Four months after Wagner-Steagall's passage, Lim P. Lee ruefully admitted that "it is a question if the Chinese can get the backing of the municipal authorities for a low-cost housing project in Chinatown."[17]

While young Chinatown residents sought housing projects, many white San Franciscans rejected them. Homeowners' organizations from working- and middle-class neighborhoods such as the Divisidero and the Mission met with Mayor Angelo Rossi to express their opposition to SFHA site choices. Public housing opponents in the comfortable Richmond district demanded that Rossi keep their neighborhood a "first class residential district," rather than "a Slum Housing Project." The Republican mayor, hostile to much of the New Deal, responded by appointing a large number of public housing opponents to the new Housing Commission, which oversaw the SFHA. The Authority eventually began work on three developments, but all of them were in lightly populated outlying districts.[18]

After ignoring Chinese American requests for months, the SFHA in late 1938 finally responded to *white* requests for a Chinatown housing project. Alice Griffith, a longtime housing advocate and new member of the Housing Commission, supported the idea, as did public health director J. G. Geiger. Sanitary Commission member Eunice Gibson also backed the project. An ebullient *Chinese Digest* declared in November 1938 that with such support, "the [housing] solution is seemingly just around the corner."[19] The *Digest* celebrated far too quickly, however. Money was a tremendous problem: land values in Chinatown were exorbitant, greatly exceeding the federal project limits of $1.50 per square foot.

As Lim P. Lee had predicted, most municipal officials expressed little interest in the project or in solving its underlying financial problem. In order to silence Geiger and his allies, SFHA officials eventually suggested putting a Chinese American project in Hunters Point, an isolated site they knew was unacceptable. Public transportation between downtown and Hunters Point was poor, and the city showed no inclination to improve it. At the same time, the vast majority of Chinatown residents worked in Chinatown, because discrimination limited opportunities elsewhere. Few could afford cars.[20] In other words, a project in Hunters Point would imperil the livelihood of its residents. Regardless, the commission and the SFHA refused to budge from this final offer of a Hunters Point development.

THE WAR AGAINST JAPAN

As Chinese American housing activists struggled with the SFHA, Chinatown's larger concerns began to shift. In July 1937, Japanese forces launched a full-scale invasion of China proper. Soldiers swept down the east coast, earning a reputation for brutality as they moved from city to city. Capturing Nanjing, the Nationalist Chinese capital, the Japanese army subjected inhabitants to a nightmarish six weeks of rape, torture, and murder that horrified the world. During 1938, the Japanese continued their southward movement, taking Hankou, Xiamen, and Xuzhou and intensively bombing Guangzhou, the capital of Guangdong Province. By the end of that year, the city and the entire Pearl River Delta had fallen to the invaders. The ancestral home of the vast majority of Chinatown residents was now in Japanese hands.

The Japanese invasion of China quickly soured relations between Japan and the United States. Beginning in the 1890s, the United States supported an "open door" policy of foreign access to China, while European powers and Japan tried to carve out exclusive spheres of influence in the weak empire. Successive U.S. presidents, including Franklin Roosevelt, supported the open door policy, which the Japanese invasion of China threatened. In 1939, after lodging fruitless diplomatic protests with Japan, the United States expressed its anger by choosing not to renew the two nations' 1911 trade treaty.[21]

Once Japan and the United States began to quarrel, most Americans moved from expressing neutrality about the Sino-Japanese war to siding with China. While the vast majority still wanted to stay out of any foreign conflicts or entanglements, this isolationism coexisted with growing compassion for the Chinese. In September 1937, a public opinion poll showed that only 47 percent of respondents favored China in the war, while 51 percent expressed no preference. Less than two years later, only 24 percent of Americans remained neutral, while 74 percent now supported China. More than half of 1939 respondents also favored boycotting Japanese goods and halting shipments of armaments to Japan. In both polls, only 2 percent of respondents expressed sympathy for Japan.[22]

The ongoing shift proved crucial to relief efforts on behalf of China. In June 1938, the United Council for Civilian Relief in China (UCCRC), whose members included Albert Einstein, Herbert Hoover, Henry Luce, and Theodore Roosevelt, Jr., sponsored the first Bowl of Rice fundraising parties in seven hundred American towns and cities, including San Francisco. The event's name reflected its major purpose: filling the "rice bowls" of starving war refugees in China. Chinatown residents and activists worked closely with the UCCRC, marching in the group's parade and organizing a Chinatown street festival to coincide with Bowl of Rice. Barricades surrounding Chinatown blocked car traffic, while UCCRC volunteers sold 50¢ "Humanity" badges to all tourists who wished to enter the district. Neighborhood businesses stayed open until four in the morning to serve the two hundred thousand San Franciscans who poured into Chinatown during the event. A reporter for the *Young China* newspaper described the cheerful chaos that resulted: "There were oceans of people, shoulder to shoulder and heel to toe, so crowded as to be impassable. . . . [T]he number of people was so great, they pressed forward with tremendous force and could not stop, and the police cars were hard pressed to cope with them." By the end of the festivities, the UCCRC in San Francisco had raised more than $50,000 for Chinese refugees.[23]

LOCAL WAR

Not all San Franciscans sympathized with China, however. During the 1930s, many of the city's six thousand Japanese Americans cheered Japan's rise in Asia and its colonization of China. Japanese American newspapers often supported Imperial Japanese policy and reprinted verbatim that government's propagandistic press releases. Nisei and Issei women sent care packages to Japanese soldiers at the front in China, while Japanese American organizations pledged funds for the invasion. As historian Mae Ngai has observed, many Issei and Nisei "held complicated, divided loyalties, a set of allegiances that sustained commitment to life in America alongside affective and cultural ties, even patriotic sympathies, with Japan." White marginalization of Japanese Americans only helped foster such sentiments; indeed, many Issei and Nisei pointed to Japan's success as proof of Japanese racial equality with whites.[24]

At the same time, Japanese American shops on Grant Avenue relied on white tourists' assumptions about "Oriental" sameness or visitors' misperceptions of store owners' ethnicity, something that increasingly infuriated Chinese American competitors. Chinatown community groups held mass meetings to call for a boycott of all Japanese-owned businesses in the neighborhood and placed signs in their windows proclaiming "This is a Chinese Store." According to Japanese American journalist Kazumaro Uno, "the children of San Francisco's Chinatown have been responsible for distribution of vicious and unfriendly handbills, they have been responsible for acts of vandalism, and activities leading to boycott."[25]

Ironically, it was San Francisco nativism that originally fostered business competition between Japanese Americans and Chinese Americans. Beginning in the late nineteenth century, San Francisco's Chinese Americans responded to nativist hostility by carving out economic niches in which they did not compete directly with whites, such as Asian art good sales, Chinese restaurants, and, by the 1910s, Chinatown tourism. As the anti-Japanese movement mushroomed in the 1900s and 1910s, San Francisco's growing Japanese American population adopted the same strategy. Since whites controlled so much of the economy, Issei started entering Chinese American–dominated fields, such as laundries and Chinatown art goods shops. Initially, Chinese Americans saw little harm in this; Chinese American and Issei merchants even advertised together in a 1909 Chinese Consolidated Benevolent Association guidebook.[26] But by 1936, no one could imagine such cooperation any longer.

Nativism aside, the transnationalism of the Chinese American community also played a role in this shift away from friendly relations. Sun Yat-sen, the

Chinese revolutionary who became the first president of the Republic of China, famously said that "the overseas Chinese are the mother of the Revolution."[27] Activists like Sun raised hundreds of thousands of dollars from the overseas Chinese communities scattered throughout Southeast Asia, North and South America, and other parts of the globe, with Chinese San Franciscans contributing their fair share to every campaign.[28] As elsewhere, the financial ties that bound San Francisco's Chinatown to China were often very personal, as well: most of the "bachelor" laborers in overwhelmingly male Chinatown supported parents, wives, and children in the Pearl River Delta counties of Guangdong.

For these reasons, the Japanese American presence in Chinatown signified much more than just heightened business competition. It threatened the economic ties that linked Chinatown residents to the Chinese nation at a time of war. It imperiled the financial security of families in China who suffered when Grant Avenue businesses lost money. Less tangibly, many Chinese Americans who had little or no stake in Grant Avenue businesses viewed Chinatown as hard-won Chinese space—for some, it was even part of a larger Chinese nation in the same general way they were themselves.[29] The painful parallels between Chinatown's embattled history in San Francisco and China's experience with Western and Japanese exploitation also helped many Chinese Americans imagine a larger purpose in Issei and Nisei business activity. In addition, Chinese Americans had, in the face of segregation and hostility, created a thriving tourist economy ostensibly based on Chinese culture. The idea of Japanese Americans profiting from Chinese struggles and Chinese culture while cheering on the destruction of China was intolerable.[30]

Chinese American citizens did not perceive their transnationalism or activities on behalf of China as compromising their loyalty to the United States. Regardless of their formal citizenship status, many Chinatown residents saw themselves as both Chinese and American—a bridge between the two cultures. They could belong to a larger Chinese nation and be patriotic American citizens at the same time, and few worried about contesting loyalties. Japanese Americans in the late 1930s were not so fortunate. Their activities in support of Japan were not illegal, nor did they differ greatly from Chinatown's efforts on behalf of China. "The majority of the American people resent the Japanese contributing American-earned money" to Japan, complained Nisei columnist Tad Uyeno. "At the same time they feel it is quite right for the Chinese to donate huge sums of money to the Chinese government . . . [or] return to China to join the Chinese Republican army." Indeed, California's politically influential white nativist organizations used evidence of pro-Japan sentiment to fuel their neverending war on the state's Asian Americans. San Francisco nativism had always thrived in times of economic distress; in 1935, the progressive journalist Carey McWilliams reported that once again, the anti-Asian Hearst newspapers were rumbling about "inequitable Oriental competition sapping the economic life of America and retarding recovery."[31] Sensing the growing public sympathy for China, however, anti-Asian nativists began focusing more on Japanese Americans this time.

As the relationship between Japan and the United States worsened, the state's influential white supremacists began to describe Nisei and Issei as a potential fifth column in a future war. Their campaign helped thwart Nisei attempts to claim a place in an American society largely hostile to Asian Americans. As historian Lon Kurashige has shown, until the very late 1930s, Japanese Americans tried to cast "Nisei as a new breed of American citizen who was at home in both Japan and the United States." In the face of shrill accusations, Japanese Americans by 1940 abandoned what Kurashige terms this "biculturalism" and adopted hyper-patriotism instead.[32] Chinese Americans could still be bicultural, but that no longer remained an option for the Nisei.

MRS. ROOSEVELT INTERVENES

The tension on Grant Avenue and the flurry of China relief activities helped distract frustrated Chinatown housing activists, whose plans for a neighborhood project remained stalled. By April 1939, SFHA officials were soliciting bids for the Holly Courts project in Bernal Heights and drawing up plans for two other outlying developments, Potrero Terrace and Sunnydale. However, they continued to avoid discussion of a Chinatown project as the federal government's January 1, 1940, deadline for final submissions neared. Worried Chinese Americans urged the Housing Commission to use the city-owned site of the former Washington School in Chinatown. Commission members refused, claiming that the site was too small for a project. More likely it was too close to the boundaries of all-white Nob Hill for commissioners' tastes.[33]

In rejecting Washington School, the commissioners tacitly acknowledged what they saw as the political reality of their city. While nativist agitators in the 1930s focused largely on Japanese Americans, they did not entirely spare the Chinese American population. In 1933, a San Francisco supervisor suggested boosting revenue by charging all Asian American residents a $5 head tax. The slow and grudging extension of relief money to Chinatown and the denial of lights for the Chinese Playground reflected the same mindset. In order to make a Chinatown project possible, the city needed to provide extra funding to cover the district's high land costs. Mayor Rossi refused to consider such an outlay. A Native Son and a thrifty, pragmatic politician, he knew that scarcely one in four Chinatown residents could vote.[34] To him, money for Chinatown was money wasted.

First Lady Eleanor Roosevelt shattered this belief, however. Beginning in 1935, Mrs. Roosevelt wrote "My Day," a popular daily newspaper column in which she described her everyday life and discussed issues that interested her. On July 5, 1939, she devoted most of her column to her Fourth of July picnic at the president's estate in Hyde Park, New York, but in the last paragraph she turned to another subject:

> I have just received a most interesting report prepared by a study group of fifteen in the School of Social Studies in San Francisco, California. It is called "Living Conditions in Chinatown," and I should think it would make San Francisco officials anxious to get a more detailed report and then take some action. I always enjoy my trips to Chinatown when I am in San Francisco, but I have always been conscious, that just as in our own rather picturesque quarters in New York City, there were undoubtedly dangers to the whole city there because of poor housing and living conditions.[35]

In fact, the School of Social Studies (SSS) report called Chinatown "a slum, a confined area largely unfit for human habitation . . . [and] comparable to the worst in the world."[36]

Mrs. Roosevelt's comments deeply embarrassed San Francisco officials, who reacted with a mixture of defensiveness and denial. They already knew about the situation in Chinatown; a Community Chest survey in the early 1930s had documented it, and in 1938, the liberal daily *San Francisco News* described the district as a "slum" crying out for public housing. But when Mrs. Roosevelt's column betrayed San Francisco's dirty little secret to the rest of the nation, city leaders feigned surprise or powerlessness. A. D. Wilder, the city's director of works and a onetime member of the Housing Commission, claimed that conditions in Chinatown would improve if Chinese American building owners "themselves would cooperate." San Francisco's chief administrative officer, Alfred J. Cleary, asked "if anybody expected these Chinatown people to have gold plumbing." Then, in an ill-conceived attempt to deflect responsibility, he blamed Dr. Geiger for the poor conditions, publicly contending that the health director never reported the problem. Geiger, who by 1939 had been fighting for several years to improve Chinatown housing, refused to play along.

Instead, he told reporters that conditions were even worse than the SSS had described.[37] As the storm continued, Mayor Rossi wisely kept his mouth shut.

Fearful of reviving old stereotypes of Chinese filth and disease, an array of Chinese Americans also publicly questioned the SSS study's truthfulness and its motives. Kenneth Lee, former secretary of the powerful CCBA, rejected the group's findings entirely. A majority of Chinese American families lived in only one or two rooms, but Lee maintained that "Chinatown's younger generation—and it is by far the greater percentage—live as do average American families. Crowding is almost a thing of the past." Looking back a decade later, liberal journalist Gilbert Woo contrasted such responses with the reactions of young Chinese American housing advocates; they were "not influenced by 'face' . . . and arose unanimously to support the SSS report," he claimed. Actually, even Lim P. Lee distanced himself from the SSS study, belittling its methodology and contending that "airing our dirty laundry to the public view will not help us solve our social and human problems."[38]

Within Chinatown, however, residents frankly acknowledged the truth of the report. The conservative *Young China* newspaper printed a three-part summary of the study and Mrs. Roosevelt's response. The citizen-run *Chinese Times* noted that "in reality, this abominable and dirty situation was reported six years ago by young Chinatown property owners to achieve reform," but the city took little action. The *Chinese Times* also informed readers of the disheartening news that "San Francisco authorities say [the SSS report] will serve to strengthen overall improvement plans and not especially those connected to overseas Chinese."[39] History appeared to be repeating itself.

Yet Mrs. Roosevelt's column resonated with many white San Franciscans, who read it with a mixture of embarrassment and recognition. A decade of shifting racial perceptions and the larger international situation had made an impact even in the heartland of anti-Asian nativism. Equally significant, by the late 1930s, a growing number of white businessmen began to appreciate that Chinatown, as Lim P. Lee put it, was a "precious jade that draws tourists." Among such people, the members of the San Francisco Junior Chamber of Commerce (the Jaycees) stood out. In the run-up to the World's Fair, they helped form a separate Chinese Jaycee organization whose members included *Chinese Digest* publisher Chingwah Lee and Lim P. Lee. The white Jaycees' failure to integrate their own group suggests that the organization's leaders had not completely broken with the past. Still, when the SSS report became public, the Junior Chamber of Commerce did not follow city officials in disavowing it. Rather, they announced plans to conduct their own study of housing conditions in Chinatown.[40]

The organization turned for help to its young affiliate, the Chinese Jaycees. Members of the latter group already possessed much of the necessary data, which they had been compiling and discussing since the mid-1930s. Together, the Jaycees and the Chinese Jaycees prepared a report about the low wages, high tuberculosis rates, and other problems of the Chinatown population. Three months after the SSS called Chinatown one of the world's worst slums, the Junior Chamber confirmed these findings in its own study. While the SSS focused mainly on the impact of poor living conditions on Chinese Americans, the Junior Chamber made a more economic appeal at the end of its report: "If [Chinatown] degenerates further, even the sham front along Grant Avenue will be useless. . . . How many people from the west have gone to New York to see the slums and spend their money there?" Then the group proposed a solution that business groups rarely embraced: public housing.[41]

A CHINESE PROJECT

The Jaycees endorsed public housing in part to stop Chinatown's slow expansion. The Junior Chamber of Commerce report from October 1939 euphemistically concluded that "the inhabitants of San Francisco appear to desire that the Chinese remain in the area now called Chinatown." A *San Francisco Chronicle* article published the next month described Chinatown as "incapable of expansion. . . . [T]here is but one direction to grow—and that one is up." Laura Reed, president of the city's International Institute, was more straightforward: "the attitudes of other races prevent the expansion of the present Chinatown boundaries."[42]

Actually, the Depression persuaded a few white homeowners and landlords on Chinatown's edges to break with nativist tradition. After 1930, some wealthier Chinese Americans purchased or rented homes west of Mason Street, the border of Nob Hill and Chinatown at that time. In 1935, a handful of Chinese Americans lived as far west as Taylor Street; by 1940, some passed Taylor and were approaching Jones Street. Alarmed, a number of white residents on Nob Hill and elsewhere began to create racially restrictive covenants rather than depending on the city's pervasive nativism, as they had always done in the past.[43] Civic leaders also hoped to stop this slow creep, and public housing offered one of the few ways to eradicate slum housing while preserving the very segregation that created it.

Pragmatic Chinese American activists understood the mixed motives of their supporters but worked with such people anyway. As Gilbert Woo concluded, "at least, underneath all the slogans about housing reform, there isn't the intention [this time] to get rid of the Chinese." Chinese Americans joined the Junior Chamber of Commerce in urging San Franciscans to write to USHA head Nathan Straus to demand that he waive the $1.50 per square foot price limit for Chinatown. The Jaycees' support, along with Mrs. Roosevelt's column, won Chinese Americans the audience that had eluded them in the past. Newly attentive reporters reprinted Theodore Lee's pleas for support and covered the activities of Chee S. Lowe's new Chinese housing advisory committee. Lim P. Lee, speaking yet again to the League of Women Voters, now convinced the group to contact Straus in support of the waiver.[44]

Behind the scenes, Eleanor Roosevelt remained involved as well. Housing advocates such as Laura Reed sought her help in obtaining the waiver, while Gilbert Woo contacted her when a few Chinatown landlords resisted the project campaign. "Ninety-nine percent of our countrymen in Chinatown are for the project. Don't lat [*sic*] a few profiteers smoke-screen the issue," he urged. Spurred on by such letters, Mrs. Roosevelt asked Nathan Straus about the $1.50 per square foot limit and "if Congress would consider an exception in this case." Straus proved more than helpful, assuring her that "the land cost question as it applies to Chinatown . . . [is] a completely special case to which established USHA policy need not necessarily be applied."[45] Soon after, Straus publicly announced that if San Francisco contributed an additional $75,000, the USHA would put up an extra $150,000 to make a Chinatown project possible.

With the decision now up to local officials, China relief organizations unwittingly ramped up the pressure on them. In early February 1940, the UCCRC organized a second Bowl of Rice party, which once again took place almost wholly within the borders of Chinatown. While the first party was a success, the second was a runaway hit. Along with tourists, a cross-section of San Francisco officials and civic leaders attended, including the city district attorney, municipal judges, and Jaycee president Truman Young. Bank of America president A. P. Giannini, former U.S. senator William Gibbs McAdoo, and other notables also pledged money to the cause. Scores of businesses from around the city donated items for the Bowl of Rice auction, with all proceeds going to the UCCRC. Hundreds of thousands of San Franciscans and other visitors attended three days of Chinese and Western musical performances, lion dances, firecrackers, a fashion show, and an art exhibition. Local radio stations offered live coverage of the festivities and broadcast some portions to affiliates across the West.[46]

The party cast Chinatown as a surrogate for China and its residents as representatives of their ancestral nation, an equation crucial to the housing

FIGURE 4.2. A diverse crowd thronged the Chinese Music Pavilion during the May 1941 Bowl of Rice festivities to raise money for Chinese war refugees. The popularity of such events highlighted white residents' changing views of the Chinese, and of San Francisco's Chinese American population: the 1940 festivities even helped prod the board of supervisors to provide extra funding for a Chinatown housing project. (San Francisco History Center, San Francisco Public Library.)

project's success. Nayan Shah has argued that the project relied on Chinese Americans' attempts to prove their community "'worthy' and 'deserving'" of public housing by emphasizing the presence of families in the neighborhood and their "desire to acculturate to American norms, values, and standards of living."[47] Certainly, project proponents rarely discussed the "bachelor" men, still a majority of Chinatown's population, who would have no access to any development that housed only families and American citizens. This strategy was only part of the story, however. While community leaders had long known that Chinatown was a slum, only in the late 1930s did they begin to care. Mrs. Roosevelt exposed San Francisco's secret to the nation, but significantly, she did so at a time when far more Americans, and San Franciscans, were willing to listen.

In other words, by February 1940, international events were playing a major role in the fate of Chinatown housing. The Bowl of Rice Party provided the board of supervisors with overwhelming evidence that the white public supported the Chinese. In early March, board members voted to approve $75,000 for the housing project. When Mayor Rossi failed to include the money in the city budget, the supervisors promised to appropriate the money themselves.[48] The board hoped that the extra funding would counter the negative publicity from Mrs. Roosevelt's column. At the same time, their vote was a gesture of sympathy and support for the Chinese, both in San Francisco and in China—or at least an attempt to please their thousands of white constituents who openly supported the Chinese cause.

PUBLIC HOUSING AND RACIAL BOUNDARIES

The presence of large Asian American populations shaped the public housing program in San Francisco in unique ways. Public housing was never neutral anywhere in the United States. Politics—especially the politics of race—played a huge role in site selection and project allocation everywhere.[49] But racial politics in San Francisco had always meant anti-Asian nativism more than anything else. In one way, the international situation threatened this tradition, forcing reluctant city officials to acknowledge the importance of Chinatown and the growing popularity of the Chinese. At the same time, authorities in San Francisco used the Chinatown project in the same way officials elsewhere employed public housing: to prevent a nonwhite group from challenging racial boundaries and residential segregation. Indeed, SFHA officials initially decided to segregate projects on the basis of race in order to keep Chinese Americans out of all of them.[50]

Even outside Chinatown, San Francisco's diversity, the Sino-Japanese War, and the impact of the Depression and the New Deal on racial traditions complicated issues of tenant selection and siting. The Great Depression eroded the relatively privileged position African Americans enjoyed, compared to Asian Americans, in San Francisco. Already clustered in low-wage, service sector jobs, many blacks lost their tenuous economic foothold when the Depression began. To make ends meet, some who lived in other neighborhoods now doubled up in the Western Addition. By 1941, a growing number of black migrants were also streaming into San Francisco because of new government defense spending in the area.[51] Many white residents responded with concern and disgust to the increasingly visible black population, a scenario replayed throughout the Bay Area during World War II.

The debate about housing for the multiracial Western Addition area of San Francisco highlighted the importance of this slow demographic shift. Located west of downtown, the Western Addition survived the 1906 earthquake but slowly deteriorated when rebuilding began elsewhere. Landlords eventually divided the area's old homes into apartments, especially in the Hayes Valley section, and rented them to tenants who often lacked the mobility of other San Franciscans. In the mid-1930s, HOLC surveyors described what they considered to be the results. "It is what might be termed the 'melting pot of the West' and is the nearest approach to a slum district in San Francisco," officials wrote, tellingly ignoring Chinatown. "It has a highly congested population consisting of Japanese, Russians, Mexicans, Negroes, etc. having a very low income." Substandard homes comprised more than half the residential structures in some sections of the Western Addition and more than 80 percent in the Hayes Valley/Jefferson Square area.[52]

When the Housing Authority announced plans in 1939 to purchase and develop the old Calvary Hill Cemetery on the western border of the Western Addition, white neighbors to the west and south flooded the board of supervisors with complaints. Other districts had resisted public housing before, but this was the first overtly racial protest. The cemetery divided a racially-mixed area to the north from a white neighborhood to the south. In 1937, HOLC surveyors described the burial ground as a racial buffer zone; if developed for *private* housing, they noted, it would improve areas to the south and west and protect them from the "threat of [racial] infiltration in the future." In response to the protests, the SFHA quickly assured the press and the public that "only whites would be admitted" to any Calvary project. Regardless, the mayor and the board of supervisors forced the SFHA to abandon its plans for the site after months of community protest.[53]

The policies of the FHA help explain this resistance, a relatively uncharacteristic development in light of San Francisco's unusual racial history. Congress established the FHA in 1934, about a year after inaugurating the HOLC. The HOLC granted direct low-interest mortgages to homeowners on the verge of default and also developed standard methods of assessing mortgage risk. Equally significant, it pioneered fifteen-, twenty-, and even thirty-year mortgages, terms far longer than private banks had ever offered. Eventually, Congress created the FHA to get the government out of the direct mortgage business. The new agency insured mortgages made by private banks and savings and loans, enabling such institutions to offer mortgages with HOLC-length terms to far more Americans. To make the mortgage market less risky, the HOLC conducted extensive city surveys, rating the soundness of neighborhoods using factors that included race. Officials of the agency routinely designated areas in which nonwhite people lived as high-risk "D," or "red," districts. The FHA relied on the same rating criteria as the HOLC, grading neighborhoods on the basis of racial composition, among other factors, and *requiring* the use of racial restrictions and covenants in insured properties. Enthusiastic about this process of risk reduction, most banks and savings and loans adopted the FHA's ratings system for all their mortgages, not just those the agency underwrote.[54]

In most places these practices helped institutionalize existing patterns of racial segregation, but in San Francisco, they also created new ones. Since the FHA required racial restrictions, white homeowners and builders quickly learned that proximity to *any* racial "concentration" hurt buyers' ability to use FHA insurance.[55] FHA policy thus made white San Franciscans far more interested than before in promoting and enforcing the segregation of all non-whites, not just Asian Americans. Mayor Rossi's housing commission, which he packed with real estate agents, bankers, and other businessmen, almost certainly favored greater residential racial segregation in principle; it was already standard real estate practice in other cities without San Francisco's unusual history.[56] Commission members' intimate knowledge of FHA practices informed their eventual decision to bolster whites' property values by segregating blacks as well as Chinese Americans in public housing.

Housing Commission members thus formalized what they called a "neighborhood pattern" policy to help them preserve the property values and FHA eligibility of white San Franciscans. The policy already existed in practice, since the Housing Authority had quietly restricted its first three projects in order to keep out Chinese Americans, the worst-housed people in the city. Now, however, SFHA executive director Albert J. Evers began to explain and elaborate on it. According to Evers, the policy meant that "families . . . will not be forced, through no fault of their own, to live in neighborhoods to which they are unaccustomed and in which they have no family, religious, and social ties." SFHA representative Marshall Dill claimed that projects would "be placed at strategic points in the City where they will be suitably located for the persons whom they are intended [*sic*] and not concentrated to oversupply any one portion of the city."[57] Projects were supposed to serve low-income residents in their own neighborhoods.

In theory, this meant that the neighborhood pattern policy would help replicate San Francisco's unusual racial geography in diverse neighborhoods, but the Housing Commission had learned from its Chinatown experience. City officials and the commission ignored Chinatown for so long in part because spending public money on the district seemed politically foolish. It won few votes inside Chinatown (only a small number of Chinese Americans could vote) and none outside, since it benefited only Chinese Americans. The public outcry over Mrs. Roosevelt's column revealed some softening of San Francisco nativism; it did not, however, demonstrate any support for Chinese American integration. Ardent backers of the Chinese project included neighboring white homeowner groups that hoped to stop the expansion of Chinatown's borders.[58] As the Housing Commission and the board of supervisors discovered, such organizations considered money for Chinatown public housing to be an investment in their own housing values as well.

In other words, properly gerrymandered public housing developments could both reinforce existing residential segregation and build white support for the SFHA. After Calvary and Chinatown, then, the Housing Commission and the SFHA essentially created two definitions of "neighborhood" to guide tenant selection under the neighborhood pattern policy. For white San Franciscans, the city was their neighborhood; for nonwhites, their neighborhoods were rundown areas where their presence could not "harm" property values. Because of early site selection controversies, the SFHA built its first three projects (Holly Courts, Sunnydale, and Potrero) in sparsely populated outlying areas. To fill the developments, the Housing Authority recruited tenants from across the city. It soon set up an office in the middle of the low-income Western Addition, where it signed up white families but rejected their black, Filipino, and Japanese American neighbors. The policy continued even though few whites expressed interest in the projects. With almost five hundred units sitting empty at Sunnydale and Potrero, the local authority even tried to raise the maximum allowed income for tenants.[59] The tactic failed to fill the projects, but the SFHA still refused to integrate them.

Having moved to stop the expansion of Chinatown, the SFHA created the foundations for another racially restricted neighborhood in the city—this one for poorer blacks and Asian Americans of all classes. By recruiting white families from the Western Addition, the SFHA segregated people who had never segregated themselves. Color alone comprised the "family, religious, and social ties" that Albert Evers and the SFHA described so glowingly. Those left behind iń the Western Addition had no access to any housing project, however. Officials publicly claimed that land costs in the Western Addition were simply too high to build there.[60]

WITHOUT MRS. ROOSEVELT

During 1940, a group of Western Addition residents formed a multiracial coalition to fight for fairness in public housing and open occupancy in all city projects.[61] The group, which called itself the Western Addition Housing Council (WAHC), included African Americans, Japanese Americans, European immigrants, and progressive white labor leaders. Outside of Communist circles, the organization was unprecedented; San Francisco had no real tradition of interracial activism. Unions had always been racially exclusive, rejecting Asians and either barring blacks or segregating them in nonvoting auxiliaries. Civic groups, from the Jaycees to the Native Sons, also followed this pattern.

Indeed, some of the city's conservative African American leaders viewed the WAHC with suspicion. Blacks and Japanese Americans in the Western Addition shopped at each others' businesses, and African American, Nisei, and white children attended the district's integrated schools together. In fact, they often lived side by side—the black-owned *San Francisco Spokesman* called "the blocks between Filmore and Octavia, and Bush and O'Farrell" in the Western Addition an "amalgamation of Japan with Africa in the majority of its population." Still, blacks found housing with far greater ease than Asian Americans, even during the Depression. Politicians at least paid them lip service, and only in San Francisco could a black editor claim that "a large Oriental population in this state will strengthen the sentiment against letting down the bars of intermarriage." In other words, many African Americans understood the benefits that accrued to them because of San Francisco-style nativism. In fact, the San Francisco NAACP branch secretary worried that unless his group worked to influence the SFHA, "the Housing Authority [will] sandwich us in with the other race groups" in a project.[62] Such an outcome might hasten the erosion of blacks' relatively privileged position in the housing market.

Although lacking the support of the NAACP, the WAHC pressed on, heartened by the board of supervisors' decision to allocate extra money for a Chinatown project. The Western Addition needed similar additional funding if the district was to get its own project. To gain the backing of the city supervisors, WAHC members held public meetings in the Western Addition and circulated pro-housing petitions to local merchants. Group spokesmen also criticized the SFHA for practicing segregation in existing projects and for ignoring the housing needs of many San Francisco residents, particularly nonwhites. In addition, they pressed the SFHA to clearly explain the "neighborhood pattern," which officials hesitated to do. Finally, in early 1942, Albert J. Evers informed the WAHC that "we have good reason to believe that any policy involving enforced com-mingling [*sic*] of races would not necessarily be evidence of equal rights but would undoubtedly jeopardize public peace and good order." In spite of plentiful evidence to the contrary, the SFHA had declared integration a menace. Yet the WAHC's activism also forced the Housing Authority to admit that it was secretly buying land for a project in the Western Addition. In October 1940, SFHA officials filed an application to build a project there, which they called West Side Courts.[63]

Japanese Americans initially expressed great interest in West Side Courts. In Los Angeles, Japanese American elites paid little attention to public housing and seemed determined to distance themselves from its program. However, San Francisco's combination of anti-Asian nativism and urban congestion closed off most other housing options for all Asian Americans. At the same time, San Francisco city officials rejected Los Angeles County's draconian tactics, such as deporting aliens who used public assistance. Under these circumstances, the USHA program proved quite appealing to many of the city's Japanese Americans, including elite Issei and Nisei, who supported the housing program and the WAHC. *Japanese American News* publisher Yasuo Abiko even sat on the WAHC's board, while the *News*'s rival, the *New World-Sun Daily*, devoted substantial attention to the housing program.[64]

But Japanese Americans quickly stopped fighting for a project obviously off-limits to the vast majority of them. The WAHC leadership urged Nisei to attend the SFHA's first public meeting about West Side Courts, held in November 1940. After the meeting, Japanese American interest in West Side waned considerably. Once the SFHA discussed tenant requirements, Japanese Americans discovered the truth: just as in Los Angeles, the head of household regulations disqualified all but a few Japanese Americans from living in the project. In the face of such disheartening news, Yasuo Abiko tried in vain to stir community enthusiasm, and Nisei and Issei listened with growing skepticism to the WAHC's assertions that "the Federal low-cost housing program should be of vital interest to all Japanese residents."[65]

Further marginalizing the Japanese American community, most of the housing advocates concentrated on African American needs. Writing a few years later, Alice Griffith confirmed that the SFHA chose Jefferson Square for West Side Courts in order to serve the area's black population. The NAACP had already expressed its interest in a project that excluded "the other race groups." Even the white progressives who helped organize the WAHC focused largely on improving black housing conditions, despite the presence of a far larger Japanese American population in the crumbling Jefferson Square area and the Western Addition as a whole. America's worsening relationship with Japan—and anti-Asian nativists' use of this animosity—also made Japanese American involvement a risky proposition for the WAHC. While Yasuo Abiko remained active in the WAHC into 1942, neither he nor any other Japanese American ever played a public role in the battle for a Western Addition project.[66]

Opposition to the development continued to build, however, even as the SFHA acquired almost all the land it needed for West Side Courts. Project opponents still hoped to stop the development by persuading the board of supervisors not to grant the Housing Authority additional funding for the last few parcels of land. In March 1941, four hundred interested San Franciscans attended a board of supervisors meeting to fight for or against the additional funding. Opponents of the development included an area businessmen's group, the city apartment house owners' organization, the vice president of the Central Council of Civic Clubs, and a neighborhood improvement organization. Representatives of the WAHC, the NAACP, the League of Women Voters, the Negro Civic Council, and several academic pro-housing organizations spoke in favor of a development.[67]

The rancorous three-and-a-half hour meeting showed that the SFHA's earlier manipulation of race had undermined its credibility. SFHA officials publicly claimed that any Western Addition project would reflect the neighborhood by housing all races together. But the SFHA's opacity about its racial policies in other projects and its discussions of "co-mingling" had already become notorious. City officials who supported West Side Courts "shifted uneasily in their seats" as Communist Emma Cutler endorsed the development. Opponents of the project never mentioned her political affiliation; instead, they pounced on the thorny issue she raised: the race of the proposed project's tenants. According to reporters, once Cutler mentioned race, "opponents . . . declared flatly that the West Side Courts would be for Negroes alone."[68] Albert Evers denied the charge, but the Housing Authority's own track record undermined his arguments. Why would the SFHA recruit whites from the Western Addition to live in outlying projects if the Housing Authority planned to admit them to a neighborhood project?

Project opponents condemned what they assumed would be a segregated public housing project, but not because they believed in integration. Most lived or owned businesses in neighborhoods west of the proposed site. The growth of the African American community to their east during the 1930s alarmed these residents and businesspeople, who had ignored the concentration of black businesses before that time. The FHA's racial rating system explains this growing white unease. Local developers planned to subdivide Laurel Hill Cemetery to the west of the proposed public housing site. Residents and real estate agents who feared the blighting influence of the crumbling Western Addition hoped that such activity would raise property values.[69] A segregated, low-income housing project would not only thwart this goal but could even spell the end of the private development. Under its own guidelines, the FHA would not underwrite mortgages for white purchasers in a subdivision that sat too close to a racial "concentration." Indeed, because of the FHA's policies and its growing importance in the housing market, no developer would even attempt to build such a subdivision to begin with.

In the Western Addition, federal public and private housing programs challenged San Francisco's nativist order and created new racial interest groups. White residents to the west of the proposed West Side Courts suddenly feared the growth of a visible black population to their east; they also resented the SFHA's purported use of public housing to solidify and anchor a black population in the Jefferson Square area. Conservative black groups fought for a segregated project in order to keep the presence of other "race groups," especially Japanese Americans and Filipinos, from diminishing their comparatively privileged status. Issei and Nisei worked to build a cross-racial housing coalition until they realized that USHA regulations barred most of them from the program to begin with. Surveying the debate, the board of supervisors voted against providing extra money for West Side Courts. Without these funds, the SFHA could not purchase the remaining land it needed to begin construction in Jefferson Square.

THE LONG SHADOW OF WAR

The war overseas not only influenced local housing policy in San Francisco but also poisoned relations between the Chinese American and Japanese American communities. Chinese American merchants understood that the public's view of the war gave them the upper hand, and they rarely hesitated to exploit their advantage. In 1939, *San Francisco Chronicle* columnist Garrett Graham explained to readers that "every Chinese place of business—shop, market, or restaurant—conspicuously displays a sign announcing that it is a Chinese establishment" because of public opinion about the war. National publications like *Business Week* applauded the city's "Chinese merchants [and] their competitive battle with the Japanese" and placed the issue in context of the Asian conflict. As one Japanese American shop owner complained, "some enterprising Chinese merchants solicit business by passing out literature condemning the Japanese merchants for supporting the cold-blooded murder of innocent Chinese people."[70]

By 1941, the deteriorating U.S.-Japanese relationship had irrevocably damaged Japanese American businesses, with whites consciously favoring Chinese Americans in the business war. "Nine out of 10 Caucasian customers who came into the store began to ask us if we were Chinese or Japanese," recalled a Nisei clerk who worked in a Grant Avenue art store before the war. "The Japanese goods were never put on exhibit in the windows because they might have chased the tourists away." Adding to Japanese American difficulties, the U.S. government imposed an embargo on Japanese imports in October 1940. The trade ban forced Japanese American business owners on Grant Avenue to purchase Chinese-made products, but many white tourists still avoided their stores.[71]

In using the war this way, Chinese Americans helped undermine certain central tenets of San Francisco nativism. The city's traditional brand of white supremacy always denied Asians and Asian Americans the right even to live in California, which local nativists declared to be white man's country.[72] White San Franciscans never managed to expel the Chinese American population and largely stopped trying to do so by 1910. Still, their actions during the late 1930s and early 1940s signified a shift from resignation to more positive acceptance. By siding with Chinese Americans in the business dispute and pushing federal officials for Chinatown housing money, white San Franciscans acknowledged that Chinatown *belonged* to the Chinese—not just legally, but spiritually as well. This quiet recognition of an indisputable and affirmative Chinese American claim to a small piece of California soil represented a marked break with the city's nativist past.

Still, San Francisco's Chinese Americans inadvertently reaffirmed and strengthened other traditional racial beliefs by internationalizing local business competition and by casting themselves as surrogates for China. Their strategy reflected their deep-seated transnationalism and, arguably, offered the most direct and obvious way to improve their situation. Besides thwarting Japanese American competition, it also strengthened the crucial association between Chinatown and China that attracted tourists. After Mrs. Roosevelt's intervention, it helped them win a housing project for Chinatown. Yet the tactic also reinforced existing perceptions of Asian Americans as eternal foreigners, something that Japanese Americans soon discovered could be very dangerous indeed.

Chinese Americans had few other tenable options, however. They lacked the independent political power to challenge white privilege, since they comprised less than 3 percent of the city's population and citizenship laws greatly limited their political power. They had to rely on powerful white allies who, while supporting a Chinatown housing development or Chinese refugees, continued to keep Chinese Americans at arm's length in other ways. Despite Bowl of Rice fundraisers and housing projects, Chinese Americans in 1941 still could not join most unions, find jobs outside their ethnic economy, live outside Chinatown, or even become members of the main Jaycee organization.

As in Los Angeles, the public housing program in San Francisco revealed the problematic place of Asian Americans in (or outside of) the emerging welfare state. Chinatown was a perfect candidate for a public housing program to alleviate slum conditions. Almost half its residents were American citizens, many of them heads of households. But as three half-empty, whites-only projects demonstrated, need did not determine SFHA site and tenant policies—racial politics did. Chinatown received a housing project because of growing white American sympathy for war-torn China—not because Chinese American citizens were entitled to one. Even with white sympathy, the Chinatown project was still a "special case," dependent on the goodwill of people such as Nathan Straus and Eleanor Roosevelt. In Los Angeles, officials wrote Asian Americans out of the new welfare state altogether. In San Francisco, they admitted Chinese Americans not as Americans but as representatives of a sympathetic foreign land. Neither approach acknowledged or took seriously Asian American citizenship rights. When the United States entered World War II in late 1941, this became even more obvious.

CHAPTER FIVE

The Subdivision and the War: From Jefferson Park to Internment

Speaking to the audience in a packed council chamber in 1940, Los Angeles City Councilman Evan Lewis claimed that "this subdivision might get us into war with Japan."[1] The council was addressing a routine matter: a developer's application to subdivide a tract in west Los Angeles. But in an unprecedented move, the company in question planned to offer lots in the proposed Jefferson Park subdivision to Nisei buyers. White residents of neighboring tracts initially used familiar arguments about race and property values to express their opposition to the development. In the summer of 1940, however, they discovered a more effective tactic: framing the central question of Jefferson Park as one of national security. The ensuing debate demonstrated white legislators' and residents' contempt for the Nisei and their rights. As citizens, adult Nisei escaped the Alien Land Act–based harassment that their parents faced in the 1920s. Yet by casting all Japanese Americans as potentially disloyal, white segregationists in 1940 thwarted the housing ambitions of the Nisei as successfully as they had those of the Issei almost two decades earlier.

Japanese immigration patterns and American immigration law together created the Nisei generation that came of age in Southern California in the late 1930s and early 1940s. Most Issei men immigrated to the United States alone, establishing themselves economically before sending for wives, bringing over "picture brides," or returning to Japan to marry. In 1904, when almost 46,000 Japanese men lived in the continental United States, the Japanese female population numbered only about 2,500. It began to increase quickly after 1910, however, and by 1920, more than 15,000 Japanese-born women lived in the three Pacific Coast states alone. Issei birthrates on the Coast skyrocketed in the 1920s, a fact that nativist agitators used to predict imminent Japanese takeover. The numbers actually reflected the high percentage of Japanese immigrant women in their prime childbearing years; after peaking between 1921 and 1923, the birthrate began to fall, first slowly and then rapidly. By 1940, the 24,393 Nisei who lived in Los Angeles County comprised fully one-quarter of the state's Japanese-origin population and more than a third of its Japanese American citizen population. Because of the demographics of immigration, however, the vast majority of these American citizens were in their late teens, with a substantial minority in their very early twenties. Only a quarter were old enough to vote.[2]

By 1940, these Nisei Angelenos had already confronted racial discrimination and the Depression; now, they faced an international situation with grave domestic repercussions. High school and college graduates alike searched in vain for low-wage jobs even inside the Japanese community, while white employers, never welcoming, became downright hostile. In March 1941, the English-language section of the Japanese American daily *Rafu Shimpo* reprinted letters from major area businesses discussing race and hiring practices. Most of the replies subtly discouraged Nisei applicants, but an agent of the American President Lines answered more frankly: "In the present state of international relations between Japan and the United States, I most certainly would not employ any Niseis [*sic*] in our Los Angeles office."[3]

Such statements reflected prevailing views in Los Angeles by 1941. In Southern California, general racial discrimination long narrowed Nisei horizons as much if not more than specifically anti-Asian or anti-Japanese sentiment. Anglo Los Angeles never really accepted the Nisei as American, regardless of their formal citizenship status; still, Northern California's nativist organizations never managed to establish themselves as a real presence in L.A., despite their attempts to do so in the 1920s. By 1940, however, the debate over the Jefferson Park housing development revealed an ongoing shift in attitudes. As the relationship between Japan and the United States worsened, a growing number of white Angelenos became more and more receptive to the old contention that Japanese Americans, regardless of citizenship, were a disloyal and fundamentally inassimilable element of the population. White Angelenos who were determined to thwart Nisei housing ambitions readily exploited this belief, whether or not they really shared it.

Their willingness to use issues of loyalty to stop the construction of Jefferson Park caught the development's elite Nisei boosters off guard. It also revealed the limits of their strategies for fighting anti-Japanese American sentiment in Los Angeles. While Japanese Americans received some support from blacks in the fight for Jefferson Park, Nisei leaders avoided the kind of interracial activism that might have helped them win their housing battle. Their defeat essentially limited their housing choices to the same older, interracial neighborhoods in which many of their parents settled after the housing controversies of the 1920s.

THE CHANGING—AND UNCHANGING—HOUSING MARKET

The battle over Jefferson Park occurred in the midst of a housing market resurgence that FHA activity sparked. While the USHA was one of the Roosevelt administration's most controversial programs, the FHA was among its most popular. In the late 1930s, more FHA activity took place in California than in any other state. According to federal officials, the agency produced particularly extraordinary results in Los Angeles. "Because of . . . recent residential building activity (primarily under F.H.A. type financing), it is believed that the home ownership ratio is now substantially larger than 1930—possibly as high as fifty percent," reported federal field agent T. H. Bowden and analyst D. W. Mayborn.[4]

Nationally and in California, however, federal officials largely excluded nonwhite Americans from the FHA program. In 1949, three African American agency officials concluded that "there is no evidence that throughout the entire history of the FHA-aided program of 'private' housing have Negro families been able to occupy as much as even 1 per cent or 2 per cent of all the new private housing developed for rent or for sale." Across California, nonwhite groups other than African Americans received similar treatment. Furthermore, HOLC and FHA policies that favored racially and socially homogeneous districts left Los Angeles's multiracial central city neighborhoods at a particular disadvantage.[5]

To assess neighborhood soundness, federal officials relied on likeminded members of L.A.'s white real estate industry, and these men constantly grappled with the same racial definitions that frustrated PWA agents in the early 1930s.[6] In the suburb of Claremont, surveyors speculated that one neighborhood might contain "a few better class Mexicans" and rated it a "C," ("yellow"). This designation connoted risk but was better than a "D" ("red") rating that rendered a neighborhood unfit for FHA insurance. The heavily Mexican American San Gabriel Wash area received such a rating because of what one inspector called an "infiltration of goats, rabbits, and dark-skinned babies." An assessor spelled out the difference between Claremont and areas such as the Wash, where "the vast majority of the population, while American-born, are still 'peon Mexicans,' and constitute a distinctly subversive racial influence."

Reflecting the lingering Nordicism of the 1920s, some, but not all, Los Angeles assessors considered Jews, Russians, and Southern Italians problematic. One of the surest signs that residents remained "low-class Southern Europeans" in the minds of surveyors was their proximity to definite nonwhites.[7]

To assessors, blacks and Asian Americans were the most "subversive" racial influences of all. For southern and eastern Europeans and some Mexicans, social class, occupation, and skin color provided a ladder to whiteness. Blacks and Asian Americans enjoyed no such option; authorities considered their very presence highly undesirable, regardless of income. Assessors who rated a Hollywood neighborhood "D" noted that "were it not for a scattering of Japanese and Filipino residents this section would be entitled to a higher grade." Surveyors also recorded every African American family they came across, from the "four Negro . . . families" in one section of Pasadena to "10 owner occupant Negro families located in center of area north and south of Bell St. between Marvista and Catalina Aves." Official descriptions demonstrated assessors' dismay about the continuing diversity of central Los Angeles, where "the population is highly heterogeneous with more than a sprinkling of subversive racial elements, there being several concentrations of Japanese and Negroes."[8]

The FHA occasionally underwrote developers who created housing tracts for nonwhites, but only if such tracts were new construction and upheld segregation. In Los Angeles, the agency insured the segregated Blodgett Tract, which catered to blacks exclusively and was built adjacent to an existing black area of Watts in southern L.A. Such subdivisions remained extremely uncommon, however. Squeezed by job discrimination and the Depression, only a handful of black Angelenos had the money to buy new homes in the FHA price range until after World War II. Further complicating matters, a segregated development required far too many pieces to fall into place: a developer interested in building it, a private financial institution willing to finance it, a racially unrestricted piece of property, proximity to an established minority neighborhood, and significant physical distance from white-owned FHA homes, the race-based property values of which agency officials saw as their first priority. To Nisei Angelenos, who necessarily sought homes in unrestricted older neighborhoods, FHA financing thus seemed irrelevant.[9]

JEFFERSON PARK

The Pacific Investment Company (PIC) offered Nisei home seekers a chance to take advantage of FHA financing for the first time. In 1938, William Cannon, Ralph Edgerton, and their business partners created the PIC and drew up plans for Jefferson Park, a new, FHA-endorsed development they marketed solely to Japanese Americans. The FHA's approval of the project once again reflected the way Asian Americans' compromised citizenship status affected their relationship to the state. The FHA not only underwrote individual buyers but also worked closely with developers. Those builders who met FHA standards and cooperated with the agency, as Gail Radford notes, "were able to get an advance commitment that the FHA would insure mortgages for all the homes they built." In the process, they attracted much-needed private financing quite easily. Just as in San Francisco, then, Asian Americans in Los Angeles gained access to federally underwritten housing (private homes in this case) only after well-connected whites like Cannon and Edgerton supported such access.[10]

The tract the PIC hoped to develop was located near the Baldwin Hills oil fields and the swampy environs of La Ballona Creek. Although the HOLC (and presumably the FHA) had not rated the uninhabited parcel, the PIC paid just $35,000 for it, a price that reflected its proximity to areas that assessors considered undesirable. Cannon claimed that he chose to build and sell homes there to Japanese Americans because of his longtime acquaintance with them. The Japanese American Communist paper *Doho* took a less charitable view, one that the location of the development confirmed: "Mr. Cannon knows that he can sell his land to Japanese with more profit than to whites." Indeed, HOLC surveyors described the surrounding districts unfavorably, designating one section "D" ("red") and the rest "C" or "C-" ("yellow" and "low yellow"). In criticizing these neighboring areas, assessors pointed to their age, a level of construction "inclined to be low grade standard to substandard," the proximity of industry, and the unattractive and unfashionable location. The surveyors concluded that "the stage is set for a rapid decline in this area."[11]

Still, the proposed tract thrilled leading Nisei, and they embraced it as their cause. Togo Tanaka, the editor of *Rafu Shimpo*'s English-language section, believed that the development would show an increasingly suspicious white public that the Nisei shared their values and living standards. Tanaka not only invested in the development but also promoted it in *Rafu Shimpo*. The newspaper even wove the tract into its campaign to prove the patriotism of the Nisei, arguing that "home owners make better citizens."[12] Either way, Jefferson Park offered relatively well-off Nisei a chance to do something that was denied to many of their parents: own a home without fear of legal reprisal. Moreover, the tract promised a standard of living that many of their parents had been unable to achieve.

Racial tensions already simmered in the neighborhoods near the proposed development, however. According to HOLC surveyors, since "deed restrictions [in West Jefferson] expired some 10 years ago it has rapidly become infiltered [*sic*] with negroes and Japanese." The white homeowners' association in neighboring West Adams fought to keep blacks and Japanese Americans east of Arlington Boulevard, the dividing line between the two neighborhoods. HOLC surveyors declared the West Adams area to be "in a 'state of flux'" that "constitutes a most interesting study in trend [*sic*] of residential desirability."[13]

By endorsing Jefferson Park, the FHA endorsed and essentially decreed racial transition in West Adams as well. Of course, the FHA cooperated with Cannon and Edgerton in part because they were good risks, established developers with strong financial industry connections. Edgerton's son even ran California Federal Bank, a fledgling institution that became one of Jefferson Park's largest backers. But the FHA's endorsement of Jefferson Park also demonstrated the agency's decision to contain nonwhite community expansion by directing it into a specific area.[14] The FHA routinely refused to underwrite mortgages for white homeowners trying to purchase even new homes in older neighborhoods abutting nonwhite tracts. West Adams fit this pattern exactly, and the HOLC description of it further suggests that officials had already written it off as a white neighborhood.

Other FHA decisions in the area support the view that local FHA agents decided to channel nonwhite expansion in a particular direction in order to protect "A"- and "B"-rated areas of western Los Angeles. In 1936, Anita Baldwin, the daughter of colorful Angeleno businessman and rancher Elias "Lucky" Baldwin, sold most of her late father's Baldwin Hills ranch to a syndicate led by *Los Angeles Times* owner Harry Chandler and his son, Norman. The group planned to subdivide its part of the ranch, which sat to the immediate east of Jefferson Park. The Chandlers obtained FHA support for their project—two separate developments—at almost exactly the same time that Cannon and Edgerton did. The first Chandler initiative, Sunset Hills, abutted the newer, more desirable neighborhoods to the east of Lucky Baldwin's old ranch. While not as high-class as those areas, the modest single-family homes of Sunset Hills served a purpose for the FHA. Together with a nearby railroad line, they provided a suitable, racially restricted buffer between an "A"-rated white district and the "D"-rated, racially mixed West Jefferson neighborhood to the northeast. The second Chandler development, Thousand Gardens (later renamed Baldwin Hills Village), was located to the west of Sunset Hills and to the south of West Adams. A rental development of garden apartments, it too revealed the FHA's approach to race and space, as well as the agency's lack of enthusiasm for West Adams. FHA officials, planners, and developers, especially in Los Angeles, believed that rental developments were a significant step down from single-family homes.[15] The FHA expressed this spatially in Thousand Gardens. Its white, working-class housing, together with La Ballona Creek, buffered Sunset Hills from the Japanese American Jefferson Park.

While *Doho* claimed that the Chandlers organized the opposition to Jefferson Park, the family likely endorsed rather than opposed the FHA's actions in west Los Angeles. The *Los Angeles Times* maintained a fairly moderate tone throughout the debate, although it could easily have blasted the Japanese American development. More significantly, the Chandlers undoubtedly knew what the FHA was doing. As two of the most powerful men in L.A. real estate, they were very familiar with the FHA's procedures and their racial aspects. In addition, the Chandlers and other civic leaders with millions of dollars invested in downtown real estate not only excluded wealthy Jews from elite Los Angeles institutions but also opposed their financing of West Side development, which competed with downtown. By the mid-1930s, eastern European Jews of far more modest means comprised close to half of the West Adams population, and the casual anti-Semitism of civic elites suggested that they would pay little attention to the complaints of these residents. In this context, the muted response of the *Times* to Jefferson Park suggests acquiescence and even approval of FHA attempts to channel nonwhite housing into the southern part of the west side.[16]

West Adams's white residents expressed outrage at the prospect of Jefferson Park. To some, the FHA decision reflected the persistence both of anti-Semitism and of "Nordic ideology" in a city long associated with both. Public familiarity with FHA racial guidelines apparently sparked residents' anger as well.[17] FHA practices reflected prevailing racial "common sense" in the real estate industry and among most white Americans by the late 1930s. West Adams's residents shared this faith in the connection between property values and segregation. They understood that the proximity of definite nonwhite housing, regardless of quality, almost certainly rendered their own neighborhood ineligible for FHA funding. This, in turn, made area homes less attractive to Los Angeles's white buyers, the majority of whom used FHA insurance during this period.[18] Eventually, a neighbor desperate to move would almost certainly agree to sell to a nonwhite purchaser with ready cash, prompting the rest of the neighborhood to transition.

In essence, whites in West Adams viewed Jefferson Park as potentially sealing the area's racial fate. If sandwiched between a Japanese American neighborhood and a multiracial one, West Adams would lose the ability to keep nonwhites out. Inevitably, it would integrate. "This home of ours is the one big financial venture of our life, and there must be some way to protect us from this particular Japanese invasion," complained a West Adams couple. Angry white residents and the Midwest Community Service League homeowners' group began to hold mass meetings and circulate anti-Japanese American petitions in May 1940. As the protests mounted, local city council members joined the fight against Jefferson Park. Yet as a reporter conceded, they "all knew that dislike of a Japanese colony [wa]sn't a legal reason" to block the approval of the tract plan.[19]

AN ISSUE OF LOYALTY

Throughout the spring of 1940, most Japanese Americans remained unaware of the growing opposition to Jefferson Park. The relatively high price of its tract homes put them beyond the reach—and likely the interest—of the average Nisei. *Doho* contended that initially "only a handful of Japanese were involved [in Jefferson Park]—about 15 who intend to move into the district, the two Nisei real estate agents, and the Japanese newspapers who carried the advertisement of the subdivision." Whatever the case, throughout April and May the mainstream Japanese American press never mentioned growing white hostility to the tract. *Doho* even claimed that the other papers had made a "gentlemen's agreement" to hide white resistance to the development.[20]

Political opposition to the tract also developed rather quietly, at least in the beginning. In June, city councilman Harold Harby began to complain about Jefferson Park to city planning officials. Many of Harby's constituents lived in "C"-rated, white, working-class areas west of the Baldwin Hills. The FHA underwrote a number of mortgages in the area, despite its unfashionable location and blocks honeycombed with industry. But Harby and his white constituents apparently feared that the agency's attitude and the area's residential future would change with the construction of Jefferson Park. As Harby contended at one council meeting, "I have heard of a private housing project in this district for Caucasians only . . . which would cost $3,500,000. If the Japanese subdivision is approved this larger housing project would have to go elsewhere."[21]

Opposition to Jefferson Park grew more strident as members from districts in the throes of racial transition jumped on the bandwagon. While Harby addressed the concerns of his constituents for the future of their neighborhood, these other politicians articulated the deeper and more immediate racial fears of their voters. Evan Lewis, who represented West Adams, spoke out most forcefully.[22] Among other things, he contended that the Nisei imperiled the nation's security and planned "to stab America in the back." Such language and the white opposition's vehemence shook even those council members with little at stake. Jefferson Park received narrow council approval on July 16, but when white constituents flooded members with protests, the councilmen met the very next day to overturn the earlier vote. The PIC quickly brought suit against the city and also pushed council members to revisit the issue, which they eventually did in early August.[23]

By that point, Jefferson Park's more moderate opponents began to recognize the effectiveness of Lewis's alarmist accusations. A year earlier, the councilman's bloviations might have attracted more scorn than respect, but international events suddenly gave them a veneer of legitimacy in the eyes of a jittery public. During the summer of 1940, France fell to the Nazis, Japan began to forge close ties to the Axis powers, President Roosevelt imposed an embargo on selling or shipping fuel, munitions, and scrap metal to Japan, and the federal government announced a program to control aliens and fifth-columnists at home. Conservative congressman Martin Dies and his House Un-American Activities Committee crisscrossed America, holding hearings and making headlines with their allegations about widespread internal subversion. Echoing Dies' own words, Councilman Lewis called the Nisei the "entering wedge" for the "Trojan Horse" of subversion. In doing so, he astutely played on the jumbled fears and suspicions of many white Angelenos. Those who initially complained about "Jap shacks" now joined Evan Lewis in connecting their resistance to the larger international conflict. Soon, councilmen Roy Hampton and Harold Harby joined the chorus, accusing the PIC of "selling our country to the Japs."[24]

STRUGGLING TO RESPOND

The potency of these tactics surprised Nisei spokesmen, who struggled to respond forcefully yet unthreateningly to their opponents' tactics. In late July, groups of angry white residents announced plans to attend the court hearings in the PIC's case against the City Council. PIC agent James Hisatomi explicitly called on Nisei not to follow this example. "As good Americans, we prefer . . . to conduct ourselves properly without resort to exhibitionism," he noted.[25] In reality, Hisatomi, Togo Tanaka, and other Japanese American spokesmen understood the perils of "exhibitionism." With the Nisei increasingly under suspicion, opponents would surely distort the meaning of any group action, even though white organizations faced no such questions about their patriotism.

Rather than rallying in front of their white opponents, the PIC and a small group of Nisei elites instead organized an Equality Committee to drum up support among Japanese Americans themselves. Jefferson Park had attracted only about 50 Nisei buyers for its 120 lots. More than twice as many Japanese American families on the east side alone earned so little and lived under such poor conditions that they qualified for the Ramona Gardens public housing project. In other words, Jefferson Park's elite backers needed to create enthusiasm for their fight among Nisei who could not afford to buy a home in the development. On August 1, the new Equality Committee invited supportive white politicians and the entire Japanese American community to attend its first rally, a four-hour marathon that *Doho* editor Shuji Fujii ridiculed. "Everything was crammed in," he complained. "Oratorical contest, Pre-election rally, reports on the housing discrimination and then the formation of the Committee"—indeed, everything but an explanation of how the committee would proceed.[26]

During the rally, two of the city councilmen in attendance revealed that the Jefferson Park tract contained racial restrictions barring African Americans and Mexican Americans. The restrictions have since become a bone of scholarly contention. Sociologist John Modell sees them as part of the attempt of Nisei Angelenos to prove that "if they weren't quite like the whites, at least they were more similar than some other groups." Historian Scott Kurashige counters that Nisei leaders accepted the restrictions grudgingly and were elitist but not racist. They "were far more likely to look down upon lower-class Japanese Americans and other Asians than their educated black and Mexican peers," he contends. In later years, he notes, Togo Tanaka described the restrictions as "a practical matter already decided by the developer."[27] And certainly, white backers and underwriters, not Nisei home seekers, determined Jefferson Park's restrictions.

Still, Nisei spokesmen chose to hide the racial bar from the public, in part because of the tenor of white opponents' arguments. Groups like the Midwest Community Service League routinely cited the state law prohibiting marriage between whites and Asians, the only two groups allowed under Jefferson Park's restrictions, as a major reason for their opposition to the tract. Nisei understood from growing up in Los Angeles that white residents there deeply feared the interracial intimacy many connected with neighborhood integration.

Eventually, however, Nisei spokesmen publicly lied about the existence of race restrictions. James Hisatomi claimed at the final August 12 council meeting that "there would be no race restriction on the proposed subdivision and whites as well as any other group could build homes there." Hisatomi's contention won Jefferson Park the welcome and much-needed backing of the *Los Angeles Sentinel*, an activist, liberal black newspaper. The morning of the final council vote, the *Sentinel* criticized both Evan Lewis and undecided Watts councilman Wilder Hartley, who seemed unfavorable to the tract. *Sentinel* editors ramped up the pressure on Hartley, encouraging African American voters to watch his actions carefully and vote against him if he opposed Jefferson Park. Hoping to win Hartley's backing, Nisei spokesmen did not correct Hisatomi's false statement about Jefferson Park's inclusiveness.[28]

The restrictions demonstrated how the strength of legal, federal, and white public support for residential segregation in L.A. encouraged different groups to jockey for position rather than unite for greater political power. The *Sentinel* editorial referred to the problems of racial discrimination and residential segregation that all minorities in the city shared. Yet before World War II, few nonwhite Angelenos saw these common issues as a logical basis for organization, and Japanese Americans were no exception. In the east-side suburb of San Gabriel, for example, the Japanese Association responded to new racial restrictions not by fighting them but by trying to convince white civic leaders to exempt Issei and Nisei. At Jefferson Park, too, Nisei elites struggled with the issue of segregation. A *Rafu Shimpo* editorial contended that "conditions among the American citizenry of Japanese extraction are sufficiently advanced to work actively for the elimination of all restrictions" against them, but it did not reject the need for all such restrictions. Togo Tanaka later argued that at Jefferson Park, many Nisei "privately believed . . . they would remove or circumvent the restrictions against blacks and Mexicans when they took occupancy." Still, tract sympathizer and city councilman Arthur Briggs felt the need at one point to warn Nisei to "refrain from acts which would antagonize the Negroes, or Mexicans."[29] In any case, the primary loyalty of Nisei elites always lay not with other minority communities but with the white-owned PIC, which had created both the tract and the restrictions. Whatever their personal feelings about the racial bar, Nisei elites accepted it in order to secure better housing immediately.

Japanese American elites' concerns about community image further discouraged interracial housing activism. The Citizens' Housing Council, the multiracial group that monitored the Los Angeles Housing Authority, offered Nisei a potential forum for their housing grievances. Japanese American organizations never joined, however. As the international situation worsened, leading Nisei tried to promote a certain image of their community, and it did not include tenancy in low-income public housing projects. Chinese Americans in San Francisco embraced public housing with little fear of white backlash; in contrast, Togo Tanaka reminded L.A.'s city council during the Jefferson Park debate that "we [Nisei] . . . avoid criminal and relief rolls."[30] In other words, Japanese Americans were good citizens and a thus not a detriment or a threat to Los Angeles.

The PIC eventually won its lawsuit against the Los Angeles City Council, but by that point, the victory hardly mattered. Most of Jefferson Park's subscribers had already pulled out of the tract, which ended as a financial failure. By then, the response of white homeowners and officials to the tract campaign had sent a chill through the Japanese American community. While white homeowners in the 1920s sometimes used vigilante tactics to force Japanese Americans out of neighborhoods, anti-Asian laws and the political powerlessness of the Issei did most of the work for these segregationists. By 1940, such laws had lost much of their effectiveness. The Nisei were citizens, so the city council had no legal grounds for rejecting Jefferson Park. But tract opponents had one very powerful tool—the war overseas—and the most outspoken anti-tract councilmen quickly deployed it. Although some local papers gently mocked the overblown rhetoric of anti-tract legislators, these councilmen's claims and the pleas of their white constituents persuaded much of the rest of the city council to ignore the rights of Nisei citizens. Issei who believed their children would one day enjoy the citizenship benefits denied their elders must have been horrified. The Nisei—despite their citizenship, despite the rights it supposedly entailed—had to retreat, as their parents had twenty years earlier, to the safety of the old, mixed neighborhoods. The Jefferson Park controversy showed just how little the majority of city councilmen and many other white Angelenos valued Nisei rights.

Even when the Nisei returned to more familiar neighborhoods, the Jefferson Park debate and the larger issues of the war overseas still shadowed them. JACL national president Saburo Kido claimed in early 1941 that while "those of the Japanese race have run into the problem of neighbors protesting[,] . . . home buying among the Nisei is going on as usual" in Los Angeles.[31] But the Jefferson Park debate drew unwanted attention to Japanese Americans, whom white homeowners began to single out for hostile treatment. Real estate agents and homeowners cited Jefferson Park and the Japanese "menace" to argue for strengthened restrictions in other places, such as the exclusive Crestmore tract on the west side. In Tujunga, a suburb northwest of Pasadena, vandals responded to rumors of Japanese home buying by spattering two homes with red paint and posting signs reading "No Japs." The Tujunga-Sunland Chamber of Commerce endorsed the vigilantism and called a mass meeting of property owners to renew expiring racial restrictions in the area. Adding insult to injury, developer Fritz Burns announced plans to develop the site across the street from the failed Jefferson Park tract. However, the homes at Rancho 57 would be available only to whites.[32]

Where neighbors did not protest, the federal government and the looming war increasingly squeezed Nisei out of the housing market. Kido noted that many young Japanese Americans lacked the funds to purchase homes, especially the kind to which they had access: "houses which are too old for federal loans," a reference to the FHA's bias toward new construction. Increased defense spending in Los Angeles was enabling many white residents to buy homes for the first time. In contrast, as journalist Tad Uyeno complained, the "boom hasn't reached the Japanese." Not only did they receive few if any of the new defense-related jobs, but as the daughter of an Issei businessman from Pasadena complained, by 1941, "some of the customers would refuse to trade with us when they found that it was a Japanese store."[33]

FROM "JAP INVASION" TO JAPANESE ATTACK

Word of Pearl Harbor reached Los Angeles on the afternoon of December 7, 1941, a few hours after the Japanese attack on Hawaii. The news stunned Nisei as much as it did other Angelenos. Japanese Americans had closely followed the war in China and its 1941 expansion into Southeast Asia; still, they expressed disbelief when it finally came to the United States. As a Nisei fruit stand worker admitted, "I was shocked.... I still continued to think that it was impossible for such a thing to happen." A Japanese American typist described her family's reaction as similarly incredulous: "we thought that maybe it might be a mistake or some kind of play," like Orson Welles' *War of the Worlds.*[34]

Although the Federal Bureau of Investigation quickly rounded up hundreds of Japanese American community leaders, many white politicians and residents initially demonstrated at least some faith in Nisei and Issei loyalty. Teachers and university professors called for calm and for the fair treatment of Japanese American students. Many church leaders expressed their belief in Japanese American blamelessness for the attacks. Both Governor Culbert Olsen and Mayor Fletcher Bowron instructed Californians not to lash out at people of Japanese ancestry because of Pearl Harbor. Simultaneously, however, the Native Sons of the Golden West, the State Grange, the American Federation of Labor, the American Legion, and similar nativist groups swung into action with anti–Japanese American smear campaigns. The Hearst and

McClatchy newspaper chains also relentlessly attacked Japanese Americans in their Southern California dailies. Not to be outdone, the Chandlers' *Los Angeles Times* joined the chorus as well.[35]

White Jefferson Park opponents had already done their part. In predicting a "Jap invasion," they spoke both to general racial fears and to the specific nagging doubts of white Los Angeles in the months before Pearl Harbor. White real estate agents, FHA and HOLC officials, and homeowners throughout the nation routinely used martial metaphors to talk about all nonwhite residents; they worried about "racial infiltration," "subversive racial elements," "encroachment," and "neighborhood invasions."[36] Such phrases reflected different local racial experiences. In Los Angeles, the warlike language of white homeownership expressed Anglos' general economic, racial, and psychosexual fears of integration. Yet as the U.S.-Japanese relationship deteriorated, these words began to convey something even more troubling: whites' equation of what they called neighborhood "Jap invasion" with actual Japanese military invasion.

By January 1942, Evan Lewis's bloviations seemed prophetic to many white Angelenos. The United States was losing the war, and, confident in white racial superiority, many Angelenos struggled to explain the destruction at Pearl Harbor and the loss of Guam and the Philippines. The press and pressure groups accused Japanese Hawaiians of sabotage, a baseless allegation that the federal government, which knew better, did not rebut. Jefferson Park could have been a dress rehearsal for the ensuing sequence of events. Officials who had initially supported Japanese Americans or remained neutral now began questioning Nisei loyalty. Even many liberal California politicians publicly turned on the Nisei. When the State Personnel Board suspended all Japanese American civil servants, Governor Culbert Olson approved its actions. Mayor Bowron called for the imprisonment of all people of Japanese ancestry, an action for which he would apologize years later. Attorney General Earl Warren, who sought and won the endorsement of prominent Nisei during his 1938 campaign, led the charge for the internment of all people of Japanese ancestry.[37]

The politically savvy Franklin Roosevelt listened to the rumblings coming out of the West Coast instead of the pleas of his wife and of Francis Biddle, his attorney general. On February 19, 1942, he issued Executive Order 9066, which authorized the Secretary of War and his military commanders to designate areas of the country "from which any or all persons may be excluded." Despite this race-neutral language, Roosevelt intended Executive Order 9066 specifically for Japanese Americans, both alien and citizen. Army commanders declared the entire West Coast a military zone from which they planned to exclude all people of Japanese ancestry. Although a handful of Issei and Nisei

FIGURE 5.1. The last group of Japanese American residents to leave Los Angeles waited in May 1942 to board buses that would take them to the temporary assembly center at the Santa Anita Racetrack. After the completion of permanent internment camps, most of these people ended up at the Manzanar camp in eastern California. (Herald Examiner Collection /Los Angeles Public Library.)

voluntarily packed up their belongings and left, most lacked the ability or were not willing to do so. In addition, residents of areas outside the military zone harassed the travelers, making a voluntary evacuation hazardous. Finally, on March 2, 1942, Western Defense Area commander General John DeWitt put a stop to the voluntary phase, ordering all Japanese Americans to register with authorities and report to temporary assembly centers.[38] The internment had begun.

HOLDING ON TO HOME

On the eve of the internment, Japanese Americans owned about 1,100 homes in Los Angeles, mostly in integrated, rundown central city and east-side neighborhoods. Fewer than 10 percent of these Japanese American homeowners sold their property during the rush to evacuate. Japanese American churches and other organizations often stepped in to protect Nisei and Issei homeowners. In one arrangement, the JACL helped forty Japanese American neighbors create a trust company in which a white American wielded power of attorney. Of course, without owners present, at least some of these houses deteriorated during the war. In numerous cases, the "friends" who promised to collect rent for evacuees pocketed such money instead and also stole household appliances, furniture, and fixtures.[39]

The treatment of departing Japanese Americans also highlighted the mix of interracial friction and friendship that characterized Los Angeles's multiracial central and east-side neighborhoods. In late 1942, local Urban League director Floyd Covington reported that "both Alien and American Japanese left much of their properties to Negroes either by gift or sale." Some African Americans, such as attorney Hugh MacBeth, both helped and vouched for the loyalty of Japanese Americans throughout the internment process. Other blacks took advantage of the evacuation to purchase Nisei and Issei property for pennies on the dollar. Throughout integrated neighborhoods, the pre-internment fire sale atmosphere tested the strength and sincerity of friendships. Many persevered, but people of all races exploited Japanese American misfortunes. One Nisei woman remembered that "we had a lot of things scattered around the house and the people in the neighborhood went right through our house like vultures after we left." A Terminal Island Nisei described how "when we started to dispose of some of our enormous quantity of store supplies, Mexicans, Jews, Slavs, Italians—people of practically every nationality rushed into our stores to buy the goods which we sold for almost nothing."[40] Chinese Americans profited as well, despite the relative lack of animosity between the two communities. "[Japanese Americans] were being locked up at that time, so everyone went to buy up the Japanese businesses," recalled Oak Yip Gee, a Chinese Angeleno. "They were relatively cheap." Jackman Hom, another Angeleno, noted that Chinese Americans used the war to make greater inroads in the produce industry. "There [were] . . . many grocery stores which were run by Japanese and sold to Chinese," he recalled.[41]

Los Angeles County's Japanese American farming families lost more than almost anyone in the pre-evacuation panic, although those fortunate enough to own their parcels of land often managed to hold on to them. In Gardena, where the mayor and some local officials apparently sympathized with evacuees, Japanese American nurserymen, gardeners, and truck farmers usually kept their acreage, as did a scattering of Japanese Americans living in other agricultural suburbs, such as Culver City, Torrance, and Whittier. But few families owned their plots, a reflection both of general land tenure patterns in the county and of the 1913 and 1920 Alien Land Acts. The internment order underscored the vulnerability of Issei who made illegal deals with white landowners to farm undeveloped tracts on the city's fringes and in unincorporated areas and agricultural suburbs. Ten years after the war, sociologist Midori Nishi noted that "leased and rented land often had valuable improvements including houses, barns, greenhouses, underground water pipes and wells which had to be abandoned with almost complete financial loss as well as the sacrifice of rights and privileges." In truth, nativist legislators had long before made sure that Issei farmers enjoyed no rights to the property they tilled. The dispossession of such farmers was usually permanent: Los Angeles developed so quickly during the war that housing and factories swallowed up many formerly agricultural areas by 1945.[42]

The evacuation also decimated the Japanese American fishing community. At the turn of the century, Japanese fishermen established a settlement on Terminal Island, a manmade island in Los Angeles Harbor. More than thirty years later, the Navy took over nearby East San Pedro's Allen Field, a civilian airstrip dating to the 1920s. Regardless of such timing, military officials viewed with suspicion the established, insular Japanese American fishing and cannery community there. After Pearl Harbor, FBI agents detained a large number of the island's Japanese American fishermen, believing, as Nisei Amy Uno Ishii recalled, that "they could send signals and . . . were going to commit sabotage."[43] Military officials announced on February 17, 1942, that all Issei and Nisei had to leave Terminal Island within four weeks. Nine days later, authorities changed their minds and told Japanese Americans to be out within forty-eight hours. The shift caused even more panic than the initial command. Fishing families, cannery workers, and the business community of the island scrambled to sell or pack up belongings and find someplace to live overnight. The U.S. government, which owned the island, never allowed them to return.

By the fall of 1942, Japanese Americans had completely disappeared from Los Angeles, leaving just a few traces. The shops of Little Tokyo stood vacant, many adorned with peeling advertisements for steep discounts, or signs quietly protesting "This Is an American Store." Less obviously, hundreds of homes sat empty throughout the older districts of Los Angeles. Weeds sprouted in the vacant lots that Issei and Nisei once farmed on the city's fringes. Throughout the state, anti-Japanese agitators rejoiced, having at last achieved one of the long-standing goals of San Francisco nativist organizations: the expulsion of the Japanese American population from California.

THE EVOLUTION OF ANTI-JAPANESE SENTIMENT IN
SOUTHERN CALIFORNIA

During the Jefferson Park debate, the latent, opportunistic anti-Japanese senti-ment of L.A.'s past changed into something far more virulent and dangerous. In the 1920s, the Japanese threat that so obsessed Northern nativists seemed, to most white Angelenos, to be quite abstract, a grab bag of dire warnings that few of them could grasp. Having successfully limited Japanese American resi-dential mobility, the white homeowners who once collaborated with northern nativist groups lost interest in the larger anti-Asian agenda. Others never paid attention to such organizations at all, since they provided no help in checking the movement of African Americans.

The same opportunism was on display in West Adams in 1940, but the war overseas gave the grassroots campaign against Jefferson Park a larger context and immediacy missing from previous anti-Asian endeavors. The West Adams homeowners and their representatives faced a handicap their predecessors had not: the citizenship of the Nisei. Indeed, most councilmen initially acknowl-edged Nisei rights, voting to approve Jefferson Park at their first meeting in July. After that, opponents completely abandoned the milder language of the 1920s. Rather than invoking "silent invasions" and "Jap shacks," they labeled the Nisei fifth-columnists, reserve officers in the Imperial Japanese Army, and a welcoming committee for a Japanese landing party. This shrillness took many councilmen by surprise, but even those who did not share the deeper fears of their constituents understood the political costs of ignoring them. In this sense, Jefferson Park both foreshadowed the tragedy to come and fueled the ideas and prejudices that made it possible.

Sadly, the PIC's racial restrictions on occupancy, for which the Nisei bore no responsibility, probably helped wavering councilmen justify their opposi-tion. In the 1920s, anti-Japanese campaigns curtailed Issei opportunities but did not close off housing altogether. Instead, Japanese Americans followed other nonwhite groups that were opening previously all-white areas, includ-ing, eventually, West Jefferson. Jefferson Park was different. Had Cannon, Edgerton, and their associates planned it as a tract for middle-income Nisei, African Americans, and Mexican Americans, they would still have encoun-tered white resistance. However, opponents succeeded in killing Jefferson Park because the development served Nisei alone. African American newspa-pers offered a few supportive articles but none of the legal or organizational skill that might have benefited the project. Mexican Americans apparently ignored the development altogether.[44] The exclusion of these other groups enabled white opponents to cast Jefferson Park as a "Japanese colony" at a time when Japan was actively colonizing other places.

Still, only the looming threat of war, and then its actual outbreak, produced the results that northern California nativist groups and their sympathizers had sought for decades. After years of trying to capture the attention of white Angelenos, California's nativist organizations, newspapers, and politicians finally managed to do so in the space of a few months. With America losing the war, anti-Asian activists offered Californians a simple explanation for U.S. defeats and a convenient target for their anger and fear. Most white Angelenos, like their peers across the nation, still believed that the different races were biologically distinct and incompatible. After Pearl Harbor, many white Americans took this "logic" even further with respect to the hated Japanese. According to historian John Dower, they "resort[ed] to nonhuman or subhuman representation, in which the Japanese were perceived as animals, reptiles, or insects."[45]

So when city residents turned on the Nisei and Issei, most did so with the same lack of remorse they might have felt in smashing a fly. Those who exploited Japanese Americans even acted with a sense of self-righteous patriotism, a sentiment their political leaders shared. Indeed, anti–Japanese American politicians and newspapers helped fuel a racial hysteria so intense that even the national office of the American Civil Liberties Union pressured its local branch to abandon Japanese Americans.[46] The local group did not, but aside from a few church organizations and conscientious citizens, Los Angeles wholly supported the internment.

Ironically, at the apex of their power, anti–Japanese American forces in California faced the same dilemma with which they grappled after the successful passage of the 1920 Alien Land Act. They needed to keep anti–Japanese American sentiment at a fever pitch to achieve one final goal: stripping the Nisei of their citizenship in order to permit the mass deportation of all people of Japanese ancestry after the war. Over the next three years, these agitators and their political allies strove to keep the Japanese American issue before the public. But in Los Angeles, which by 1942 was experiencing a massive influx of people of all racial backgrounds, the question quickly lost its immediacy after internment. The issue of migration—particularly of blacks and Mexican Americans—completely eclipsed it.

* 2 *

Foreign Friends

CHAPTER SIX

"Glorified and Mounted on a Pedestal": San Francisco Chinatown at War

At the end of World War II, Joseph James of the San Francisco NAACP complained that during the conflict, "Caucasian San Francisco turned to the machinery already at hand for the subjugation of the Oriental and applied it to the Negro." The charge hinted at the depth of San Francisco's wartime transformation and its impact on the city's old racial order. During World War II, about twenty thousand African Americans and almost ten times as many whites streamed into San Francisco, while the entire Japanese American population left for internment camps. At the same time, China became a wartime ally, altering perceptions of Chinese Americans and prompting sociologist Rose Hum Lee to joke that "as violently as the Chinese were once attacked, they are now glorified and mounted on a pedestal."[1] By 1945, pro-China sentiment, together with wartime civil rights activism and the political gaffes of anti-Asian organizations, greatly eroded public support for the city's traditional nativism. Yet its decline did not undermine the residential segregation it had created in San Francisco. At the end of the war, most white San Franciscans not only still supported the residential segregation of Chinese Americans but also favored the similar segregation of blacks.

Public policy, changing real estate practices, and the China alliance contributed to this seemingly paradoxical outcome. During the war, federal housing policies introduced in the mid-1930s continued to reshape the racial geography of San Francisco. FHA manuals and guidelines, which helped standardize real estate and banking practices across the country, encouraged growing numbers of white San Franciscans to see their housing market in white-nonwhite, rather than white-Chinese, terms. Of course, World War II, in which the United States faced avowedly racist foes, also forced many white Americans to acknowledge for the first time the destructive power of racism in their own country. Yet whites' changing ideas about race did not produce more open housing markets. "The postwar decades saw most Northern whites argue that the American metropolis was segregated and unequal not because blacks were inferior, but because they were unable or unwilling to play by the rules of the marketplace [for] . . . whatever cultural or market-driven reason," historian David M. P. Freund has contended.[2] Concerned about their property values, white San Franciscans applied a similar logic to Chinese Americans, a group long considered foreign and culturally distinct. The wartime equation of Chinese Americans with China merely reinforced such ideas.

During World War II, Chinese Americans enjoyed new opportunities, but only those that did not fundamentally challenge perceptions of their foreignness or threaten white privilege. After the Japanese American internment, a number of Chinese American entrepreneurs took over vacated stores on Grant Avenue; those who hoped to set up shop outside Chinatown faced hostility and resistance, however. Thousands of Chinese Americans also streamed into the shipyards and other defense industries of the East Bay. Still, employers who welcomed these useful "allies" often created segregated work units for many of them, and public housing remained closed to the vast majority. America's wartime alliance with China reaffirmed Chinese American transnationalism, which was often both personally and politically empowering; at the same time, however, it deterred Chinese American leaders from participating in new, multiracial organizations dedicated to nonwhite civil rights. In the worst cases, such reluctance betrayed a deeper disdain for blacks and Japanese Americans, or community fears of provoking whites by associating with these reviled groups.

"ALL OF US WERE STUNNED"

On December 7, 1941, two shaken and disheartened Nisei drove through Golden Gate Park, absorbing the grim news from Hawaii. A white patrolman stopped their car at a beach near the Great Highway, but after interrogating them at length, he let them go. When the pair returned to Nihonmachi, the Japanese section of town, they noticed that "the policemen were on all the corners and the whole area was roped off." In Chinatown, less than two miles away, police did not stand guard, but most residents expressed as much shock at the turn of events as did their Japanese American peers. "All of us were stunned," admitted Jane Kwong Lee, who heard of the attack that day from her cousin. May Lew Gee, who first found out in church, struggled to fully comprehend the news from Pearl Harbor. It finally sank in that afternoon, she recalled, when she saw "this giant headline that said, 'WAR!'"[3]

The coming of war to America affected the two communities in extraordinarily different ways. As in Los Angeles, FBI agents in San Francisco quickly rounded up Japanese American community leaders, froze Issei bank accounts, and confiscated cameras, radios, and similar equipment. The Treasury Department shut down the major Japanese-language papers, while the JACL scrambled to create some way of relaying news to the community.[4] With authorities targeting Japanese Americans, the *Chinese Press* newspaper urged Chinese Americans to carry multiple forms of identification, from driver's licenses to Social Security cards, to prove their ethnicity. "Scores of Chinese have been stopped on bridges and highways," warned the editors. "Many are reported to have been refused streetcar services." To further protect Chinese Americans, the city's Chinese consulate began issuing identification cards to verify that "the holder of this certificate . . . is a member of the Chinese race." Other Chinatown residents bought buttons declaring "I Am Chinese." Tired of being identified as Japanese, one irate Chinese American even donned a hand-lettered sign that said "No, I'm Not!"[5]

When San Francisco officials imposed a curfew on all Japanese Americans, a few slipped into Chinatown to pass the long nights. Back in Nihonmachi, "almost everyone had lost their jobs and the stores were all closed," complained a young Nisei.[6] By the middle of March 1942, however, the eerie quiet that gripped the Japanese section after December 7 gave way to frantic activity. Residents now hastened to wrap up their affairs and store their belongings before the Army announced the dates for their removal to assembly centers. On April 1, the details came: the military directed the first groups of Japanese Americans to assemble at two different offices on April 7 for transportation to the Tanforan Racetrack in nearby San Bruno. By mid-May, officials had moved the remainder of the city's Japanese American population to this assembly center south of San Francisco.

With Pearl Harbor and the internment, Chinese Americans handily defeated their Japanese American business rivals on Grant Avenue. After the attack, "many [customers] left after asking if we were Japanese," complained a Nisei clerk at a Japanese-owned tourist bazaar. Frightened by constant harassment, numerous Japanese American businesspeople quickly shuttered their shops. A Chinese American reporter noted with satisfaction that within a week of Pearl Harbor, "all the[ir] stores were silent, empty, and dark." By mid-1942,

Chinatown had recovered from a post–December 7 lull in tourism. Now, thousands of servicemen and civilians with cash to burn spent their free hours in the neighborhood's nightclubs, restaurants, and shops. Sensing an opportunity, a number of Chinese Americans leased formerly Japanese-occupied properties, creating new curio shops, hotels, and nightclubs. Workmen quickly cleared away the last traces of the prewar Japanese American presence, disposing of the Japanese art goods left at one store and ripping out a miniature Japanese garden at another.[7] The erasure proved permanent; after the war, Japanese American businesses never returned to Grant Avenue in any significant way.

Few Chinese Americans expressed much concern about the internment, and many watched the Japanese American retreat from Grant Avenue with great satisfaction. "There was a spirit of revenge everywhere," said Jane Kwong Lee of the Grant Avenue buyout. "The Chinese hated the Japanese and the Caucasians would have nothing to do with them." Ultimately, white Californians demanded the internment, but many Chinese Americans supported the decision. As historian K. Scott Wong notes, "They helped to perpetuate false accusations of fifth-column activity among Americans of Japanese descent," accusations that whites used to justify the mass incarceration. The *Chinese Times*, an anti-nativist, American citizen–owned paper, lampooned Issei leaders whom the police arrested, while the *Chinese Press* mocked a JACL suggestion that whites' inability to tell the Japanese from the Chinese might necessitate the internment of all Asian Americans. "The U.S. public knows the difference between a slap on the back and a stab in the back," noted editors, calling Japanese Americans the "enemy of China and the United States." Even a year after the internment, popular Chinatown journalist Gilbert Woo received threatening mail from other Chinese Americans for writing a column sympathetic to the Nisei.[8]

Yet most white San Franciscans used the same arguments to explain Chinese American worthiness as they did to confirm supposed Japanese American disloyalty. Casting Chinese virtues in racial terms, they spoke of all Chinese Americans as if they were foreigners, albeit suddenly welcome ones. Describing the new Chinese American workers at the Bay Area's defense plants, reporter Marie Carey noted that "the Chinese go about their war work with the same patient, enduring spirit that built the China wall, the Burma road, and the courageous defense of the last seven years." At the Mare Island shipyard in the East Bay town of Vallejo, accountant Sue O'Connor won a Navy contest when she suggested having one of the yard's Chinese American women christen a ship. "It would be a good way for our people to show their appreciation and reaffirm their faith in China," O'Connor said.[9] To many white residents, Chinese Americans during World War Two remained as racially and culturally alien as ever, albeit in a more positive way than in the past.

Chinese Americans' own understandings of loyalty, citizenship, and racial identity often complemented such views. The *Chinese Times* expressed this in a March 1942 discussion of the war. "We overseas Chinese recognize that today, the United States is our ally," the American-born editors proclaimed. "Our shared goal is a united front of resistance against the invading Axis nations, and in wartime America working together to protect the nation." The article did not speak for every Chinese American, but it reflected the feelings of many that they were part of the Chinese nation in a larger racial and cultural sense, even if they claimed formal U.S. citizenship. The English-language *Chinese Press*, which mainly served the American-born and educated segment of the community, offered a similarly transnational view. "Bound by the ties of race to the people of that Republic across the Pacific, [they] can do no less than to bend their every effort in helping China emerge victorious from her present war with Japan, and later aid her in the gigantic task of reconstruction," wrote its editors of their readership.[10] The lines were never clear, for few Chinese Americans neatly compartmentalized their lives and identities. Nor did the war, or white San Franciscans' lionization of China, encourage them to do so.

ENDURING FOR THE DURATION

Transnationalism gave many Chinese Americans a sense of personal empowerment, but it offered little more than high self-esteem when they had to compete for scarce wartime resources. In early 1941, the San Francisco Board of Supervisors approved extra funding for the Chinatown public housing development, now dubbed Ping Yuen ("peaceful garden" in Chinese). To obtain land for the project, local housing officials spent the year cobbling together small parcels purchased from individual Chinatown building owners. As the SFHA completed this phase of the project, however, the war overseas began to drive steel prices far beyond the project's original budget. After Pearl Harbor, Housing Authority officials asked the federal government for a quota of rationed building materials so that they could complete Ping Yuen. But the project would not serve newly arrived war workers, a problem in the eyes of defense planners. Anticipating such resistance, USHA head Leon Keyserling highlighted "the international significance of this proposed project to the Chinese, generally and officially." Charles Palmer, the housing coordinator for the Office for Emergency Management (OEM), even suggested that the USHA ask the State Department for assistance in making its case. "The building of this project has real importance from the standpoint of our international relations with China," he argued.[11]

The Roosevelt administration's Europe-first strategy, together with federal housing officials' often hypocritical use of race, determined Washington's response. Although China's armies proved crucial to keeping Japanese troops pinned down in Asia, China was far more dependent on the United States than vice versa. Indeed, Chinese Nationalist leader Chiang Kai-shek spent much of the war urging Roosevelt to move more troops and weapons to the Pacific theater. When Leon Keyserling approached the State Department, assistant secretary of state Adolph Berle offered only tepid support for the Chinatown project. The State Department "believes that any such project which would benefit nationals of China who are in this country would fall within the framework of activities tending to further the friendly relations which exist between the United States and China," Berle ventured.[12] However, by law, project residents had to be American citizens, not "nationals of China."

Suddenly, housing officials who had never really acknowledged the legitimacy of Chinese American citizenship discovered it, and instead of approving construction, the War Production Board postponed Ping Yuen for the duration of the war. As the *Chinese Times* lamented, "said public housing is irrelevant to promoting national preparedness and is therefore forbidden." In any case, by defending the Chinatown development in the way they had, Leon Keyserling, Charles Palmer, and other housing officials reiterated the link between Chinese American "foreignness" and access to federal social programs. In fact, almost every federal official involved in the matter, even the hesitant Adolph Berle, treated Ping Yuen as a matter of foreign rather than domestic policy; certainly the Department of State played no role in other domestic housing issues.[13]

BOOMTOWN DELUXE

In January 1943, journalist Lucius Beebe called San Francisco a "boom town de luxe." Because of the war, "the town is in the chips, the fleet is always in; the plush cord is up at the hot spots and you can't find your way to the bar at cocktail time at the Top of the Mark or the Fairmont," he wrote. Always a maritime hub, the Bay Area during the war became central to naval and defense production, as well as a transit point for soldiers and sailors heading to and from the Pacific theater. The population of the nine-county metropolitan area swelled by half a million during the conflict as civilians flocked to the region looking for work. More than ninety thousand newcomers arrived in

San Francisco alone between early 1940 and December 1942, increasing the city's population by 15 percent.[14]

Most of these migrants faced far greater hardships than missing cocktail hour at the Fairmont, however. The massive influx of so many people in such a short time strained city resources, especially housing. Housing shortages were familiar elsewhere in the country during the war, especially in the major defense production areas. Still, the West, where wartime cities grew exponentially, suffered far more than most other parts of the nation. One and a half million newcomers streamed into wartime California alone, most of them settling in Los Angeles or the Bay Area.[15]

Nevertheless, San Francisco civic leaders refused to acknowledge the resulting housing shortage until it became a crisis. By 1940, federal preparedness activities were attracting thousands of job-seeking migrants to the Bay Area. The San Francisco Chamber of Commerce denied that the newcomers placed any sort of burden at all on city housing, however, even as President Roosevelt himself declared an "acute shortage of housing" in San Francisco. Mayor Rossi also ignored housing advocates' pleas to create a War Public Housing Center to coordinate housing resources.[16] When the war began, San Francisco officials thus had no real plan for dealing with a housing shortage that even the federal government already recognized as severe.

Federal agencies and private interests addressed the shortage instead. Under the direction of the National Housing Agency (NHA), which coordinated and directed the various federal housing programs for the duration of the war, the San Francisco Housing Authority converted its unfinished low-rent projects into war worker housing. Washington also financed several new temporary projects at Hunters Point for the sole use of workers at the area's naval shipyard and announced plans for the FHA to underwrite thousands of single family homes and apartments for defense workers in the Bay Area. Many landlords responded to the migrant influx far more opportunistically, cutting apartments and houses into ever smaller units and charging a premium for them.[17]

BUILDING SEGREGATION

About sixty thousand blacks arrived in California between 1941 and 1944, and the ten thousand who moved to San Francisco during this period struggled even more than white migrants to find decent homes.[18] Federal housing policy in the 1930s had already begun to encourage white homeowners in San Francisco to discriminate against blacks far more than they had in the past. With wartime housing scarce, white landlords also started rejecting black tenants they might have welcomed a decade earlier. Lacking other options, thousands of blacks eventually settled in the Western Addition, including in Nihonmachi.

Migrant desperation and landlord opportunism combined to worsen an already deteriorating district. Many property owners converted old Japanese storefronts into inadequate dwelling units; tenants who arrived earlier in the war sublet rooms to latecomers. In the most rundown sections of the Western Addition's migrant settlements, almost half the units lacked toilets and kitchens. More than fifteen percent of migrant families in the area lived in single rooms, rather than in multi-room apartments. Observers conducting a survey in the area in 1943 described incredible overcrowding, trash-filled yards, dank basement cubicles, and rooms without windows or access to light and air. In a revealing comment, Joseph James lamented that the area's "Negroes are now living under conditions indistinguishable in most respects from the Chinese."[19]

The sudden, rapid growth of the black population heightened the anti-black sentiments that the federal housing policies of the late 1930s helped enflame. James, the new local NAACP president and a wartime migrant himself, noted that before the conflict, "Negroes were so widely scattered that the visitor to San Francisco at that time would have easily received the impression that there were almost no Negroes in the city." By 1943, most white San Franciscans could not help but notice that the black population tripled in the space of three years and had reached 25,000 by war's end. On the streetcars, in the shops, and on the factory floors, the presence of African Americans was far more evident than in the past. Overwhelmed with patrons, some businesses in San Francisco began to discriminate covertly or openly against blacks. African Americans also complained of growing police brutality in the city.[20]

The growing concentration of blacks in the rundown Western Addition further heightened racial tensions and African American visibility. City officials had long neglected the area's Nihonmachi section with little fear of political reprisal. A 1943 *San Francisco Chronicle* series finally broke the silence, informing the public that "fifty percent of the housing in the district is unfit for human habitation" and emphasizing that the worst-housed tenants were African American.[21] While meant to stir the city's conscience, such coverage also linked the presence of blacks in the district to deteriorating conditions there.

White San Franciscans who had never considered housing restrictions now scrambled to cover their neighborhoods with covenants to keep out African Americans. The rush to restrict blacks was unprecedented. Before the war, San Francisco's neighborhood covenants, where they existed, usually focused on Asian Americans. In contrast, the new residential restrictions applied to all nonwhites but were drawn up with African Americans in mind. Sociologist Charles S. Johnson worried that the proliferation of covenants in the city would soon create a black ghetto in San Francisco.[22]

FHA policies in San Francisco encouraged segregation in other ways as well. By early 1944, the agency had underwritten thousands of units of private housing for white defense workers in the Bay Area, but nonwhites could not live in any of these homes. With black defense workers growing increasingly desperate, the NHA pushed the local FHA office to insure at least some private housing for nonwhites. As a further inducement, NHA officials even found a contractor who expressed great interest in building such homes. Regardless, local FHA head D. C. McGinness rejected the idea, arguing that he wanted "to protect the community and commitments already made by FHA in San Francisco." According to McGinness, African Americans had poor attitudes about financial matters and the property of others and would not be fit for agency insurance for many years. Although the NHA supposedly oversaw the FHA, McGinness prevailed, despite his decision's impact on defense production. During the entire war, builders only produced 150 units of privately financed housing for nonwhites in San Francisco. The FHA did not underwrite any of it.[23]

The San Francisco Housing Authority also continued its prewar campaign to confine African Americans to a few set neighborhoods. Because of wartime migration, the SFHA finally filled the empty units in Holly Courts, Sunnydale and Potrero, but only with white tenants. Even African American war workers with pleading letters from military officials received no consideration. To justify its actions, the SFHA recruited some of the black community's most conservative leaders, forming a Negro Advisory Council that endorsed the "neighborhood pattern" and called for a segregated, blacks-only West Side Courts. Although the federal government granted the SFHA necessary building material priorities for West Side Courts, the SFHA lacked the supplemental city funding it needed to begin construction; like many white San Franciscans, numerous city leaders viewed the growing African American population with great unease.[24]

With the project stalled, the WAHC again demanded that the SFHA open other public developments to people of all races. In response, SFHA board members defiantly voted to reaffirm the discriminatory neighborhood pattern policy. Exasperated, the WAHC finally decided to sue the SFHA to force integration of every project in the system. Days later, however, a riot broke out in Detroit when white residents protested the placement of a black housing project near their neighborhood. Detroit's racial history and geography differed markedly from San Francisco's, yet the riot confirmed local and federal officials' beliefs about the dangers of racial unrest over housing. Suddenly, Washington and San Francisco found the money to finish West Side Courts, short-circuiting the WAHC's lawsuit and ensuring that other SFHA developments remained all-white.[25]

West Side Courts, the first nonwhite public housing facility in San Francisco, hardly satisfied the desperate need of black migrants for decent homes. When completed in 1943, at the height of wartime migration to California, the development contained only 136 units. The project quickly filled, with the SFHA somewhat ironically including five white families—apparently to prove that it had maintained the Western Addition's "neighborhood pattern" after all. The federal government also built three all-black projects and three slightly integrated ones at Hunters Point. These developments together added fewer than five hundred additional units to San Francisco's nonwhite housing pool, and almost eighty of the new "homes" were actually dormitory beds.[26]

NEW OPPORTUNITIES

While local housing shortages fostered racial segregation, Bay Area labor shortages forced many companies to rethink old discriminatory hiring practices. Before Pearl Harbor, white men monopolized the defense industry jobs that Roosevelt administration preparedness initiatives produced in the Bay Area. Before and even during the war, racially exclusionary American Federation of Labor (AFL) locals also dominated most defense industries in northern California. Under pressure from black leaders, President Roosevelt in 1941 prohibited racial discrimination by defense contractors and created the Fair Employment Practices Committee (FEPC) to investigate violations; however, the body wielded little power and enjoyed only token support from the president.[27]

Labor shortages thus played a greater role than the FEPC in opening many of the region's workplaces to nonwhites (and to women). After Pearl Harbor, the federal government announced plans to almost double defense spending within months. But new federal contracts created hundreds of thousands of defense-sector jobs at a moment of massive military expansion. By late 1942, more than six million men of all backgrounds had joined the armed forces, creating a shortage of labor throughout much of the nation.[28] The Bay Area experienced a particularly severe labor shortage, because shipbuilding, one of its major industries, grew faster in 1942 than almost any other area of defense production. The region's shipyards, once the province of white men, now turned in desperation to women and minorities. Some employers, such as Kaiser Shipyards, even sent recruiters throughout the United States to attract black as well as white workers. Nonwhite employment also grew in other sectors of the region's economy, especially civilian government work. In fact, nonwhite employment in the Bay Area ballooned by 1,600 percent between September 1942 and May 1943.[29]

Stereotypes and discriminatory treatment still limited opportunities for nonwhite workers. In national polls, whites frequently labeled blacks as incompetent and lazy. These same ideas shaped employers' practices: "Negro workers are almost never used in supervisory and administrative capacities," a black-authored study of wartime San Francisco complained. Still, blacks at least worked at various tasks throughout the shipyards. In contrast, non–defense-related firms in the Bay Area often hired African Americans only for service and janitorial positions or refused to employ them at all, regardless of labor shortages. In interviews, managers repeated the same excuses for such policies: blacks were "not sufficiently skilled"; they were "not sufficiently educated, intelligent, and healthy"; they were "undependable and indifferent"; they showed "a tendency to shirk responsibility and be lazy."[30]

The shipyards that integrated black workers often segregated Chinese Americans, especially men. Katherine Archibald, a sociologist who worked at Moore Dry Dock in Oakland, confirmed that her company placed most of its Chinese American employees in an all-Chinese electrical unit. Mare Island Shipyard integrated its Chinese Americans, but Western Pipe and Steel, Marinship, and Kaiser organized their Chinese American male workers into separate, all-Chinese crews. Foremen, many of them longtime members of historically anti-Asian AFL unions, justified this segregation in ways that revealed nativism's perseverance in area labor markets. At Moore Dry Dock, managers blamed segregation on Chinese American language difficulties, even though almost eighty percent of the Chinese Americans at the company spoke English.[31] In reality, the system of segregation both paralleled the isolation of Chinese Americans in the prewar Bay Area and perpetuated it: black and white employees in the same crews at least interacted, while Chinese American men had far less contact with people of other backgrounds.

White managers in the shipyards also made race- and gender-based decisions about the type of work nonwhite employees could do and how well they could do it. Employers preferred to place women rather than men in clerical positions; with opinions about the Chinese improving, many companies hired some Chinese American women for such jobs but almost never offered the

same kinds of positions to African Americans—another reflection of stereotypes about racial competency and industriousness. Historian Marilynn Johnson has also found that "Chinese American workers were often placed in electrical work," because employers thought the "lighter, detail-oriented trade . . .
more suitable for [them]." Blacks, in contrast, frequently received the harder
and dirtier jobs that managers considered appropriate for their station and
racial abilities.[32] Prevailing stereotypes about Chinese passivity, fatalism, and
unsuitability for modern industry shaped employers' perceptions as well.[33]
Bob Myer, the assistant yard superintendent at Kaiser, credited his Chinese
American employees with great intelligence but claimed that "they are not so
easily adapted to streamlined mass-production methods."[34]

SHOP FLOOR IDENTITY

Still, shop floor debates, workers' interactions, and international relations
weakened the appeal of San Francisco-style nativism to the same types of
workers who had deployed it decades earlier. Many longtime white California
residents blamed simmering racial tensions in the wartime state on the Southern origins of most of the white migrants; hundreds of thousands came from
places such as Oklahoma, Louisiana, and Texas in the 1930s and 1940s.
Katherine Archibald questioned such pat explanations. "Except for the greater
emotionality of the Southerner, and his more frequent talk of lynchings, riots,
and reprisals, the attitudes of the two groups [white Southern migrants and
other white workers] were hard to distinguish," she said. Indeed, Archibald
shuddered at the violent anti-black sentiments of the majority of her fellow
workers. "Many [white] shipyard workers expressed satisfaction with the
bloody Detroit race riots of 1943, and boasted of the greater carnage that
would have taken place had they been there," she recalled.[35]

If anything, white Southern migrants bonded with their Northern and
Western white coworkers through shared racial attitudes. A few years earlier,
Californians had ridiculed and harassed the penniless and hungry Okies and
Arkies who camped on state roadsides and sometimes took the place of Mexican workers in the fields. Thousands of shipyard workers of Southern origin
remembered such slights, as well as the occasional violence they faced during
the Depression. Even those who came later knew that many Californians saw
them as illiterate rubes. Skin color, for such people, became a badge of belonging, a way to shake off the contempt of other whites. Because of their
race, they received promotions denied to equally deserving blacks and Chi-

nese Americans; they also took part in a shop floor culture based on shared understandings of black inferiority. Indeed, they could even draw on their Southern experiences to cast themselves as experts on the "Negro problem."[36]

White workers in the shipyards and other industries lacked this common currency of contempt for Chinese Americans. The South's small Chinese American population occupied a status somewhere between blacks and whites; unable in many places to attend white schools or mix socially with whites, they still strove to preserve their peculiar position through avoiding black institutions and association with African Americans.[37] Of course, many white Southerners in Bay Area factories saw nothing except the racial difference of their Chinese American coworkers. Indeed, Chinese Americans reported that white workers sometimes called them "Chink," and managers promoted white migrants based on racial considerations alone. As one exasperated Chinese American asked, "I have been here many months. Do you think I can become a leaderman?"[38] Still, by World War II, the anti-Asian nativism once so central to white working-class identity on the Pacific Coast was losing its power to bind white newcomers together on the shop floor, and by extension, in other areas. In part, this shift reflected the different stereotypes of blacks and Chinese then current. It also mirrored the way the U.S. government loudly celebrated the nation's allies, including China, while more circumspectly calling for racial tolerance inside the United States. But the segregation of Chinese American men and the integration of black ones in many work units probably played a role as well. White Southerners accustomed to Jim Crow and black submission feared and hated the African American integration they saw everywhere in the Bay Area. Chinese Americans, on the other hand, appeared to stay in their "place," both on the shop floor and in residential areas. As a result, Katherine Archibald noticed that at Moore Dry Dock, "Chinese, either as a people or as individuals employed in these years, were accepted without resistance or dislike, though with little positive friendliness." Similarly, while wartime polls showed some lingering white resistance to Chinese American employment on the West Coast, opposition to black coworkers had become far more pronounced there.[39]

COURAGEOUS ALLIES

Following Pearl Harbor, China became an official American ally and gained even greater stature in the United States than it had enjoyed in the late 1930s. The popular press lionized the Chinese and their immense courage in the face of Japanese occupation. *Time* and *Life* magazines published their now-infamous articles about how to distinguish between Japanese and Chinese people—"how to tell your friends from the Japs," as *Time* editors put it. *Ladies' Home Journal* assured readers that "Generalissimo Chiang Kai-shek is not a dictator." Comic strips, such as Milton Caniff's *Terry and the Pirates*, and American films like *Flying Tigers* and *The Lady from Chungking* portrayed China as struggling valiantly against fiendish Japanese invaders. The China installment of Frank Capra's government-funded *Why We Fight* series reminded viewers that "China has been fighting our enemy, Japan, for seven long years" and praised the nation's "indestructible spirit." By and large the public agreed, donating millions of dollars to China relief and naming Chiang Kai-shek and his wife two of the most admired living people.[40]

Widespread adulation of ally China eroded support for the most hardcore California nativist groups, whose high profile anti–Japanese American activities could not completely hide their wider anti-Asian agenda. Nativist organizations had failed in the past to amend the U.S. Constitution to exclude from citizenship the children of ineligible aliens; now, they focused on producing a court ruling they could use to achieve the same goal. As a first step, John Regan, the secretary of the Native Sons of the Golden West, sued Cameron King, San Francisco's registrar of voters, for keeping 2,600 Nisei on the voting rolls after Pearl Harbor. U. S. Webb, the nativist former attorney general who represented Regan, tried to persuade a lower court and then a federal appellate court to overturn the 1898 *U.S. v. Wong Kim Ark* decision recognizing the citizenship of all people born on U.S. soil, regardless of their parents' eligibility for citizenship. In making his pitch, Webb relied on arguments first honed against the Chinese, calling the 1898 ruling "one of the most injurious and unfortunate decisions" the Court ever made and declaring that the nation essentially belonged to white Americans only. Such language, although common enough among whites at the time, jarred the judge and court observers familiar with government propaganda and its emphasis on racial tolerance; a representative of the left-wing Lawyers Guild even compared Webb's statement to Adolf Hitler's racist screed *Mein Kampf*.[41]

Webb made another critical error when he argued that the case also "involves the citizenship and right to citizenship of all people and all races who do not fall within the characterization of . . . White people." Participants in the hearing, and, later, members of the press and the public, pounced on the statement, seeing it as an indirect reference to the Chinese American population. Backed into a corner, the former attorney general grudgingly conceded that if the court found for Regan, Congress could still pass a law granting citizenship to Chinese Americans. However, Webb had already blown his case by letting slip the entire nativist program. The judge ruled against Regan without even leaving the bench, and in May 1943, the U.S. Supreme Court upheld the decision.[42]

The high court's ruling came at the apex of wartime pro-China sentiment: the visit of Generalissimo Chiang Kai-shek's wife, Soong Mei-ling, to the United States. China's First Lady was the perfect spokesperson for a nation most Americans still regarded as exotic and inscrutable. An attractive Wellesley graduate who spoke perfect English, she put a Westernized, Christian face on China's government and people. Behind the scenes, her husband and his cronies pocketed millions of dollars of American wartime aid and constantly frustrated U.S. military leaders with their incompetence and corruption. But hundreds of thousands of Americans, ignorant of these facts, turned out in city after city to greet and cheer Madame Chiang, who brought senators and congressmen to their feet and to tears with her speeches on Capitol Hill.[43]

Madame Chiang also received a hero's welcome and the key to the city of San Francisco, once America's most anti-Chinese metropolis. The historical contrasts were striking. Thousands turned out to cheer China's First Lady on the same avenues where white San Franciscans once murdered Chinese in broad daylight. Generations of California politicians had called for the expulsion of the entire Chinese American population; now, Madame Chiang rode with a beaming Mayor Rossi and Governor Earl Warren through the streets of San Francisco. "Missimo," the First Lady of China, later spoke before an audience of 2,500 labor union members at the invitation of the AFL's San Francisco Central Labor Council, whose evocations of "yellow peril" had bound white workingmen together for more than a half century.[44]

Madame Chiang's reception highlighted the contradictions between white San Franciscans' simultaneous appreciation of China and of the economic and social privileges they gained from nativism. Many of the same union leaders who cheered the First Lady at the Central Labor Council refused to allow Asian Americans and other nonwhites into union locals. Most of the white San Franciscans who waited in the morning fog to catch a glimpse of Madame Chiang's car lived in districts where Chinese Americans could not buy property, whether because of homeowner resistance or restrictive covenants. The hypocrisy was not lost on many Chinese American observers. Such people "are inconsistent and have ulterior motives," journalist Gilbert Woo warned his readers. "We shouldn't be taken in."[45]

THE STRAIN OF HYPOCRISY

As Woo understood, the nation that went to war in 1941 was a starkly, brutally segregated country, a reality that clouded the meaning of the conflict for many nonwhite Americans. In its wartime propaganda, the U.S. government sometimes reminded its people that the Axis powers considered themselves racial supermen and longed to destroy America's multiracial democracy. Posters urged citizens to buy war bonds "for freedom's sake," showed black and white workers "united," and proclaimed that "Americanism is not, and never was, a matter of race or ancestry."[46] At the same time, millions of blacks in the South lacked even the basic right to vote and faced the constant threat of white violence. In the North, white Americans maintained a less violent racial order in which people of color could vote but lived in segregated areas and worked in the most menial occupations. In the West, Japanese Americans languished in concentration camps because of their ancestry. The reality of life for most nonwhite Americans thus cruelly belied the nation's propaganda.

This hypocrisy extended to the making of war itself. Mexican Americans served in integrated units; so did Chinese Americans and Filipinos, largely because of their "allied" ancestry. But African American soldiers were shunted into all-black units, and military officials also segregated Japanese American enlistees. While blacks volunteered for service at an extraordinary rate, secretary of war Henry Stimson and many of his generals privately disparaged their courage and abilities and avoided placing many in combat for the first years of the war. The armed forces required black soldiers in military camps throughout the country to use segregated and invariably inferior facilities, from post exchanges and commissaries to movie theaters. Conditions were particularly bad in the South, where white residents often treated captured German soldiers with far greater respect than African American troops. Black historian John Hope Franklin, a young man during the war, concluded at the time that "the United States, however much it was devoted to protecting the freedoms and rights of Europeans, had no respect for me, no interest in my well-being." After initially volunteering for service and being rejected because of his race, a disgusted Franklin found ways to stay out of the military once drafted. Most African American men did not follow his lead, yet they expressed many of the same sentiments about the nation's hypocrisy. Determined to fight for real freedom, they rallied behind the *Pittsburgh Courier's* campaign to achieve a "Double V" or "Double Victory": victory against Fascism abroad and racism at home.[47]

Wartime outbreaks of interracial violence prompted a growing number of white Americans to face the nation's hypocrisy. The 1942 Detroit housing riot foreshadowed far worse: in 1943, major race riots broke out not only in Detroit once again, but also in Los Angeles, New York, and elsewhere. Although each riot differed in its details, the racial tensions that sparked them were harrowingly familiar. In cities across the nation, migrants of all backgrounds toiled long hours in newly integrated workplaces and competed for scarce housing, commodities, and recreational opportunities. Small racial incidents, from fistfights to screaming matches to hate strikes, occurred with frightening regularity. Civic leaders around the country watched the riots elsewhere and shuddered, fearing that their towns could be next.

In San Francisco, as in many other urban areas, the mayor and independent activists created interracial "civic unity" groups to help prevent race riots. The first such San Francisco group, the Bay Area Council Against Discrimination (BACAD), dated to 1942 and the initial Detroit disturbances. Officials with San Francisco's War Production Board helped organize the group, together with black and white progressive leaders concerned about rising racial, ethnic, and religious tensions in the area. The organization quickly stepped into the civil rights activism void that San Francisco's conservative NAACP, by then in disarray, had created through its inaction. Despite BACAD's quasi-official origins, it publicized and criticized discrimination not just by trade unions and private businesses but by government agencies as well; its exposés eventually pushed the United States Employment Service, a federal agency, to form its own Bay Area Advisory Committee on Discrimination. Roger Lapham, a moderate Republican who trounced Angelo Rossi in the 1943 mayoral election, also set up his own short-lived Civic Unity Committee after taking office. The new San Francisco Council for Civic Unity eventually superseded the three other organizations, continuing its interracial activism for decades after the war.[48]

COUNTERING PROPAGANDA

As civic unity groups pushed for greater nonwhite civil rights, they highlighted the Japanese government's frequent exploitation of America's racial situation. Japan cast itself as Asia's liberator, driving European and American colonialists from their holdings in Southeast Asia and incorporating these territories into a "Greater East Asia Co-Prosperity Sphere" of which it was the leader. Of course, Japanese officials also viewed other Asians as inferior to the Yamato race; they enslaved Indonesians, Koreans, and Chinese, among others, and tested biological agents on the population of Manchuria. Still, as historian John Dower has shown, the "Japanese exploited every display of racial conflict in the United States in their appeals to other Asians." One of the most effective examples of American hypocrisy was the nation's immigration policy, which banned Asians from entry and declared those immigrants already residing in the United States to be racially ineligible for citizenship.[49]

The Roosevelt administration and many legislators eventually questioned the wisdom of continued Chinese exclusion. Sympathetic congressmen such as Warren Magnuson of Washington and Walter Judd of Minnesota worked closely on the issue with the Citizens Committee to Repeal Chinese Exclusion (CCRCE). A private organization of Asia scholars and racial progressives, it advocated repeal of the Chinese Exclusion Act of 1882 and the granting of naturalization rights to resident Chinese aliens. In addition to crafting a bill that would assuage doubters in Congress, these allies worked to win over civic groups and local governments throughout the United States. The CCRCE focused much of its energy on the Pacific Coast, and especially the Bay Area, where nativist organizations lined up to resist repeal.[50]

The CCRCE's success in convincing thousands of white Californians to support repeal demonstrates the limited way national security imperatives overrode local racial traditions during the war. Scores of West Coast organizations, from the League of Women Voters to local city councils, eventually endorsed repeal—but only as a measure to help win the war rather than as a repudiation of the nation's racist immigration policy. The bill's stipulation that China would receive only a 107 person per year immigration quota proved crucial to its passage, assuring potential supporters that the legislation would have virtually no real impact on the composition of the U.S. population. Indeed, the tiny quota convinced both the San Francisco Board of Supervisors and the city's chamber of commerce to support the repeal bill, despite initial hesitation. The *San Francisco Chronicle* also got behind the campaign, publishing seven editorials favoring repeal.[51] As pressure mounted, Congress finally passed the Chinese Exclusion Repeal Act in December 1943.

Although significant, repeal was also a cheap political gesture from legislators unwilling to address or discuss the larger racial problems of wartime America. It was certainly cheap in a financial sense, for it offered no tangible benefits to Chinese in war-torn China. The one group it directly affected was Chinese Americans, enabling many to gain citizenship and the right to vote for the first time. For this reason, the CCRCE excluded Chinese Americans from joining the organization so that no one could question its motives.[52] And by focusing solely on repeal's impact on China's morale, the organization hoped to distract attention from the legislation's actual effect on Chinese Americans in the United States. CCRCE members apparently worried that white Americans would oppose a move that empowered a minority group, even a small and increasingly well-regarded one.

A TRANSNATIONAL FUTURE?

Repeal signaled that Chinese American civil rights were tied to China and its relationship with the United States, even in the midst of vibrant progressive activism for greater nonwhite rights in San Francisco. The continued link rarely worried San Francisco's Chinese Americans, affirming as it did their transnational identities and nativism's decline in the city. Indeed, the nascent San Francisco civil rights groups that sought Chinese American support had little to offer them in comparison. To begin with, such organizations focused primarily on the problems of the African American migrants, and by 1945, Japanese Americans, largely ignoring the needs of Chinatown's thousands. Nor did the interracial activists impress Chinese Americans with their achievements. The local Council for Civic Unity and a newly activist NAACP branch each pressed for better housing and an end to racial discrimination in industry and in AFL unions. Both organizations attained some of these goals after the war, but during the conflict they remained locked in a stalemate with intransigent union leaders and white housing officials. BACAD, the one civil rights group in which Chinese Americans actively participated, promised to push housing authorities to open the East Bay's war housing projects to people of Chinese ancestry. Since Chinese American workers often commuted twenty or thirty miles from San Francisco Chinatown to the shipyards in Richmond, Vallejo, and Oakland, the issue was a major one for them.[53] BACAD's failure to deliver on its promise merely reinforced the comparative benefits and success of Chinese American transnational politics.

Indeed, going it alone seemed to pay off for Chinese Americans during the war. The Sino-American alliance and the repeal of Chinese exclusion prompted both Democratic and Republican leaders to reach out to a community they had once vilified. In early 1943, with repeal a distinct possibility, the Republican County Committee appointed a Chinese American to its board. A few months later, district attorney-elect Edmund G. "Pat" Brown named Jack Chow, a Chinese American and Democratic activist, one of his new assistant district attorneys. Not to be outdone, Mayor Roger Lapham asked Henry Shue Tom to join his Civic Unity Committee. National political figures also took note of the newly empowered community: then senator Harry S

Truman toured Chinatown during the 1944 presidential campaign, forging a public friendship with local Democratic leader Albert K. Chow, Jack Chow's brother.[54]

These small moments of recognition drew leading Chinese Americans closer to a city establishment in which they already had something of a stake, and simultaneously pushed them further away from the new interracial organizations. Beginning in 1939, a number of white politicians cited their support for Chinatown's housing project in order to win the support of the growing Chinese American citizen population of voting age. In 1944, the Council for Civic Unity and the NAACP challenged the SFHA's continued segregation of its projects.[55] Most Chinese Americans deplored residential segregation in general, but they had won the promise of a project for their district by working within the Authority's system. Few wished to lose any of the precious promised units of housing to integration, especially as the city's racial demographics changed.

Mutual suspicions between the city's two largest nonwhite communities further undermined the potential for them to cooperate in the fight against segregated housing or anything else. In the late 1930s, "the Chinese . . . were segregated more than the blacks," recalled pioneering black San Francisco journalist Thomas C. Fleming. "But in some of those [Chinese] restaurants, they [the owners] would flatly tell you to leave. They did it because they thought the white people wanted it that way." Many Chinatown restaurants continued the practice during the wartime period. The black-owned *San Francisco Reporter* described one such incident in which a group of African Americans went to a Chinatown nightclub to celebrate a friend's birthday. The restaurant's host informed them that no tables were available, even though they could see several vacant ones in the dining room. Waiting for a table to clear, the group watched the host seat parties of whites who arrived after they did. Commenting on the case, a *Chinese Times* columnist asserted that "the Chinese nightclub perhaps didn't have the mentality of discriminating against blacks. Perhaps all those seats were reserved or were saved for regular customers. During the war, this has been a common restaurant practice." The *Chinese Times* refused to acknowledge that, as historian Yong Chen has pointed out, Chinese Americans of this era often viewed blacks with "contempt." Arnold Shankman, Rose Hum Lee, and other scholars of this period confirm Chen's assertion. "Chinese were reluctant to hire blacks, to have Negro neighbors, or to develop friendships with Afro-Americans," argued Shankman.[56]

Chinese American restaurant owners who discouraged black patronage only worsened the relationship between the two largest minority communities in the city. Stories of Jim Crow treatment in Chinese American businesses especially angered black civil rights activists. "Our feelings against nonwhites who do this sort of thing are stronger than our feelings against the white man," noted one who had experienced such discrimination. The NAACP's magazine *The Crisis* expressed similar feelings, referring at war's end to the "kowtowing Chinese" who "follow the established policy of the dominant group in dealing with Afro-Americans."[57] The mutual suspicion and dislike boded poorly for interracial activism; with Chinese American workers segregated in the shipyards and in Chinatown tenements, interactions in the district's shops and restaurants remained the major point of contact between blacks and Chinese Americans during the war.

SAN FRANCISCO, I AM ASHAMED OF YOU

In the early 1930s, a group of white Nob Hill neighbors signed a racial restrictive covenant after a handful of well-off Chinese Americans tried to buy nearby homes from their bankrupt white owners. A few years later, a Chinese American named Mabel Tseng purchased one of the covenanted homes at 1150 Clay Street. When she moved into it during the war, her white neighbors quickly filed suit against her in a local court. In late May 1945, just a few weeks after Nazi Germany surrendered to the Allies, a San Francisco judge upheld the restrictive covenant and ordered Tseng's eviction.[58]

The timing was particularly ironic. Delegates from fifty nations, including the Republic of China, were at that very moment meeting in San Francisco to discuss the formation of the United Nations and to draft a charter that expressed "faith in fundamental human rights, in the dignity and worth of the human person, in the equal rights of men and women and of nations large and small." During the conference, several delegations stayed at two major Nob Hill hotels where huge banners proclaimed, "Welcome, Citizens of the World." Simultaneously, the hotels quietly bankrolled the Nob Hill residents' lawsuit against Mabel Tseng. "If Americans intended for the delegates to know about the sincerity of American social and economic progress, I'm afraid they'll have no more powerful proof than this eviction case," wrote Gilbert Woo. "San Francisco, the meeting place of the United Nations! I am ashamed of you."[59]

The Nob Hill incident, and the lack of attention it received in the mainstream press, suggested that even at war's end, most white San Franciscans still rejected the aspirations and individuality of the city's Chinese Americans. The once-common desire to excise Chinatown and its inhabitants had disappeared, of course. As journalist Harold Isaacs observed, during the war

"Chinatown life became more than ever quaint, fascinating, and sentimentally attractive" to white Americans. But *San Francisco Chronicle* columnist Bill Simons self-mockingly observed that like many other residents, "I couldn't even think of Chinatown without feeling that warm, patronizing glow come over me."[60] That glow masked Chinatown's complex symbolic appeal as a place not just in spatial terms but in the city's racial, economic, and social order. The district dated to a seemingly simpler era, before massive black migration and nascent civil rights activism challenged San Francisco's smug and contradictory progressivism. Many white San Franciscans liked Chinatown not only for its novelty but because its residents stayed in their place, in all meanings of that word. The supposed docility of the Chinese American population resulted from decades of repression and segregation, something few white San Franciscans cared to acknowledge. But when Chinese Americans stepped out of their place—when they bought property in another district, for example—the warm glow that Simons described swiftly turned cold. Even on the shop floor, white workers who no longer bonded over the "yellow peril" still treated Chinese American coworkers with little friendliness. Whatever their ancestry, they were not white. In other words, when Chinese American aspirations exceeded what was acceptable to mainstream society, white San Franciscans quickly forgot the courage of China's millions.

However psychologically empowering, then, Chinatown's transnationalism proved ill-suited to achieving fairness or equality for Chinese Americans in housing and many other areas. Instead, it encouraged the view that Chinese American rights were linked to Sino-American relations, not the U.S. Constitution. This fostered political opportunism and a cavalier view of Chinese American claims on the state: as the history of Ping Yuen demonstrated, officials recognized Chinese American citizenship when it suited them, and rejected it when they wished. They also clung to pernicious stereotypes about Chinese American difference and residential undesirability. In fact, city officials in 1946 expressed great surprise at their discovery that Chinese Americans could live in regular American homes and had "no special preferences in housing because of nationality or belief."[61]

Despite transnationalism's limits, however, most Chinese Americans after the war continued to avoid San Francisco's new multiracial activist organizations and their high-profile challenges to residential segregation. In part, this approach was rooted in prewar strategies. It also reflected the way a number of Chinese American leaders were forging ties to the city's establishment during the 1940s. Yet the absence of Chinese Americans in San Francisco's fledgling civil rights coalition left people like Mabel Tseng at the mercy of white opinion and caprice. Without the backing of vocal advocates for equal rights, homeowners like Tseng remained vulnerable to the shifting interests and sentiments of white neighbors and the mainstream press. Indeed, this was a major problem with using Chinese transnationalism to achieve domestic political goals: public opinion, always fickle, inevitably shifted, and alliances changed.

Equally significant, most white San Franciscans showed a general unwillingness to sacrifice racial privilege for the war effort. Indeed, as David M. P. Freund has noted, the very language that white homeowners used to talk about race in this era was changing in ways that denied racism's role in the allocation of urban space, all while preserving and extending that role. A Bay Area homeowners' committee member used this language when he said, "We don't feel that it is our patriotic duty to take a loss in property values."[62] Like most Americans, white San Franciscans saw World War II as a battle for values dear to them, and in many cases, those values included racial segregation. Moreover, by the 1940s, racial restrictions had become a common and accepted practice nationwide, affirmed and supported by U.S. government programs. By separating segregation from its anti-Chinese past, federally mandated housing practices allowed white San Franciscans to isolate Chinese Americans without guilt—or fear of criticism from the millions of Americans who now praised their ally China. Despite civic leaders' calls for greater tolerance, then, many white residents took concrete steps during the war to contain all the city's nonwhite populations in specific neighborhoods. Together with federal officials, they helped lay the foundations in San Francisco for a segregated black neighborhood and showed no interest in easing restrictions on Chinatown, the nation's oldest segregated slum.

If anything, the outcome of the Tseng case suggested that Chinese American housing opportunities might actually contract after the war. White residents of other Nob Hill blocks also created restrictive covenants during the Depression. The judge's ruling in the Tseng case motivated such people to file suit against Chinese Americans who tried to move into the neighborhood. Chinese Americans also faced similar resistance elsewhere in city; even the Geary Boulevard Merchants Association and the Park Presidio Improvement District sought to oust a Chinese American veteran who purchased a Richmond District laundry, reasoning that he would want to live in the neighborhood where he worked. Chinese Americans reported similar incidents in Oakland and other parts of the Bay Area, as well.[63]

Surveying this persistent segregation, a frustrated Gilbert Woo recalled how he and other reporters encouraged soldier friends during the war by telling them that they were fighting for equality and freedom. "But then we saw our veteran friends return, and because of the color of their skin, they couldn't even occupy the homes they'd bought," he said. Now, instead of just being ashamed of San Francisco, he admitted, he was also ashamed of himself.[64]

CHAPTER SEVEN

Becoming Equally Unequal:
The Fight for Property and Housing
Rights in Postwar California

In December 1944, General Henry C. Pratt of the Western Defense Command announced that all but a handful of Japanese American "evacuees" could return to the West Coast after the new year. For the former internees, the proclamation sparked a mixture of excitement, fear, and uncertainty. Between 1942 and 1944, race-baiting officials and members of Congress from the western states held numerous hearings, made countless speeches, and pushed a raft of legislation calculated to keep anti–Japanese American sentiment inflamed. When the military finally opened the West Coast to the Nisei and Issei, the *Los Angeles Times* proclaimed that "we shall not pretend to like it. . . . Japs in large numbers on the Pacific Coast are dangerous."[1] The thousands of Japanese Americans who decided to return in spite of such rumblings faced vandalism and violence in many rural areas. But the Issei and Nisei who arrived in California's major cities, now packed with wartime migrants and brimming with racial tensions, experienced relatively little violence; instead, they grappled with everyday problems already familiar to other nonwhite residents. In the process, Japanese Americans joined with these people for the first time to fight the legal restrictions that limited their ability to buy land and homes. This budding civil rights coalition successfully challenged racially restrictive covenants and land laws, but its victories in the courts did not end the housing discrimination so common throughout urban California.

Interracial organization was far from inevitable in either Los Angeles or San Francisco. Japanese Americans in prewar L.A. usually avoided collaborating with other minority groups; in San Francisco, tensions between Chinese Americans and African Americans simmered during the war. By the end of the conflict, social service workers reported friction between various minority groups in different parts of Los Angeles. When Japanese Americans returned to urban California, they competed for scarce resources—especially housing—with other nonwhites who could also not live outside racially unrestricted neighborhoods. Community activists even feared that blacks and Japanese American returnees might come to blows in some of the districts where both sought housing.

Instead, groups representing many of California's minority communities eventually came together, initially to prevent interracial violence during the war but then to fight for equal rights after it. Chinese Americans, Filipinos, Korean Americans, and Mexican Americans participated to varying degrees in wartime civic unity groups that elsewhere in the nation included only blacks and whites.[2] As a member of the mayor's Civic Unity Committee of San Francisco reminded his colleagues, "it would be well to bear in mind that the committee is to deal with the problems of all Minority Groups [sic] and not with the Negro situation alone." Established African American organizations in California, such as the NAACP, worked closely with the new civic unity organizations, while progressive residents of the state's few integrated housing projects sought to foster such cooperation at the grassroots.[3] By the end of World War II, interracial cooperation had begun to replace prewar patterns of minority group isolation or competition. Organizations that supported "fair play" for Japanese American returnees drew Nisei into these growing interracial coalitions as well.

These loose-knit progressive networks attacked racial inequality throughout the urban state and scored some major legislative and legal wins for nonwhite residents between 1945 and 1948. Activists successfully fought to overturn both *de jure* educational segregation and the longstanding bar on interracial marriage in California, picketed at segregated public facilities, and held mass meetings to protest discrimination against nonwhite citizens. In 1945, "fair play" group leaders also spoke before hundreds of their fellow Californians, urging them to support the rights of Japanese American returnees.[4] Because of the massive shortage of shelter, however, housing and land rights soon emerged as central issues for these civil rights activists, who participated in a successful 1948 lawsuit against racially restrictive covenants, mobilized voters to defeat an anti-Japanese American ballot initiative, and helped persuade the U.S. Supreme Court to overturn part of the Alien Land Act.

After achieving some major wins, many of California's activist organizations stumbled in the late 1940s. As Soviet-American tensions increased, emboldened conservatives labeled a number of progressive groups Communist-supported, a particularly lethal accusation in the political climate of the time. Part of a national trend, attempts to equate civil rights proponents with Communist sympathizers never completely succeeded in California, where moderate groups appropriated anti-Communist language to justify their own goals. However, conservatives' accusations and insinuations prompted many civil rights and labor organizations to force out members with suspected left-wing ties.[5] Even without conservative pressure, the clarity of purpose that bound civil rights groups together in the fight against racial restrictions scarcely outlasted the 1948 court decision. White flight to California's burgeoning suburbs undercut the victory, since almost every new subdivision barred non-white homebuyers without ever resorting to restrictions. California's white legislators also expressed little interest in addressing the resulting suburban segregation, which the vast majority of their constituents supported.

The legal changes of the 1940s did alter urban California's racial geography, however. The end of the legal racial hierarchy gave Asian Americans much greater residential mobility than they had enjoyed before 1948. In addition, the continued influx of black migrants into the urban Bay Area, and nativism's decline there, further eroded the region's distinctive racial traditions. By 1950, San Francisco's racial dynamics had come to resemble those of Los Angeles: an overwhelming number of whites in both places now made their opposition to *any* kind of residential integration obvious, either through their own choices of residence or through their willingness to use a variety of methods—including vandalism and sometimes violence—to limit the choices of others.

A CITY TRANSFORMED

Fully one-third of the interned Japanese Americans originally lived in Los Angeles County, and the tens of thousands who returned in 1945 and 1946 found that the wartime transformation of Southern California had not greatly altered patterns of residential discrimination there. If anything, the migration of close to half a million people into the Los Angeles metropolitan area during the war simply intensified the segregation so common before the conflict.[6] The Japanese American internment and the rapid influx of blacks also homogenized many of the city's formerly multiracial areas; white residents left the old Central Avenue district in droves as more and more black migrants arrived during the war.[7]

New and existing racial restrictions hemmed in tens of thousands of these newcomers, who moved out of desperation into the rundown, abandoned Little Tokyo area. Once a Japanese American business district, it quickly became a majority African American residential area during the war. Little Tokyo's storefronts "were boarded up and people were living here in the ground and second floors," recalled Kango Kunitsugu, a Nisei soldier allowed to visit Los Angeles in 1944. "Basically, it served as a residential area for the blacks, as opposed to a commercial area." The converted retail properties made poor housing, however, and intense overcrowding burdened the neighborhood's infrastructure. In 1943, Arthur F. Miley, an assistant to L.A. county supervisor John Anson Ford, predicted that "unless some action is taken immediately on a large scale . . . we are going to be subject to disease, epidemics, race riots, and a general breaking down of the home front in this area."[8]

By the time Miley wrote his report, Los Angeles's simmering interracial tensions had already exploded in the "Zoot Suit Riot" of 1943. For a week in early June, white servicemen and civilians roamed through Los Angeles, attacking Mexican American youths and some African Americans as well. Scores of military, police, and civic leaders tolerated and even encouraged the violence, rather than trying to curb it. Incredibly, city officials then denied that race had anything to do with the riot or the reaction of law enforcement officers to it. This response laid bare what historian Edward Escobar has described as "the dire economic conditions under which Mexican Americans lived, the hostility they faced from their white neighbors, and the discrimination—or at best, indifference—they endured from police, school, and other governmental officials" in Los Angeles.[9]

Federal officials and many of their local counterparts also spent the war paying lip service to racial tolerance while quietly supporting white supremacy in L.A.'s housing market. By mid-1943, thousands of African Americans were arriving monthly in a Los Angeles already desperately short of housing. Still, the city council responded to the fears of white homeowners in southern Los Angeles rather than to the plight of the black newcomers who crowded into neighboring areas. In a typical instance, the Council persuaded the NHA to change the tenancy of a new private development at 104th Street and Avalon Boulevard from black to white. A year later, local officials also convinced the NHA to convene FHA officials, real estate agents, contractors, and businessmen—none of them African American—to fix 124th Street as the southernmost border for black housing in L.A. Although such racial boundaries had long existed in the mental geography of many Angelenos, federal authorities' decision to quietly but officially sanction them infuriated African Americans in the city and created a grim precedent.[10]

Federal and local officials never managed to solve the problem of shelter for the hundreds of thousands of migrants of all backgrounds who streamed into

Los Angeles during the war, but their record on black housing was particularly dismal. Between 1940 and 1945, about 150,000 African Americans migrated to Los Angeles County. During the same period, the NHA authorized the construction of just 1,257 privately financed housing units for blacks in the county, less than 3 percent of all such housing it allocated in the area. Worse yet, builders had only completed *eight* of those units by July 1944. Public developments picked up little of the overflow, with only about three thousand units open to African Americans in Los Angeles County by war's end. In mid-1945, local officials estimated that they needed one hundred thousand additional units of family housing to satisfy the needs of the entire Los Angeles population at that moment. However, race determined the severity of the need: the number of black families in L.A. exceeded the number of housing units open to them by almost 30 percent; for whites, the overflow was 8 percent.[11]

Japanese Americans thus returned to a Los Angeles housing crisis worsened not only by the demobilization of veterans and the continued in-migration of other Americans but by racial tensions and resentment. In the hunt for housing, they had always been at a disadvantage compared to other Angelenos, including other nonwhites. Now, many worried that their ancestry would prove too great a handicap to overcome, even in the diverse, unrestricted areas in which many had once lived. Worse yet, a number of white journalists and citizens were working to incite anti-Japanese American sentiment among Los Angeles's African Americans, at least some of whom knew they faced eviction when Japanese Americans returned to claim homes and property.

BITTERSWEET HOMECOMING

Nevertheless, the Nisei and Issei were not without vocal allies. Pro-internee groups, including Friends of the American Way and the Pacific Coast Committee on American Principles and Fair Play, worked closely with civic unity organizations, the ACLU, the federal government's War Relocation Authority (WRA), and the JACL to ensure decent treatment for the returnees. The WRA also secured the cooperation of Governor Earl Warren, an early proponent of internment who now urged Californians to accept the returnees and treat them fairly. To win over regular citizens, however, pro-returnee organizations largely relied on the sterling record of the Nisei soldiers, with which returnee advocates hoped to dispel longstanding accusations of Japanese American disloyalty.[12]

In particular, fair play groups highlighted the heroics of the all-Japanese American 442nd Regimental Combat Team, which earned more decorations for valor than any other unit of its size during the war.[13] With the cooperation of the WRA and of the army, which wanted to preserve peace in the Western Defense Region, fair play groups brought Japanese American soldiers, such as "a young Nisei G.I. who lost one arm overseas and is covered with ribbons and wears a purple heart insignia," to speak before groups of civic leaders and other Californians. National journalists also covered the exploits of the 442nd, whose dramatic rescue of a battalion of white Texans in Italy captured the imagination of thousands of Americans. In late 1944, the American Legion of Hood River, Oregon, inadvertently helped the Japanese American cause as well when it removed the names of Nisei soldiers from its honor roll of local troops. The decision, and the subsequent death in battle of one of the Hood River Nisei, outraged white soldiers and citizens across the nation and heightened sympathy for Japanese American evacuees. Prominent military leaders, such as General Joe Stilwell of the China-Burma-India theater of operations and General Mark Clark of the European theater, added to the chorus when they hailed the Nisei soldiers and called on the West Coast public to treat the returnees with respect. Recognizing Nisei military service, even the California State American Legion, a member of the arch-nativist California Joint Immigration Committee, quietly supported the right of Nisei veterans to return to the coast.[14]

Still, in the first half of 1945, many local officials in rural areas turned a blind eye to vigilantes attacking Japanese Americans. In Fresno County, nightriders shot at returnees and set fire to their property. In Placer County, a series of suspicious blazes destroyed a number of Japanese Americans' homes and barns. In the delta region south of Sacramento, white vigilantes burned down Japanese American–owned buildings and shot at Nisei and Issei returnees in Florin, Mayhew, and Acampo. Vigilantes also struck Japanese Americans' homes in San Jose, Salinas, Watsonville, and other farming communities throughout California.[15]

In San Francisco and Los Angeles, however, Japanese Americans faced more indifference than hostility, especially by mid to late 1945. These cities' energetic civil rights and fair play groups used speakers' bureaus, meetings, and press releases to convince the public to respect the rights of returnees. Equally important, the WRA secured the vital support of major urban officials, including mayors, police chiefs, and city councilmen and supervisors. Although such authorities expressed little overt sympathy for the former internees, they were desperate to prevent any interracial violence that might erupt into something larger, especially another race riot. In San Francisco, city officials moved quickly to investigate incidents of anti-Nisei home vandalism, and Mayor Roger Lapham personally defused a hate strike at the Municipal Railway by speaking to workers there who objected to a new Nisei machinist. L.A. mayor Fletcher Bowron, who had called for internment in 1942, now urged city residents to respect the returnees. Under strict orders from Bowron, the Los Angeles Police Department also protected Japanese Americans from initial hostility in several neighborhoods. By September 1945, WRA head Dillon Myer contended that "except for the housing battle, we have no battles left in the cities" of California.[16]

As Myer noted, housing rather than violence proved to be the biggest problem for the Nisei and Issei who came to Los Angeles and San Francisco in 1945. The handful of internees who traveled west in January and February usually stayed with members of sympathetic church or fair play organizations.[17] By March and April, as the pace of return picked up somewhat, internee support groups and Japanese American organizations created hostels to serve as way stations for Nisei and Issei until they could find homes of their own. Most hostels were located in church buildings or on property that Japanese American groups owned. Although the majority sheltered ten or twenty returnees at a time, some, such as the American Friends Service Committee hostel on Evergreen Street in L.A. or the Buddhist Hostel on Pine Street in San Francisco, housed from ninety to one hundred fifty people each. These hostels were often filled to capacity; clients frequently stayed for weeks, unable to find even a shack in which to live. The Japanese American housing situation soon grew even worse. In mid-1945, when the WRA publicly confirmed its plans to close all but one internment camp by the end of the year, thousands of Issei and Nisei began streaming out of the camps and into California.[18]

WRA officials refused local authorities' requests to keep the camps open until the housing situation in California improved, but agency staffers soon realized that they had a potential public relations disaster on their hands. In June 1945, after having done very little up to that point to help returnees obtain housing, the WRA quietly contacted military authorities throughout California about any surplus barracks, Quonset huts, or trailers they might be able to provide to Japanese Americans. The agency also secured apartments, usually for Nisei veterans and their families, from public housing officials. The WRA relied on such housing in the Bay Area, where the federal government built far more wartime public developments than in Los Angeles. Hundreds of Japanese Americans soon settled in projects in Richmond and San Francisco's Hunters Point.[19]

In Los Angeles, the WRA created an exclusively Japanese American public housing program for the very same Nisei and Issei whom federal public housing officials ignored before the war.[20] Initially, the WRA provided temporary housing to 2,100 Japanese Americans at six former army barracks in Los Angeles County. In early 1946, as the city's housing crisis persisted, the WRA and the Federal Public Housing Authority (FPHA) opened trailer camps in north Burbank and Long Beach for the large number of barracks dwellers who still could not find other homes. The agency also placed many of the larger returnee families in jobs at the California Seafood Corporation, which set up a trailer camp for the group in Harbor City near Lomita and Torrance.[21]

The former internees who moved to the WRA's barrack and trailer housing and remained there into 1948 and 1949 tended to be Issei, or older, less financially secure Nisei, often with children. About half of the Japanese American internees left camp during the war to resettle in the Midwest or on the East Coast; in contrast, a large number of the trailer park and barracks families remained in the camps for the entire war, coming west at the end of the conflict with just $25 from the WRA.[22] Conditions in the trailer settlements exacerbated such differences in economic status. When members of the L.A. County Committee on Human Relations visited the Burbank camp in May 1946, they described it as a firetrap and a health hazard. The floors of the communal restrooms had rotted out, children played just yards from speeding traffic and piles of trash, and the boilers and stoves leaked. California Seafood's camp was no better. Worst of all, trailer park sites were located far from central Los Angeles and its job opportunities; numerous trailer park families accepted county relief for the first time, while others commuted hours each day for work.[23] They also felt the sting of contempt from other returnees. "I hear too often the expression backwash and residue from the young nisei [*sic*] who are safely situated in town," complained California Seafood camp resident Estelle Ishigo.[24]

Indeed, the younger and more mobile Japanese American returnees largely avoided the trailer parks. Much of the small, prewar Nisei middle class returned to homes purchased before the conflict in areas such as West Jefferson, Boyle Heights, and the Central Avenue district. Some Japanese Americans managed to rent houses in the same residential areas, often doubling up with other families. Such accommodations were in short supply, however, and hundreds of Japanese Americans eventually sought rooms in the former Little Tokyo area instead. Before the war, the only residents the Japanese business district usually attracted were single Issei laborers, who rented rooms in the cheap hotels and apartment buildings there. But now scores of young Nisei moved in, drawn by the prospect of vacancies and nearby job opportunities and transportation. Other returnees, especially young women, took domestic

FIGURE 7.1. The Winona Trailer Park in Burbank, north of Los Angeles, housed hundreds of Japanese American returnees who could not find homes in the over-crowded metropolis after World War II. Many of the Nisei and Issei who moved to such facilities stayed there until at least 1948. (Department of Special Collections, Charles E. Young Research Library, UCLA. Collection 1387, *Los Angeles Daily News.* Temporary Japanese post-war housing. Uclamss 1387 b87 36081-4.)

positions with white families who offered free housing in upscale areas of L.A., such as Beverly Hills and San Marino.[25]

Nisei who found homes in the central areas often remained dissatisfied with them. Numerous returnees blamed their conditions on Little Tokyo's hotel owners; those of Japanese ancestry attracted particular scorn, accused of "getting 'blood' money" from other, less fortunate Japanese because of the inflated prices they charged. Potential hotel proprietors, many of them Japanese Americans who returned to L.A. in mid-1945, engaged in bidding wars to obtain increasingly expensive hotel leases. Hotel guests inevitably paid the price, since landlords of all backgrounds required each day's high rent in advance, and in cash. Whole families crowded into single rooms: a Japanese American church leader discovered fifteen people living in some units. Further angering their tenants, many hotel owners skirted Office of Price Administration restrictions on room fees by calling hotels "hostels," enabling them to increase the rents they charged. Some "hostel" managers put up flimsy partitions and crammed so many people into each room that the cubicles resembled nothing more than the old internment camp barracks. Even many returnees who avoided the hotels and "hostels" still ended up in crowded, substandard, or overpriced homes. A number of families paid multiple rents since they lived apart, either because of the lack of family housing or to take advantage of far-flung job opportunities.[26]

LOOKING FOR WORK

Despite their willingness to commute long distances for work, many returnees struggled to find places for themselves in Los Angeles's economy, especially in 1945. The internment wiped out the prewar Japanese American niche economy, with its base in truck farming and produce retailing. The growth of chain stores and the occasional white boycott prevented Japanese Americans from reopening fruit stands or nurseries, at least when they first returned to the coast. Sprawling new housing tracts now covered many of their old plots on the city's margins, as well.[27] In 1945, only a few Nisei managed to purchase or rent land farther out in Los Angeles County or Orange County, or to recover prewar leaseholds.

Instead, most returnees to both Los Angeles and the Bay Area sought work in other fields, where they faced the same kind of job discrimination that other nonwhites routinely encountered. Female Nisei, whom potential employers perceived as less threatening and more publicly acceptable than nonwhite men, encountered the least resistance. City and county agencies across the urban state hired numerous Nisei women as clerks and secretaries, since many had done similar government work for the WRA. Private businesses eventually followed suit. Japanese American men, on the other hand, struggled to find decent positions. Right after the war, significant numbers of them took jobs in manufacturing, often in L.A. factories that stamped phonograph records. Thousands eventually went into business for themselves in one way or another, entering fields where they could escape the discrimination they faced in the mainstream job market. Some started dry cleaners, restaurants, or groceries in mid-1945, with scores more launching such establishments in the years that followed.[28]

The largest group flocked to contract gardening, both in San Francisco and Southern California. Contract gardening required almost no capital and conveyed a sense of independence, and the need for only limited English skills attracted many Issei and Kibei (Nisei who received their education in Japan before returning to America) to the trade. Contract gardening paid fairly well, and many Japanese Americans with significant experience in other fields became gardeners because of a lack of other options. "Mr. Leo Ishikawa, who owned a drug store [before the war] . . . had to turn to being a gardener," noted a Japanese American observer in 1945. "Mr. S. Mayeda, who was in the fish business also had to become a gardener."[29]

The importance of gardening for Nisei men reflected the perseverance of old assumptions about racial aptitudes. White residents often expressed a preference for Japanese gardeners, as sociologists Leonard Bloom and Ruth Riemer noted at the time. "The Japanese Americans' prewar reputation for horticultural proficiency stereotyped them and made it possible for those who had never done gardening to get contracts," they remarked. Right after the war, almost half of the Japanese American men in Los Angeles County worked as contract gardeners. As Rev. John Yamazaki discovered during a mid-1945 fact-finding trip to Los Angeles, "practically all who have returned have become gardeners except three persons who were able to find employment of their own choice." The percentage of Japanese Americans who worked in the trade eventually shrank to about one-quarter of the male population in the early 1950s, but many stayed in the business for the rest of their working lives. Since Nisei boasted a rate of education that matched or surpassed that of their white peers, the popularity of gardening as a career revealed the depth of employment discrimination Japanese American men continued to face long after the war.[30]

Work opportunities eventually drew some Nisei and Issei back to agriculture on the semirural fringes of Los Angeles, albeit farther out than many had lived before the war. A number of Issei and Nisei started farming again on a very small scale beyond the city's limits as anti–Japanese American boycotts eased. In addition, some Nisei leased or bought land in areas such as Venice, Gardena, and Culver City, where they established (or reestablished) nurseries that served a handful of remaining truck farms in those places. Others worked as farm laborers or managers for white landowners, especially since such jobs usually included housing. Still, Japanese Americans who returned to outlying areas right after the war often had to sleep in old barns and garages, many without running water.[31] If Nisei in the central city hostels felt like they were back in the internment camps, Issei sleeping in shacks in the outlying areas sometimes lived as they had forty years earlier.

INCIPIENT RACE WAR?

Because of housing shortages, Japanese American returnees to the Pacific Coast usually competed directly with other nonwhites for the limited supply of dwelling units in the racially unrestricted neighborhoods of the region's cities. At the end of the war, *Ebony* magazine worried that for this reason, the old Japanese districts of West Coast cities were sites of "an incipient race war." Sensing the same possibility, the anti-Asian press in California tried to whip up interracial conflicts, reporting on alleged plans to "evict Negroes to make way for Japs."[32]

But if these agitators ever had a real chance to sow widespread anti–Japanese American hatred among blacks, they had lost it by 1945. As historian Cheryl Greenberg has shown, in 1942, leading African American civil rights groups either supported or only weakly questioned Executive Order 9066. In 1945, however, anti–Japanese American agitators swayed few of the black residents of the Bay Area and Los Angeles. By then, civilian and military leaders, the civic unity movement, and leading African American organizations had all swung to the side of the returnees. Moreover, the groups most interested in fomenting interracial discord wielded little influence over the state's black population. Most anti-Asian organizations, such as the Native Sons of the Golden West, barred African Americans from membership and spouted white supremacist rhetoric. The most anti–Japanese American newspapers, including the *Los Angeles Herald* and the *San Francisco Examiner*, counted far fewer blacks among their readers than the African American press, and black-owned papers became increasingly supportive of both returnee rights and interracial cooperation in 1945. Indeed, a growing number of blacks echoed the rhetoric of African American journalists by this point, terming the internment a "dirty shame" and a warning to other minorities.[33]

In San Francisco, robust civic unity groups and progressive black activists thwarted any major problems from developing between Japanese American returnees and the African American population. During the conflict, the city's black community grew from around 4,000 to about 25,000, many of whom found homes in the Western Addition's old Japanese American businesses and dwellings. The influx also transformed African American politics, with progressive migrants forcing out conservative prewar NAACP leaders, including those who backed segregated public housing that excluded Japanese Americans. Prewar attempts to foster interracial activism left a more enduring mark on the city. Although the Western Addition Housing Council disbanded during the war, group alumni, including State Senator Jack Shelley and Booker T. Washington Community Center leader Robert Flippin, worked in civic unity groups and behind the scenes to foster better race relations. Several prominent participants in the civic unity movement also served in or maintained close ties to dedicated "fair play" organizations for Japanese Americans. These associations, together with organizations representing numerous ethnic groups, even held a conference in January 1945 to discuss ways to assist Japanese Americans returning to San Francisco.[34]

San Francisco's racial geography and the availability of public housing in the Bay Area also played significant roles in helping defuse interracial tension. The WRA secured a significant amount of public housing for Bay Area returnees, who thus did not compete for housing with blacks as often as they did in Los Angeles. In addition, the thousands of African American migrants who streamed into L.A.'s Little Tokyo arrived in a business district with few community-based organizations. Conditions in San Francisco's Nihonmachi resembled those of wartime Little Tokyo, with migrants living in storefronts under terrible conditions. Still, the heavily nonwhite areas of San Francisco's Western Addition had always combined homes, businesses, and various groups' institutions. These community centers, churches, and similar organizations provided some stability and cool-headed leadership to a neighborhood in tremendous flux.

Indeed, African Americans in San Francisco largely welcomed Japanese Americans back to the city in 1945. Some of the city's African American old-timers opened their homes to Japanese American friends coming back from the camps. With strong community support, Robert Flippin also set up a hostel for returnees, becoming one of the only African Americans in the state to do so. San Francisco's NAACP branch soon became a staunch champion of the Nisei and Issei; when anti–Japanese American violence flared in rural California, the branch fired off letters of protest to Governor Warren and met with Attorney General Robert Kenny. Its president also served on the advisory board of the local Japanese American Citizens League. In the end, the Washington Community Center could not even find anyone to argue "no" when it sponsored a debate on the question, "Should Japanese Be Returned to the West Coast?"[35]

The outlook for Los Angeles was not as positive, however, for tensions between other minority groups in the city had already boiled over by the time Japanese Americans began returning in significant numbers. In Watts, the rapid growth of the black population angered many returning Mexican American veterans, some of whom threatened to use force to expel the newcomers. In Hollenbeck, on the east side, Mexican American and African American youths came to blows after a fight between two girls at a junior high school. Community members also reported friction between Jewish and Mexican American residents of the same neighborhood.[36]

Civic leaders worried about the impact of the Nisei influx on this already volatile situation. No one expressed concern about middle-class Japanese American homeowners reclaiming their houses in traditionally diverse residential areas such as West Jefferson. The social composition of such neighborhoods barely changed during the war, and residents there often formed friendships across racial lines. Instead, social workers saw the potential for disaster in Little Tokyo, which lacked the infrastructure and institutions of San Francisco's Western Addition or the west side's history of racially integrated residence areas and schools. Little Tokyo also attracted the most underprivileged migrants and provided them little outlet for recreation or social interaction. Sensing a need for a steadying force, the city's Welfare Council set up an interracial social service facility called Pilgrim House in Little Tokyo in 1943, after the Zoot Suit Riot and during the peak of black migration to L.A. Having weathered the remainder of the war with minimal strife, Pilgrim House staffers now worried that the return of Japanese Americans might create new problems in a district that black wartime migrants had renamed Bronzeville.[37]

Realizing that they might displace other residents, some Japanese Americans also expressed fears about how other nonwhites would respond to them. Local JACL head Scotty Tsuchiya admitted that "most of us were afraid to come back here [to Los Angeles] because we knew that colored people were in our homes and stores." L.A.'s anti–Japanese American papers also publicized the early attempts of Japanese American organizations, such as the Hongwanji Buddhist Temple, to evict African American tenants to make room for returnees. With housing at a premium, many wartime renters refused to leave Japanese American–owned property unless served with official eviction orders. Numerous Nisei and Issei hesitated to take this step, fearing more bad publicity and an increase in anti–Japanese American incidents. Tenants occasionally threatened their Japanese American landlords as well, further worrying returnees.[38]

Regardless of these concerns, and some initial tension over evictions, Little Tokyo and Bronzeville managed to coexist, if not commingle. Black and Japanese American residents rarely mixed outside the multiracial Little Tokyo clinic, Pilgrim House, or area shops. The composition of the population, much of it transient, encouraged neither institution building nor the formation of stable relationships. As a reporter for the black *Pittsburgh Courier* newspaper observed, "one may see Japanese and colored members of the district apparently mingling, but close observation will reveal that the association of the two groups is merely one of forced mingling." Still, by mid-1946, *Ebony* dubbed the Little Tokyo–Bronzeville situation "the race war that flopped."[39]

At the same time, the comments of Scotty Tsuchiya and other Nisei reflected their lingering unease about the African American migrants who now thronged the streets that Japanese Americans still considered their own. Reverend Art Takemoto, a Nisei returnee, suggested that Japanese Americans often shared negative views about the African American newcomers with white Angelenos and many black old-timers. "[The black Southerners] in Bronzeville were thought of as being . . . uneducated" and seen as wasting their newfound earnings on liquor and entertainment, he observed. Whatever the case, Issei and Nisei quietly began to reassert their claim to Little Tokyo by late 1945. A few Japanese American hotel owners renovated their buildings to justify raising the rents and forcing out poorer black tenants. Nisei and Issei entrepreneurs also contacted the white property owners who controlled the district, convincing a number to ease out their African American tenants to make way for Japanese American businesses.[40]

Perhaps to justify their displacement of black migrants, numerous Nisei and Issei contended that Japanese Americans simply made better tenants than African Americans. Tom Sasaki, who conducted a study of Little Tokyo for the WRA, claimed that "building owners were glad to have the Japanese back because it meant that the buildings would be kept up better." Years later, journalist Katsumi Kunitsugu agreed, recalling that Japanese Americans "kept the place clean, they paid the rent on time and everything [and] were preferable to the blacks as tenants." Yet the district's longtime white landlords, although never part of Los Angeles's anti–Japanese American cohort, most likely acted out of self-interest rather than racial preference. Nisei Harry Honda suspected as much. "The landlords were able to get these black Americans out so that their places could be resumed as businesses, as opposed to housing," he argued.[41] Japanese American businesses made better tenants than African American migrants because the use of business property for residential purposes took such a heavy toll on Little Tokyo's buildings and infrastructure. Under the circumstances, S. K. Uyeda's Ten Cent Store was inevitably a far "cleaner" tenant than a group of migrants living in a storefront without proper bathing or cooking facilities.

MAKING COMMON CAUSE

Even as some Japanese Americans tried to ease blacks out of Little Tokyo, the JACL began cooperating closely with African American organizations throughout the state. In prewar days, the JACL usually focused on creating an image of Japanese Americans as loyal and patriotic model citizens whose rate of crime and delinquency was the lowest of any group in the population. The idea of ethnic desirability persevered in postwar Nisei ideas about Little Tokyo's black residents.[42] But after Pearl Harbor, Japanese American leaders began to understand the pitfalls of this strategy, which isolated Japanese Americans from other minority groups and the support they could render. Within months, the national JACL started reaching out to the NAACP and other civil rights organizations, pleading for their help in defeating anti–Japanese American legislation in Congress.[43]

Three years' experience with internment camps and scapegoating further transformed the JACL. In Los Angeles, local JACL leaders fought for the rights of the trailer camp dwellers and proposed a permanent public housing project to accommodate them—a far cry from the group's prewar ambivalence about Ramona Gardens. The San Francisco JACL proved even more enthusiastic, seating black and white progressives on its board, supporting a campaign to integrate public housing in the city, and helping fight for a non-segregation clause in the proposed Western Addition redevelopment program.[44] The war did not radicalize the JACL, but its leaders emerged from the conflict determined to confront rather than accommodate white supremacy and to forge the kinds of alliances they lacked in 1942.

In the process, JACL officials hoped to salvage the group's reputation among other Japanese Americans by contesting discriminatory state and federal laws. Many Japanese Americans after the war continued to condemn the JACL for having supported internment and cooperated with the U.S. government in carrying it out.[45] A small but vocal group of Japanese American progressives also began to challenge the JACL from the left, urging it to fight more actively for racial justice and to make common cause with other nonwhite groups. Such Nisei decried the "Old Guard [Japanese American] leaders who have regained power on the national scene" and contended that "we Japanese Americans together with all other minority groups in America are duty-bound to this great nation of ours to be among its severest critics." Under pressure from many sides to deliver real change for Japanese Americans, the JACL joined the loose-knit network of civic unity organizations, fair play groups, and civil rights activists fighting for racial equality in postwar California.[46]

The coalition faced a major challenge in 1946, when state senators Jack Tenney and Hugh Burns coauthored Proposition 15, a measure to include in the state constitution the various anti-Asian land laws that the legislature and voters had passed beginning in the 1910s. Anti–Japanese American zealotry served Tenney and Burns quite well until late in the war, when publicity about the 442nd Regimental Combat Team's stunning record undermined this tactic. As a Palo Alto woman explained in November 1944, anti–Japanese American agitators "don't realize that what they consider 'the best people' are [now] largely against them." But Tenney and Burns hoped to revive anti–Japanese American sentiment and its political benefits—hence their support of an initiative, the only purpose of which, in the words of the ACLU's Ernest Besig, was to "afford . . . a basis for a race-baiting campaign."[47]

As the civil rights coalition mobilized to fight Proposition 15, its diverse members discovered growing public support for Japanese American rights, at least in urban areas. The Congress of Industrial Organizations (CIO), the ACLU, the NAACP, the new California Federation for Civic Unity, the American Veterans Committee, Christian and Jewish groups, and a host of local associations all joined the JACL to fight the measure in publications, speeches, meetings, and voter outreach. They focused their campaign largely on the urban parts of the state where little anti-returnee violence or vandalism occurred in 1945. Harry Truman tacitly weighed in by awarding the 442nd Regimental Combat Team a Presidential Unit Citation in July 1946 and telling the soldiers that "you fought not only the enemy, but you fought prejudice— and you have won." The president's words underscored the way a growing number of white urbanites viewed the Alien Land Act—not as protection for the sacred land of white California, but as a mean-spirited assault on a group of deserving veterans. Indeed, as sympathetic federal officials argued, by 1946 "the term 'Nisei' [had] come to connote loyalty, just as the term 'Jap' carried a derogatory meaning."[48]

The final outcome of the 1946 election reflected the stunningly rapid demise of anti–Japanese American sentiment in urban California, where a large majority of voters endorsed the rights of "Nisei," not the punishment of "Japs." Although Proposition 15 won most of the state's 58 counties, it still lost statewide by 350,000 ballots. Voters in every major urban center except San Diego made the difference, rejecting the proposition by large margins. Los Angeles

County residents alone provided two-thirds of the votes to defeat the measure. This outcome was a testament both to the work of the civil rights coalition there and to the traditionally shallow roots of anti-Asian sentiment in Southern California. But even San Francisco voters, with their nativist traditions, overwhelming rejected the initiative, a sure sign of the weakening hold of anti-Asian ideology in its onetime heartland. Jack Tenney, ever the opportunist, quickly shifted the focus of his State Fact-Finding Committee on Un-American Activities (often known as the "Tenney Committee") to investigating the Communists he saw behind every civil rights organization. Still, for the moment, the JACL savored one of the first political victories Japanese Americans had ever won in California.[49]

THE MOST IMPORTANT ISSUE

Anti-Asian sentiment was dying in urban areas, but white support for the residential segregation of all nonwhite Californians did not decline nearly as quickly. Although the white public rejected overtly mean-spirited measures like Proposition 15, most still demanded the housing segregation that was by now a cornerstone of real estate practice, federal policy, and racial "common sense" in California. As thousands of demobilized Asian American veterans poured into the Bay Area and Los Angeles after the war, they joined other nonwhites desperately searching for one of the few homes open to them. Having fought overseas for democracy, they returned to California to find that racially restrictive covenants continued to limit their housing options.

Still, by 1946 and 1947, a number of white homeowners in areas bordering the racially unrestricted neighborhoods of San Francisco and Los Angeles began to sell to nonwhite buyers, covenants or not. The massive wartime growth of the nonwhite populations of unrestricted areas convinced many whites in neighboring districts that racial transition was inevitable—and that they should cash in while they could. As Lloyd Fisher of the American Council on Race Relations observed, a number of whites in such border areas happily "receiv[ed] the premium prices the Negroes are willing to pay for their property." Indeed, these "transition neighborhoods" frequently attracted nonwhite doctors, dentists, lawyers, and other professionals with ready cash—people for whom race, rather than income, limited home choices.[50]

Other white neighbors turned to the law to preserve the racial "purity" of their neighborhoods, however. Between 1944 and 1947, white homeowners throughout the urban state created a host of new restrictive covenants and used many existing ones to sue their nonwhite neighbors. Sometimes, whole cities or regions moved to write or reinforce restrictions against nonwhite occupancy. After the war, white real estate agents and civic leaders in both South Pasadena and the San Fernando Valley tried to bar nonwhites entirely. Farther north, prominent real estate agent Harry Carskadon publicly advocated restricting the entire San Francisco peninsula south of the city of San Francisco to whites only. "Any attempt to move Negroes or Chinese into areas occupied by the whites will result in a serious depreciation of property values," he claimed. "Such social equalization is undesirable."[51]

Racially restrictive covenants soon become *the* major issue for space-starved nonwhite residents of urban California. Judges upheld restrictions against Chinese Americans on Nob Hill, a huge blow to the thousands of servicemen bringing fiancées and wives to San Francisco from China after decades of exclusion. Those who hoped to escape crowded Chinatown discovered that their service to the nation failed to move the city's courts. In a worrisome ruling, San Francisco judge James G. Conlan claimed that the very presence of Chinese Americans on Nob Hill would "lower . . . the social and living standards" there. A discouraged Gilbert Woo explained just how powerful restrictive devices still were: "You must prepare to move out or hope for World War Three to break out soon and an atomic bomb to blow up the city government (by all means don't blow up Chinatown!) and burn down the deed and contract registry office," he joked.[52]

White homeowners in Los Angeles invoked restrictive covenants more frequently than anywhere else in the state.[53] The most famous of the Los Angeles lawsuits involved several well-known African American businessmen, professionals, and actors, including Hattie McDaniel and Louise Beavers, who bought property in the formerly all-white Sugar Hill area of West Adams during the war. But covenants afflicted a host of lesser-known homebuyers as well. Between 1943 and 1947, whites throughout the southeastern and western parts of Los Angeles brought scores of suits against nonwhites for breaking covenants. To make their point, white residents worked outside the courts as well as through them; in early 1946, vigilantes even burned a cross on the lawn of an African American family who purchased a restricted home on West 56th Street.[54]

By the late 1940s, however, lawsuits and vandalism only stiffened the resolve of many middle-class nonwhite residents, often war veterans, who now united to enjoy some of the democracy for which they had fought overseas. In casual conversations and meetings with civic unity and other interracial activist groups in the years after the war, they discussed their frustrations and their disappointment with continuing legal support for racial restrictions in housing. These meetings led to legal tests as well as grassroots activism to stymie white homeowners' groups and their restrictive devices.

Strategies differed from region to region, depending both on local politics and racial geography. In cities where the wartime migration transformed demographics, such as San Francisco, judges generally upheld racially restrictive covenants; in areas with significant prewar black populations, including Los Angeles and Oakland, a growing number of justices, although certainly not all of them, began to question the legality of the devices. In the three years after World War II, several Los Angeles judges, including Stanley Mosk, Thurmond Clarke, and Frank Swain, ruled covenants against blacks, Chinese Americans, Nisei, Filipinos, Mexican Americans, and Jews unconstitutional or at least unenforceable.[55] In contrast, nonwhite San Franciscans fared less well in local courts, often fighting for their rights in front of older nativist judges like James G. Conlan.

San Francisco organizations thus avoided court challenges when possible. In 1946, a group of white residents in the Portola Heights neighborhood organized to sue two Asian Americans who purchased homes there. During the war, such segregationist activity flourished but attracted relatively little attention, as Mabel Tseng's experience on Nob Hill demonstrated. By 1946, however, the Council for Civic Unity sensed the potential of a new tactic—publicizing such incidents—because the mood of white San Franciscans seemed to have shifted in response to a confluence of events and trends: the campaign against Proposition 15, civic pride in the founding of the United Nations in the city, public horror over revelations about Nazi concentration camps, and growing outrage over the abuse of black servicemen returning to the South. In addition, the protagonists in the Portola Heights case could not have been more perfect: two honorably discharged veterans with attractive wives and families. Like so many white servicemen in overcrowded urban California, they merely wanted decent homes for their children. Even better, the Pulanco family was Filipino and the Yees were Chinese American, two ethnic groups widely seen as American "allies" during the war. Working with a new, multiracial area residents' group, the council informed the media about the proposed suit and the names of its backers. The council also held a rally in support of the buyers, eventually embarrassing the segregationists into dropping their lawsuit.[56]

The situation in Portola Heights was ideal for this approach. Both families had bought homes in Silver Terrace, a newer development in a neighborhood given an overall "D" grade by the HOLC because of the age and condition of its other homes, most of them at least thirty years old. The proximity of Hunters Point, its thousands of temporary wartime housing units, and their many black occupants made the neighborhood fairly undesirable to race-conscious whites. Some who supported the Yees and Pulancos did so out of conviction; others, anticipating possible racial transition, likely just wanted to keep their options open. In the more expensive and distant Lakeview and Monterey Heights neighborhoods, the Council for Civic Unity achieved little with its strategy of shame.[57]

In Los Angeles, the rulings of a growing number of judges emboldened nonwhite homeowners, who not only fought for their property in court but also organized to defeat covenants in less formal ways. The impending threat of lawsuits brought middle-class homeowners of different backgrounds together. In the mid-city area, black leader H. Claude Hudson and Korean American Yin Kim founded the Wilshire Defense Committee, a group of twenty-eight nonwhite families determined to hold on to their covenanted homes. The organization eventually helped twenty more nonwhite families buy in the same neighborhood by teaching them to circumvent white residents' legal strategies. Kim brought his furniture into his new home at night; when the sun rose, his neighbors served him with a court injunction forbidding him from taking possession of the property, but his late night move-in rendered the injunction moot. Wilshire Defense Committee members soon helped a number of other nonwhites surreptitiously move into their new homes as well, since courts often refused to uphold covenants in neighborhoods with substantial nonwhite populations.[58]

Kim also joined the Los Angeles Committee Against Restrictive Covenants, a citywide group of six nonwhite families that sought public support and funds for members' ongoing covenant suits. The composition of the group suggested the wide reach of racial restrictions in Los Angeles: besides Kim, founding members included three black families, a Chinese American named Tommy Amer, and Tsuneo Shigekuni, a Japanese American. One of the group's backers, the American Friends Service Committee, itself faced a lawsuit for allowing nonwhite students to live in a rooming house it owned on a restricted block just west of the University of Southern California.[59]

These individuals and small groups soon became part of a larger national struggle for housing rights. Since the early 1930s, the NAACP had been waging a successful step-by-step assault on different types of racial segregation, winning challenges to white primaries and segregated graduate education in the South. At the end of World War II, the NAACP, the ACLU, and other progressive organizations decided to revisit racially restrictive covenants as well. Lawyers for the ACLU and the NAACP eventually appealed the constitutionality of adverse covenant decisions from Michigan, Missouri, and the

District of Columbia all the way to the U.S. Supreme Court. As the cases progressed, Southern California ACLU counsel A. L. Wirin managed to con-vince the national ACLU to include Asian Americans in its challenge.[60] The organization's officials were initially skeptical; Clifford Forster, the national staff counsel, even dismissed the *Kim* and *Amer* appeals as a waste of valuable time and money. "I have no reason to think that the court does not know that restrictive covenants apply to persons other than Negroes," he complained.[61] But Wirin and other local civil rights lawyers such as the NAACP's Loren Miller understood California's legal racial hierarchy far better than Forster. In view of California's anti-Asian traditions, local attorneys believed that they needed a clear ruling from the Supreme Court about the applicability of covenants to Asian Americans as well as blacks.

Local civil rights lawyers did not include the Tsuneo Shigekuni lawsuit among their Asian American test cases almost certainly because of Shigekuni's Japanese ancestry. The Alien Land Acts continued to limit the property rights of both citizen and alien Japanese Americans, complicating any challenge of covenants that involved a Nisei. Indeed, by 1947, the Alien Land Acts posed an even bigger problem for Japanese Americans than they had in the years before the war. In attacking Pearl Harbor, Japan had abrogated its U.S. treaty, a document that protected the rights of the Issei to lease residential and com-mercial property in the United States. After the war, Issei entrepreneurs who returned to California hoping to restart their lives and businesses struggled to overcome this new problem.[62] Worse yet, after a spate of anti-internee hear-ings in mid-1943, the state legislature gave law enforcement officials greater powers to investigate alien land holdings and "escheat," or confiscate, the property of Japanese Americans found to have violated the Alien Land Act. State attorney general Robert Kenny quickly announced plans to create a spe-cial alien land unit to investigate what he called Japanese "subterfuges to retain possession of the State's agricultural lands." By late 1944, the unit had already escheated about $300,000 worth of Japanese American holdings. A July 1945 law directed the state to split escheatment profits with counties, giving local authorities a far greater stake in land law investigation than before. California legislators, many of whom represented rural areas where anti–Japanese Amer-ican sentiment still ran high, authorized more money for the alien land unit in 1945 and 1946.[63]

Kenny's ongoing support for land investigations revealed his own political ambitions. Kenny knew that Earl Warren's support for internment helped him become governor in 1942, and he planned to run for governor himself against Warren in 1946. Those Japanese Americans whom Kenny sued that year included decorated Nisei veterans, but in each instance, his office contended that Japanese American citizen ownership of property hid Issei interest in and profit from it. Through such claims and prosecutions, Kenny seemed determined to appeal to rural residents and to cloak his overall record of racial liberalism in parts of the state where it was a liability.[64]

Robert Kenny lost the June 1946 primary anyway, but L.A. County District Attorney Frederick N. Howser, who became state attorney general that year, refused to call off the land law prosecutions.[65] Howser promised during his campaign to "get tough" on Japanese American land cases, and he also relished any chance to "get his picture in the paper," at least according to colleagues. Even after voters rejected Proposition 15 in November 1946, Howser continued the state government's high-profile quest to investigate every Japanese American title in California. By early 1947, the alien land unit had brought more than seventy new escheatment cases against Japanese American property owners, almost all of them Nisei.[66]

Hoping to stop the prosecutions, the JACL challenged the racial basis of the Alien Land Act in the courts, selecting as a test case the state's escheatment of land belonging to Fred Oyama, a Nisei minor.[67] Japanese Americans had not disputed the legal validity of the act for more than two decades. However, JACL leaders knew that the record of the 442nd Regimental Combat Team and other Nisei troops was eroding old beliefs about Japanese American inassimilability and disloyalty. The recent war against Fascism cast further doubt on racialist laws; indeed, the white supremacist views of organizations such as the Native Sons of the Golden West and the California Joint Immigration Committee now sounded enough like Hitler's own doctrines to unsettle many white Californians horrified by newly released photos of Nazi concentration camps. Taking advantage of these shifts, the JACL and its attorneys contended that the Alien Land Act was unconstitutional, and they obliquely referred to Japanese American wartime military service as well.[68]

The California Supreme Court remained unmoved, citing U.S. Supreme Court cases from the 1920s and ruling that California had every right to escheat Oyama's land. But there was more. Prewar nativists long used the Alien Land Act to persuade Japanese Americans not to purchase even urban residential property, although the issue had never been fully settled through litigation. Now, the court contended that state law barred ineligible aliens from purchasing *any* type of real property, not just agricultural land. In taking this step, the court transformed a case that originally applied only to farmland and made it into one that affected the property of thousands of Nisei and Issei throughout urban California. Attorney General Howser certainly grasped the importance of the ruling; he began to target not only rural hold-ings but some urban residential property as well. Title insurance compa-nies also understood the case's significance: many now refused to work with Japanese Americans anywhere in the state, even in urban areas.[69]

The broadened enforcement of the Alien Land Act made the law's invalida-tion the JACL's top priority. The California court's new reading of the Alien Land Act placed far greater limits on urban Japanese Americans than even restrictive covenants. Although the JACL submitted an amicus brief to the Supreme Court in the restrictive covenant cases, the group's leaders put most of their time and money into challenging the California Supreme Court's deci-sion in *Oyama*. Appearing before the U.S. Supreme Court, attorneys for Fred Oyama argued that the Alien Land Act violated the Fourteenth Amendment by imposing burdens on Japanese American children that no other group had to bear. This was a novel argument, but in the end a convincing one, and in January 1948, the Supreme Court ruled in favor of Oyama. Although the justices upheld the basic right of California to restrict landholding to citizens and aliens eligible for citizenship, they found that one part of the Alien Land Act violated the U.S. Constitution. This half-victory saved Fred Oyama's land and persuaded California officials to end their aggressive escheatment campaign against the Nisei.[70]

Oyama was just one sign of the U.S. Supreme Court's growing impatience with supposedly race-neutral laws and practices that were acutely racial in re-ality. Less than three months after the *Oyama* ruling, the Court also refused to enforce racially restrictive covenants any longer. An extensive list of civil rights groups, progressive organizations, and veterans' associations submitted ami-cus briefs that opposed the restrictions; so did the State Department, which be-lieved that they embarrassed the United States abroad, especially in the devel-oping world where the United States now hoped to counter Soviet influence. The magnitude and breadth of the opposition, and the court's strong opinion, suggested the deeper changes the war had wrought. "It is clear that but for the active intervention of the state courts, supported by the full panoply of state power, petitioners would have been free to occupy the properties in question without restraint," noted Chief Justice Fred Vinson in his May 3 ruling on the most well-known case, *Shelley v. Kraemer*. "States have made available to such individuals the full coercive power of government to deny to petitioners, on the grounds of race or color, the enjoyment of property rights."[71]

The JACL rejoiced in the Court's covenant decision, but the group's leaders worried about its universality. The Court had not ruled on the *Kim* and *Amer* cases in its May 3 session, although Justice Vinson noted in his

Shelley decision that "we are informed . . . such agreements [covenants] have been directed against Indians, Jews, Chinese, Japanese, Mexicans, Hawaiians, Puerto Ricans, and Filipinos, among others." The vagueness of this footnote troubled Japanese American leaders, and they pushed the Court to clarify its position. The JACL newspaper *Pacific Citizen* portrayed the issue as one of education, contending that a ruling on *Kim* and *Amer* "would illustrate how the enforcement of racial deeds affects the well being of people other than those of Negro birth." Given California's history, and the mixed *Oyama* verdict, the JACL had a far more pressing motive: obtaining a verdict on the state's longstanding legal racial hierarchy. In *Shelley*, the Supreme Court contended that "the difference between judicial enforcement and nonenforcement of the restrictive covenants is the difference to petitioners between being denied rights of property available to other members of the community and being accorded full enjoyment of those rights on an equal footing."[72] But with Court sanction, California had denied Asian and Asian American residents full and equal enjoyment of property rights for almost forty years, a practice the *Oyama* decision did not wholly question. The justices likely understood the JACL's concerns, for they quickly remanded the *Amer* and *Kim* cases to the California Supreme Court with instructions to use *Shelley* in its reconsideration.[73]

The decision dealt a near fatal blow to the old legal racial hierarchy and emboldened the JACL to launch a final campaign to eliminate once and for all the influence of San Francisco-style nativism on California property rights.[74] Because of the 1946 California court ruling, aged Issei in the state could not buy any type of real property for their own use, prompting the JACL and ACLU to initiate two new land law challenges in California after the 1948 *Oyama* ruling. Significantly, both tests dealt with essentially residential property in the Los Angeles area—a far cry from the agricultural focus of earlier cases.[75] In the first and most significant case, *Sei Fujii v. California*, the Issei community leader and publisher Sei Fujii sued the state over its escheatment of land he purchased in East Los Angeles in 1948. Most of the same justices who rejected Fred Oyama's argument just days before the 1946 Proposition 15 vote now heard Fujii's case. Increasingly mindful of growing U.S. Supreme Court opposition to race-based laws, the justices this time reversed the lower court decision to escheat the Issei-owned property. In his ruling, Chief Justice Phil Gibson finally admitted the truth about California's old land statute: "by its terms the land law classifies persons on the basis of eligibility to citizenship but in fact it classifies on the basis of race or nationality." Using this decision, the same court three months later quieted the title to a home that JACL leader Mike Masaoka and his four brothers bought for their widowed

Issei mother in Pasadena.[76] Congress almost simultaneously passed the Immigration Act of 1952, creating small immigration quotas for all Asian nations and naturalization rights for the Issei. Together, the measure and the California court decision finally destroyed the old legal racial hierarchy once and for all.

THE SLOW PACE OF CHANGE

Civil rights and civic unity organizations throughout California hailed the U.S. Supreme Court's rejection of land laws and covenants, but the justices' decisions did not quickly alter residential patterns in the urban state. Most immediately, the rulings saved the property of scores of nonwhite homeowners facing covenant and escheatment suits. Under pressure from the NAACP and other groups, the FHA also changed its regulations in 1950, omitting from its manual the section that required racial restrictions on the homes it underwrote. However, this alteration of FHA regulations made a far smaller impact on the real estate industry than had almost two decades of federal policy that institutionalized and standardized the use of race in lending, sales, and planning decisions. By originally supporting restrictions as a way to reduce risk for lenders, federal authorities legitimized the idea that the mere presence of nonwhite residents reduced property values. In doing so, they entrenched the residential racial segregation that in 1934 was just a decade or two old in most American cities. And in places such as San Francisco, the federal government actually helped foster a new kind of discrimination—in this case, against African American home seekers—with such racial policies.

Despite the Supreme Court's covenant ruling, public agencies and private institutions also helped maintain all-white communities in numerous ways after 1948. Veterans Administration G.I. Bill provisions operated through the same private institutions that routinely redlined nonwhites. The FHA's bias towards new construction favored home buyers in the suburbs—suburbs that almost always excluded blacks and Asian Americans, and sometimes Mexican Americans and Jews, through sales practices and homeowner cooperation rather than racial restrictions. More obviously, federal agencies essentially underwrote many of these large suburban developments, such as the community of Lakewood in southern Los Angeles County, despite the practices of builders who openly discriminated against minorities.[77]

The persistence of widespread housing segregation after 1948 revealed the fundamental weakness of the *Shelley* ruling. Although it forbade court enforcement of covenants, it did not declare housing discrimination itself illegal. Back from his service in the military, San Francisco Chinatown housing activist Lim P. Lee described the case's outcome as an important first step, but too timid regardless. The Supreme Court justices "only had to make the essence of such contracts illegal and signing them punishable," he contended, yet they refused to do so.[78]

As Lee and others knew, the same white residents who supported abstract notions of "fair play" for Nisei veterans or Chinese "allies" still routinely refused to live alongside such people. Asian American homebuyers and renters thus continued to face extensive racial segregation in the post-1948 housing market, just as blacks and many Mexican Americans did. And such discrimination, widespread enough in older urban areas, was almost universal in newer suburban districts. In the northeastern section of South San Francisco, a city on the San Francisco peninsula, white residents threatened both black and Chinese American families who tried to buy homes in a previously all-white neighborhood. Vigilantes in L.A. burned down the home that an African American family bought on West 48th Street and the one a Nisei family rented in the suburb of Glendale. Tract developers throughout Los Angeles County and the Bay Area also refused to sell to any nonwhite buyer. In 1949, newly elected L.A. City Councilman Edward R. Roybal, a leader in the emerging civil rights coalition and the first Mexican American elected to the council in the twentieth century, discovered that only six of the county's hundreds of real estate firms would sell new suburban homes to nonwhites.[79]

For blacks and Asian Americans in particular, the end of restrictions and land laws thus meant the expansion of the neighborhoods in which they already lived rather than a newfound ability to buy anywhere they chose. The covenant decision had an especially marked impact on San Francisco; in less than three years, thousands of Chinese Americans moved out of Chinatown. Although racial discrimination continued to limit their choices, many Chinese Americans bought houses in the northeastern areas of the city or in other parts of the Bay Area.[80] The majority still lived close to Chinatown, which remained the center of their social and often their economic lives; its nearness also helped ease the culture shock that thousands of Chinese-speaking "war brides" experienced when they came to the United States after 1945. But their exodus from Chinatown belied old arguments that they liked living in the district's squalid, overcrowded tenements.

In the city of Los Angeles, as in much of the rest of the urban North, white resistance to integration grew increasingly ugly as the old unrestricted neighborhoods spread outward. Black and Asian American families began moving south and east from Watts and southern Los Angeles into formerly all-white areas of western Compton. Scores of African Americans, Chinese

Americans, and Japanese Americans also bought homes in the once restricted areas south of Slauson and west of Vermont, the rough boundaries of the integrated Central Avenue district in 1948. Many white homeowners simply left such neighborhoods as more attractive homes became available in the rapidly mushrooming suburbs. Others banded together to oppose integration with vandalism and sometimes violence. In the Leimert Park area near Santa Barbara Avenue and Crenshaw, whites formed Neighborly Endeavor, a benign-sounding residents' association that severely vandalized the home of the Wilson family, the first African Americans to move to the area. "When [the Wilsons] have learned to flood their neighbor's home, to leave dead rats on their neighbor's front porch or, better still, to throw dead rats through their neighbor's open window," wrote a sarcastic critic of the vigilantes, "they will be better equipped to meet the stringent standards of the white neighborhood." White residents of such areas saw little humor in the situation, however. "The only way to protect yourselves is to make sure that none of your neighbors sells to a non-Caucasian," argued a leading member of Neighborly Endeavor. "The law doesn't protect you so we will have to rely on each other." White homeowners in southern areas of the city and Compton soon joined the crusade, helping create a citywide segregationist organization they called Citizens United. Among other activities, group members spread sharp rocks and glass on the lawns of nonwhite homeowners and scattered threatening notes in transitional districts.[81]

While such white homeowners consistently opposed any kind of residential integration, their behavior suggested that they viewed African Americans as a particular threat to all-white neighborhoods. In most reported cases of housing vandalism or violence, the victims were black homeowners or renters. Asian American home seekers also faced intense resistance outside unrestricted areas; still, while a handful encountered direct intimidation, most tended to experience discrimination in the form of a real estate agent's or salesman's rejection. "They just tell you right off 'we don't sell it to you,'" recalled Charles Chinn, a Chinese American sheet metal worker.[82]

White perceptions of blacks as the major threat to white neighborhoods reflected predominant racial stereotypes and the growth of the African American population during the war, but they were also rooted in the old legal racial hierarchy. Before the war, anti-Asian laws and organizations gave white Californians inordinate power over their Asian American neighbors. A white man who grew up in the prewar Bay Area described the resulting "San Francisco stereotype of the Chinese" as one "who knows his menial place and sticks to it." In Los Angeles, white residents before the war used the tools that San

Francisco nativists created to keep Japanese Americans out of white districts—and to eject them from areas in which they had lived longer than most of their white neighbors. In contrast, only violence or restrictive covenants stopped black movement in many cases. Because whites generally preferred covenants (the legal option), the devices proliferated in Los Angeles, a city with a significant black population, but not in San Francisco, where the black community was small. The widespread use of restrictive covenants in wartime San Francisco highlighted the way nativism there had structured and preserved racial boundaries so effectively before the conflict. The swift wartime growth of the black population and its civil rights activism stunned white San Franciscans, accustomed as they were to Chinese Americans whose compromised citizenship status, political weakness, and social isolation kept them in their "place." Many whites reacted in an almost violent fashion to the new "threat": Katherine Archibald recalled that in the wartime shipyards, "physical repression, continually threatened and occasionally active, seemed to [white workers] the only means of keeping the Negro in his place."[83]

Postwar white Californians who had long employed legal methods to restrict Asian American residential ambitions were thus accustomed to using (or at least considering) more extreme techniques largely where African Americans were concerned. Deep-seated stereotypes about black criminality, aggression, and sexuality, and Asian passivity, informed these different approaches, but they also reflected traditional patterns of racial interaction in urban California. In Los Angeles, sociologist Wen-Hui Chung Chen noted that after 1948, "the white people do not run away from the Chinese as they do in the case of Negro invasion." The *San Francisco Chronicle* also described the "popular belief . . . that there is a hierarchy of property values, based upon the race of the occupant—with the white occupying top place in this hierarchy, the Oriental being less financially satisfactory, and the Negro occupying the bottom position." Yet as the *Chronicle* observed, whites hardly welcomed the arrival of Asian Americans. While not African American, they were certainly not white, or wholly "financially satisfactory." White residents usually reacted to them by leaving newly integrated neighborhoods eventually, if not immediately. In fact, many of the urban areas Asian Americans "pioneered" before 1951 became heavily nonwhite districts by 1960.[84]

THE END OF CLARITY

By the late 1940s, the multiracial progressive organizations that fought for integrated housing in California after the war faced growing hostility from conservative politicians and commentators both locally and nationally. Such antagonism was part of a national trend, a conservative response to increased fears of Soviet power, more than a decade of Democratic presidential administrations, and what historian Michael S. Sherry has called "Americans' quarrelsome, anxious mood" after the war. Republicans in particular took aim at the legacy of the New Deal, labeling it "socialism under the guise of liberalism" and the 1946 election a contest "between 'Communism and Republicanism.'" Richard Nixon, a young Whittier attorney, embraced such rhetoric, Red-baiting and ultimately defeating a popular liberal congressman, Democrat Jerry Voorhis. State officials, including state senator Jack Tenney, quickly followed Nixon's lead. As head of California's Fact-Finding Committee on Un-American Activities, Tenney, after the defeat of Proposition 15, turned his attention from Japanese Americans to Communists, using a series of 1947 and 1948 hearings across the state as a forum for his racial and political views. In a typical hearing, Tenney fulminated against "the intermarriage of races, Negroes and whites, which is part of the Communist philosophy of breaking down the races." Tenney echoed other conservatives determined to use the issue of Communism to roll back postwar civil rights achievements. Although they did not achieve this goal, the conservatives' fulminations often prompted CIO locals, race relations groups, and civil rights organizations to moderate their agendas and purge members perceived as too leftist or progressive.[85]

Almost simultaneously, the clarity of the struggle to defeat restrictive covenants gave way to the vaguer objective of achieving open and integrated housing. Interracial cooperation continued after 1948, at least at the organizational level; still, activists struggled to agree on goals in a state where different communities faced different kinds of discrimination. In Los Angeles and the Bay Area, Mexican Americans generally found homes more easily than Asian Americans or African Americans because of differing perceptions of their "whiteness"; a salesman at a Los Angeles-area development even told Councilman Edward Roybal that "we can't sell to Mexicans, but if you say you are of Spanish or Italian descent we will sell you the house." In contrast, accounts of vandalism and sometimes violence in transitional neighborhoods crowded the pages of California's African American newspapers.[86]

The differences between San Francisco's Chinese American and black and Japanese American populations vividly illustrated the way divergent interests divided nonwhite communities after 1948. Almost every nonwhite resident of San Francisco supported the struggle against racially restrictive covenants, which affected all minorities. Still, in the late 1940s, the local NAACP and

JACL branches and the Council for Civic Unity angered many Chinese Americans when they revived the old Western Addition Housing Council's challenge to the San Francisco Housing Authority's segregated "neighborhood pattern" system of tenant selection. By the time Congress passed the Housing Act of 1949, which gave the SFHA the funds to complete projects planned before the war, a number of civic leaders and housing advocates also supported complete integration of all public housing developments. Most Housing Authority officials were not among this group, however. In cities from Detroit to Chicago to Los Angeles, opponents of public housing after World War II exploited white fears of integration to thwart local housing authorities. SFHA officials were determined that the same thing would not happen in San Francisco. Defying a board of supervisors resolution that supported integration, the Housing Authority not only decided to keep the segregated "neighborhood pattern" but even hired a publicist to conduct a survey of avowedly pro-segregation groups, such as white homeowners' associations, to create an illusion of public support for the approach.[87]

Facing criticism of its racial policies, the SFHA also sought out credible minority allies, just as it had in 1942 with the Negro Advisory Committee. This time, however, the Housing Authority turned to Chinese Americans, the very people it had tried to ignore before the war. Chinese American leaders made no secret of their continued desire for a housing project that would serve Chinatown alone, and Housing Authority officials reassured them—and a still supportive white public—that the first project built with new federal funding would be such a development, despite land, material, and architectural costs that exceeded what Washington allowed. When builders completed Ping Yuen's first units in October 1951, the Housing Authority even threw a gala opening ceremony, complete with firecrackers and Chinese dragon dancers. In California and across the nation, huge numbers of white residents were turning against public housing, yet five thousand San Franciscans of all races attended the Ping Yuen festivities. Not coincidentally, the celebration generated much favorable publicity for the embattled SFHA. The most effusive commentators were members of the Chinese American press, but even the *San Francisco Chronicle*, a frequent critic of the Housing Authority, called the new project a "spacious, sunny, attractive . . . humanitarian enterprise."[88]

The controversy over public housing impeded the efforts of San Francisco's new interracial civil rights coalition to attract Chinese American organizations and activists. Such collaboration might have proved mutually beneficial: Portola Heights showed that Chinese Americans were perfect protagonists for the Council for Civic Unity's strategy of shame, but when they acted alone,

FIGURE 7.2. The front gate of the Ping Yuen federal public housing project in San Francisco's Chinatown (1956). At a time when the white public increasingly rejected such developments, five thousand people of all races attended Ping Yuen's opening ceremonies. (San Francisco History Center, San Francisco Public Library.)

they failed to defeat the segregationists of Nob Hill. Regardless, most Chinese Americans who chose to battle covenants before 1948 turned for help to traditional Chinatown groups, such as the CCBA, whether out of habit or a lack of familiarity with other organizations. Greater knowledge only came in the context of the housing project struggle, however, and it frustrated civil rights groups' attempts to make inroads in Chinatown. When Chinese American representatives attended a 1950 rally in support of open occupancy public housing, they refused to endorse the meeting's anti-segregation resolution; the Japanese American Citizens League, the Urban League, and the Council for Civic Unity all publicly signed the statement. Similarly, neither the Chinese American Citizens Alliance nor any other prominent Chinese American group backed a planned NAACP lawsuit to desegregate existing and future San Francisco public housing. In contrast, the JACL, the Council for Civic Unity, and similar groups endorsed the suit. Like many of their readers, *Chinese Press* editors saw the issue not as a civil rights problem, but as an issue that would "affect some 500 Chinese families in Chinatown" who would live in the Chinatown project. The debate eventually affected the 1952 mayoral campaign as well. Candidate John J. Sullivan, a city supervisor, ran advertisements in the Chinese-language press, claiming to be a "good friend of the Chinese, and opposed to racial discrimination," despite his widely-publicized vote *against* the board of supervisors' integration resolution. Sullivan won the endorsement of major Chinatown newspapers not in spite of the vote but because of it.[89]

Different nonwhite communities' wartime experiences and relationships with local and federal officials deeply influenced their perceptions of the issues at stake. During World War II, black San Franciscans lost the residential mobility that once distinguished their community, while Japanese Americans lost everything. Groups representing both communities associated the "neighborhood pattern" with increased segregation under government sanction. Chinese Americans, on the other hand, benefited markedly from the war and established ties with local authorities by highlighting their ethnicity and links to China. While civil rights groups called Ping Yuen a symbol of discrimination, a Chinese American reporter echoed sentiments in his community when he described it as "a strong, handsome, living memorial to a dream and its happy realization after more than fifteen years of 'blood, sweat and tears'. . . [and] America's pledge that a century-old wrong is being righted."[90] To Chinese Americans, Ping Yuen was official recognition of their importance to San Francisco and their unique place in it.

Chinese American opposition to public project integration also reflected economic and demographic realities, however. Like other war workers, including an inordinate number of nonwhites, thousands of Chinese American defense-sector employees lost their jobs at the end of World War II. Making matters worse in the heavily unionized city, numerous AFL locals continued to bar Asian Americans from membership.[91] The economic picture was not completely bleak; Chinatown's wartime and postwar tourist boom enriched many merchants, and hundreds of Chinese American veterans used the G.I. Bill to acquire the skills and education that made them newly desirable to white employers during the postwar economic expansion. Still, many Chinatown residents remained dependent on the low wage jobs available to them in the district's restaurants and shops. Thousands earned far too little to move to newly opened and more spacious areas outside Chinatown, yet Chinese American housing advocates knew that because of the wartime migration of African Americans, any changes in SFHA racial policy could result in needy blacks securing many of the units in Ping Yuen. If this occurred, the project would fail to relieve Chinatown's continuing housing shortage, especially for the district's many low income people.

Residents' sense of Chinatown as a uniquely Chinese space and a haven from white hostility also motivated their spirited defense of a homogenous Ping Yuen. Outside the district, as a woman who grew up in the Mission recalled, "I sensed [that] . . . being Chinese . . . was a vulnerability. At any moment you could be thrown out."[92] Having struggled to remain in San Francisco and to defend war-torn China from abroad, area residents took great pride in their district and their ethnicity; they also expressed a deep sense of ownership over the neighborhood. Many thus responded quite negatively to the prospect of outsiders residing in large numbers in the area—especially a neighborhood that still depended on perceptions of its "Chineseness" for economic survival.

The identity of the potential outsiders provoked particular concern. A multiracial Ping Yuen would bring African Americans into Chinatown as neighbors, an idea that created unease among many Chinese Americans and provoked outright resistance from others. In one pointed column, Gilbert Woo challenged what he saw as the anti-black sentiments of his community. "When it came to angrily protesting white discrimination against the yellow race, didn't we always speak out loudly and clearly?" he asked. "Perhaps, do the loud voices that ten years ago cried out to build Ping Yuen, today deeply regret it?" According to Woo, the issue was so touchy that some participants in Chinatown community housing meetings intentionally avoided it, while others made openly anti-black statements.[93]

EQUALLY UNEQUAL

While urban California's longtime legal racial hierarchy collapsed between 1943 and 1952, the residential racial segregation of all nonwhites persisted. Some racial dynamics had changed, of course. In Los Angeles, Japanese Americans began for the first time since the early 1920s to "pioneer" areas on the city's west side, with blacks then following—a reversal of prewar patterns. The SFHA even tried to thwart civil rights groups by "integrating" several all-white housing projects with a few token Chinese American and Japanese American families—but no African Americans. Such shifts revealed the amazingly rapid demise of anti-Asian nativism and the incredible shift in white racial perceptions, especially in San Francisco. After all, the SFHA had created the neighborhood pattern just a few years earlier in order to keep Asian Americans, not blacks, out of its projects.[94] Still, the gradual white exodus from areas Asian Americans pioneered between 1947 and 1951 demonstrated that in the private housing market, most whites remained fundamentally unwilling to live with nonwhites of any race or ancestry.

This continued white resistance to residential integration, together with a growing trend of violence against African Americans in particular, suggested that Asian Americans in the 1950s would become the vanguard of housing transition in urban California. Asian Americans with money, courage, and luck now pioneered many older white neighborhoods, and blacks often followed once the threat of violence and vandalism had subsided. The pattern was already apparent in Los Angeles's west side, in parts of Pasadena, and in sections of San Francisco and other Bay Area cities. Indeed, numerous areas that Asian Americans opened after 1948 rapidly filled with African American families who also sought decent homes for themselves. But the growing involvement of the United States in Asia, and ever-present fears of foreign and domestic Communism, soon spurred white Californians to reconsider the impact of their segregationist decisions. In the end, the deepening cold war short-circuited the emerging pattern and replaced it with a far different one.

"The Orientals Whose Friendship Is So Important": Asian Americans and the Values of Property in Cold War California

In late February 1952, residents of the Southwood tract of South San Francisco gathered to vote to accept or reject a new neighbor. The unofficial poll was the brainchild of the neighbor himself, a Chinese American named Sing Sheng. When he and his family purchased a home in all-white Southwood, they discovered that a number of other residents objected to their presence because of their race. Sheng, an aircraft mechanic, veteran of the Chinese Nationalist armed forces, and ardent believer in American democracy, had immigrated to the United States as a student just a few years earlier. He could not believe that the threats of a few white neighbors represented the feelings of the majority, but the poll soon set him straight: the Sheng family lost the "referendum" by 174 votes to 28. Within days, however, the local and national press picked up the story, sparking public outrage and a wave of sympathy for the Shengs. The family received hundreds of supportive telephone calls and letters and scores of offers of homes from white Americans who believed, as California senator William Knowland argued, that Southwood "will undoubtedly be put to the worst possible use by Communist propaganda in Asia."[1] Such attitudes eventually opened the mainstream housing market to Asian Americans, a process hastened by the publicity that a series of episodes similar to Southwood generated. By the 1960s, the supposed Asian American "foreignness" once used to defend residential segregation became white Californians' new rationale for Asian American inclusion.

In his 1947 Truman Doctrine, President Truman promised aid for nations fighting Communism, yet he simultaneously tried to disengage from Chiang Kai-shek's corrupt and incompetent Nationalist regime. After the 1945 defeat of Japan, China's Communist-Nationalist civil war, which dated to the late 1920s, started anew. Despite concerns about the spread of Communism, Secretary of State George Marshall and his advisors believed that the Kuomintang could not defeat the strong, disciplined, and comparatively uncorrupt Communists. Because Congress connected the Truman Doctrine directly to the China situation, however, legislators pressured the administration to continue assisting Chiang. Congressional and citizen support for "Free China" also remained strong enough to thwart frank public discussion of the Nationalists' shortcomings.[2]

In late 1949, the Chinese Communists surged to victory on the mainland, stunning an American public that still clung to wartime images of Chiang Kai-shek as China's beloved, unifying leader. During the late 1940s, the House Un-American Activities Committee (HUAC) had fueled public concerns about internal Communism by holding a series of hearings to investigate the alleged influence of subversives in the entertainment industry and other fields. Now, conservatives in the House and Senate, including Senator Joseph McCarthy, claimed that Truman administration tolerance of Communists within the federal government itself, and particularly the State Department, had led to the "loss" of China.[3]

In this poisonous environment, the U.S. public soon came to fear internal subversion as much, if not more, than the external threat that the Soviet Union posed to the nation. Some of the people who faced Senator McCarthy and his colleagues or HUAC committed real crimes against the nation. Many others were simply targets of the baseless witch hunts that McCarthy and his allies pursued against Americans whose politics they disliked, especially liberals and New Dealers. The nature of the cold war encouraged this increasingly paranoid domestic climate, as historian Stephen Whitfield has argued. "Unable to strike directly at the Russians, the most vigilant patriots went after the scalps of their own countrymen instead," he contends. This focus on internal subversion sent waves of fear through Chinese American communities across the nation, especially after the People's Republic of China entered the Korean War on the side of North Korea in late 1950. The example of the Japanese American internment was recent and raw, and some Chinese Americans faced persecution and even deportation for their political beliefs.[4]

Yet the nature of the cold war shielded Chinese Americans from a repeat of the internment. To begin with, McCarthy's focus on State Department elites—almost all of them white Protestants of northern and western European ancestry—contrasted with the racial assumptions of 1941 and 1942.[5] Equally significant, the geopolitical climate had also changed: the United States now sought to draw into its sphere the newly-independent, non-aligned nations of post–World War II Asia. The American government simultaneously helped rebuild Japan into what officials hoped would become a "bulwark of democracy" and a prime American ally in a region where several Communist insurgencies were already developing.[6] Domestic racial problems greatly complicated America's task, especially since the Soviets and the Chinese Communists both disavowed racism and exploited America's racial record in their propaganda. Black civil rights leaders encountered great resistance when they tried to use international opinion to advance their cause; Southern white politicians frequently equated black activism with Communism, while federal officials and policymakers usually tried to silence civil rights protesters rather than acknowledge their grievances. Still, according to scholar Mary Dudziak, "in the years following World War II, racial discrimination in the United States received increasing attention from other countries," fed Soviet propaganda, and "led to particular foreign relations problems with countries in Asia, Africa, and Latin America." Equally significant, a growing number of white Americans recognized this, whether or not they accepted the need for racial change.[7]

Longtime white perceptions of Asian Americans as perpetually foreign, biologically and culturally alien regardless of formal citizenship, took on new meanings in this context. During the 1950s, the United States provided millions of dollars of aid to anti-Communist regimes in countries like Taiwan, the Philippines, and Japan. Moreover, American troops fought and died in Korea and guarded U.S. bases throughout Asia, all in an attempt to contain Communism and preserve "democratic" (although often authoritarian) governments there. The U.S. government and many of the nation's cultural elites strove to explain such sacrifices to the public, portraying the people of "Free Asia" as America's partners in the anti-Communist struggle. As scholar Christina Klein observes, "the waging of the Cold War was as much a domestic endeavor as a political or military one [because] the American public . . . needed to be persuaded to accept the nation's sustained engagement in world affairs, its participation in international organizations, and its long-range cooperation with other governments."[8] By sacrificing American lives and money for Asian freedom, successive presidential administrations signaled the particular worthiness and value of Asians, while tolerating continued European colonization in Africa and the South's brutal Jim Crow practices.

During World War II, the frequent equation of Chinese Americans with China produced little improvement in Chinese American housing opportunities, but the particular circumstances and ideological tenor of the cold war changed the terms of the equation. The United States was no longer helping

China fight a common enemy but was instead competing with the Soviets and the Chinese Communists for the friendship of skeptical Asian nations. White Americans during the 1950s identified the suburban good life as part of the democratic capitalism they were offering to Asia, and that soldiers were fighting and dying to defend there. As historian Lizabeth Cohen has noted, there was "powerful symbolism . . . [in] the prosperous American alternative to the material deprivations of Communism." No one expressed this view better than Vice President Richard Nixon. During his 1959 "kitchen debate" with Soviet leader Nikita Khrushchev, the vice president "insisted that American superiority in the cold war rested not on weapons, but on the secure, abundant family life of modern suburban homes."[9]

By the mid-1950s, those who barred Asian Americans from sharing this kind of life faced a growing outcry from other white Californians, many of whom saw such discrimination both as a vehicle for Communist propaganda and as the belittling of American troops' sacrifices. Not all white Californians shared such ideas, to be sure; housing discrimination against Asian Americans continued throughout the state. Still, it began to decline noticeably, both because of the perceived need to include Asian Americans in the suburban good life and because American involvement in the cold war increasingly influenced white Californians' ideas about Asian worthiness and "values." The shift took place throughout the urban state, first becoming evident in the Bay Area and later in Los Angeles.

In both regions, perceived national security imperatives eventually overrode older local racial traditions. A series of publicized incidents reminiscent of the Southwood affair reflected this shift and also helped accelerate it by shaping white public opinion and reaffirming the social acceptability of Asian American integration. Because of the massive public reaction to each such event, a growing number of white homeowners not only began to consider the international ramifications of anti–Asian American discrimination but also the negative reactions their neighbors might have to it. Remarkably, this transformation took place at a time of intense black-white tension over housing integration throughout the urban North and much of the South. In cities such as Chicago, Detroit, Atlanta, Cleveland, Birmingham, Dallas, and Miami, African American neighborhood "pioneers" and home seekers faced violence and vandalism as white residents tried to preserve neighborhood racial homogeneity.[10] In contrast, the arrival of a few Asian American residents in a neighborhood in the late 1950s no longer prompted gradual racial transition and sometimes outright white flight the way it had in the late 1940s. Instead, by this point, the cold war was creating unique housing opportunities for people of

Asian ancestry in urban and suburban California—opportunities that African Americans did not usually share.

OUR RIGHTS ARE EQUAL TO YOURS

Few Asian Americans would have anticipated such an outcome in October 1950, when forces of the new People's Republic of China entered the Korean War on the side of North Korea. The involvement of China in the Korean War terrified many Chinese Americans already reeling from the implications of the Communists' 1949 victory on the mainland. By the late 1940s, large numbers of Chinese Americans had become disillusioned with the Kuomintang's corruption and incompetence. Conservative Chinatown leaders refused to acknowledge widespread anti-Kuomintang feeling, however, instead lashing out at anyone who questioned the legitimacy of Chiang Kai-shek's government. After Mao Zedong declared the founding of the People's Republic of China, thugs aligned with the San Francisco Kuomintang and its close ally, the CCBA (also known as "Chinese Six Companies"), even attacked a celebratory meeting at the Chinese American Citizens Alliance hall and posted the names of left-wing "bandits" marked for death. Once China entered the Korean War, Chinese Americans struggling to avoid the political infighting in their own community began to worry about attacks from other Americans as well. Worse yet, as Japanese American journalist Larry Tajiri tactfully noted, "Grant Avenue is particularly sensitive to talk of mass evacuation because there were a number of Japanese American businesses . . . in operation in San Francisco's Chinatown at the time of Pearl Harbor."[11]

The lack of widespread public demand for the internment of Chinese Americans demonstrated the stunning erosion of anti–Asian sentiment in California after World War II. By 1950, a growing number of white Californians and Americans in general questioned the earlier Japanese American internment and rejected the legitimacy of mass imprisonment on the basis of race or ethnicity. The publication of books like Milton Grodzin's *Americans Betrayed*, Rose McKee's *Wartime Exile*, and Mine Okubo's *Citizen 13660* within a few years of the war revealed the degree to which the white public was rethinking internment. So did the success of the 1951 film about the 442nd Regimental Combat Team, *Go for Broke*, the premier for which was attended by Vice President Alben Barkely. "Name a congressman in California or Oregon or Washington who has not heard of the 442nd," contended JACL official Richard Akagi in 1950. "Name a racist who will today question the loyalty of

Japanese Americans." Indeed, no major California politician demanded the incarceration of Chinese Americans in 1950. Governor Earl Warren, who had lobbied for Japanese American internment in 1942, publicly reassured Chinese Americans of his faith in their loyalty, as did Senator Richard Nixon.[12]

Still, the federal government quietly increased its surveillance of Chinese Americans and strengthened the power of Chinatown conservatives in the process. As historian Mae Ngai has shown, "the local Kuomintang, which overlapped with the Six Companies leadership . . . colluded with the FBI and INS to harass and deport Chinatown leftists." This combination of external and intracommunity pressure eventually forced publishers to close the *China Weekly* and the *Chung Sai Yat Po* newspapers, both of which expressed sympathy for the People's Republic of China. Gilbert Woo, now operating his own newspaper, also ran afoul of Kuomintang leaders for his balanced coverage of the Chinese civil war and its aftermath. His publication survived, but even Woo joined a Chinatown merchant and labor organization, the Ying On Association, for protection.[13]

San Francisco's distinctly transnational Chinese American community struggled to reinvent its identity and politics as the Korean War continued. Gilbert Woo urged his fellow Chinese American citizens not to slip into passivity or forget that they were now legally equal to whites. "This sentence, 'Our Rights Are Equal to Yours,' should be displayed in each Chinese citizen's home, and he should be made to memorize it day and night," Woo contended.[14] But the new political environment created deep uncertainty in Chinatown. Chinese Americans' transnational identity and white perceptions of their ties to China had facilitated their entry into San Francisco politics in the 1930s, making possible the success of the Bowl of Rice parties, the campaign for a Chinatown housing project, lighting for the Chinatown school playground, and local officials' appointments of Chinese Americans to various boards and commissions. The repeal of exclusion in 1943 helped remedy the problem of disfranchisement that originally forced Chinese Americans to leverage white sympathy for China into political gains in San Francisco. At the same time, Chinatown's thousands of new votes would count for little if hostile whites linked Chinese Americans to "Red China." In the years after 1949, then, numerous Chinese Americans tried to recast the image of their community, a process that provoked internal disagreements and helped muffle progressive voices.

Chinese politics cast a long shadow over every effort, since despite widespread community skepticism about the Kuomintang, most Chinese Americans in San Francisco publicly supported the government in Taiwan out of fear of being labeled Communist. Larry Tajiri observed that Chinese Americans "are caught in the jaws of an ideological nutcracker," because Nationalist officials often seemed to speak for them, yet any "disavowal [of such statements] may be mistakenly interpreted in some quarters to mean an avowal of the Peiping government." Indeed, the Republic of China's existence was a double-edged sword for Chinese Americans. On the one hand, the Republic of China acted as a non-Communist "homeland," an important role because so many whites still considered all Chinese Americans essentially foreigners. At the same time, the presence of the Republic of China–backed American Kuomintang in Chinatown and the support it received from the U.S. government empowered the very conservatives who at the end of World War II were losing influence in the community.[15]

In the early 1950s, many prominent Chinese Americans worked to distance San Francisco's Chinatown from the People's Republic of China and to revive tourism in the district at the same time. After 1949, Chinatown businesses struggled, for the Communists' victory and the Korean War temporarily soured public opinion of things Chinese and also cut merchants off from their suppliers on the mainland. Ironically, some of the same stores that fought Japanese American business "invasion" ten years earlier now offered Japanese goods for sale. To bring in more tourists, the members of the Chinese Chamber of Commerce and other community groups started holding colorful New Year's festivals and beauty pageants with political undertones. As historian Chiou-Ling Yeh notes, these festivals helped business and community leaders promote Chinese Americans "as nonthreatening and contented with the existing social order," as well as people who "embod[ied] the 'authentic' Chinese culture." Judy Wu contends that such celebrations also "promoted an exotic image to fulfill the expectations of white tourists."[16] In other words, the new strategy was much like the prewar one: it depended on and thus often reaffirmed white views of Chinese American difference, foreignness, and passivity.

This strategy, together with the renewed strength of Chinatown conservatives, both marginalized Chinese Americans who fought for social change and concealed the continued political diversity of the community. Members of leftist organizations, such as Min Qing, suffered because of their politics, becoming prime targets of the FBI in the years after 1948. But business leaders' emphasis on Chinese American "passivity" even undermined the efforts of liberals and moderates. Lim P. Lee remained a critic of segregation and moved in the city's progressive Democratic Party circles, yet his friend Gilbert Woo noted years later that while Lee "fought for admission into white society and resisted discrimination, his greatest obstacles came from his own Chinatown." Woo's liberal *Taipingyang* newspaper successfully withstood conservative boycotts, belying the image of passivity, conformity, and conservatism that community leaders attempted to create. At the same time, however, Woo felt the need to constantly urge his readers to assert their rights as American citizens. "Just because our ancestors were Chinese, we can't beg others for mercy," he wrote. "This only brings about greater bullying."[17]

THE MEANING OF "VALUES"

The Southwood vote came at a particularly awkward moment, not only for Chinese Americans struggling with issues of identity, but for all nonwhites in California. Two months before the Sheng affair, an organization called America Plus announced plans to gather signatures to place a "Freedom of Choice" initiative on the November 1952 ballot in California. The organization was a conservative rejoinder to the state's progressive civil rights coalition and reflected the kind of post-*Shelley* housing tensions now palpable throughout the urban state and much of the rest of the nation. The group's initiative promised to invalidate the state's existing civil rights laws and guarantee every citizen the right to discriminate against anyone else in employment, housing, and other areas. Civil rights groups worried that America Plus could win in California by using the ongoing red scare to legitimize white resistance to integration, casting it as the right to freedom of association.[18]

America Plus's backers hailed the Southwood referendum as just what they had in mind. State senator Jack Tenney, a major supporter of the initiative, praised Sing Sheng for submitting to a vote and said, "if people don't have the right to vote on their neighbors, they don't have the right to vote on their president." Echoing America Plus's rhetoric about freedom of association and choice, Southwood's defenders also claimed that democracy equaled the right to select one's own friends and neighbors. Jack Stockton, who lived on the street where the Shengs hoped to move, argued that, "I, as an American, like to live with my own race of people." According to William Grapengeter, Jr., another resident, "now that the world is criticizing Southwood for this election, I have come to feel that the world is trying to take away my vote and my right to say what I think."[19]

To bolster their arguments, Southwood residents used the kind of property values language they felt many other white Americans, especially Californians, would understand. After the *Shelley* decision, real estate agents, bankers, and insurers continued to claim that nonwhites hurt property values, so

Southwood resident and spokesman Clinton Kenney assumed a sympathetic audience when he argued that "when one oriental or any one of a minority group comes into an area others follow. The property value then drops correspondingly." The Southwooders even blamed their property value concerns and their votes not on personal prejudice, but on the sentiments of other white people. According to Kenney, the Shengs' arrival would have left Southwood families with homes "materially depreciated through no fault of [our] own but through the racial prejudices of others."[20]

But like so many other white Americans, the Southwooders' property "values" involved much more than money. White segregationists across the United States considered home ownership symbolic not just of their financial stability, but of their morality, character, and social status. In his study of postwar Detroit, historian Thomas Sugrue describes this world view:

> To white Detroiters, the wretched conditions in Paradise Valley and other poor African American neighborhoods were the fault of irresponsible blacks, not greedy landlords or neglectful city officials. . . . Many Detroit whites interpreted [these] poor housing conditions as a sign of personal failure and family breakdown.[21]

In other words, the "values"—or lack of them—that many white Detroit residents ascribed to blacks contrasted markedly with the values they saw themselves embodying. Similarly, as Becky Nicolaides has shown, postwar white working-class homeowners in Los Angeles County simultaneously "embraced self-reliance, independence, Americanism, familism, and racial separation." The first four ideals depended to a significant extent on the fifth.[22] White homeowners like the Southwooders feared that racial mixing—with interracial marriage the inevitable endpoint—threatened the rest. It certainly threatened their ability to claim these values as racially unique.

By using arguments about property "values" against the Sheng family, however, the Southwooders stumbled into a cold war trap. In 1952, much of the black population of the South still could not vote; in the North, many local officials and community leaders openly fought residential integration. Yet at the same time, American policymakers were sacrificing American lives and money for Asian freedom and democracy. This was a strong statement. If Asians did not share the very American "values"—independence, individualism, and self-reliance—that white Americans so often refused to see in blacks, then this sacrifice was pointless.

America's deepening involvement in the "hot" cold war in Asia thus forced the many white Californians who thought of Asian Americans as essentially foreign to choose between two competing fears. The first was an older, but very powerful, concern about integration and its impact not just on whites' literal property values but also on their social status and racial and sexual "purity." The second fear was a newer, but equally compelling, dread of Communism and the almost supernatural power that many Americans attributed to it. During World War II, America's enemies were almost entirely outside its borders, either literally (the Axis powers) or figuratively (the Japanese American population that so many other Californians identified as an enemy presence). In contrast, historian Elaine Tyler May notes, "it is well to recall that McCarthyism was directed against perceived internal dangers, not external ones."[23] Some of those dangers came from Communist spies and domestic subversives consciously acting to weaken America, but others supposedly derived from the unwitting actions of well-meaning Americans—including the Southwood neighbors, now supposedly exposed as Communist dupes.

Coming in the midst of the Korean War, Southwood thus marked a turning point for numerous white Californians, who began to deem the cost of preserving Asian American segregation too high for the nation to bear. The incident was so powerful in this regard that it effectively undermined growing white support for America Plus in California. Once the organization's leaders publicly embraced the Southwood neighbors, the initiative lost much of its backing in the state. Unable to gather enough signatures for "Freedom of Choice," the group's sponsors left California for the more welcoming environment of Oklahoma.[24]

REFRIED RICE

Despite the national outrage over Southwood, Gilbert Woo warned his readers that the incident was unique and that it had no larger significance. "After the uproar is over, this new and unusual flavor will be gone," predicted Woo. "This rice can't be fried again." A jarring event that occurred just weeks after Southwood appeared to support Woo's view. In March 1952, white vigilantes firebombed the home of a black teacher who had moved into a formerly all-white neighborhood on the west side of Los Angeles. When three state assemblymen introduced a resolution arguing that "such incidents are not in keeping with the American tradition and way of life and furnish material to be used as propaganda by the Communists," the measure died in committee.

Although its language mirrored the words critics used to denounce the Southwood voters, the resolution's demise attracted little attention. Nor did scores of editors, citizens, and elected officials across the country rush to condemn the vigilantes of Los Angeles.[25]

Woo's own experiences gave him no reason to differentiate between Southwood and the Los Angeles bombing. During World War II, the journalist watched angrily as white San Franciscans praised Chinese Americans while maintaining their strict residential segregation inside Chinatown. Whatever ethnic advantages Woo's readers enjoyed in wartime quickly evaporated after V-J Day, and such benefits never extended to the private housing market anyway. When Chinese Americans defied racial boundaries, white residents increasingly lumped them together with other Asian Americans as undifferentiated and undesirable "Orientals."[26] Either way, they were not welcome in most districts; San Francisco's Chinese Americans only managed to move into neighboring Nob Hill after restrictive covenants lost legal force. Even war veterans with college and graduate degrees and G.I. Bill financing struggled to find anyone willing to sell to them in the suburbs.

In other words, lingering anti-Asian sentiment continued to inform white attitudes about Asian Americans despite nativism's decline as a political force in California. White homeowners in racial border areas reacted to black neighborhood "incursions" with a degree of violence uncommon in cases involving Asian Americans, but they still saw the latter as undesirable. After the Southwood controversy died down, white residents of the South San Francisco tract who discussed their feelings about the Sheng family revealed the way old nativist tropes endured:

[Sheng] should live with his own people in a Chinese district. . . . Sheng would be paving the way for his own countrymen and for Negroes. Our children don't know the difference and might marry one someday. . . . Chinamen can live on ten cents a day and save lots of money. They would move three families into one house in order to finance it.[27]

These statements reflected the same ideas about Asian racial inassimilability, low living standards, foreignness, and disloyalty that San Francisco nativists helped embed in state and federal law and local custom in the nineteenth century. Although anti-Asian organizations no longer wielded much political power, then, their beliefs endured in other ways. Little wonder the JACL's *Pacific Citizen* agreed with Gilbert Woo and criticized Sing Sheng for "establishing a precedent in a neighborhood vote to accept or reject a minority group."[28]

What Woo and JACL officials did yet not perceive, however, was the way that Asia's newfound importance to America's global interests was slowly reshaping California by the early 1950s. The defeat of Japan ended Californians' worries about Japanese invasion, but the rise of Chinese Communism stoked new fears. And perched on the edge of the Pacific, Californians encountered constant reminders of America's involvement in cold war Asia: the growing number of military facilities and defense contractors within the state; civic leaders' focus on increasing trade with the Pacific region; stridently anti-Communist politicians such as Senator Knowland, with deep ties to "democratic" regimes in Asia; and even a trickle of Asian military brides joining white or African American husbands. The state also boasted the largest population of war veterans in the nation, a fact historian Lisa McGirr contends "reinforced a sense of commitment to defending America against perceived threats from within and without." Some of these factors were present during World War II, when concerns about Japanese propaganda motivated many white Californians to support the repeal of Chinese exclusion. But that legislation received public support in large part because its tiny quota for Chinese immigration made no real impact on white lives, jobs, and neighborhoods. Now, however, the United States was not simply helping ally China fight a shared enemy but in fact competing with the Soviet Union and the People's Republic of China for the hearts and minds of Asian peoples. In order to win this conflict, Americans needed to sell their values to a skeptical Asian public.[29]

Crucially, California's history—as a place where the rights of much of the nonwhite population had always been tied directly to relations with Asia—shaped how and where its white citizens fought this new kind of war. Before the 1950s, white Californians strictly limited Asian American property rights with little concern for the consequences of such choices. But accustomed to linking Asian Americans to their nations of origin, a growing segment of the white population now started paying a great deal of attention to what many saw as the possible ramifications of the poor treatment of Asian Americans. White Californians did not shed traditional ideas about Asian American undesirability overnight. Still, a growing segment showed a real willingness to make the racial "sacrifices" they now deemed necessary to win the cold war. Such sacrifices included integrating Asian Americans into the otherwise all-white communities that epitomized the prosperity and independence for which the United States was supposedly fighting. If white homeowners excluded Asian Americans from these neighborhoods, a growing number argued, how could they expect Asian nations to spurn Communist suitors and join the American-led community of democratic countries?

Near the end of 1952, another incident of anti–Asian American residential discrimination revealed the impact that Southwood, and the cold war in Asia, had begun to make on the housing market in California. This episode took place in San Jose, a fast-growing community with strong military and defense industry ties. In early October, a disabled Nisei veteran of the 442nd, Sam Yoshihara, put a deposit on a home in an all-white residential area of the city. Soon after, twenty-four white neighbors of Thornton Way, Yoshihara's new street, signed a petition rejecting the Nisei buyer because of his race. Once the press caught wind of the story, however, scores of white San Jose residents, a host of area veterans' groups, and a local Congressional Medal of Honor winner all publicly excoriated the segregationists. While a civic unity group spokesman described the incident as an example of the pervasive discrimination all nonwhites faced, most Yoshihara supporters publicly condemned the petitioners for "allow[ing] the Communists to make propaganda from an incident like this," as one told reporters.[30]

Although cultural elites and the U.S. government worked to portray Asian allies in a favorable light to the American public, even many of Yoshihara's supporters believed that Asian Americans might harm property values. The twenty-four signers of the petition insisted that they acted "not because of any feeling of discrimination . . . but rather, under the laws of our country that each man has the right to protect the value of his property and his home." Instead of refuting the argument, a number of Yoshihara's backers simply accepted lower property values as the cost of freedom. Speaking to reporters, Thornton Way resident Vivian Gardner, who refused to sign the petition, argued that "my property values aren't as important as my principles." Like many Yoshihara supporters, Gardner accepted a loss in property values as necessary for a larger purpose. That purpose, according to the *San Jose News*, was to prevent another Southwood, where neighbors had already done too much to help "Communist propaganda . . . prove that Americans are intolerant toward the Orientals whose friendship is so important." Fearful of paying a different kind of price as newly outed Communist dupes, the Thornton Way twenty-four quickly drafted a new petition apologizing for any "misunderstanding" and welcoming Yoshihara to the neighborhood.[31]

Despite Gilbert Woo's skepticism, then, this rice could be fried again, and it was throughout the rapidly developing suburbs of northern California. In a series of incidents involving attractive, financially secure, and well-educated Asian American families with unquestionably solid "values," white journalists, civic leaders, and regular citizens reaffirmed the cold war links that thousands of homeowners had begun to make. In 1953, Earl Goon and his wife received a threatening letter as they built a home in a Watsonville subdivision. The *Watsonville Register-Pajaronian* berated the anonymous author and asserted that "it takes only a few crackpots to give a community a lasting black eye [and] to do immeasurable damage to the cause of the United States." In 1954, local papers reported that white residents were protesting the plans of Dr. William Lee, a Stanford University research chemist, to purchase a home in Palo Alto Scores of white Bay Area residents contacted Lee and his family to support them and offer them homes, while the *Daily Palo Alto Times* lambasted the segregationists for violating "the American sense of fair play [and] Christian brotherhood." The following year, a white homeowner received a death threat when he sold his San Leandro home to Japanese American dentist Satoru Larry Aikawa. Once again, dozens rushed to the aid of the Aikawa family, offering homes and support.[32]

Unlike Sing Sheng, none of these Asian Americans linked their personal encounters with discrimination directly to the larger global fight against Communism, nor did groups such as the JACL make such claims. Whatever their transnational ties, both Chinese Americans and Japanese Americans in California had, by the 1950s, experienced tremendous difficulties because of the way others connected them to international relations. The families in question merely expressed their frustration at ongoing housing discrimination. Earl Goon and his wife asked their anonymous opponent: "Why do you resent us? Because our ancestors came from China? Where did yours come from? Are you so certain that they were so much better than ours?" Skirting any mention of global politics, the San Francisco-born William Lee simply noted that after attending graduate school in the Midwest, "I had forgotten what things could be like here [in California]." Satoru Larry Aikawa complained that "I've been trying for three months to find a home close to my offices, but the real estate agents say they are afraid if they sell to an Oriental they will be kicked off the Southern Alameda County Real Estate Board."[33]

In contrast, a white public that saw Asian Americans as surrogate Asians embraced cold war conceptions of such incidents far more readily than the reality of housing segregation in California. The media's portrayal of Southwood-style episodes as embarrassing aberrations contributed to such an interpretation. Editorials sought to isolate segregationists in each instance and to highlight the groundswell of public sentiment for Asian American acceptance. In San Jose, the petitioners of Thornton Way withdrew their complaint because of a "snowballing display of public disapproval of their original stand," according to the *San Jose Mercury*. The *Watsonville Register-Pajoranian* contended that the Goon family's "unsigned letter is the work of a crank, a crackpot." Commenting on William Lee's experience in Palo Alto, the *Daily Palo Alto Times* informed readers that "this type of prejudice is on its way out . . . [and] manifestations of it now run up against outspoken public opinion." The *Oakland Tribune* emphasized that the Aikawa family had received "dozens of offers of homes throughout the Metropolitan Oakland area" after the incident of discrimination in San Leandro.[34] In writing this way, editors helped shame the white residents involved, but they also whitewashed the extent of anti-Asian discrimination that still existed.

Like some of these editors, a number of the citizens who participated in Southwood echoes seemed more interested in absolving their communities of culpability for segregation than of actually challenging the practice, as Dr. Aikawa learned. White residents of San Leandro, where he hoped to buy a home, worked constantly to keep out nonwhites, particularly African Americans from neighboring Oakland. Facing national scrutiny for discriminating against the Aikawas, a number of San Leandrans publicly disavowed prejudice, but only while the spotlight shined on them. A builder who offered the Aikawas a home in another part of San Leandro later raised the price by $1,000 when the couple actually tried to take him up on the deal. After willing sellers in a different neighborhood began negotiations with the Aikawa family, other residents quickly balked at even this token integration. When three real estate firms started knocking on doors in the area in an attempt at blockbusting, the Aikawas quickly withdrew their bid.[35]

But overall, media coverage of Southwood's echoes, as well as the massive public responses these incidents prompted, reflected the genuine popular indignation and concern that grew with each new episode. Christina Klein has argued that during the cold war, anti-Communism became "a structure of feeling and a set of social and cultural practices that could be lived at the level of everyday life." As a consequence, "ordinary Americans could take part in the 'world struggle' by naming names, testifying before investigatory committees, enlisting their local community groups in the crusade, and keeping an eye on their neighbors." Throughout the Bay Area, hundreds of white citizens found other, more positive ways to participate, responding to Southwood echoes out of a desire to do something to help win the vast, frightening, and open-ended cold war whose evidence littered their everyday lives. Dozens of these people made good faith home offers to the Asian American families involved in Southwood and its echoes. After the initial uproar, the Shengs found a house in an all-white neighborhood of Menlo Park, where neighbors welcomed them. The Lees were able to buy a home just a few blocks away from the location of their initial choice, while the Aikawas eventually settled in one of the houses offered to them after their plight became public.[36]

Other white residents, unable to help the home seekers find a place to live, sought different ways to assist them. Several veterans' organizations offered Yoshihara formal membership so that they could fight more effectively on his behalf. The Lee family's Menlo Park neighbors contacted the press to vouch publicly for the family's desirability. A television shop owner who lived near the Aikawas' first choice of home was so angry about their treatment that he even went door to door on his own block to gauge other residents' feelings. "We spend millions of dollars all over the world to combat Communist propaganda and then some little incident like this helps to destroy all the good we've done," he explained.[37] In taking such actions, he and others who shared his ideas felt that they were doing their part to win the cold war in Asia.

THE LIMITS OF COLD WAR RACIAL CHANGE
IN CALIFORNIA

By the mid-1950s, a growing number of white community leaders and businesspeople had come to fear the kind of publicity that anti-Asian housing incidents could generate. The embarrassed city officials and businesspeople forced to make stammering apologies in the press or to publicly condemn discrimination long tolerated in private were a wake-up call to community leaders elsewhere. No city legislature wanted to be like the South San Francisco City Council, which in the wake of Southwood had to declare defensively that "the overwhelming majority of the residents of this city are actuated by the principles of democracy and are opposed to racial prejudice." Nor did real estate agents wish to emulate Roy Hoefler, the manager of the company that employed Sam Yoshihara's real estate agent; when Hoefler quietly fired the man for selling to a Nisei, media attention forced him to make a public statement denying any connection between his decision and the Yoshihara affair. Less than three years later, the Southern Alameda County Real Estate Board could not even pull a Hoefler and discipline the broker involved. Instead, Dr. Aikawa's accusations against the organization forced it to publicly disavow the racial segregation it privately helped create.[38]

The JACL soon learned to use communities' fears of adverse publicity to its advantage. In 1956, Gladwin Hill of the *New York Times* argued that the organization "has not . . . made a public issue out of instances of discrimination in the real estate field, on the theory that such friction can better be worked out privately." In fact, JACL legal counsel Frank Chuman used this tactic because he realized that real estate agents and civic leaders increasingly feared public exposure if they discriminated against Asian Americans. Although Chuman did not openly connect his strategy to Southwood, it was intimately linked to that incident: he successfully deployed it for the first time less than a month after Southwood made headlines. In the years that followed, he contacted developers, lending institutions, military officers, state and federal officials, governors, civic leaders, and U.S. senators to press for the quiet resolution of anti-Nisei bias cases throughout the Los Angeles area, and he almost always succeeded.[39]

Although scholars in recent years have explored the connection between domestic civil rights and international relations, many Americans in the 1950s were already well aware of foreign criticism of the nation's racial record. As journalist Harold Isaacs noted in 1958, "we hear a great deal nowadays about the effect of American race relations on American standing in world affairs." Still, international opinion itself, rather than American knowledge of it, created whatever change occurred. As Mary Dudziak has shown:

> Domestic racism and civil rights protest led to international criticism of the U.S. government. International criticism led the federal government to respond, through placating foreign critics by reframing the narrative of race in America, and through promoting some level of social change. . . . in order to make credible the government's argument about race and democracy.[40]

In other words, foreign opinion itself—not American citizens' concerns about it—effected some token shifts for blacks.[41]

But in instances involving Asian Americans, white Californians took the initiative, criticizing other white homeowners and worrying about Asian public opinion before it even materialized. While scholars today contend that citizens of Asian nations at the time focused on America's treatment of its black population, many white Californians never made such a connection.[42] Instead, their actions betrayed their assumption that Asians cared mainly about the treatment of Asian Americans. If anything, such a belief reflected the kind of race consciousness and tacit sense of white solidarity necessary to maintain segregated neighborhoods in the first place.

While a growing number of white neighborhoods and civic leaders thus tried to avoid Southwood-style embarrassments, far fewer worried about the implications of anti-black discrimination, public or not. Less than a month after Southwood, white residents of the Rollingwood tract of San Pablo, a Bay Area suburb, organized to oust an African American family that had just purchased a home there. Publicity did not discourage white Rollingwood in the least; receiving tacit support from law enforcement officials, segregationists continued their resistance for weeks, even stoning the family's home and burning a cross on its lawn. In late 1953, white residents of a South San Francisco neighborhood less than three miles from Southwood took an informal poll that showed overwhelming resistance to a black family that was moving there. Regardless of the strong Southwood overtones in their vote, white neighbors met openly to plan strategy and to tell reporters that "we won't serve [the family] ice cream every night." Four months after Bay Area residents flooded William Lee and his family with calls offering them homes, all twenty-one white buyers in a slow-selling Benicia subdivision accepted the developer's offer to refund their deposits; he had decided to offer homes to African Americans as well as whites. Just a few months after the Aikawa family received home offers throughout the region, real estate firms in Menlo Park openly participated in the blockbusting of the Belle Haven section, which transitioned from all-white to almost completely African American within two years.[43] Each of these cases received token press coverage, and some even elicited angry editorials from local papers. Still, few journalists and even fewer members of the public discussed the cold war ramifications of these episodes. Equally significant, none of the African American families involved received the scores of phone calls, letters, and home offers that marked each Southwood echo.

White homeowners who of their own accord linked Asian American discrimination to the cold war expressed far greater suspicion about the motives of African American home seekers. At Southwood, a few tract residents contended that subversives caused the uproar, but no one dared accuse the Shengs themselves of malevolent motives. Yet white neighbors frequently did just than when describing African American neighborhood "pioneers." The accusations of white Rollingwood resident Fred Steger, who contended that "the moving of [the Gary family] into Rollingwood was a Communist conspiracy to mix up races," received loud applause from other neighbors. In South San Francisco, white residents claimed that the black family in question "was put there by a group," the NAACP, that they deemed highly suspicious.[44]

The Korean War and Southwood-style incidents thus helped spur a degree of racial transformation that was far from inevitable in the urban Bay Area, with its nativist past. Within a year of Southwood, residents of some all-white Bay Area communities began to express far greater acceptance of potential

"Oriental" neighbors than of black ones. Real estate agents, a group particularly sensitive to their image and to white community sentiment, confirmed
the growth of this attitude among their clients by the mid-1950s. "Orientals
are generally accepted, but the Negro is a special problem," contended a
San Francisco broker. Another argued that "Japanese and Chinese are often
accepted almost like whites," while a third claimed that "generally, the feeling
is against non-Caucasians, but most people will qualify this by saying they
mind Orientals less than Negroes." Within just three or four years, then,
white opinions about racial desirability had changed remarkably, and within
two decades, perceptions of Asian American and black desirability had been
almost transposed. Frank Quinn, the San Francisco Council for Civic Unity's
executive director, revealed the extent of this change when he discussed an
incident involving "a Negro doctor . . . who offered $24,000 for a home and
was turned down because of his race by the owner. The same home was sold
the next week for $22,000 to a Chinese American family."[45]

Such attitude shifts influenced the decisions of some critical institutions as
well. "Insurance firms will accept Orientals, but they will not accept Negroes,"
confirmed a man familiar with the Bay Area housing market. The preference
extended only so far: lenders continued to discriminate against Asian Americans, although not as much as against blacks. This was particularly the case
in northern California's older neighborhoods, where because of age, neither
the FHA nor the VA would underwrite financing for available homes. Cal-
Vet, the state's own mortgage program for veterans, also refused to disavow
discriminatory developers, creating even more problems for Asian Americans
and other nonwhites trying to arrange financing.[46] Yet the willingness of so
many Bay Area brokers to sell to Asian Americans once they obtained financing suggested the growing importance of economics, rather than race, to the
residential mobility of Chinese Americans and Japanese Americans.

Indeed, the fact that an increasing number of whites were willing to see
Asian Americans as potential neighbors created some of the very incidents
that exposed lingering discrimination against people of Asian ancestry. Just
a few months after Southwood, Sam Yoshihara managed to find a real estate
agent who would sell him a home in an all-white neighborhood. Less than two
years later, builder John Mackay told William Lee and his family that he "was
sure it would be all right" with other tract residents to sell to Chinese Americans; the negative reaction of the Palo Alto neighbors took him by surprise.
By 1955, U.C. Berkeley sociology students discovered that twice as many
brokers would sell to "Orientals" as to blacks in neighborhoods where members of neither group lived. When an undercover white investigator visited

a real estate agent and asked if the homes he planned to show her "were in all white areas" of San Mateo, his reply suggested the racial accommodations that white real estate professionals had begun to make. "Well, there are no 'jigs' there—if that is what you mean," he said, using a derogatory term for African Americans but indirectly acknowledging the presence of some Asian Americans. When a few residents of an all-white San Mateo neighborhood threatened new resident Patrick Sun, San Francisco's Chinese consul-general, no one expressed more surprise than the home's seller. She had bragged to her neighbors about the identity of the buyer, assuming that they would be pleased and proud.[47]

Southwood and its echoes reflected perceived cold war national security imperatives and created real and long-term changes in the housing market of the Bay Area, once the state's most anti-Asian region. Such transformations occurred not just in "progressive" San Francisco but in its suburbs, and among groups notorious for racial conservatism, such as real estate agents, developers, and insurers. And such shifts were more than just aberrations: after a Southwood-style incident took place in a neighborhood, the Asian American population of the area in question grew substantially, while the population of blacks did not. At the same time, noticeable white flight did not occur in any of these neighborhoods. In essence, Southwood and its echoes, together with the larger cold war, broke the pattern of racial succession that developed in the urban state after 1948.[48]

THE SEGREGATED SOUTH

In Southern California, where the housing market was traditionally divided along white-nonwhite lines, change occurred far more slowly. JACL Pacific Southwest regional director Tats Kushida blamed Japanese Americans themselves for some of the problems that all of them faced in Los Angeles. "The Nisei who is refused a home acts like a scolded dog with tail between his legs and conceals his embarrassment and shame at having been racially rejected so no one else knows about it," complained Kushida. "Instead of fighting bigotry, he is encouraging it because the discrimination succeeds by forfeit."[49] Yet the JACL's own approach to housing discrimination in the Los Angeles area kept such incidents out of the public eye, inadvertently isolating those involved. In exploiting the power of Southwood, Frank Chuman also helped prevent any Southwood-style episodes from occurring in Southern California. Even in northern California, the Japanese Americans involved in Southwood echoes came to the notice of the press not through the JACL but through other avenues—such as the death threat to the white home seller in San Leandro.

In any case, racial discrimination in housing was just one of the many hurdles Japanese Americans faced in 1950s Los Angeles. Because of the internment, thousands of Issei who returned to L.A. after the war often had little to show for a lifetime of work. The Alien Land Acts prevented even those with some savings from leasing commercial or agricultural property or helping their children buy homes, land, or businesses until the late 1940s and early 1950s. Partly as a result, home ownership rates in heavily Japanese American neighborhoods remained well below those in the city as a whole, as well as those in majority black neighborhoods. Elderly Issei suffered the most; unlike many younger members of the immigrant generation, the oldest Issei were often too frail or ill to seek employment again. As ineligible aliens once employed in agriculture, they also had no access to Social Security retirement benefits.[50]

Nisei men and women also struggled to regain their footing. Historian Evelyn Nakano Glenn contends that the youngest members of the Nisei generation enjoyed far greater social and economic opportunities than their older peers, many of them the trailer dwellers of the late 1940s. "Those who were adults and entered the labor market *before* the war remained stuck in the traditional Japanese job market after the war," she notes. "Those who became adults and entered the labor force *after* the war were able to enter the white-collar job market at the beginning of their careers." Either way, many bore tremendous family responsibilities, supporting both impoverished and elderly parents and young children while trying to reestablish lives in Los Angeles.[51]

Like their African American peers, few such Japanese Americans chose to become neighborhood "pioneers," but the city's transformation in the 1950s forced many to fight for greater residential mobility. After 1948, nonwhite housing demand slowly enlarged the area of the city's multiracial central neighborhoods, which pushed steadily south, west, and east in the wake of white flight. Simultaneously, however, white civic leaders with tremendous financial investments in the downtown area demanded redevelopment in many of these same places. They also called for construction of freeways to allow white suburbanites easy access to the stadiums, office towers, and other new creations they envisioned. The Red-baiting of Los Angeles's public housing program in the early 1950s meant that no large-scale program of home construction would serve the displaced in such areas. Nevertheless, city leaders pushed ahead with freeway building and urban redevelopment in neighborhoods such as Bunker Hill, Boyle Heights, and West Adams, all areas with substantial Japanese American populations. Multiracial coalitions challenged many of these plans but generally failed to stop them.[52]

By the mid-1950s, then, redevelopment and the desire for newer and better homes pushed Japanese Americans and African Americans beyond West Adams to other western L.A. neighborhoods, as well as south of the West 50s, the rough border of the integrated districts in 1950. Since Japanese American pioneers tended to face less violence than their black counterparts, they often formed the vanguard of transition in many such areas, especially Crenshaw on the west side; significant numbers bought homes in several of the city's westernmost tracts with few if any African American residents up to that point. As in the late 1940s, these areas bordered more heavily black districts from which white populations had fled or were fleeing, and they eventually transitioned as well. "That was the start—I didn't realize it then—of what they call the 'white flight,'" remembered George Abe, who purchased a home in such an area around 1950. "Just about then, all my [white] neighbors started to just move away. They just took off."[53]

The west side's "integration" never matched the stability of Los Angeles's prewar rundown multiracial areas, but the new neighborhoods like Crenshaw were sources of greater pride to their residents. Unlike in prewar days, ethnicity and religion no longer really limited the housing opportunities of Jews and residents of southern European origin, who left the area in large numbers in the 1950s. As a result, Crenshaw's integration was a momentary snapshot in a slower process of racial transition, with Japanese Americans and their middle-class African American peers replacing fleeing whites. Still, Crenshaw's fairly new Spanish-style stucco homes and highly rated high school made it popular with middle-class blacks and Nisei alike. For these nonwhites, Crenshaw was preferable to older, less expensive neighborhoods such as Boyle Heights, where poorer Japanese Americans still lived in significant numbers. By the late 1950s, Crenshaw had developed into a heavily Japanese American neighborhood, anchored by the Nisei-owned Crenshaw Square, businesses such as the Holiday Bowl bowling alley, and a Japanese American credit union. "It was a one step up [*sic*] . . . from living in the ghetto that you could buy a real house and live in it," remembered Katsumi Kunitsugu. "The [homes that] whites were moving out of were sold to Japanese. The Japanese just sort of moved in wholesale in the Crenshaw area."[54]

Crenshaw offered a sense of security and belonging to its Japanese American residents, who still enjoyed only limited acceptance in white Los Angeles. In surveys, the area's residents expressed deep satisfaction with the social outlets that the concentration of Japanese American–owned homes, businesses, and social and religious institutions in their neighborhood made possible. The large number of Japanese speakers also benefited the many Kibei and Issei who called the neighborhood home. But even Nisei educated in California's public schools appreciated the kinds of relationships and networks the area helped foster. Nisei Marion Manaka, who raised her children in Crenshaw, enjoyed a social network that included her Japanese American church, a Japanese American social club at Dorsey High School, and an informal group of other Japanese American mothers whose children attended school together. Certainly, some Nisei understood the area's significance in larger political terms; Scott Kurashige has even described the "tight-knit bonds . . . [that] developed between blacks and Japanese Americans in Crenshaw."[55] Still, far more Nisei seemed to value the kinds of comfortable Japanese American social networks available to a community still grappling with the economic and psychological impact of the wartime internment.

SOUTHWOOD IN SOUTHERN CALIFORNIA

By the mid-1950s, white flight to the suburbs was creating both opportunities and potential problems for such Japanese Americans. The movement of whites out of central and western Los Angeles opened areas such as Crenshaw, and, further west, Leimert Park, giving Los Angeles's Nisei access to much higher quality and newer housing than their parents had ever enjoyed. Although segregation persisted—or resegregation eventually occurred—the homes in Crenshaw and other western and southern areas were often just a decade or so old. For gardeners and nurserymen, who comprised a significant proportion of the Nisei and Issei male population in Crenshaw, Gardena, Boyle Heights, and Pasadena, the mushrooming suburbs of Los Angeles also meant thousands of new customers. Yet rapid real estate development simultaneously threatened Japanese American livelihoods. Nursery proprietors and truck farmers who leased rather than owned their land often faced eviction when landlords sold holdings to a developer or subdivided the land for tract homes. Some farmers survived by living in urban areas and commuting between far flung plots of open land, but the practice became less and less tenable as the city grew.[56]

Industries and residents were also relocating north to the San Fernando Valley, south to the southern part of Los Angeles County, and even farther south to Orange County. Neither younger white collar and professional Nisei, nor older Japanese American gardeners, farmers, and nurserymen could follow, because housing tracts in such areas continued to bar most nonwhite residents. White homeowners resisted Japanese American integration even in the modest suburbs where Nisei-owned nurseries and truck plots greatly contributed to the tax base. Aiko Tanamachi Endo's experience was revealing. When she and her husband Bob tried to buy a tract home in Culver City, on whose fringes many Nisei farmers still grew celery, the bank denied their loan, and threatening white residents chased their Japanese American real estate agent down the street.[57]

Such treatment even occurred in Gardena, a once rundown suburb south of Los Angeles that gained a reputation as a haven for middle-class Japanese American strivers in the 1950s. Often called "Little Las Vegas," Gardena had the somewhat dubious distinction of being the only city in the entire state where poker clubs operated legally and openly. Before the war, a few hundred Japanese Americans ran nurseries and truck farms in the area. After the conflict, the unusually welcoming attitude of the city administration drew a number back; though nonwhite, they provided a more desirable tax base than card clubs. In the late 1940s and early 1950s, hundreds more Japanese Americans followed, opening nurseries that served the new tract homes of southern Los Angeles County. By the 1950s, Japanese Americans comprised a major portion of the city's population, with Nisei working in many professions and even serving in the city government.[58] Regardless, white residents of Gardena's and neighboring Torrance's newer and more desirable tracts kept those areas all-white.

In 1955, however, a Southwood-style incident finally helped pry open Southern California. The episode occurred in Orange County, a former agricultural center where housing tracts and defense industries were rapidly replacing chili and citrus growers. As nonwhite Angelenos knew, Orange County's suburban tracts were even more restricted than those of neighboring Los Angeles County. After World War II, a number of Japanese Americans bought agricultural land in the county and farmed there, but real estate agents and developers kept Asian Americans, including highly educated defense workers, out of the area's new housing tracts. It was one thing for Japanese Americans to cultivate large parcels in the county's rural districts, but as a white real estate agent explained, in the suburbs "people live eight feet apart" and "are not open-minded." By the mid-1950s, Orange County had gained a reputation not only for political conservatism but for such racial practices. When "you filled out an application" for an Orange County house, Kazuo Inouye of Kashu Realty remembered, "as soon as you leave they put it in the round file."[59]

As county development increased, subdividers began offering to buy out Nisei farmers in order to build housing that was almost always racially exclusive. JACL officials urged these growers to think twice before cashing in, citing the case of Amy Motodani, a Nisei from Los Angeles County's San Fernando Valley. Motodani's family bought its parcel in 1948, when the area was largely farmland. After the Motodanis sold some of their land to developers, the whites who purchased homes in the new tract began to harass and threaten them. "With houses mushrooming here in Orange County, it could possibly happen here," warned Orange County JACL chapter president George Kanno. "Moral of the story? Don't sell, farmers, don't sell."[60]

Kanno perhaps understood the racial climate in Orange County better than Sammy Lee, another Southern California native. In 1955, Lee, a Korean American Army major, doctor, and two-time Olympic diving gold medalist, made plans to leave the military and set up a private practice in Santa Ana, the Orange County seat. However, agents at two new tracts in nearby Garden Grove refused to sell a home to the world-famous "Diving Doctor" and his Chinese American wife, Rosalind. While Sammy Lee dined with President Eisenhower in Washington, another developer called Rosalind Lee to reject the couple's application for a home.[61]

The incident exposed the post-1948 inner workings of California housing discrimination, which involved a host of different parties acting separately for the same ends. A salesman at the Anaheim Village Home Fair told the Lees that "I have to eat, and I'd lose my job for selling to a non-white." Developer David Johnston, whose upscale Lee Lane tract rejected Sammy Lee, claimed to have no personal prejudice but said that other contractors told him "it would be suicidal . . . to risk selling to Dr. Lee." Several doctors in Garden Grove also informed Johnston that they objected to Lee practicing in the area, and as far as Lee Lane's white residents, "they sure wished I would not sell," he recalled. Neighbor Robert Miller argued that accusations about residents' objections to Lee were unfounded. Johnston "asked me what I would think if he sold one of the houses on the street to a 'Chinaman,'" contended Miller. "I told him that I would have no objection . . . [but] that it might reduce the value of his property." Another resident defended Johnston, asserting that "people should live with their own kind." A second white salesman who turned away the Lees claimed that "I'd rather have Dr. Sammy Lee myself than half the families here, but if you have one—a nice one—then you'll have others, including a little guy from a produce market who smells like hell."[62]

For the Lees, the incident posed a wrenching dilemma, and the couple spent several weeks deciding how to proceed. Had Lee been Japanese American rather than Korean American, he might have contacted JACL counsel Frank Chuman and settled the whole incident privately. Instead, he wrote for advice to his friend Bob Pierpoint, a journalist at CBS. Sammy Lee had traveled extensively for the State Department, promoting the United States and its system of government in a series of diving exhibitions across Asia. If he went public with his story of discrimination, he might embarrass America and perhaps create propaganda fodder for the Soviets and Chinese Communists. Regardless, Pierpont told him that "you are in a position . . . to really make a fight against discrimination, especially in California." After thinking the matter over, Sammy Lee contacted his sister, Dolly Rhee, an employee of *San Francisco Chronicle* editor Scott Newhall. Newhall's newspaper had been responsible for framing almost every Southwood-style incident in the Bay Area in terms of Communism versus democracy. Now, the editor assured Lee that he was going to "attack the disease," and he made the Lees' plight front-page news with editorials that could have come directly from the paper's Southwood coverage. "Here was an American of Oriental descent demonstrating to Asians that despite Communist propaganda the United States is a land of tolerance and opportunity," scolded the *Chronicle*. "The story of Major Lee's reception in Garden Grove will embarrass our country in the eyes of the world."[63]

Despite Chuman's behind-the-scenes strategy, JACL branch officials who increasingly understood the kind of impact that Southwood echoes could make jumped to exploit this one. Cognizant that white Orange County residents regularly discriminated against all "Orientals," local JACL leaders George Ichien, Hitoshi Nitta, and George Kanno hastily arranged a meeting with *Santa Ana Register* publisher R.C. Hoiles, whom they urged to make a strong pro-Lee statement in his paper. Hoiles, an extremely influential conservative voice in Orange County, hardly sympathized with civil rights activism. Still, he understood the implications of the Sammy Lee story and published an unusual editorial that struggled to reconcile what he saw as the right to discriminate with the immorality of discrimination. The nearby *Long Beach Press-Telegram*, a newspaper that contemporary scholars described as "ultraconservative," took an even more forthright stand: its editors promised to fly Lee back to California from his post at Fort Carson, Colorado, and help him find a house.[64]

The Lee incident challenged Orange County's suburbs by forcing white homeowners who normally demanded residential segregation to face what they now perceived as its broader consequences. Historian Lisa McGirr notes that white Orange County residents often harbored "deep-seated racial biases" and opposed racial "changes [that] would impinge on their affluent white havens and would undermine their prosperity . . . and way of life." Yet these same residents also had a reputation for strident anti-Communism; indeed, Orange County was a stronghold of the John Birch Society, a Far Right organization dedicated to fighting Communism internally as well as externally. When the Lee story appeared, numerous white Orange County residents suddenly grappled with the apparent incompatibility of their two priorities. As in the Bay Area's Southwood echoes, just a few players set events in motion—in this case, the Lees, their friends, and the editor of the *Chronicle*—yet the incident resonated far more broadly. Hundreds of local residents telegrammed, wrote, or called the Lees to express their support, condemn those who had rejected the family, and offer the couple homes in other parts of the area. The incident mushroomed to such an extent that Governor Goodwin Knight and Vice President Richard Nixon both became involved. In the end, the embarrassing blizzard of condemnations even compelled the kinds of local institutions that usually supported segregation to renounce it, at least publicly. The Garden Grove Chamber of Commerce, the West Orange Real Estate Association, the local FHA, and city leaders all welcomed the Lees, while representatives of the offending tracts announced that the couple could purchase homes in them.[65]

Once again, perceived national security imperatives had overridden local racial practices because of the Asian ancestry of the victim of discrimination. The Sammy Lee incident occurred during a tumultuous year in American race relations. In February, white students at the University of Alabama rioted over the court-ordered integration of the school. Just weeks after Sammy Lee's case became news, two white men in Mississippi kidnapped and beat to death a visiting black Chicago teenager named Emmett Till, who had whistled at a white woman in a local store. In November, police arrested Rosa Parks, a black seamstress, when she refused to give her seat to a white man on a Montgomery, Alabama, bus; a young clergyman named Martin Luther King, Jr., began his rise to fame as the leader of the ensuing movement to boycott the bus system. In each of these cases—even in Till's brutal murder—the outraged response of Northerners and the international community infuriated white Southerners, who closed ranks to defend their Jim Crow racial order.[66] In Orange County, however, national condemnation failed to stop the local groundswell of sentiment in favor of Sammy Lee. The region's anti-Communist politics simply proved stronger than residents' aversion to integration.

The assumed international implications of the Sammy Lee incident, rather than the light it cast on discriminatory local practices, prompted a growing number of white Southern Californians to consider the racial ramifications of their housing choices. According to Nancy MacLean, "in the South . . . anti-Communism offered the best defense for segregation, so the two causes were mutually reinforcing." For Asian Americans in Southern California, the opposite proved true. Within a year, dozens of Asian American families began buying homes in previously all-white Garden Grove, including the areas that earlier rejected Sammy Lee. In contrast, when a black Air Force officer and Annapolis graduate named Harold Bauduit attempted to purchase a house in the same suburb for his family, fifty white neighbors gathered on his lawn in protest, formed a homeowners' association to stop the sale, and threatened him with violence. The incident highlighted the contours of racial change in California: other black families avoided the area for more than a decade, while Asian Americans continued to move there.[67]

HISTORICAL AMNESIA AND SHARED VALUES

As Asian Americans gained greater access to formerly all-white areas, a growing number of white Californians began to speak of them as people who shared the kinds of values that whites usually identified exclusively with themselves and their neighborhoods. Such ideas about values motivated Southwood and its echoes in the first place, but the concepts coexisted with other, older beliefs—especially the idea that the presence of any Asian Americans in a neighborhood lowered property values there. Now, however, many white observers started to deny the latter charge. The change was stunning in its swiftness; twenty years earlier, racist pronouncements about Asian inassimilability and filthiness blocked the construction of Los Angeles's Jefferson Park, maintained the hyper-segregated San Francisco Chinatown, and justified the Japanese American internment. Now, however, many whites tried to describe the same groups in ways that rhetorically preserved the social status and property values that Asian Americans once supposedly imperiled. In other words, a growing number of white Californians accommodated racial change in ways that preserved their racialized self-esteem.

White Californians' recognition of commendable Asian "values" both reflected and contributed to a larger national project of explaining cold war imperatives to the American people. Historian Naoko Shibusawa has shown that after World War II, lingering American hatred of Japan complicated that nation's role as America's major ally in Asia. By the early 1950s, however, "a broad range of governmental and nongovernmental actors . . . transform[ed] the Japanese enemy into an acceptable ally in American culture" through films, articles, novels, and other cultural products. According to historian Lon Kurashige, "the relationship between victor and vanquished [in Japan] produced a mutual admiration and familiarity, a goodwill that would radically revise American attitudes toward Japan and, by extension, Japanese in the United States."[68] *Time* and *Life* magazines, which had featured glowing portrayals of Chiang Kai-shek and his wife, played a similar role in reminding Americans that despite the Communist victory in 1949, "Free China" and its people persevered with Christian, Westernized leadership.

By the mid-1950s, many white Californians similarly sought to rationalize the presence of Asian Americans in their neighborhoods (and workplaces and schools) in ways that preserved the racialized economic value—and social values—of those places. As Southwood and its early echoes suggested, even white residents who supported Asian American integration out of geopolitical concerns often considered people of Asian ancestry a drag on housing prices. But as the cold war in Asia continued with no end in sight, many white residents in the urban state moved to accommodate its apparent permanence; they rhetorically transformed Asian Americans from tolerable to desirable neighbors while largely accepting the common perception of such people as fundamentally foreign.

To render Asian Americans acceptable, white Californians began to actively ignore the recent past, reshaping once negative ideas about Japanese Americans and Chinese Americans into new forms of praise. In a particularly breathtaking example, a San Francisco development company executive explained the difference between racial groups' desirability. "The majority of Negroes are poor credit risks and have no feeling of ownership," he contended. "Orientals often have a heritage of ownership and some understanding of what it brings." Only six years earlier, California's Supreme Court had struck down the state's Alien Land Act, which had denied two generations of Asian Americans any "heritage of ownership" that was not criminal. San Francisco's Mayor George Christopher also rewrote history when he informed the U.S. Commission on Civil Rights in 1959 that "we are determined San Francisco will not develop a segregated minority core area with its attendant social problems."[69] In the process, he denied Chinatown's history as America's first segregated district and a longtime center of poverty and substandard housing.

This new language often reflected the ways in which many white Californians saw themselves and what they wanted from the suburbs to which millions moved in the 1950s and 1960s. Historian Kenneth T. Jackson has shown that most white Americans who left cities during this era "were looking for good schools, private space, and personal safety" in order to avoid dangers such as "interracial violence and interracial sex." Public discussions of Asian Americans in California harmonized these concerns with ongoing local racial change. A *Los Angeles Times* journalist describing Chinese Americans in the suburbs assured readers that for such people, "intermarriage . . . just seldom occurs because of cultural differences," a contention that ignored California's anti-miscegenation law, overturned just a few years earlier. The police chiefs of Los Angeles and San Francisco tacitly addressed the racialized security concerns of white Californians by explicitly comparing what they called African Americans' high crime rate to Asian Americans' low one.[70]

Some white Californians also recast the troubled relationship of Asian Americans to the social welfare state in order to affirm "Oriental" desirability. Federal housing and highway construction programs in the 1950s enabled white suburbanites to flee the racialized threats they associated with urban areas. Regardless, many of the same white homeowners saw themselves as paragons of self reliance and disparaged nonwhites for their supposed dependence on government handouts. In Southern California, such rhetoric dated to the "Mexican Problem" of the 1920s, but it found new life in the white flight of the 1950s. This time around, however, white critics targeted blacks too but discounted Asian American campaigns for inclusion in the social welfare state. The increasingly common characterization of Los Angeles's public housing as a "Negro housing" program ignored the attempts of postwar Japanese Angelenos to gain a public project for the Little Tokyo area. An observer who acknowledged the existence of a Chinese-only public housing project in San Francisco suggested that the ethnicity of its tenants ennobled it. "When low-cost housing came at last to Chinatown, it came not as a sterile concrete pile, but as a sanctuary known as Ping Yuen, tranquil garden, an apartment house girdled with terraces and guarded at the entrance by sacred dogs," he contended. In 1955, a journalist even claimed that "San Francisco had [only] two in 10,000" Chinatown residents on relief during the Depression. In reality, thousands of the city's Chinese Americans depended on state and federal relief programs in the 1930s.[71] Regardless of the truth, the mythology of a Chinatown that rejected charity fit better with emerging ideas about the confluence of Asian and white values.

In other words, Asian Americans' cultural differences made them better neighbors than members of other minority groups. By the mid-1950s, white Californians who praised "Oriental" values began to contrast them to the lack of values and the alarming militancy they attributed to other nonwhite people, particularly blacks. "Race and color no longer need be a barrier to social and economic equality," argued white Gardena resident Irene Dalrymple. Japanese Americans "have earned their position because they are industrious, clean, considerate, and reliable; and because they do not go around with a 'built-in' chip on the shoulder" the way blacks supposedly did. L.A. officials told a reporter from *U.S. News and World Report* that Japanese Americans "want to solve their problems in their own way—through hard work, education, and high moral standards, more than by court actions or publicity," while "a contrasting attitude of militancy and suspicion . . . often turns up among top Negroes." An official with the San Francisco Real Estate Board, parrying criticism of black housing segregation, reiterated such sentiments during the 1959 U.S. Civil Rights Commission hearings in the city. Eighteen years earlier, "the minority group of Chinese in the city of San Francisco, I believe, was in the same position that the minority group is here today—at least the one we are talking mostly about," he argued, referring to blacks. "As of today, and this is some 18 years later, we have absolutely no difficulty placing that particular minority group anywhere, and they have become a credit to San Francisco."[72] Actually, Chinese Americans still faced housing discrimination in some parts of the city, but the real estate agent used their example to dismiss housing segregation as the fault of the segregated. Once blacks became a "credit to the city," he implied, they too would find acceptance and homes.

RACIAL CHANGE AND INTERRACIAL RELATIONS

In 1963, sociologist Cy Wilson Record observed that in the Bay Area, "Negroes resent the white's more ready 'acceptance' of Japanese as students, workers, and neighbors," and he pointed to growing black hostility towards Chinese Americans as well.[73] By the early 1960s, African Americans in the San Francisco and Los Angeles areas readily understood that white Californians treated them differently than Asian Americans. The most obvious manifestation of this was spatial: Asian Americans now moved to places where African Americans could not follow, and their arrival no longer prompted the beginnings of white flight. According to Berkeley scholars, by the mid-1950s "nine out of ten [Bay Area real estate agents] felt free to sell to other minorities if Negroes were already in the neighborhood, [but] just one-half as many would sell to Negroes in neighborhoods in which other minorities were present."[74] While all nonwhites continued to face housing discrimination, then, the growing number of Asian Americans in many neighborhoods closed to blacks offered ample proof of racial differentiation.

In San Francisco, the city's public housing program also provided forceful evidence both of this racial parsing and of the interracial friction it sometimes caused. In 1952, the NAACP finally sued to integrate San Francisco's housing projects and eventually triumphed in the U.S. Supreme Court. The Court's decision challenged the Chinese American community's sense of ownership over Ping Yuen, however, and exposed continuing hostility in Chinatown toward the possibility of black neighbors. A large percentage of the people living in substandard conditions in San Francisco, and thus eligible for public housing, were African American. At community meetings in the early 1950s, the Chinatown residents who spoke out against Ping Yuen's integration imagined it as a black phenomenon and at times used ugly stereotypes to describe the African American population. Yet while the California appellate court decision singled out Ping Yuen as one of seven segregated projects whose pattern the Housing Authority needed to change, it remained all-Chinese into the 1960s. Indeed, federal officials knew that the SFHA was flouting the court's decision but allowed it to do so without interference, just as they permitted the Authority to gerrymander its projects to concentrate blacks and whites in certain developments.[75]

Black activists protested Ping Yuen's segregation for years but managed to change nothing. At the 1959 Civil Rights Commission hearings, Franklin Williams, a former NAACP activist and a new assistant state attorney general, complained that "this city's so-called Chinatown is officially recognized, if not encouraged, by the erection and maintenance of public housing facilities in the heart of the area complete with pseudo-Chinese architectural trappings and occupied solely by Chinese Americans." One of the real estate board's vice presidents snapped back, "I think it is beautiful. And as a matter of fact, I laid it out." When NAACP president Terry Francois raised the issue at a Housing Authority meeting in 1962, the Housing Commission promised to study the issue and then ignored it for another year. In May 1963, the local NAACP tried yet again, this time comparing the situation in San Francisco to Birmingham, where white supremacist city leaders were then attacking Martin Luther King, Jr., and his peaceful followers. Angry housing commissioners denied the connection and pushed off the issue for further study.[76]

The controversy revealed the starkly different ways that the city's African Americans and Chinese Americans now understood and defined racial segregation. Responding to black complaints, Chinatown community leaders argued that the district's homogeneity was not exclusionary but was simply the product of cultural forces. In some ways, the argument was quite ironic: Chinatown was originally the creation of nativism and racial discrimination, and it owed its transformation from racially restricted area to ethnic enclave to the legal victories of the progressive civil rights coalition of the postwar era—a coalition in which few Chinese Americans participated. Still, Chinatown proper by the 1960s *was* an ethnic enclave and home mainly to less mobile Chinese Americans, especially newcomers. After 1948, and especially by the 1950s, American-born and educated Chinese Americans streamed out of Chinatown, moving to a host of other San Francisco neighborhoods and to the suburbs and belying stereotypes about Chinese "clannishness" in the process. Chinatown's remaining residents tended to be poorer people, often recent immigrants who spoke little if any English and depended on Chinatown businesses and tourism for their livelihood and social life. Referring to Ping Yuen's residents, a *Chinese Times* columnist asserted that "they have always been accustomed to living in Chinatown and for this reason are happy to live together with the same race."[77]

Rejecting arguments about Chinatown's cultural distinctiveness, African Americans accused its residents of simple bigotry. To black critics, Chinatown was not hard-won Chinese space in the way many of its residents believed; it was merely symbolic of the way Chinese Americans were adopting the same practices as white homeowners who also preferred to "live together with the same race." Perhaps Chinese Americans could exclude others from privately owned parts of Chinatown, argued African American leaders, but they could not keep blacks out of a publicly funded housing project. As Solomon Johnson, the Housing Commission's only African American member, contended, Chinese Americans "have no more right [in Ping Yuen] than anyone else." But at a time when white Americans increasingly linked central city decay to the presence of African Americans and the public housing associated with them, San Francisco civic leaders were determined to "protect" Chinatown, one of the city's top tourist draws.[78]

So was T. Kong Lee, the Housing Commission's sole Chinese American member. A product of Depression-era Chinatown, a transnational island in a hostile city, Lee embraced ideas of ethnic desirability with particular ease. A former president of the Chinese Chamber of Commerce, Lee had helped craft the body's post-1949 tourism strategy and Chinatown's cold war image. In 1961, when the San Francisco Board of Supervisors considered passing a city fair housing ordinance, Lee publicly opposed it, using his former title as Chinese chamber president to enhance his influence. The move worried some of Lee's old colleagues on the chamber and convinced many African Americans that Chinese Americans in general refused to associate with blacks. Of course, Lee was just one voice in the community, but the charge was not completely without merit—or irony. In prewar days, conservative black leaders afraid of jeopardizing their unusual residential mobility opposed any housing project that mixed, and thus associated, African Americans with Asian Americans. Now, Chinatown residents and their leaders acted similarly to protect their community's positive image, which derived in part from white civic leaders' comparisons of Chinese American crime and delinquency rates to those of the black population. In light of Gilbert Woo's many comments on the issue—he once noted that "there are some overseas compatriots who confuse 'different races' with 'strangers'"—the *Chinese Times*' assertion that Ping Yuen's residents "are absolutely not rejecting other races [and] . . . are not ashamed to associate with black people" seemed more defensive than entirely truthful.[79]

WATTS AND BEYOND

In the early 1960s, Asian Americans had still not come close to achieving the ease of movement that whites took for granted in every field. People of Asian ancestry continued to encounter residential segregation and employment discrimination far more often than civic leaders and politicians cared to admit. A much larger number still worked in traditional "ethnic niche" occupations— gardening, nursery work, or farm management for Japanese Americans, and restaurants, laundries, and similar small businesses for Chinese Americans— than in prestigious and highly paid professional positions. To be sure, Asian American employment rates exceeded those of other minority groups and even of whites. However, the median income of Asian American men in California was only slightly higher than that of African American men and was less than the median income of Hispanic men—and Asian American education rates far surpassed those of both blacks and Mexican Americans.[80]

Still, by 1960, Asian Americans enjoyed significant residential mobility throughout urban and suburban California, a mobility that laid the foundation for future gains in other fields. While African Americans in the Bay Area and metropolitan Los Angeles became more segregated and isolated after 1940, Asian American segregation rates fell between 1950 and 1960, and again between 1960 and 1970. Mexican Americans' contested racial status continued to give them greater mobility than blacks and Asian Americans during much of the same period; indeed, according to historian Eric Avila, "families of Mexican descent who willingly identified themselves as 'Spanish'" could often move to neighborhoods such as Lakewood, where Asian Americans long remained unwelcome. Yet by 1960, Asian American and Mexican American dissimilarity rates in the L.A. area had become almost identical, and Asian American isolation rates there were far lower than Mexican American rates. Indeed, Los Angeles's Asian Americans were now more likely to own their own homes than the area's Mexican Americans or blacks, a marked shift from just a decade or two earlier.[81]

Asian Americans' unusual residential mobility gave them access to the parts of the Bay Area, Los Angeles County, and Orange County that were experiencing the greatest economic growth during this era. Ironically, their continued

TABLE 8.1 Indices of Segregation for Asian Americans, African Americans, and Hispanics, 1940–1970

	Isolation index				Dissimilarity index			
	1940	1950	1960	1970	1940	1950	1960	1970
San Francisco								
Asian Americans	52	39	33	32	76	47	52	39
African Americans	6	26	41	49	71	· 40	71	68
Bay Area⁺								
Asian Americans	43	30	20.5	18	70	61	52	44
African Americans	16	38	50	53	73	50	81	77
Los Angeles Metro Area⁺⁺								
Asian Americans	13	9	11	11	59* (63*)	61* (65*)	58.5 (63)	46 (52)
African Americans	47	56	65	71	83* (83.5*)	84* (85*)	89 (91)	89 (91)
Hispanics	25*	30*	42	37	63*	61*	57	50

Source: Indices based on Minnesota Population Center, *National Historical Geographic Information System: Pre-release Version 0.1.* Minneapolis: University of Minnesota 2004; Bureau of the Census, *1950 Census of Population: Census Tract Statistics, Los Angeles, California and Adjacent Area* (Washington, DC: USGPO, 1952), 9-53; Bureau of the Census, *1960 Census of Population: Census Tract Statistics, Los Angeles-Long Beach SMSA* (Washington, DC: USGPO, 1962), 576–602.
Note: Numbers in parentheses indicate dissimilarity indices when Hispanics are not included in the white population. All calculations for Hispanics do not include them in the white population.
⁺1940 includes San Francisco, Contra Costa, Alameda Counties; Santa Clara added 1950; Marin, San Mateo added 1960.
⁺⁺Includes Orange County beginning 1960.
*Indicates estimate.

concentration in traditional ethnic niches also made them far less dependent than both blacks and Mexican Americans on the kinds of manufacturing jobs that were disappearing from places like Los Angeles and Oakland.[82] Furthermore, the many Asian American children who gained access to decent, well-funded suburban schools during the 1950s and 1960s began to break into the mainstream economy in the 1960s and 1970s—something their parents' residential mobility made possible.[83]

Racial perceptions and racial discrimination—not economics—thus played the key role in the mobility of Asian Americans and the thwarted opportunities of blacks, and to a lesser extent, Mexican Americans. African Americans suffered disproportionately, because as Josh Sides observes, in those years "middle-class blacks encountered racism and discrimination as often as poor blacks did."[84] Housing trends revealed as much. While diverse communities such as Crenshaw and parts of the Western Addition continued to exist, the growing Asian American middle class increasingly chose to live in the newer and more exclusive suburban areas, with their superior services and schools. Scores of Japanese Americans and Chinese Americans purchased newly built tract houses in the San Gabriel Valley town of Monterey Park; numerous Mexican Americans also found homes there, but ongoing resistance to black buyers prompted the Congress of Racial Equality to picket area housing developments.[85] More of Gardena opened to Nisei, but not to blacks, and hundreds of Asian Americans also bought homes in southwestern Los Angeles County cities such as Hawthorne and Inglewood where whites sometimes used violence to keep out African Americans. Similarly, the Asian American populations of Bay Area neighborhoods that excluded blacks, including parts of cities such as Berkeley, Castro Valley, Fremont, Hayward, San Leandro, San Bruno, and South San Francisco, grew substantially during this period. Even in downtown San Francisco, Asian Americans often lived in apartment buildings whose landlords rejected black tenants. The Richmond District, completely off limits to Chinese Americans in prewar days, gained so many former Chinatown residents that they began calling it the "west side family area" or the second Chinatown; African Americans, however, struggled to gain access to homes there.[86]

Frustrated with the ongoing segregation of African Americans in California, black assemblymen William Byron Rumford and Augustus Hawkins took turns during the late 1950s and early 1960s sponsoring a bill to prohibit racial discrimination in the sale or rental of any private dwelling with more than four units. The legislation predictably failed to pass each year until 1963, when growing civil rights activism throughout the nation finally prodded the state legislature's Democratic majority to approve what by then had become known as the Rumford Fair Housing Act. Although Governor Pat Brown signed the bill into law, the California Real Estate Association and a host of conservative groups, including some white supremacist organizations, launched a drive in 1964 to repeal the act through a ballot initiative called Proposition 14. The nasty, racially charged campaign in support of the initiative, which won by a landslide, took place against the backdrop of intensifying African American anger about the slow pace of change in California.[87] In the summer of 1965, this frustration exploded at Watts, a once-diverse area of southern Los Angeles that had become a black ghetto in the years after World War II.

The Watts Riot, which raged for five days, came to epitomize the racial upheavals that devastated more than one hundred American cities during the

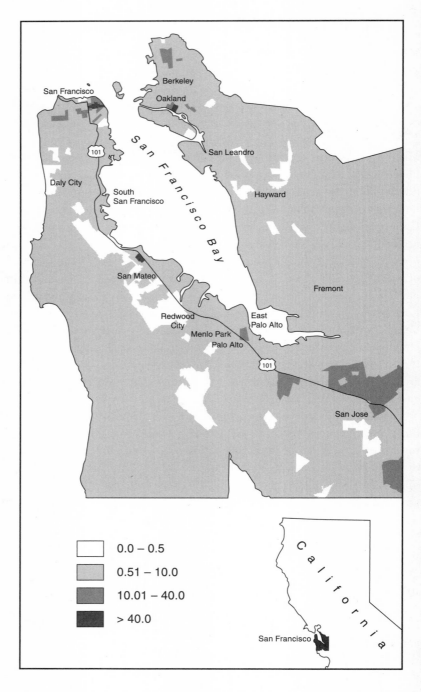

Asian American population by census tract (percent of total population), Bay Area, 1960. (Map by Harry D. Johnson, based on Minnesota Population Center, *National Historical Geographic Information System: Pre-release Version 0.1.* Minneapolis: University of Minnesota, 2004.)

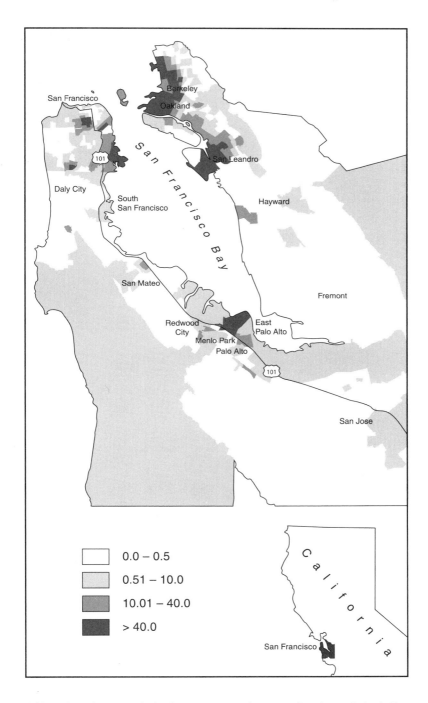

African American population by census tract (percent of total population), Bay Area, 1960. (Map by Harry D. Johnson, based on Minnesota Population Center, *National Historical Geographic Information System: Pre-release Version 0.1.* Minneapolis: University of Minnesota, 2004.)

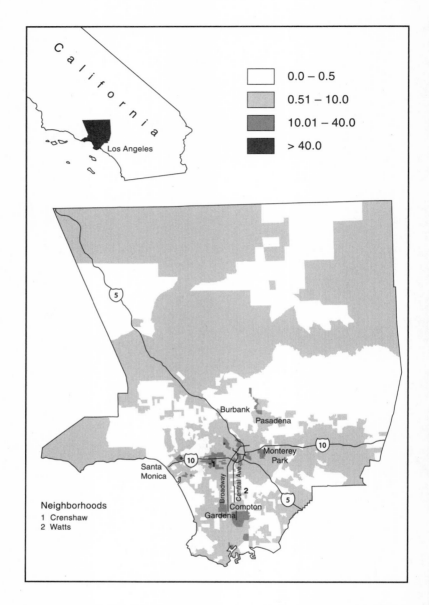

Asian American population by census tract (percent of total population), Los Angeles County, 1960. (Map by Harry D. Johnson, based on Minnesota Population Center, *National Historical Geographic Information System: Prerelease Version 0.1.* Minneapolis: University of Minnesota, 2004.)

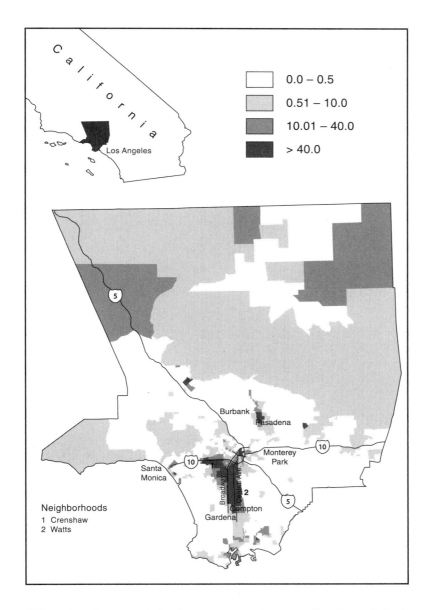

African American population by census tract (percent of total population), Los Angeles County, 1960. (Map by Harry D. Johnson, based on Minnesota Population Center, *National Historical Geographic Information System: Pre-release Version 0.1*. Minneapolis: University of Minnesota, 2004.)

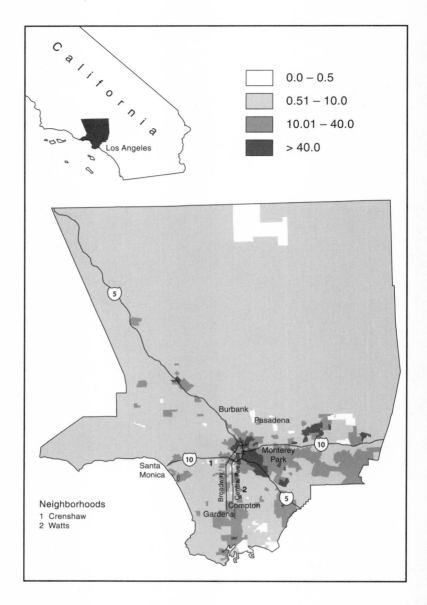

White population with Spanish surname by census tract (percent of total population), Los Angeles County, 1960. (Map by Harry D. Johnson, based on Minnesota Population Center, *National Historical Geographic Information System: Pre-release Version 0.1.* Minneapolis: University of Minnesota, 2004; Bureau of the Census, 1960 *Census of Population: Census Tract Statistics, Los Angeles-Long Beach SMSA* (Washington, DC: USGPO, 1962), 576–602.)

late 1960s. The riot began as an altercation between two white officers from the Los Angeles Police Department and a black motorist from the neighborhood. The policemen's treatment of the driver stirred African American anger over police brutality, but it also catalyzed deeper black frustration about limited job opportunities, underfunded public services, and segregated housing. Within a day of the original incident, thousands of African Americans were rioting, burning buildings, and looting stores in Watts and neighboring areas. At the end of the riot, more than nine hundred buildings had been damaged, thirty-four people had died, and over one thousand had been injured.[88]

News reports and studies of the riots focused on their most obvious effects—property damage, looting, the withdrawal of many merchants from riot-scarred areas—but few noted their impact on the diversity of Los Angeles's central city neighborhoods. After the riots, Asian American residents poured out of the old integrated areas of South Central. A special census of L.A. showed that by November 1965, seven hundred of the thousand Asian American residents of Green Meadows, to the immediate west of Watts, were gone. Only six hundred of the Central district's more than 1,800 Asian Americans stayed, and even the western Exposition area lost a quarter of its Asian American residents. The riots stunned many African Americans as well, including the middle-class residents of Compton, Crenshaw, and Leimert Park, but fewer could leave. They simply enjoyed less mobility than their Asian American neighbors in the racialized housing market.[89]

Just two years before Watts, Gilbert Woo, now a veteran of thirty years of Chinatown journalism, cautioned his readers to keep their recent history in mind when they considered the current state of race relations in California. "Now that [white reactionaries] have made blacks their sworn enemies, they have no time to deal with us and even go so far as to be a little polite to us," he noted. "But this isn't their real intention. If they had a day, white Southerners and the North's ultra-rightist factions would form a huge front, take blacks and settle scores with them, and Chinese would also receive the same treatment. Our future in America is closely bound to the future of other minority groups." Within a few short years, the children of the Chinese Americans and Japanese Americans who endured the Depression and fought World War II began to take these words to heart. Many such young people grew up in predominately white neighborhoods, yet as they reached their late teens, they began to sense the way pervasive stereotypes and insidious discrimination still limited their parents' and their own opportunities. Thousands participated in the African American civil rights groups that talked about the racial oppression they felt. Still, few could really express their discontent until they mobilized against American involvement in the Vietnam War, which many perceived as an extension of white America's contempt for Asian Americans.[90]

Despite their growing residential isolation from other minorities, these young Asian Americans increasingly understood their own experiences as part of a larger pattern of racial oppression in the United States. In the process, they challenged moderate and conservative community leaders, from the CCBA to the JACL. At colleges and universities throughout the nation, thousands also joined multiracial student coalitions to fight against the Vietnam War and for more diversity in admissions, greater democracy on campuses, and the creation of ethnic studies departments. Central to these coalitions was their identification with the "third world" nations of Africa and Asia, where leftist revolutionaries attacked American power.[91]

In the 1950s, numerous white Californians began to favor the residential integration of Asian Americans because they identified such people with the nonaligned nations of Asia, where American involvement was so deep and prolonged. The inclusion of Asian Americans in the suburban good life was never on an equal basis, however, nor was it complete: stereotypes, rather than a belief in racial equality, created this integration. The Vietnam War and American responses to it helped Asian American youths express their anger at this half-hearted inclusion. Ironically, then, while foreign policy in the 1950s enabled Asian Americans to move out of the segregated areas in which most had once lived, their growing disgust with that same foreign policy eventually pushed many to make common cause with those they had left behind.

Epilogue

Struggling to come to grips with the racial upheavals and urban unrest of the late 1960s, a number of white commentators in the national press began to draw direct comparisons between Asian Americans and their African American peers. Within two years of Watts, *U.S. News and World Report* and the *New York Times Magazine* both published extensive articles describing Chinese Americans and Japanese Americans as groups that, in the words of one author, "challenge . . . every generalization about ethnic minorities." Written in a period of growing white backlash against civil rights activism and the War on Poverty, both pieces cast Asian Americans as people who, unlike blacks, quietly succeeded through hard work and without asking for handouts. "At a time when it is being proposed that hundreds of billions be spent to uplift Negroes and other minorities," wrote *U.S. News and World Report*, "the nation's 300,000 Chinese-Americans are moving ahead on their own—without help from anyone else." When the article's authors called Chinese Americans "an important racial minority . . . becom[ing] a model of self-respect and achievement in today's America," the term "model minority" was born. The phrase became particularly popular among white conservatives opposed to civil rights legislation, affirmative action, and anti-poverty programs.[1] If Asian American "model minorities" could make it on their own, such people argued, why did other nonwhites demand government assistance?

Scholars generally date the idea of Asian Americans as a "model minority" to this period and to these articles, but the essays merely drew on beliefs current in urban California a decade earlier.[2] Some of the concepts they used reflected the ideas of the American elites who strove to explain cold war imperatives to rest of the nation in the late 1940s and 1950s. However, much of what the "model minority" authors wrote echoed the beliefs of the thousands of ordinary white Californians who by the mid-1950s were trying to justify as a positive good the Asian American integration they had initially accepted as a necessary cold war sacrifice.

Like many white Californians before them, those Americans who embraced the model minority myth blithely ignored the nation's own recent history. One of the fundamental flaws of the myth was its conception of the relationship of Asian Americans to the state. At its heart, the model minority myth was an attack on African Americans' and Hispanics' use of government authority to fight racial inequality, whether through social welfare programs, litigation in the courts, or civil rights legislation. Asian Americans had supposedly demonstrated that such government intervention was unnecessary by rejecting it and achieving success solely through hard work. As this book has shown, however, such a characterization was deeply at odds with real events. Beginning in the 1930s, Asian Americans tried, albeit with limited success, to gain access to the federal social welfare programs available to other groups. They also supported and greatly benefited from the legal battle against restrictive covenants. And in 1964, they voted overwhelmingly against Proposition 14, thus embracing the power of the state to enforce fair housing.[3]

The central irony of the "model minority myth" was that Asian Americans actually owed much of their postwar success to a federal policy, albeit one less apparent in its domestic impact than the civil rights laws of the 1960s. American foreign policy, although not a social welfare program or a single piece of legislation, created unique opportunities for Asian Americans in California's housing market and, eventually, in other areas as well. Indeed, foreign policy imperatives—or, at least, white Californians' perceptions of them—proved far more effective tools for Asian American advancement after World War II than domestic programs and laws that mirrored legislators' ambivalence about civil rights. After 1950, the FHA stopped requiring white homeowners to use racially restrictive covenants, but the agency still underwrote explicitly segregated developments. Federal officials allowed local governments to use urban renewal money to displace nonwhites and destroy their neighborhoods. City councils and state officials debated fair housing legislation but rarely passed it. Local politicians pledged to respect residents of all backgrounds but worked quietly to maintain racial boundaries. In contrast, the goal of American foreign policy in Asia during the same period seemed far clearer, with thousands of Americans fighting and dying to protect Asian nations from Communism and to draw them into the capitalist "free world."

With federal officials in the 1950s largely turning their backs on brutal Jim Crow in the South and the residential segregation of blacks in the North, the government's message to white Americans was that some people were worth fighting for, and some were not. Some people deserved inclusion in the suburban lifestyle that symbolized American freedom, and some did not. In California, the deserving increasingly included Asian Americans, while the undeserving were, more often than not, blacks and Mexican Americans. In the end, then, American foreign policy was the most effective domestic civil rights program of all—at least for Asian Americans.

In 1958, the journalist Harold Isaacs observed that "the very idea that world affairs have an impact on our race relations here at home sounds oddly startling at first, even to people intimately involved in race problems."[4] Asian Americans, of course, would not have been the least bit surprised. More than one hundred thousand Japanese Americans had spent much if not all of World War II in concentration camps because of widespread assumptions about their loyalty to Japan. The establishment of the People's Republic of China and its involvement in the Korean War heightened scrutiny of Chinese American loyalty to the United States and resulted in the investigation of many people of Chinese ancestry. And as this book has shown, international relations affected the most mundane aspects of Asian Americans' lives, including where they could live.

Today, the argument that world affairs affect domestic race relations would surprise far fewer Americans. In 1965, Congress passed legislation that eliminated the old national origins system of immigration preferences and quotas once and for all. Within a few years, people from Asia and Latin America, many fleeing political unrest and economic hardship, began streaming into the United States. Among the millions of newcomers were immigrants from predominately Muslim and Arab nations, people who currently find themselves the focus of suspicion the way Asian Americans did in the 1940s and 1950s. History does not repeat itself, but the parallels between then and now are striking. As it turns out, California at mid-century foreshadowed America at century's end: a place where race was far more complicated than black and white and where international conflicts affected domestic race relations. We ignore its example at our peril.

NOTES

1. Carey McWilliams, "Critical Summary," *Journal of Educational Sociology* 19:3 (November 1945): 187; Marilynn S. Johnson, *The Second Gold Rush: Oakland and the East Bay in World War II* (Berkeley: University of California Press, 1993), 8; L. D. Reddick, "The New Race-Relations Frontier," *Journal of Educational Sociology* 19:3 (November 1945): 137; Bureau of the Census, *Sixteenth Census of the United States, 1940—Population—Vol. II: Characteristics of the Population, Part One* (Washington, D.C.: USGPO, 1942), 516.

2. Ideas about race are not static, but reflect specific economic, political, social, and international contexts and conditions. As a result, the terms used to describe "races" of people also change over time, creating challenges for any historian who attempts to explore the development of such ideas across an extended period. For the sake of clarity, I use a single set of terms throughout the book. I use the term "white" to describe people wholly of European ancestry, including people of southern and eastern European descent whose "white" identity was sometimes disputed in the early twentieth century. I use the term "nonwhite" to describe African Americans, Asian Americans, and Mexican Americans, while noting the contested whiteness of that last group. I use the term "Asian American" in this book to describe people of Asian ancestry, regardless of citizenship. When citizenship is a salient issue, I refer more specifically to "immigrants" and "citizens."

3. See, for example, Thomas J. Sugrue, *The Origins of the Urban Crisis: Race and Inequality in Postwar Detroit* (Princeton, NJ: Princeton University Press, 1996), 33–88; Arnold R. Hirsch, *Making the Second Ghetto: Race and Housing in Chicago, 1940–1960* (Chicago: University of Chicago Press, 1998), 9–10; Andrew Wiese, *Places of Their Own: African American Suburbanization in the Twentieth Century* (Chicago: University of Chicago Press, 2004), 111–42; Rosalyn Baxandall and Elizabeth Ewen,

Picture Windows: How the Suburbs Happened (New York: Basic Books, 2000), 171–209.

4. Bureau of the Census, *Racial and Ethnic Residential Segregation in the United States: 1980-2000* (Washington, D.C.: USGPO, 2002), 96–97, http://www.census.gov/hhes/www/housing/housing_patterns/pdftoc.html (accessed May 6, 2007). The only nonwhites less segregated than Asian Americans in 2000 were Native Americans/Pacific Islanders.

5. Josh Sides, *L.A. City Limits: African American Los Angeles from the Great Depression to the Present* (Berkeley: University of California Press, 2003), 101; Becky M. Nicolaides, *My Blue Heaven: Life and Politics in the Working-Class Suburbs of Los Angeles, 1920-1965* (Chicago: University of Chicago Press, 2002), 6; Robert O. Self, *American Babylon: Race and the Struggle for Postwar Oakland* (Princeton, NJ: Princeton University Press, 2003), 166.

6. See, for example, Sides, *L.A. City Limits*, 17; Douglas Flamming, *Bound for Freedom: Black Los Angeles in Jim Crow America* (Berkeley: University of California Press, 2005), 66–67; Bureau of the Census, *Sixteenth Census of the United States, 1940—Population—Vol. II: Characteristics of the Population, Part One*, 516.

7. See, for example, K. Scott Wong and Sucheng Chan, eds., *Claiming America: Constructing Chinese American Identities during the Exclusion Era* (Philadelphia: Temple University Press, 1998); Brian Masaru Hayashi, *For the Sake of Our Japanese Brethren: Assimilation, Nationalism, and Protestantism among the Japanese of Los Angeles, 1895-1942* (Stanford, CA: Stanford University Press, 1994); Xiaojian Zhao, *Remaking Chinese America: Immigration, Family, and Community, 1940-1963* (New Brunswick, NJ: Rutgers University Press, 2002); Renqiu Yu, *To Save China, To Save Ourselves: The Chinese Hand Laundry Alliance of New York* (Philadelphia: Temple University Press, 1992); Yong Chen, *Chinese San Francisco, 1850-1943: A Trans-Pacific Community* (Stanford, CA: Stanford University Press, 2000).

8. Ira Katznelson, *When Affirmative Action Was White* (New York: W. W. Norton, 2005), 42–48; Kenneth T. Jackson, *Crabgrass Frontier: The Suburbanization of the United States* (New York: Oxford University Press, 1985), 197–203.

9. Asian immigrant property rights were not consistent between 1849 and 1912 because of changes in naturalization rights, the California state constitution, and treaties between the United States and China and Japan. California's 1849 constitution guaranteed all resident foreigners the same property rights as citizens, a guarantee subsequent litigation upheld. Chinese were denied naturalization rights in the federal circuit ruling *In re Ah Yup* (1 F. Cas. 223) in 1878, and the U.S. treaty with China at that time guaranteed them "most favored nation" status only with regard to travel and residence. Exploiting this, the 1879 California state constitution gave aliens "of the white race or of African descent" the same property rights as American citizens, language that would have allowed the legislature to restrict Chinese property ownership. Yet as far as I can determine, the state legislature did *not* attempt at this time to pass any laws depriving Asian aliens of the right to own real property. In 1894, the state constitution

was amended to deny *all* non-naturalized aliens, regardless of race, the right to own real property. However, this conflicted with some U.S. treaties with foreign nations. In any case, the U.S.-China treaty, also amended in 1894, somewhat expanded the most-favored-nation status (and potentially the property rights) of Chinese nationals, as did the revised 1903 treaty, and both would have prevailed over the California constitution. Either way, I have found no litigation to indicate that the state enforced the 1894 measure against Chinese. Curbing Asian land ownership only became an issue with significant Japanese immigration after the turn of the century.

10. See, for example, Yuji Ichioka, *The Issei: The World of the First Generation Japanese Immigrants, 1885–1924* (New York: Free Press, 1988), 226–43; Lon Kurashige, *Japanese American Celebration and Conflict: A History of Ethnic Identity and Festival in Los Angeles, 1934–1990* (Berkeley: University of California Press, 2002), 17–19; Tomás Almaguer, *Racial Fault Lines: The Historical Origins of White Supremacy in California* (Berkeley: University of California Press, 1994), 184–87. In *Between Two Empires: Race, History, and Transnationalism in Japanese America* (New York: Oxford University Press, 2005), 62–79, Eiichiro Azuma devotes about two paragraphs of his extensive exploration of the impact of land laws to urban issues.

11. Mae Ngai, *Impossible Subjects: Illegal Aliens and the Making of Modern America* (Princeton, NJ: Princeton University Press, 2004), 2–8.

CHAPTER ONE

1. Mrs. Frank Leslie, *California: A Pleasure Trip from Gotham to the Golden Gate* (New York: G. W. Carleton and Company, 1877), 153–54; "Communication from the Mechanics State Council of California in Relation to Chinese Immigration," March 12, 1868, Chinese in California collection, Bancroft Library, University of California, Berkeley, http://content.cdlib.org/ark:/13030/hb1779n497/ (accessed September 11, 2007).

2. Arnold R. Hirsch, "With or Without Jim Crow: Black Residential Segregation in the United States," in *Urban Policy in Twentieth-Century America*, ed. Arnold R. Hirsch and Raymond A. Mohl (New Brunswick, NJ: Rutgers University Press, 1993), 73.

3. Douglas S. Massey and Nancy A. Denton, *American Apartheid: Segregation and the Making of the Underclass* (Cambridge, MA: Harvard University Press, 1993), 19, 20. Residential segregation actually became common in the urban South later than in the North.

4. See, for example, Thomas Sugrue, *The Origins of the Urban Crisis: Race and Inequality in Postwar Detroit* (Princeton, NJ: Princeton University Press, 1998); Andrew Wiese, *Places of Their Own: African American Suburbanization in the Twentieth Century* (Chicago: University of Chicago Press, 2005); John T. McGreevy, *Parish Boundaries: The Catholic Encounter with Race in the Twentieth-Century Urban North* (Chicago: University of Chicago Press, 1998); Arnold Hirsch, *Making the Second*

Ghetto: Race and Housing in Chicago, 1940–1960 (Chicago: University of Chicago Press, 1998); and Steven Gregory, *Black Corona: Race and the Politics of Place in an Urban Community* (Princeton, NJ: Princeton University Press, 1998).

5. John Logan et al., "Ethnic Diversity Grows, Neighborhood Integration Lags Behind," Report by the Lewis Mumford Center, University at Albany, SUNY, April 3, 2001, p. 3, http://mumford.albany.edu/census/WholePop/WPreport/MumfordReport. pdf (accessed June 11, 2008).

6. Massey and Denton, *American Apartheid*, 20, 26–29; Kenneth L. Kusmer, *A Ghetto Takes Shape: Black Cleveland, 1870–1930* (Urbana: University of Illinois Press, 1976), 35–45; Thomas Lee Philpott, *The Slum and the Ghetto: Neighborhood Deterioration and Middle-Class Reform, Chicago, 1880–1930* (New York: Oxford University Press, 1978), 119.

7. Massey and Denton, *American Apartheid*, 23; *Report on Population of the United States at the Eleventh Census: 1890, Part One* (Washington, D.C.: USGPO, 1895), 452; 1880 U.S. Federal Census (Population Schedule), San Francisco, San Francisco, California, Districts 1–229, U.S. Bureau of the Census, *Tenth Census of the United States, 1880* (Washington, D.C.: National Archives & Records Administration, 19–?), microfilm pub. T9, reels 73–79 [digital scan of original records in the National Archives, Washington, D.C.], http://content.ancestry.com/Browse/list.aspx?dbid= 6742&path=California.San+Francisco.San+Francisco (subscription only; accessed September 15, 2007). Throughout this book, I use two sociological measures of segregation. The first, the isolation index, measures the average percentage of a given racial or ethnic group in the measured area (the higher the percentage, the more isolated—and segregated—the group is). The second, the index of dissimilarity, measures the evenness of different groups' distribution over the measured area (the higher the index of dissimilarity, the less even—and thus more segregated—a group is).

8. Wayne F. Daugherty, *1939 Real Property Survey, San Francisco, California*, vol. 1 (San Francisco: City and County of San Francisco, *1939*), 101, 182; Bernard Taper, *1939 Real Property Survey, San Francisco, California*, vol. 3, *San Francisco's Housing* (San Francisco: City and County of San Francisco, 1939), 30; *Sixteenth Census of the United States, 1940: Population and Housing: Statistics for Census Tracts. San Francisco, Calif.* (Washington, D.C.: USGPO, 1942), 5. No evidence exists that the "nonwhites" listed in Chinatown were anything but Chinese Americans; contemporary observers concur with this conclusion. Between 1885 and 1915, state and federal courts ruled on a variety of cases involving Chinese laundries (*In Re Wong Wing, Yick Wo v. Hopkins*, and so forth). Although the San Francisco Board of Supervisors apparently never banned living in laundries, it did stipulate that "no person or persons engaged in the laundry business within that portion of this city described in section 1 of this order shall permit any person suffering from any infectious or contagious disease to lodge, sleep, or remain within or upon the premises used by him, her, or them for the purposes of a public laundry" (*In re Yick Wo*). The U.S. Supreme Court did not strike down this section in its ruling on *Yick Wo,* and

other California cities also adopted similar regulations. The statute may have been crucial to driving laundries and their Chinese residents out of many San Francisco neighborhoods after 1885, because as Nayan Shah has shown, public health officials began to target Chinese as health threats by this point.

9. Hirsch, *Making the Second Ghetto*, 23; Massey and Denton, *American Apartheid*, 24. Massey and Denton calculate a very high 82.9 dissimilarity index in the city of San Francisco in 1940, indicating the extreme segregation of blacks (47). They also cite a very low isolation index for blacks in 1930 (26), suggesting that astronomical segregation occurred in just a decade. As I will discuss in chapter 4, blacks did become somewhat more segregated during this time. However, Massey and Denton's source uses blocks, which census officials divided on a white/nonwhite basis, not a white/Negro/other basis. Using tracts, which census officials divided on the basis of race (white/Negro/other), I have found a dissimilarity rate of about 70 percent for blacks in 1940, and 76 percent for "other." The tendency of Japanese Americans to live in mixed, heavily black neighborhoods accounts for this rate. If Chinese Americans were considered separately, the rate would probably have been in the ninetieth percentile, as I have found using enumeration districts in 1930.

10. W. B. Farwell, John E. Kunkler, and E. B. Pond, *Report of the Special Committee of the Board of Supervisors of San Francisco on the Condition of the Chinese Quarter and the Chinese in San Francisco* (San Francisco: P. J. Thomas, 1885), 5; Taper, *San Francisco's Housing*, 7; Jacob A. Riis, *How the Other Half Lives: Studies Among the Tenements of New York* (New York: Charles Scribner's Sons, 1890); Lim P. Lee [Li Panlin/Lee Poonlum], "Yu chang jian ping yuan you guanzhi renwu" [Commending Ping Yuen's Advocates and Builders], *Taipingyang Zhoubao* [Chinese-Pacific Weekly (San Francisco)], October 6, 1951 (all translations, unless otherwise noted, are mine). James Grossman, *Land of Hope: Chicago, Black Southerners, and the Great Migration* (Chicago: University of Chicago Press, 1989), 135-37, discusses conditions in the Black Belt of Chicago, the most segregated city in America. Black migrants frequently lived in substandard homes, but their apartments were fairly spacious and often had kitchen facilities.

11. Nayan Shah, *Contagious Divides: Epidemics and Race in San Francisco's Chinatown* (Berkeley: University of California Press, 2001), 66, 158.

12. Carey McWilliams, *California: The Great Exception* (Berkeley: University of California Press, 1949), 42.

13. Tomás Almaguer, *Racial Fault Lines: The Historical Origins of White Supremacy in California* (Berkeley: University of California Press, 1994), 157-58; Ronald Takaki, *Strangers from a Different Shore: A History of Asian Americans* (New York: Penguin Books, 1989), 81; Madeline Yuan-yin Hsu, *Dreaming of Gold, Dreaming of Home: Transnationalism and Migration Between the United States and South China, 1882-1943* (Stanford, CA: Stanford University Press, 2000), 59.

14. Eric Foner, *Free Soil, Free Labor, Free Men: The Ideology of the Republican Party Before the Civil War* (New York: Oxford University Press, 1995), xxv-xxvi, 9,

57–59; James Oakes, *Slavery and Freedom: An Interpretation of the Old South* (New York: Vintage Books, 1990), 135.

15. David Roediger, *The Wages of Whiteness: Race and the Making of the American Working Class*, rev. ed. (New York: Verso, 1999), 35, 57; Leon Litwack, *North of Slavery: The Negro in the Free States* (Chicago: University of Chicago Press, 1965), 71; Rowland Berthoff, "Conventional Mentality: Free Blacks, Women, and Business Corporations as Unequal Persons, 1820–1870," *Journal of American History* 76:3 (December 1989): 761, 763.

16. Almaguer, *Racial Fault Lines*, 14, 210; Foner, *Free Soil, Free Labor, Free Men*, 262; *People v. Hall*, 4 Cal. 399 (1854).

17. Hsu, *Dreaming of Gold, Dreaming of Home*, 58–60. Hsu suggests that the money to be made in California proved too enticing to pass up, even in the face of violence.

18. Jonathan D. Spence, *God's Chinese Son: The Taiping Heavenly Kingdom of Hong Xiuquan* (New York: W. W. Norton, 1997), xxi; Yong Chen, "The Internal Origins of Chinese Emigration to California Reconsidered," *Western Historical Quarterly* 28:4 (Winter 1997): 526, 541–43; Alexander Saxton, *The Indispensable Enemy: Labor and the Anti-Chinese Movement in California* (Berkeley: University of California Press, 1971), 62–63, 114; Almaguer, *Racial Fault Lines*, 171–73; Alexander Saxton, *The Rise and Fall of the White Republic: Class Politics and Mass Culture in Nineteenth-Century America* (New York: Verso, 1990), 295.

19. Shah, *Contagious Divides*, 159–61; Saxton, *The Rise and Fall of the White Republic*, 295; idem, *The Indispensable Enemy*, 71; William Issel and Robert W. Cherny, *San Francisco, 1865–1920: Politics, Power, and Urban Development* (Berkeley: University of California Press, 1986), 126–27, 129.

20. Philip J. Ethington, *The Public City: The Political Construction of Urban Life in San Francisco, 1850–1900* (New York: Cambridge University Press, 1994), 283.

21. Gertrude Atherton, *My San Francisco: A Wayward Biography* (New York: Bobbs-Merrill, 1946), 26.

22. Issel and Cherny, *San Francisco, 1865–1920*, 58.

23. Michael Kazin, *Barons of Labor: The San Francisco Building Trades and Union Power in the Progressive Era* (Urbana: University of Illinois Press, 1987), 13–14; Ray Stannard Baker, "A Corner in Labor: What's Happening in San Francisco Where Unionism Holds Undisputed Sway," *McClure's* 22 (February 1904): 366; Issel and Cherny, *San Francisco, 1865–1920*, 99–100, 213.

24. Issel and Cherny, *San Francisco, 1865–1920*, 56, 206; John Higham, *Strangers in the Land: Patterns of American Nativism, 1860–1925* (New Brunswick, NJ: Rutgers University Press, 1994), 169–86; Matthew Frye Jacobson, *Whiteness of a Different Color: European Immigrants and the Alchemy of Race* (Cambridge, MA: Harvard University Press, 1998), 80–81; Kazin, *Barons of Labor*, 20–25.

25. Higham, *Strangers in the Land*, 4, 170; Mae Ngai, *Impossible Subjects: Illegal Aliens and the Making of Modern America* (Princeton, NJ: Princeton University Press, 2004), 11.

26. Section 14 of the Chinese Exclusion Act of 1882 reaffirmed a federal circuit court's determination in the 1878 case *In re Ah Yup* (1 F. Cas. 223) that Chinese were racially ineligible to become naturalized U.S. citizens.

27. California politicians routinely joined the Native Sons of the Golden West and maintained an affiliation with one of the many parlors across the state, but most Native Sons were ordinary citizens: an 1897 roster of officers from San Francisco's Rincon Parlor includes an attorney, a surgeon, a tailor, a pattern maker, an iron worker, two machinists, a salesman, and a retail harness dealer, among others. All of these men were born in California, but their parents hailed from a range of European nations, including France, Ireland, Germany, Finland, Russia, and "Austrian Bohemia."

28. Higham, *Strangers in the Land*, 75; "History," Native Sons of the Golden West Web site, http://www.nsgw.org/history.htm (accessed August 30, 2006).

29. In the 1930s, the Native Sons criticized Mexican immigration, but their main focus remained Asians.

30. McGreevy, *Parish Boundaries*, 36; Russell A. Kazal, *Becoming Old Stock: The Paradox of German-American Identity* (Princeton, NJ: Princeton University Press, 2004), 251–52; Jacobson, *Whiteness of a Different Color*, 95–96. Jacobson mentions a San Francisco newspaper's take on race as "atypical," because it included all the various European "races" as part of the "real American population" (91).

31. Shah, *Contagious Divides*, 166.

32. Ibid., 165–66; Lucy E. Salyer, *Laws Harsh as Tigers: Chinese Immigrants and the Shaping of Modern Immigration Law* (Chapel Hill: University of North Carolina Press, 1995); John Kuo Wei Tchen, *New York Before Chinatown: Orientalism and the Shaping of American Culture, 1776-1882* (Baltimore, MD: The Johns Hopkins University Press, 1999), 225; Yong Chen, *Chinese San Francisco: A Trans-Pacific Community, 1850-1943* (Stanford, CA: Stanford University Press, 2000), 59; Eliot Grinnell Mears, *Resident Orientals on the American Pacific Coast: Their Legal and Economic Status* (Chicago: University of Chicago Press, 1928), 263–64, 402, 413.

33. Saxton, *The Rise and Fall of the White Republic*, 299–303; advertisement for the Native Sons of the Golden West, *Grizzly Bear* vol. 35, no. 208 (August 1924): back cover.

34. Connie Young Yu, "A History of San Francisco Chinatown Housing," *Amerasia* 8:1 (1981): 95.

35. B. E. Lloyd, *Lights and Shades in San Francisco* (San Francisco: A. L. Bancroft, 1875), 236; Mark Twain, *Roughing It* (New York: Penguin, 1981), 391; R. David Arkush and Leo O. Lee, eds., *Land Without Ghosts: Chinese Impressions of America from the Mid-Nineteenth Century to the Present* (Berkeley: University of California Press, 1989), 73.

36. 1880 U.S. Federal Census (Population Schedule), San Francisco Districts 27–30, 33, 35, 48–50, 52, 53; San Francisco Board of Supervisors, Special Committee on Chinatown, "Official Map of 'Chinatown' in San Francisco," ca. 1885, Chinese in California collection, Bancroft Library, University of California, Berkeley; http://

content.cdlib.org/ark:/13030/hb8j49n988/?docId=hb8j49n988&&query=map&
brand=oac&layout=printable and http://content.cdlib.org/ark:/13030/hb1p30016z/?
docId=hb1p30016z&&query=map&brand=oac&layout=printable (accessed August 30, 2006). These buildings were likely brothels, but even if they were not, the labeling of their occupants as prostitutes indicates the prevailing understanding of living near Chinese.

37. Judy Yung, *Unbound Feet: A Social History of Chinese Women in San Francisco* (Berkeley: University of California Press, 1995), 28–30; Robert G. Lee, *Orientals: Asian Americans in Popular Culture* (Philadelphia: Temple University Press, 1999), 104; Twain, *Roughing It*, 391; Yu, "A History of San Francisco Chinatown Housing," 97–99; Shah, *Contagious Divides*, 32, 81, 89–90, 107–9, 129.

38. Chen, *Chinese San Francisco*, 58; Issel and Cherny, *San Francisco*, 126; Farwell et al., *Report of the Special Committee*, 5; Shah, *Contagious Divides*, 33–37, 71–72. Ignoring the segregation the Chinese faced, most scholars have dated the first legislative attempt to zone residential segregation to Baltimore, Maryland, in the 1910s. The first litigated racially restrictive covenant was also aimed at Chinese in California. A federal circuit court in *Gandolfo v. Hartman* (49 F. 181; 1892 U.S. App.) threw out the covenant, ruling that "it would be [ridiculous] . . . to hold that, while state and municipal legislatures are forbidden to discriminate against the Chinese in their legislation, a citizen of the state may lawfully do so by contract, which the courts may enforce." Ironically, the U.S. Supreme Court ruled twenty-five years later that such contracts were, in fact, valid and enforceable by the courts.

39. Yu, "A History of San Francisco Chinatown Housing," 100; Chen, *Chinese San Francisco*, 165–66.

40. Bureau of the Census, *Fifteenth Census of the United States, 1930: Population Number and Distribution of Inhabitants* (Washington, D.C.: USGPO, 1931), 266; Mears, *Resident Orientals on the American Pacific Coast*, 422 (Mears provides figures for the entire state; the ratio of men to women was probably lower in San Francisco, where a settled family life was more possible for couples); Mae Ngai, "Legacies of Exclusion: Illegal Chinese Immigration during the Cold War Years," *Journal of American Ethnic History* 18:1 (September 1998): 3; Yung, *Unbound Feet*, 106. At least some of the population surge was due to the immigration of China-born men (and some women) with actual Chinese American citizen fathers. Such children, called derivative citizens, were born of Chinese American citizen men who married Chinese women on trips to China. Their children received their citizenship from their American citizen fathers. Paper sons all claimed to be derivative citizens, but there probably were a fair number of legitimate derivative citizens.

41. Ruth M.W. Chue and Lena A. Way, "Comments on Housing Action in Chinatown," May 1940, sec. I, p. 5 and sec. II, p. 2, "Chinatown" file, carton 6, Catherine Bauer Wurster papers, Bancroft Library, University of California, Berkeley; William Hoy, notes on Yew Toy, March 1935, folder 18, box 2, William Hoy papers, Ethnic Studies Library, University of California, Berkeley; William Hoy, notes on You Ur

Choy, 1936, folder 18, box 2, William Hoy papers, Ethnic Studies Library, University of California, Berkeley; Esther Wang, "The History and Problem of Angel Island," March 1924, p. 11, major document 150, box 26, Survey of Race Relations on the Pacific Coast (hereafter, SRRPC), Hoover Institution, Stanford, California.

42. Chue and Way, "Comments on Housing Action in Chinatown," sec. III, p. 5; Harold Isaacs, *Scratches on Our Minds: American Images of China and India* (Westport, CT: Greenwood Press, 1973), 101; Shah, *Contagious Divides*, 158; Farwell, et al., *Report of the Special Committee*, 6; Sue A. Pike Sanders, *A Journey to, on, and from the "Golden Shore"* (Delevan, IL: Times Printing, 1887), 61; "Resident Orientals, Personal Interviews: Miss Wong, Chinese Y.W.C.A., San Francisco," May 1927, "Segregation" file, box 1, SRRPC. Even later and more favorable commentators repeated these assertions about the supposed Chinese love for living in overcrowded spaces. See, for example, Carl Crow, "Our Allies, the Chinese," *Ladies' Home Journal*, January 1944, 5.

43. Judy Yung, *Unbound Voices: A Documentary History of Chinese Women in San Francisco* (Berkeley: University of California Press, 1999), 218; T. Y. Chen et al., "Social Service Needs of the Chinese Population of San Francisco," (San Francisco: Emergency Relief Administration, 1935), 39.

44. Massey and Denton, *American Apartheid*, 32-40; see also Kazal, *Becoming Old Stock*, 247; Sugrue, *The Origins of the Urban Crisis*, 22; McGreevy, *Parish Boundaries*, 34.

45. See, for example, Redwood City, California, deed in "Segregated Housing" file, box 2, SRRPC. Covenant wording differed from place to place and often targeted particular local minority groups, including Asian Americans, African Americans, Jews, Armenians, Syrians, and others.

46. "Resident Orientals, Personal Interviews: Miss Murphy," May 1927, p. 1, file "Segregation," box 1, SRRPC; Victor Low, *The Unimpressible Race: A Century of Education Struggle by the Chinese of San Francisco* (San Francisco: East/West Publishing Company, 1982), 115-22. As Becky Nicolaides, *My Blue Heaven: Life and Politics in the Working-Class Suburbs of Los Angeles, 1920-1965* (Chicago: University of Chicago Press, 2002), 164, has shown, struggles for school segregation in Los Angeles County during the same era also foundered on the issue of high costs.

47. Wang, "The History and Problem of Angel Island," 11; anonymous social worker, ca. 1924, p. 2, major document 148, box 26, SRRPC.

48. Anonymous social worker, ca. 1924, p. 2; Albert S. Broussard, *Black San Francisco: The Struggle for Racial Equality in the West, 1900-1954* (Lawrence: University Press of Kansas, 1993), 31.

49. Jerome A. Hart, "The Asiatic Peril," *Grizzly Bear*, May 1907, 24-25; Paul Scharrenberg, "The Attitude of Organized Labor towards the Japanese," *Annals of the American Academy* 93:1 (January 1921): 34-36; Kazin, *Barons of Labor*, 164; Proceedings of the Asiatic Exclusion League, San Francisco, December 8, 1907, 9; Spencer C. Olin, Jr., *California's Prodigal Sons: Hiram Johnson and the Progressives, 1911-1917* (Berkeley: University of California Press, 1968), 81.

50. "Resident Orientals, Personal Interviews: Miss Murphy," p. 1.

51. "Jap Purchases to Be Probed," *San Francisco Examiner*, October 6, 1920; "State Takes Hand in Jap Realty Probe," *San Francisco Examiner*, October 9, 1920; "Realty Firms Handle Japs' Sales, Charge," *San Francisco Examiner*, November 11, 1920; "Fight Begun to Bar Japanese on Bush Street," *San Francisco Chronicle*, August 5, 1921.

52. Charles A. Selden, "Japanese Settler Problem Paramount in California," *New York Times*, January 25, 1920; "Business Backs Hughes on Japan," *New York Times*, May 8, 1924.

53. John H. Mollenkopf, *The Contested City* (Princeton, NJ: Princeton University Press, 1983), 172; Japantown Task Force, Inc., *San Francisco's Japantown* (San Francisco: Arcadia Publishing, 1995), 9; Division of Research and Statistics, Federal Home Loan Bank Board, Area Description San Francisco D-3, ca. 1937, file "San Francisco, California Master File Security Map and Area Descriptions," box 147, RG 195, National Archives, College Park, Maryland (hereafter, NARA); Chester Rowell, "Chinese and Japanese Immigrants—A Comparison," *Annals of the American Academy of Political and Social Science*, 34:2 (September 1909): 227, 230; Broussard, *Black San Francisco*, 32–34.

54. "Local Item," *Japanese American News* (San Francisco), April 5, 1925; CH-50 interview by Charles Kikuchi, September 18, 1944, transcript, p. 35, folder T1.979, Japanese American Evacuation and Resettlement Study (hereafter, JAERS), Bancroft Library, University of California, Berkeley; CH-57 interview by Kikuchi, November 2, 1944, p. 13, folder T1.986, JAERS, Bancroft Library, University of California, Berkeley. Using enumeration data transcriptions from the Web site Ancestry.com, I have determined that the isolation index for Chinese Americans in San Francisco in 1930 was 70 percent (the dissimilarity index was a stunningly high 92 percent). For Japanese Americans, it was 27 percent, and for blacks it was 4 percent. Comparing these statistics with other cities' statistics is difficult, for 1930 isolation indices are measured by ward. San Francisco's "wards" were assembly districts and thus much larger than wards elsewhere. However, the Japanese American isolation rate was comparable to black isolation rates in heavily segregated cities such as Detroit, Indianapolis, and Philadelphia. The Chinese American isolation rate was almost identical to the black isolation rate in Chicago, where it was higher than anywhere else in America. The black isolation rate in San Francisco, measured by assembly district or enumeration district, was among the lowest in the nation.

55. Kazin, *Barons of Labor*, 163–71; Broussard, *Black San Francisco*, 107; Marilynn S. Johnson, *The Second Gold Rush: Oakland and the East Bay in World War II* (Berkeley: University of California Press, 1993), 22, 71.

56. Kusmer, *A Ghetto Takes Shape*, 235; Gilbert Osofsky, *Harlem: The Making of a Ghetto*, 2nd ed. (New York: Harper Torchbooks, 1971), 93–104, 117–20; Allan H. Spear, *Black Chicago: The Making of a Negro Ghetto, 1890–1920* (Chicago: University of Chicago Press, 1967), 83, 225–27.

57. Broussard, *Black San Francisco*, 21–23.

58. Serena B. Preusser, "Color Question in California Reveals Many Problems," *California Real Estate*, July 1927, 35, 61; Massey and Denton, *American Apartheid*, 29; Broussard, *Black San Francisco*, 30.

59. Minutes of the Sunset Transportation and Development Association, July 13 and December 12, 1925, and January 9, 1928, Records of the Sunset Transportation and Development Association, North Baker Research Library, California Historical Society, San Francisco.

60. Broussard, *Black San Francisco*, 32.

61. Ivan Light, "From Vice District to Tourist Attraction: The Moral Career of American Chinatowns, 1880–1940," *Pacific Historical Review* 43:3 (August 1974): 368, 389; Mary H. Wills, *A Winter in California* (Norristown, PA: M. A. Wills, 1889) 107, 115.

62. R. K. Newman, "Opium Smoking in Late Imperial China: A Reconsideration," *Modern Asian Studies* 29:4 (October 1995): 770–71; Ellen Oxfeld Basu, "Profit, Loss, and Fate: The Entrepreneurial Ethic and the Practice of Gambling in an Overseas Chinese Community," *Modern China* 17:2 (April 1991): 230–31; Wang, "The History and Problem of Angel Island," 11; L. Eve Armentrout-Ma, "Urban Chinese at the Sinitic Frontier: Social Organizations in United States Chinatowns, 1849–1898," *Modern Asian Studies* 17:1 (1983), 116, 121–26.

63. Shah, *Contagious Divides*, 207–9; Light, "From Vice District to Tourist Attraction," 383–85.

64. William Hoy, *The Chinese Six Companies* (San Francisco: Chinese Consolidated Benevolent Association, 1942), 22; Ruth Teiser interview with Thomas W. Chinn, "A Historian's Reflections On Chinese-American Life in San Francisco, 1919–1991," December 10, 1990, p. 13, Regional Oral History Office, The Bancroft Library, University of California, Berkeley, 1993; Light, "From Vice District to Tourist Attraction," 390; Victor G. and Brett de Bary Nee, *Longtime Californ': A Documentary Study of an American Chinatown* (Stanford, CA: Stanford University Press, 1986), 71–72.

65. *San Francisco's Chinatown* (n.p. [CCBA?]: October 1909), pp. 11–14, Department of Special Collections, Young Research Library, University of California, Los Angeles; Mrs. Clemens Wang, *Chinatown* (San Francisco: Mrs. C. Wang, 1915), 8, California Digital Library, http://sunsite.berkeley.edu/cgi-bin/flipomatic/cic/chs1014 (accessed September 1, 2006); Wang, "The History and Problem of Angel Island," 11; Sidney Herschel Small, "San Francisco's Chinatown," *Holiday*, August 1954, 100.

66. Helen Virginia Cather, "The History of San Francisco's Chinatown" (master's thesis, University of California, Berkeley, 1932), 86; School of Social Studies, "Living Conditions in Chinatown," p. 3, file "Hogan—Living in Chinatown," box 2, Records Relating to the History of the Agency ("Historical File"), 1934–1948, Records of the Central Office (Records of the Office of the Historian), RG196, NARA; Philip P. Choy,

"The Architecture of San Francisco Chinatown," *Chinese America: History and Perspectives* 1990: 49–51.

67. Shehong Chen, *Being Chinese, Becoming Chinese American* (Urbana: University of Illinois Press, 2006), 13; Sing Chong Company business card, ca. 1915, Ethnic Studies Library, University of California, Berkeley, http://ark.cdlib.org/ark:/13030/hb3779n5t3/ (accessed September 1, 2006); *1916/1917 Crocker-Langley San Francisco Directory* (San Francisco: H. S. Crocker, 1916), 2342.

68. *San Francisco's Chinatown*, 12; Grand View Garden Restaurant, menu, ca. 1920s, Ethnic Studies Library, University of California, Berkeley, http://ark.cdlib.org/ark:/13030/hb2z09n5ns/ (accessed September 1, 2006); Chinese Tea Garden, menu, ca. 1920s, Ethnic Studies Library, University of California, Berkeley, http://ark.cdlib.org/ark:/13030/hb4x0nb082/ (accessed September 1, 2006).

69. Mears, *Resident Orientals on the American Pacific Coast*, 209.

70. School of Social Studies, "Living Conditions in Chinatown," p. 6; Chue and Way, "Comments on Housing Action in Chinatown," sec. I, p. 5. Connie Young Yu argues that white Americans owned most of Chinatown until after World War Two (Yu, "A History of San Francisco Chinatown Housing," 101), based on interviews with Dr. Theodore Lee. The two 1930s studies contend that Chinese Americans owned three-fifths of the area.

71. "High Class Apartment Building Exclusively for Chinese," *San Francisco Chronicle*, January 29, 1927; School of Social Studies, "Living Conditions in Chinatown," p. 6.

72. Chue and Way, "Comments on Housing Action in Chinatown," sec. I, p. 4; Daughterty, *1939 Real Property Survey*, 182–83; School of Social Studies, "Living Conditions in Chinatown," p. 6.

73. Langston Hughes, *The Big Sea: An Autobiography* (New York: Hill and Wang, 1993), 223; A. B. Christa Schwarz, *Gay Voices of the Harlem Renaissance* (Bloomington: Indiana University Press, 2003), 8, 35–36. Hughes also alludes to this in *The Big Sea*, 237.

74. Frank Morton Todd, *The Chamber of Commerce Handbook for San Francisco* (San Francisco: San Francisco Chamber of Commerce, 1914), 67–68; Isaacs, *Scratches on Our Minds*, 140–41.

75. Spear, *Black Chicago*, 191; Osofsky, *Harlem*, 165–78.

76. Lizabeth Cohen, *Making a New Deal: Industrial Workers in Chicago, 1919–1939* (New York: Cambridge University Press, 1990), 148–49; Spear, *Black Chicago*, 83; Osofsky, *Harlem*, 170–71; Kusmer, *A Ghetto Takes Shape*, 152–53.

77. Phoebe S. Kropp, *California Vieja: Culture and Memory in a Modern American Place* (Berkeley: University of California Press, 2006), 5–6; William Deverell, *Whitewashed Adobe: The Rise of Los Angeles and the Remaking of Its Mexican Past* (Berkeley: University of California Press, 2004), 53–56, 218–22.

78. E. C. Ortega Interview by Chloe Holt, January 22, 1925, p. 3, major document 274A-2, box 30, SRRPC; J. C. Mitchell Interview by Chloe Holt, December 15,

1924, p. 1, major document 274A-16, box 30, SRRPC; A. E. Hennion Interview by Chloe Holt, December 17, 1924, p. 1, major document 274A-17, box 30, SRRPC; H. J. Barceloux Interview, October 25, 1924, p. 1, minor document 1, box 33, SRRPC; H. Ramsey Interview, "Interviews with Employers of Farm Workers," ca. 1924, p. 1, minor document 1, box 33, SRRPC; Lillian R. Thielen, "Causes of Anti-Japanese Prejudice in California," May 1923, pp. 7-8, minor document 192b, box 33, SRRPC; David Blight, *Race and Reunion: The Civil War in American Memory* (Cambridge, MA: Belknap Press of Harvard University, 2001), 220-21; M. J. Boggs Interview, "Interviews with Employers of Farm Workers"; Cletus E. Daniels, *Bitter Harvest: A History of California Farmworkers, 1871-1941* (Ithaca, NY: Cornell University Press, 1981), 72-74.

79. "The Chinese in America," *Literary Digest*, 92:11 (March 12, 1927), 81.

80. Isaacs, *Scratches on Our Minds*, 116-17; Sax Rohmer, *The Insidious Dr. Fu-Manchu: being a somewhat detailed account of the amazing adventures of Nayland Smith in his trailing of the sinister Chinaman* (New York: A. L. Burt, 1920). Lee, *Orientals*, 116-40, discusses various aspects of "Oriental" film portrayals in far greater depth.

81. Chin Bock Choy, "American-Made Chinese Photoplays," *The Trailmaker*, March 1924, no file, box 2, SRRPC; Nee and Nee, *Longtime Californ'*, 71-72.

82. Gloria Heyung Chun, *Of Orphans and Warriors: Inventing Chinese American Culture and Identity* (New Brunswick, NJ: Rutgers University Press, 2000), 26; Choy, "American-Made Chinese Photoplays," 23; Yung, *Unbound Voices*, 254.

CHAPTER TWO

1. "'Swat' the 'Jap' Goes to Bat for White America," *Swat the Jap* vol. 1—Special, June 23, 1923, cited in Koyoshi Uono, "The Factors Affecting the Geographical Aggregation and Dispersion of the Japanese Residences in the City of Los Angeles" (master's thesis, University of Southern California, 1927), 140b; Bureau of the Census, *Fourteenth Census of the United States Vol III, Population, 1920: Composition and Characteristics of the Population by States* (Washington, D.C.: USGPO, 1922), 110, http://www2.census.gov/prod2/decennial/documents/41084484v3.pdf (accessed June 27, 2008); Lon Kurashige, *Japanese American Celebration and Conflict: A History of Ethnic Identity and Festival in Los Angeles, 1934-1990* (Berkeley: University of California Press, 2002), 18-21. The San Francisco earthquake of 1906 also prompted a number of Japanese to move to Southern California.

2. W. A. Bixel, "A Nordic Census," *Commonweal*, August 27, 1930, 424; Mark Wild, *Street Meeting: Multiethnic Neighborhoods in Early Twentieth-Century Los Angeles* (Berkeley: University of California Press, 2005), 38; Mike Davis, "Sunshine and the Open Shop: Ford and Darwin in 1920s Los Angeles," *Antipode* 29:4 (October 1997): 376. The term "white spot" referred to the idea that the city was not friendly to "reds," the term many employers used to refer to union organizers.

3. Robert Fogelson, *The Fragmented Metropolis: Los Angeles, 1850–1930* (Cambridge, MA: Harvard University Press, 1967), 68–74; Carey McWilliams, *Southern California: An Island on the Land* (Salt Lake City, UT: Gibbs Smith, 1999), 157–58; Davis, "Sunshine and the Open Shop," 376–77.

4. Between 1910 and 1930, the overall population of Los Angeles County increased from 504,131 to 2,208,492. The Japanese American population increased from 4,238 to 35,390; the Mexican American population from an estimated 20,000 to 163,216; the black population from 9,424 to 46,425, and the southern and eastern European immigrant population from 11,178 to 62,993. Bureau of the Census, *Thirteenth Census of the United States: Vol. II—Population, 1910: Alabama–Montana* (Washington, D.C.: USGPO, 1913), 162, 166, 172–73, 180–81, 185, http://www2.census.gov/prod2/decennial/documents/36894832v2.pdf (accessed June 27, 2008); idem, *Fourteenth Census of the United States, 1920: Vol. III*, 109–10, 14, 118; idem, *Fifteenth Census of the United States, 1930: Vol. III, Pt. 1—Population, Alabama–Missouri* (Washington, D.C.: USGPO, 1932), 252, 260, 266–69, http://www2.census.gov/prod2/decennial/documents/10612963v3p1.pdf (accessed June 27, 2008).

5. Carey McWilliams, *California: The Great Exception* (Berkeley: University of California Press, 1999), 26, 33, 58, 136–37; Gary Brechin, *Imperial San Francisco: Urban Power, Earthly Ruin* (Berkeley: University of California Press, 1999), 95–96; William Deverell, *Whitewashed Adobe: The Rise of Los Angeles and the Remaking of Its Mexican Past* (Berkeley: University of California Press, 2004), 14–19; Fogelson, *The Fragmented Metropolis*, 43, 52, 70–74.

6. Fogelson, *The Fragmented Metropolis*, 148; Becky Nicolaides, "'Where the Working Man Is Welcomed': Working-Class Suburbs in Los Angeles, 1900–1940," *Pacific Historical Review* 68:4 (November 1999): 533.

7. Gail Radford, *Modern Housing for America: Policy Struggles in the New Deal Era* (Chicago: University of Chicago Press, 1996), 19–27; Mike Davis, *City of Quartz: Excavating the Future in Los Angeles* (New York: Vintage Books, 1992), 28–30; Nicolaides, "'Where the Working Man Is Welcomed,'" 535; Deverell, *Whitewashed Adobe*, 139; Fogelson, *The Fragmented Metropolis*, 104–5, 151, 226–27.

8. Fogelson, *The Fragmented Metropolis*, 151–53; Kenneth T. Jackson, *Crabgrass Frontier: The Suburbanization of the United States* (New York: Oxford University Press, 1985), 184–89.

9. McWilliams, *Southern California*, 135; Becky M. Nicolaides, *My Blue Heaven: Life and Politics in the Working-Class Suburbs of Los Angeles, 1920–1965* (Chicago: University of Chicago Press, 2002), 13–20, 24–29; idem, "'Where the Working Man Is Welcomed,'" 526–27; Andrew Wiese, *Places of Their Own: African American Suburbanization in the Twentieth Century* (Chicago: University of Chicago Press, 2004), 17–19.

10. *Fourteenth Census of the United States, Vol. III: Population, 1920*, 109; Bureau of the Census, *Fifteenth Census of the United States, 1930: Population Number and Distribution of Inhabitants* (Washington, D.C.: USGPO, 1931), 267, http://www2.

census.gov/prod2/decennial/documents/03815512v1.pdf (accessed June 27, 2008); T. H. Bowden and D. W. Mayborn, "Confidential Report of a Survey in Metropolitan Los Angeles, California," p. 7, file "California," box 74, Records Relating to the City Survey File, 1935–1940, Records of the Home Owners' Loan Corporation, RG 195, NARA; W. M. Fitchmiller to Harry Allen, President, California Real Estate Association, March 1, 1927, p. 1, file "Segregated Housing," box 2, SRRPC.

11. Davis, "Sunshine and the Open Shop," 358–59, 376; Wendy Kline, *Building a Better Race: Gender, Sexuality, and Eugenics from the Turn of the Century to the Baby Boom* (Berkeley: University of California Press, 2001), 34.

12. During the Great Migration, which historians generally describe as the period between 1915 and 1920, more than half a million African Americans from the South migrated to cities outside the region, especially Chicago and New York.

13. Nicolaides, *My Blue Heaven*, 24–25; Davis, "Sunshine and the Open Shop," 374; Wild, *Street Meeting*, 50; Josh Sides, *L.A. City Limits: African American Los Angeles from the Great Depression to the Present* (Berkeley: University of California Press, 2003), 14. Some Mexican Americans eventually found work in factories, but often received less than "white wages."

14. Wild, *Street Meeting*, 4; Sides, *L.A. City Limits*, 4, 14–15, 23, 25–26; Natalia Molina, *Fit to Be Citizens? Public Health and Race in Los Angeles, 1879–1939* (Berkeley: University of California Press, 2006), 54.

15. Douglas Monroy, *Rebirth: Mexican Los Angeles from the Great Migration to the Great Depression* (Berkeley: University of California Press, 1999), 35–38; Lawrence Brooks de Graaf, "Negro Migration to Los Angeles, 1930 to 1950" (PhD diss., University of California, Los Angeles, 1962), 76; Larry Tye, *Rising from the Rails: Pullman Porters and the Making of the Black Middle Class* (New York: Owl Books, 2005), 2–3, 92–93.

16. Yuji Ichioka, *The Issei: The World of the First Generation Japanese Immigrants, 1885–1924* (New York: The Free Press, 1988), 72; Ronald Takaki, *Strangers from a Different Shore: A History of Asian Americans* (New York: Penguin Books, 1989), 188–93; Michael Kazin, *Barons of Labor: The San Francisco Building Trades and Union Power in the Progressive Era* (Urbana: University of Illinois Press, 1987), 163; Carey McWilliams, *California: The Great Exception* (Berkeley: University of California Press, 1999), 99–101, 153; Robert Higgs, "Landless by Law: Japanese Immigrants in California Agriculture to 1941," *Journal of Economic History* 38:1 (1978): 207.

17. Lee D. Baker, *From Savage to Negro: Anthropology and the Construction of Race, 1896–1954* (Berkeley: University of California Press, 1998), 92; Madison Grant, *The Passing of the Great Race* (New York: Charles Scribner's Sons, 1921), 17; Molina, *Fit to Be Citizens?*, 43; Lothrop Stoddard, *The Rising Tide of Color Against White World Supremacy* (New York: Charles Scribner's Sons, 1920), 229; Raymond Leslie Buell, "Again the Yellow Peril," *Foreign Affairs* 2 (1925): 295.

18. Stoddard, *The Rising Tide of Color*, 154; Clarence M. Hunt, "Growls from the Grizzly: California Must Have Protective Laws," *Grizzly Bear* 26 no. 151 (November

1919): 10; Marshall De Motte, "California—White or Yellow?" *Annals of the American Academy of Political and Social Science* 93:1 (January 1921): 18–23; V. S. McClatchy, "Japanese in the Melting-Pot: Can They Assimilate and Make Good Citizens?" *Annals of the American Academy of Political and Social Science* 93:1 (January 1921): 29–34.

19. See, for example, *In re Buntaro Kumagui* (D.C.), 163 Fed. 922 (1908); *Bessho v. U.S.*, 178 Fed. 245, 101 C.C.A. 605 (1910); *In re Saito*, 62 F. 126 (1894). The U.S. Attorney General in 1906 ordered that no more Japanese be naturalized, because they were not white.

20. *Takao Ozawa v. U.S.*, 260 U.S. 178 (1922).

21. Eliot Grinnell Mears, *Resident Orientals on the American Pacific Coast: Their Legal and Economic Status* (Chicago: University of Chicago Press, 1928), 56.

22. See, for example, *Webb v. O'Brien* 263 U.S. 313 (1923); *Frick v. Webb* 263 U.S. 326 (1923).

23. Ichioka, *The Issei*, 243; Midori Nishi, "Changing Occupance of the Japanese in Los Angeles County, 1940–1950" (PhD diss., University of Washington, 1955), 30; Eiichiro Azuma, *Between Two Empires: Race, History, and Transnationalism in Japanese America* (New York: Oxford University Press, 2005), 79–82.

24. Higgs, "Landless by Law," 213–14; A. E. Hennion interview by Chloe Holt, December 17, 1924, p. 2, major document 274A-17, box 30, SRRPC; Mr. Ishizaki interview by Chloe Holt, February 2, 1925, p. 2, major document 274A-39, box 30, SRRPC; Nishi, "Changing Occupance," 37.

25. Azuma, *Between Two Empires*, 63; Nishi, "Changing Occupance," 32; Kurashige, *Japanese American Celebration and Conflict*, 19; J. Max Bond, "The Negro in Los Angeles" (PhD diss., University of Southern California, 1936), 148; Molina, *Fit to Be Citizens?*, 106.

26. James D. Phelan campaign poster, in Ichiro Mike Murase, *Little Tokyo: One Hundred Years in Pictures* (Los Angeles: Visual Communications, 1983), 59; "One Object, One Design," *Los Angeles Times*, September 22, 1920.

27. Uono, "Factors Affecting the Geographical Aggregation," 129. Pico Heights was roughly bounded by West Pico, South Normandie, West Olympic, and South Vermont avenues.

28. 1910 U.S. Federal Census (Population Schedule), Los Angeles, Assembly District 72, Enumeration District 211 [digital scan of original records in the National Archives, Washington, D.C.], http://www.ancestry.com/ (subscription only; accessed September 15, 2007) (all enumeration schedules cited in this chapter come from this source); 1920 U.S. Federal Census (Population Schedule), Los Angeles, Assembly District 63, Enumeration District 187; Loyola High School of Los Angeles, "The Historical Mission of Our School," http://www.loyolahs.net/files/About_Loyola/Historical_Mission_of_LHS/index.htm (accessed October 12, 2007). John T. McGreevy discusses the importance of parochial schools in attracting Catholics to a neighborhood (*Parish Boundaries: The Catholic Encounter with Race in the Twentieth-Century Urban North* [Chicago: University of Chicago Press, 1998],

21–22). Interestingly, the minister of a local Congregational church that had been bombed in a bootleg-related case in 1919 also joined the anti-Japanese movement, apparently out of resentment that other denominations—like the Methodists—were poaching his now dispersed flock.

29. Los Angeles Population Schedule 1920, Assembly District 63, Enumeration District 185–86; Rev. Herbert Johnson to Holt, August 22, 1924, p. 1, major document 111, box 26, SRRPC. The implication that Catholics dominated the association leadership was likely true. Area census schedules suggest that at least two of three leaders were first- or second-generation Irish Americans, and thus likely Catholics.

30. Johnson to Holt, p. 2; T. T. McClellan interview by Chole Holt, July 1924, pp. 1–5 major document 111, box 26, SRRPC.

31. Before World War II, Protestant denominations in California generally built separate churches for Asian immigrants and their children, often treating such populations almost like the targets of overseas missions.

32. John Modell, *The Economics and Politics of Racial Accommodation: The Japanese of Los Angeles, 1900–1942* (Urbana: University of Illinois Press, 1977), 33, 60; "Anti-Asiatics in Big Drive," *Los Angeles Times*, January 12, 1920.

33. Uono, "The Factors Affecting the Geographical Aggregation and Dispersion," 129; P.H. 2 interview by Chole Holt, 1924, p. 1, major document 111; Clarence Hunt, "'Exclusives' Now Call for Help," *Grizzly Bear* 33, no. 193 (May 1923): suppl., 21.

34. Modell, *The Economics and Politics of Racial Accommodation*, 56; Los Angeles Population Schedule 1920, Assembly District 63, Enumeration District 186, sheets 9B, 15B. Interestingly, Percy Jenkins may have either purchased his home—or rented it—from a Japanese owner, Toshiro Sakurai, who was listed as living there with his family (and owning the home) in the 1920 census.

35. Hunt, "Growls from the Grizzly," 10; P. H. 3 interview by Chloe Holt, 1924, p. 1, major document 111, Box 26, SRRPC. See also Mr. Duffy interview by Chloe Holt, July 28, 1924, in ibid.

36. Council Petition 4364, box A183, Los Angeles City Archives, Los Angeles, CA. Rose Hill is situated roughly in the area of Los Angeles along North Huntington Drive to the south of Rose Hills Park.

37. Division of Research and Statistics, Federal Home Loan Bank Board, "Security Area Map Folder," Vol. II: Security Area Descriptions, Area Description Los Angeles D-38, 1939, file "California," box 74, RG 195, NARA. All area descriptions cited in this chapter were compiled in 1939 (hereafter, "Area Description").

38. See, for example, Los Angeles Population Schedules 1910, Assembly District 74, Enumeration District 60, sheets 1A, 1B, 2A, 2B, 3A, 3B, 4A, 4B; Los Angeles Population Schedules 1920, District 66, Enumeration District 276, sheets 14A, 14B, 15B,16A, 17A, 17B, 18A, 19, 21, 21A.

39. Los Angeles Population Schedule 1920, Assembly District 66, Enumeration district 276, sheet 21A; United States, Selective Service System. *World War I Selective Service System Draft Registration Cards, 1917–1918* (Washington, D.C.: National

Archives and Records Administration), roll 1531188; "Union Statement on Shipyard Situation," *Los Angeles Times*, October 19, 1919.

40. "Rose Hill Continues Anti-Japanese Fight," *Los Angeles Times*, December 23, 1921; Hideo Oyama, "The Life History as a Social Document," June 3, 1924, p. 5, major document 60, box 24, SRRPC.

41. "A Great Victory: Funds Badly Needed to 'Carry On,'" *Grizzly Bear* 28, no. 164 (December 1920): 20; Bureau of the Census, *Sixteenth Census of the United States, 1940: Population and Housing, Statistics for Census Tracts Los Angeles-Long Beach, CA* (Washington, D.C.: USGPO, 1942), 4–5.

42. Los Angeles Population Schedule 1910, Assembly District 70, Enumeration District 276. Becky Nicolaides has called this type of suburb a "labor camp suburb," because of its origin as one of the labor camps for Pacific Electric Railway employees. Nicolaides, "'Where the Working Man Is Welcomed,'" 531–32.

43. Area Description Los Angeles D-29; Uono, "The Factors Affecting the Geographical Aggregation," 139; E. S. Bickford to William C. Smith, in "Anti-Japanese Agitation in Hollywood," ca. 1924, p. 7, major document 64, box 24, SRRPC.

44. "Japanese Invasion is Feared in New District," *Hollywood News*, January 17, 1924, p. 2, major document 231, box 28, SRRPC.

45. Denver, Colorado, Population Schedule 1920, Enumeration District 166, sheet 4B; "Anti-Jap Fight Led by Woman," *Los Angeles Examiner*, June 18, 1923; "Stronger Jap Control Urged," *Los Angeles Examiner*, June 19, 1923; "Banners Aimed at Japanese Church," *Los Angeles Examiner*, May 18, 1923, in Uono, "The Factors Affecting the Geographical Aggregation and Dispersion of the Japanese Residences," 140a. The collapse of the Hollywood movement when the city council demanded that residents pay for condemned Japanese land offers further evidence that the nativist groups provided whatever money the anti-Japanese group initially used.

46. Smith, "Anti-Japanese Agitation in Hollywood," p. 5.

47. "Association Adds to Its Activities," *Los Angeles Times*, June 24, 1923.

48. Arnold R. Hirsch, "With or Without Jim Crow: Black Residential Segregation in the United States," in *Urban Policy in Twentieth-Century America*, ed. Arnold R. Hirsch and Raymond A. Mohl (New Brunswick, NJ: Rutgers University Press, 1993), 74–76; Alison Isenberg, *Downtown America: A History of the Place and the People Who Made It* (Chicago: University of Chicago Press, 2004), 113; Nicolaides, *My Blue Heaven*, 157–58.

49. *Swat the Jap*, June 23, 1923, in Uono, "The Factors Affecting the Geographical Aggregation and Dispersion of the Japanese Residences," 140b; Smith, "Anti-Japanese Agitation in Hollywood," p. 23; "200 Join to Fight Japs in Hollywood," *Los Angeles Examiner*, April 24, 1923; Oscar Ruff interview by Chloe Holt, in "Interviews with Real Estate Dealers of Hollywood," October 20, 1924, minor document 323, box 36, SRRPC; J. Hirai interview by Chloe Holt, October 20, 1924, p. 1, major document 274-27, box 29, SRRPC. According to *Swat the Jap*, it was "combined with the

Anti-Asiatic League Press" and an advertisement for that group covered the entire back page of the publication.

50. J. O. Poole to Editor, *Hollywood Citizen*, in Smith, "Anti-Japanese Agitation in Hollywood," p. 17; Mr. Gehrkens interview by Chloe Holt, November 8, 1924, p. 2, major document 254A, box 29, SRRPC; Mrs. ***** interview by Chloe Holt, October 27, 1924, p. 2, major document 257A, box 29, SRRPC.

51. Los Angeles Population Schedules 1920; Smith, "Anti-Japanese Agitation in Hollywood," p. 26.

52. John Modell discusses this issue in connection to voting on the Alien Land Act of 1920 in *The Economics and Politics of Racial Accommodation* (47–52). The lack of zoning laws in working-class suburbs likely also attracted Japanese, for many of them farmed land that was officially residential.

53. Thomas Lee Philpott, *The Slum and the Ghetto: Neighborhood Deterioration and Middle-Class Reform, Chicago, 1880–1930* (New York: Oxford University Press, 1978), 192.

54. Schalbert and Jones interview by Chloe Holt, in "Interviews with Real Estate Dealers of Hollywood"; Mr. Gehrkens interview, p. 5; Smith, "Anti-Japanese Agitation in Hollywood," p. 7; Mr. and Mrs. Sessions interview by Chloe Holt, October 20, 1924, p. 3, major document 255, box 29, SRRPC.

55. P. H. 3 interview by Holt, p. 3; Smith, "Anti-Japanese Agitation in Hollywood," pp. 35–36; Chloe Holt, "Account of a Visit with a White Woman Married to a Japanese," August 14, 1924, p. 8, major document 104, box 26, SRRPC; L. R. Bowles, Hollywood Protective Association, to Los Angeles City Council, September 18, 1923, Council Petition 5031, box A186, Los Angeles City Archives; Mrs. J. O. Poole to Council, July 18, 1923, Council Petition 5031, box A186, Los Angeles City Archives; City Clerk Robert Dominguez to Chief Inspector of Buildings and Hollywood Protective Association, July 26, 1923, Council Petition 5031, box A186, Los Angeles City Archives.

56. Gerald Sorin, *A Time for Building: The Third Migration, 1880–1920* (Baltimore, MD: The Johns Hopkins University Press, 1995), 87; James R. Grossman, *Land of Hope: Chicago, Black Southerners, and the Great Migration* (Chicago: University of Chicago Press, 1989), 131; Azuma, *Between Two Empires*, 37–38.

57. Sei Fujii, "Letter of Warning," translated from Japanese, July 1923, major document 307, box 31, SRRPC; Los Angeles Chamber of Commerce, "Statement on Oriental and Agriculture," ca. 1923, p. 2, major document 136, box 26, SRRPC.

58. Azuma, *Between Two Empires*, 39; Adjutant M. Kobayashi interview by William C. Smith, ca. 1923, p. 2, major document 236, box 29, SRRPC; K—I— interview by William C. Smith, August 19, 1924, p. 2, minor document 55, box 35, SRRPC. African American elites also often responded to similar accusations in similar ways. See, for example, Linda Gordon, "Black and White Visions of Welfare: Women's Welfare Activism, 1890–1945," in *Unequal Sisters: A Multi-Cultural Reader*

in U.S. Women's History, ed. Vicki L. Ruiz and Ellen Carol DuBois (New York: Routledge, 1994), 169; Glenda Elizabeth Gilmore, *Gender and Jim Crow: Women and the Politics of White Supremacy in North Carolina, 1896–1920* (Chapel Hill: University of North Carolina Press, 1996), 75.

59. Victoria W. Wolcott, *Remaking Respectability: African American Women in Interwar Detroit* (Chapel Hill: University of North Carolina Press, 2000), 13; Uono, "The Factors Affecting the Geographical Aggregation," 75.

60. "State Takes Hand in Jap Realty Probe," *San Francisco Examiner*, October 9, 1920; Uono, "The Factors Affecting the Geographical Aggregation," 66; *Oyama v. California*, 332 U.S. 633 (1948). Other scholars of the 1920s echoed Uono's argument. See, for example, Kanichi Kawasaki, "The Japanese Community of East San Pedro, Terminal Island, California" (master's thesis, University of Southern California, 1931), 27; Gretchen Tuthill, "A Study of the Japanese in the City of Los Angeles" (master's thesis, University of Southern California, 1924), 27.

61. I have found only a few cases that deal with this issue, and they do not entirely agree. In *Saiki v. Hammock*, 207 Cal. 90; 276 P. 1015 (1929), the judge noted that the parcel in question was "residential property, which T. Saiki as an ineligible alien is *not* entitled to hold or possess." The judge in the second case, *Takeuchi v. Schmuck*, 206 Cal. 782; 276 P. 345 (1929), voiced the same opinion. However, in *In re Guardianship of Yano*, 188 Cal. 645; 206 P. 995 (1922), the court distinguished between farm and residential property, although mentioning both only in the context of leasing. And *Mott v. Cline* (200 Cal. 434; 253 P. 718) distinguishes between home ownership and agricultural property ownership, as well as distinguishing the treatment of Chinese and Japanese based on different treaties between the U.S. and China and Japan. The U.S. Supreme Court ruled in *Terrace v. Thompson* (1923) that the U.S.-Japanese treaty allowed citizens of one country to "own or lease houses, manufactories, warehouses, and shops." The Supreme Court in *Webb v. O'Brien* (263 U.S. 313; 44 S. Ct. 112; 68 L. Ed. 318) also conceded that ineligible aliens had the right to *own* houses and *lease* land for residential purposes, but it dealt with agricultural land. Justice Black's description of the law suggests the right to own the land upon which a house sits but nothing more. Within their own circles, nativists acknowledged that Japanese did have the right to own residential property, but at the same time they circulated misinformation about that right and used harassing investigations based on such misinformation. See, for example, V. S. McClatchy, "Japs Organizing to Force Racial Equality," *Grizzly Bear* 33, no. 193 (May 1923): suppl., 17.

62. See, for example, Kazuo Kawai, "Life History of Kazuo Kawai," March 2, 1925, p. 13, major document 296, box 31, SRRPC; CH-30 interview by Charles Kikuchi, February 8, 1944, p. 5, JAERS; Tame Narita interview, June 11, 1924, p. 3, major document 241, box 29, SRRPC; *Takeuchi v. Schmuck*; Keitoku Watanabe interview by Chloe Holt, August 22, 1924, p. 2, major document 121, box 26, SRRPC.

63. Modell, *The Economics and Politics of Racial Accommodation*, 40; Consul of Japan to William I. Traeger, March 15, 1923, major document 124, box 26, SRRPC;

J. Sato, "An American Born Japanese in America," ca. 1924, p. 3, major document 107A, box 26, SRRPC; Los Angeles County, Belvedere Township, Enumeration District 9, sheet 20B. Sato refers to a "Mr. Perry," who called himself sheriff of the district. I believe that this "Perry" is actually George Perdue, a deputy sheriff living in Belvedere at this time.

64. Brian Masaru Hayashi, *For the Sake of Our Japanese Brethren: Assimilation, Nationalism, and Protestantism among the Japanese of Los Angeles, 1895–1942* (Stanford, CA: Stanford University Press, 1995), 129; Gretchen Tuthill, "A Study of the Japanese in the City of Los Angeles" (master's thesis, University of Southern California, 1924), 23.

65. Mae M. Ngai, *Impossible Subjects: Illegal Aliens and the Making of Modern America* (Princeton, NJ: Princeton University Press, 2004), 17, 37, 49–50; Azuma, *Between Two Empires*, 52–53, 60; Richard Rubinger, "Who Can't Read and Write? Illiteracy in Meiji Japan," *Monumenta Nipponica* 55:2 (Summer 2000): 165, 176, 179–80, 184. Universal schooling was the norm by the turn of the century.

66. George J. Sánchez, *Becoming Mexican American: Ethnicity, Culture and Identity in Chicano Los Angeles, 1900–1945* (New York: Oxford University Press, 1993), 75; Uono, "The Factors Affecting the Geographical Aggregation and Dispersion of the Japanese Residences," 137–38. Belvedere was unincorporated at this time.

67. Sato, "An American Born Japanese in America," pp. 1–2; Tuthill, "A Study of the Japanese in the City of Los Angeles," 31; Watanabe interview by Chloe Holt, p. 3.

68. J. Hirai interview, p. 1; Bond, "The Negro in Los Angeles," 48. Wen-Hui Chung Chen notes the same phenomenon for prewar Chinese American residents of Los Angeles: Chen, "Changing Socio-Cultural Patterns of the Chinese Community in Los Angeles" (PhD diss., University of Southern California, 1952), 71. Area Descriptions Los Angeles D-12, D-24, D-25, D-33, D-34, D-52, D-53, and D-61 substantiate Bond's claim, as does Bessie McClenahan, "The Changing Nature of an Urban Residential Area" (PhD diss., University of Southern California, 1928), chap. 1, sec. 2.

69. Leon E. Truesdell, *Population and Housing: Statistics for Census Tracts Los Angeles-Long Beach, California* (Washington, D.C.: USGPO, 1942), 4–6; Area Description Los Angeles D-52; Douglas Flamming, *Bound for Freedom: Black Los Angeles in Jim Crow America* (Berkeley: University of California Press, 2005), 66–67; Sides, L.A. City Limits, 16–19.

70. Flamming, *Bound for Freedom*, 261–62; Scott Tadao Kurashige, "Transforming Los Angeles: Black and Japanese American Struggles for Racial Equality in the 20th Century" (PhD diss., University of California, Los Angeles, 2000), 59–60, shows the way blacks enjoyed an advantage because of the legal status of Japanese immigrants.

71. McClenahan, "The Changing Nature of an Urban Residential Area," chap. 2, sec. 1; Modell, *The Economics and Politics of Racial Accommodation*, 55; Matt Garcia, *A World of Its Own: Race, Labor, and Citrus in the Making of Greater Los Angeles,*

1900–1970 (Chapel Hill: University of North Carolina Press, 2001), 76–77; Kevin Starr, *Material Dreams: Southern California through the 1920s* (New York: Oxford University Press, 1990), 137.

72. Bureau of the Census, *Fifteenth Census of the United States, 1930: Population Number and Distribution of Inhabitants*, 260; Sides, *L.A. City Limits*, 17; Loren Miller interview, ca. 1938, p. 1, file 22, box 1, Los Angeles Urban League papers, Young Research Library, University of California, Los Angeles; Flamming, *Bound for Freedom*, 172–74; Christopher Robert Reed, *The Chicago NAACP and the Rise of Black Professional Leadership, 1910–1966* (Bloomington: Indiana University Press, 1997), 85; Cheryl Lynn Greenberg, *Or Does It Explode? Black Harlem in the Great Depression* (New York: Oxford University Press, 1997), 95.

73. Kurashige, "Transforming Los Angeles," 59–61; George J. Sánchez, *Becoming Mexican American*, 78.

74. McClenahan, "The Changing Nature of an Urban Residential Area," chap. 5, sec. 2; Bond, "The Negro in Los Angeles," 34, 38, 46; De Graaf, "Negro Migration to Los Angeles," 88; *Sixteenth Census of the United States, 1940: Census of Population and Housing, Statistics for Census Tracts Los Angeles–Long Beach, California* (Washington, D.C.: USGPO, 1942), 140–43; *Sixteenth Census of the Unites States, 1940: Housing, Vol. III: Characteristics by Monthly Rent or Value, Part 2: Alabama–New Hampshire* (Washington, D.C.: USGPO, 1943), 85–86, 89, http://www2.census.gov/prod2/decennial/documents/36911485v3p2.pdf (accessed June 27, 2008). Using totals from heavily black, heavily Japanese American, and more mixed areas, I estimate that only about 12 percent of Japanese Americans owned their own homes, as compared to about 30 percent of blacks; about 13 percent of Japanese American–occupied homes were substandard, as compared to about 8 percent of black-occupied homes; and the average Japanese American–owned home was worth about $2,400, compared to about $2,800 for the average African American–owned home. The median value of all homes in Los Angeles was $3,958.

75. Sánchez, *Becoming Mexican American*, 72–75; Deverell, *Whitewashed Adobe*, 47, 251.

76. Deverell, *Whitewashed Adobe,* 30–31; Molina, *Fit to Be Citizens?*, 10, 43. The Treaty of Guadelupe-Hidalgo insured Mexicans' right to become U.S. citizens. Federal census takers began counting Mexican Americans as white in 1940.

77. Kurashige, "Transforming Los Angeles," 63–64; Ricardo Romo, *East Los Angeles: History of a Barrio* (Austin: University of Texas Press, 1983), 69–81. Much of this activism seemed to come from European immigrants. I have not found evidence of Mexican American involvement in such activity.

78. Sánchez, *Becoming Mexican American*, 70–71; Mayborn and Bowden, "Confidential Survey," p. 7; Area Description Los Angeles D-13.

79. Wild, *Street Meeting*, 28, 40–44; John Higham, *Strangers in the Land; Patterns of American Nativism, 1860–1925* (New Brunswick, NJ: Rutgers University Press, 1994), 245–47; Modell, *The Economics and Politics of Racial Accommodation*, 74.

80. Lee Shippey, "The Lee Side o' L.A.," *Los Angeles Times*, June 23, 1934; undated clipping ca. 1926, p. 1, file "Segregation," box 1, SRRPC; Kazuo Kawai, "Life History of Kazuo Kawai," p. 3; *Sixteenth Census of the U.S., 1940: Population and Housing, Statistics for Census Tracts Los Angeles-Long Beach, Calif.*, 140-43.

81. Wild, *Street Meeting*, 35.

82. Works Progress Administration Information Division, "'Less Chance' Areas in the City of Los Angeles: Fourteen Areas Where Group Programs Could Be Instituted to Advantage," February 1941, p. 50, box 2, Los Angeles County Coordinating Councils, Inc., collection, Specialized Libraries and Archival Collections Center, University of Southern California, Los Angeles, CA. As I will discuss in chapters 3 and 5, by the 1930s, Mexican American "whiteness" became increasingly contested.

83. Area Descriptions Los Angeles D-29, D-48, C-114, C-120, C-117, D-50, C-122, C-124, C-99, C-126, D-53, D-54, D-38, C-36, D-12; *Sixteenth Census of the United States, 1940: Census of Population and Housing, Statistics for Census Tracts Los Angeles-Long Beach, California*, 140-43. These statistics deal with tracts with more than 250 "nonwhite" residents. The Census Bureau published special data for such tracts but did not differentiate between "Negro" residents and "other" residents (almost all Asian Americans). My statistics are thus rough but hold up over census tracts; indeed, tracts in which about half of nonwhites are Asian American and half are black have lower home ownership rates than more heavily black tracts.

84. Sidney Gulick, "Japanese on the Pacific Coast: A Report to the Committee on Relations with the Orient of the Federal Council of the Churches of Christ in America and to the National Committee on American Japanese Relations," ca. 1929, p. 1, file SC71, box 2, Yamato Ichihashi papers, Special Collections, Stanford University Library, Stanford, CA; Los Angeles City Council Minutes, Vol. 227, May 25, 1931, 14; "Hindu Faces Fight to Keep His Home," *Los Angeles Times*, July 11, 1928; "Japanese Case Meets Setback," *Los Angeles Times*, April 14, 1928; *Jordan v. Tashiro*, 278 U.S. 123 (1928); Area Descriptions Los Angeles C-100 and C-107; Mears, *Resident Orientals*, discusses the way school segregation functioned on the West Coast (354). Since separate schools for Japanese Americans existed in many Central Valley communities, I suspect Mears has underestimated the extent of segregation statewide.

85. Molina, *Fit to Be Citizens?*, discusses this in terms of public health (115).

CHAPTER THREE

1. Arthur Gallion to Robert D. Mitchell, "Field Notes on Los Angeles, California," November 13, 1934, p. 2, file H3500-1, Public Housing Administration Project Files, Project H-3500, box 259, RG 196, NARA; Kenneth T. Jackson, *Crabgrass Frontier: The Suburbanization of the United States* (New York: Oxford University Press, 1985), 199, 208.

2. William H. Mullins, *The Depression and the Urban West Coast, 1929-1933* (Bloomington: Indiana University Press, 1991), 10; Carey McWilliams, "Migration

and Resettlement of the People," July 1940, pp. 1–2, "Division of Immigration and Housing" file, box 67, Carey McWilliams Papers, Special Collections, Young Research Library, University of California, Los Angeles.

3. Erskine Caldwell, "Jesus Lopez," *Nation*, April 29, 1936, 546; Kevin Starr, *Endangered Dreams: The Great Depression in California* (New York: Oxford University Press, 1996), 177; Douglas Monroy, *Rebirth: Mexican Los Angeles from the Great Migration to the Great Depression* (Berkeley: University of California Press, 1999), 150.

4. Don Parson, *Making a Better World: Public Housing, the Red Scare, and the Direction of Modern Los Angeles* (Minneapolis: University of Minnesota Press, 2005), 18–20.

5. Jackson, *Crabgrass Frontier*, 193. Chapters 4 and 5 will discuss the struggles of the FHA and the HOLC in this regard.

6. Gail Radford, *Modern Housing for America: Policy Struggles in the New Deal Era* (Chicago: University of Chicago Press, 1996), 101–4; Parson, *Making a Better World*, 18–20; Mike Davis, *City of Quartz: Excavating the Future in Los Angeles* (New York: Verso, 1992), 117–19; *Housing Officials' Yearbook 1936* (Chicago: National Association of Housing Officials, 1936), 79. The Municipal Housing Commission dated to the Progressive Era. Shaw appointed a new committee when PWA funds for housing became available.

7. "Representation Asked," *Los Angeles Times*, November 13, 1933. I have not found any mention of the early housing program in Los Angeles's major Spanish-language daily, *La Opinión*, or in Japanese American papers.

8. Mark Wild, *Street Meeting: Multiethnic Neighborhoods in Early Twentieth-Century Los Angeles* (Berkeley: University of California Press, 2004), 4–5; Raphael A. Nicolais, "Elysian Park Municipal Housing Project," ca. 1934, p. 2, file H-3500, box 258, RG 196, NARA; Prof. Erle F. Young to Council of Social Agencies, Los Angeles, January 13, 1934, p. 1, file H-3500 (unnumbered), box 258, RG 196, NARA; "Resume of the Activities of the Municipal Housing Commission During the Past Twelve Months," September 1, 1935, p. 2, file H3500 #3, box 259, NARA.

9. Nancy J. Weiss, *Farewell to the Party of Lincoln: Black Politics in the Age of FDR* (Princeton, NJ: Princeton University Press, 1983), 29–32, 50–51, 181; Radford, *Modern Housing for America*, 104–5.

10. "Jobs Lure for Colored Votes," *Los Angeles Times*, May 20, 1933; John E. Prowd, "Looking Backward," *California Eagle*, October 6, 1933; Radford, *Modern Housing for America*, 104; Booker T. McGraw, "Special Note on Site Selection," May 19, 1944, p. 2, file "Materials submitted in Preparation for a May 27th Conference on the Provision of Housing to Accommodate Minority Groups, with Special Reference to Problems Faced by the Negro," box 747, RG 207, NARA; Walter H. Waggoner, "Paul Williams Dies," *New York Times*, January 26, 1980; Paul R. Williams, Gordon B. Kaufmann and Associates, Architects, Mr. C. A. Lindner, Coordinator, "East Adams Boulevard Housing Project," June 17, 1935, p. 1, file H-3500, box 258, RG 196, NARA.

11. George Adams, Walter Davis, John Kibbey, Ross Montgomery, William Mullay, Lloyd Wright, architects, "The Utah Street Project for the Los Angeles Municipal Housing Commission," ca. 1935, pp. 17-18, file H-3500 (Utah Street), box 258, RG 196, NARA; "Resume of the Activities of the Municipal Housing Commission," p. 2.

12. Works Progress Administration Writers Program, *Los Angeles: A Guide to the City and Its Environs* (New York: Hastings House, 1936), 155-56; Wen-Hui Chung Chen, "Changing Socio-Cultural Patterns of the Chinese Community in Los Angeles" (PhD diss., University of Southern California, 1952), 67-70; "New Chinatown Proposed," *Los Angeles Times*, October 18, 1933; C. Lyle Powell, "Chinese Colony—Los Angeles," January 25, 1935, pp. 1-2, file H3500 #2, box 259, RG 196, NARA. This was not Kodak's George Eastman.

13. C. Lyle Powell to Charles Lindner, January 25, 1935, p. 1, file H3500 #2, box 259, RG 196, NARA; Horatio Hackett to Lindner, April 25, 1935, p. 1, file H3500 #2, box 259, RG 196, NARA.

14. *U.S. v. Certain Lands in City of Louisville*, 78 F.2d 684 (1935); A. R. Clas to Charles Lindner, July 19, 1935, p. 1, file H3500 #2, box 259, RG 196, NARA; Radford, *Modern Housing for America*, 103.

15. Radford, *Modern Housing for America*, 105; J. Finlinson to LAMHC, July 16, 1935, p. 1, file H2500 #2, box 259, RG 196, NARA; Homer Phillips to A.R. Clas, July 28, 1935, pp. 1-2, file H3500.023, box 260, RG 196, NARA.

16. Robert D. Kohn to George Eastman, January 5, 1934, p. 1, file H3500 #1, box 259, RG 196, NARA; Arthur Gallion to Mitchell, "Field Notes on Los Angeles, California," November 13, 1934, pp. 2-3, file 2500 #1, box 259, RG 196, NARA; "Resume of the Activities of the Municipal Housing Commission," p. 2; W.W. Alley to A.R. Clas, May 28, 1935, p. 2, file H3500 #2, RG 196, NARA; B.M. Pettit to Mitchell, May 24, 1935, p. 1, file H3500 #2, RG 196, NARA; Clas to Alley, August 2, 1935, pp. 1-2.

17. Mae M. Ngai, *Impossible Subjects: Illegal Aliens and the Making of Modern America* (Princeton, NJ: Princeton University Press, 2004), 170; Bureau of the Census, *Sixteenth Census of the United States: 1940—Population: Vol. II: Characteristics of the Population, Part I* (Washington, D.C.: USGPO, 1943), 567. This rule also excluded Mexican immigrants who had not naturalized, but they were eligible for citizenship under U.S. law, unlike Asian immigrants.

18. Natalia Molina, *Fit to Be Citizens? Public Health and Race in Los Angeles, 1879-1939* (Berkeley: University of California Press, 2006), 115.

19. Eugene H. Klaber to Robert D. Kohn and Horatio Hackett, ca. 1934, p. 1, file H3500 #1, box 259, RG 196, NARA; Homer Phillips to A.R. Clas, August 20, 1935, p. 1, file H3500.021, box 260, RG 196, NARA; Clas to Phillips, September 3, 1935, p. 1, file H3503, box 261, RG 196, NARA; Phillips to Clas, September 7, 1935, p. 1, RG 196, NARA.

20. Hackett to Lindner, October 14, 1935, pp. 1-2, file H3500 #3, box 259, RG 196, NARA; Lindner to Hackett, September 25, 1935, p. 1, RG 196, NARA.

21. Elizabeth Longan, "The Present Status of Municipal Housing and Slum Clearance in the United States," *American Political Science Review* 31:6 (December 1937): 1130–31; Starr, *Endangered Dreams*, 102, 135–36, 181–86, 205, 211, 229–30; *Housing Yearbook*, 1939, 4–6.

22. Josh Sides, *L.A. City Limits: African American Los Angeles from the Great Depression to the Present* (Berkeley: University of California Press, 2003), 33; Tom Sitton, *Los Angeles Transformed: Fletcher Bowron's Urban Reform Revival, 1938–1953* (Albuquerque: University of New Mexico Press, 2005), 63; "Housing Post to Mrs. Terry," *Los Angeles Sentinel,* June 22, 1939; George J. Sánchez, *Becoming Mexican American: Ethnicity, Culture, and Identity in Chicano Los Angeles, 1900–1945* (New York: Oxford University Press, 1993), 244–50; Los Angeles Council of Social Agencies Executive Committee Minutes Digest, August 15, 1940, p. 1, file "Council of Social Agencies Executive Committee Minutes 1940," box III, Los Angeles Council of Social Agencies collection, Specialized Libraries and Archival Collections Center; "City Housing Authority Names Citizens Committee," *Rafu Shimpo*, July 28, 1940.

23. "Council Votes on Slum Project," *Los Angeles Times*, November 9, 1940; *Housing Yearbook*, 1940, 11–12; *Housing Yearbook*, 1941, 12; "El Litigio de Belvedere, Sin Solucion Aun" (Belvedere case still without a solution), *La Opinión* (Los Angeles), July 17, 1940; "Aceleran Los Trabajos en un Proyecto" (Work on project is sped up), *La Opinión* (Los Angeles), August 30, 1940; "Residents Balk on Property Offers for Slum Project," *California Eagle* (Los Angeles), August 15, 1940; "Housing Program in Danger," *Los Angeles Sentinel*, November 9, 1939.

24. Executive Board, Los Angeles County Coordinating Councils, "WPA Delinquency Prevention Project: Juvenile Delinquency and Poor Housing in the Los Angeles Metropolitan Area," December 1937, pp. 8–9, file 2, Southern California Housing Collection, Specialized Libraries and Archival Collections Center.

25. Augustus Hawkins to Ernest Besig, January 16, 1942, p. 1, file 581, American Civil Liberties Union Northern California Branch collection (hereafter, ACLU-NC), North Baker Research Library, San Francisco, CA; Howard L. Holtzendorff to A.H. Reinert, January 21, 1942, p. 1, ACLU-NC; Marilynn S. Johnson, *The Second Gold Rush: Oakland and the East Bay in World War II* (Berkeley: University of California Press, 1993), 105; Lawrence P. Crouchett, Lonnie Bunch III, and Martha Kendall Winnacker, *Visions Toward Tomorrow: The History of the East Bay Afro-American Community* (Oakland: Northern California Center for Afro-American History and Life, 1989), 47.

26. Lillian Jones to John P. Davis, May 3, 1938, pp. 1–2, in Eric Gallagher, Martin Schipper and David Werning, eds., *Records of the National Negro Congress* (microfilm, University Publications of America, 1989), part 1, series II, reel 13, frames 821–822; *Housing Yearbook*, 1939, 6; Housing Authority of the County of Los Angeles, *A Review of the Activities of the Housing Authority of the County of Los Angeles, 1938–1943* (Los Angeles: County Housing Authority, 1943), 29.

27. *Housing Yearbook*, 1939, 6; *Housing Yearbook*, 1941, 13–14.

28. Molina, *Fit to Be Citizens?*, 69, 71–72, 77. The County Board of Health apparently was a bastion of anti-Mexican racism.

29. Matt Garcia, *A World of Its Own: Race, Labor, and Citrus in the Making of Greater Los Angeles, 1900–1970* (Chapel Hill: University of North Carolina Press, 2001), 61–66, 72–74. The supervisors also similarly targeted Filipinos, eventually getting Congress to foot the bill for voluntary Filipino repatriation.

30. Housing Authority of the County of Los Angeles, *A Review of the Activities of the Housing Authority*, 29, 41, 49, 55, 63, 65.

31. William Deverell, *Whitewashed Adobe: The Rise of Los Angeles and the Remaking of Its Mexican Past* (Berkeley: University of California Press, 2004), 43; Phoebe Kropp, *California Vieja: Culture and Memory in a Modern American Place* (Berkeley: University of California Press, 2006), 208, 227–31, explores the contradictions of this. Both Kropp and Deverell trace the essentializing impulse to the nineteenth century.

32. Marge Ong interview by Beverly Chan, December 11 and December 17, 1979, p. 2, file 41, Summaries and Indices, Southern California Chinese American Oral History Project (hereafter, SCCAOHP), Young Research Library Special Collections, University of California, Los Angeles.

33. Kim Fong Tom, "The Participation of the Chinese in the Community Life of Los Angeles" (M.A. thesis, University of Southern California, 1944), 7–8; Chen, "Changing Socio-Cultural Patterns of the Chinese Community in Los Angeles," 85; Works Progress Administration Writers Program, *Los Angeles*, 154; Emily Honig, "The Politics of Prejudice: Subei People in Republican-Era Shanghai," *Modern China* 15:3 (July 1989): 245–46. I will discuss *The Good Earth* in greater depth in chapter four.

34. Peter Soo Hoo, Jr., interview with Suellen Cheng, December 15, 1979, pp. 1–3, SCCAOHP, Young Research Library, University of California, Los Angeles; Chen, "Changing Socio-Cultural Patterns of the Chinese Community in Los Angeles," 85, 87–88.

35. Housing Authority of the County of Los Angeles, *A Review of the Activities of the Housing Authority*, 26. As I discuss in chapter two, data from the 1940 census suggests that Japanese Americans were actually more likely to live in substandard dwellings than African Americans.

36. Holtzendorff to Reinert, pp. 1–2; "Scarcity of Applicants Among Nisei in Ramona Garden Project Found," *Rafu Shimpo*, February 6, 1941; Carey McWilliams, "Once Again the 'Yellow Peril,'" *Nation*, June 26, 1935, 735.

37. "Scarcity of Applicants Among Nisei in Ramona Garden Project Found," *Rafu Shimpo*, February 6, 1941; "City Housing Stress Cited," *Rafu Shimpo*, June 30, 1940; Brian Masaru Hayashi, *Democratizing the Enemy: The Japanese American Internment* (Princeton, NJ: Princeton University Press, 2004), 54; John Modell, *The Economics and Politics of Racial Accommodation: The Japanese of Los Angeles, 1900–1942* (Urbana: University of Illinois Press, 1977), 85. Asian Americans were largely

absent from the kinds of interracial coalitions just emerging in Los Angeles at the time. For more on prewar civil rights activism in L.A., see Shana B. Bernstein, "Building Bridges at Home in a Time of Global Conflict: Interracial Cooperation and the Fight for Civil Rights in Los Angeles, 1933–54" (PhD diss., Stanford University, 2003), 27–97, and Daniel Widener, "Something Else: Creative Community and Black Liberation in Postwar Los Angeles" (PhD diss., New York University, 2003), 24.

38. Holtzendorff to Reinert, p. 2; David K. Yoo, *Growing Up Nisei: Race, Generation, and Culture among Japanese Americans of California, 1924–1949* (Urbana: University of Illinois Press, 2000), 3–5; "Scarcity of Applicants Among Nisei in Ramona Garden Project Found," *Rafu Shimpo*; Robert K. Carr to the President's Committee on Civil Rights, May 19, 1947, p. 3, file "Staff Memoranda . . . Japanese Americans," box 17, RG 220, Harry S Truman Library Institute, Independence, Missouri; Molina, *Fit to Be Citizens?* 139–41.

39. K. Walter Hickel, "War, Region, and Social Welfare: Federal Aid to Servicemen's Dependents in the South, 1917–1921," *The Journal of American History* 87:4 (March 2001): 1390–91; Jill Quadagno, *The Color of Welfare: How Racism Undermined the War on Poverty* (New York: Oxford University Press, 1994), 21; Alice Kessler-Harris, "In the Nation's Image: The Gendered Limits of Social Citizenship in the Depression Era," *The Journal of American History* 86:3 (December 1999): 1257–59.

CHAPTER FOUR

1. Ernest O. Hauser, "News of the Far East in U.S. Dailies," *The Public Opinion Quarterly* 2:4 (October 1938): 651.

2. William H. Mullins, *The Depression and the Urban West Coast, 1929–1933* (Bloomington: Indiana University Press, 1991), 36–38, 45, 52, 53, 57; Carey McWilliams, *California: The Great Exception* (Berkeley: University of California Press, 1949), 189.

3. Judy Yung, *Unbound Feet: A Social History of Chinese Women in San Francisco* (Berkeley: University of California Press, 1995), 180–82.

4. Ibid., 180–83; Ethel Lum, "Chinese During Depression," *Chinese Digest*, November 22, 1935.

5. Jim Marshall, "Cathay Hey-Hey!" *Colliers*, February 28, 1942, 13, 53; "Neon Nightmares," *Chinese Digest*, December 27, 1935.

6. "Neon Nightmares," *Chinese Digest*; Nayan Shah, *Contagious Divides: Epidemics and Race in San Francisco's Chinatown* (Berkeley: University of California Press, 2001), 229; D. L. Chinn to Editor, *Chinese Digest*, November 15, 1935, 8.

7. "A Message to Chinatown Merchants," *Chinese Digest*, November 15, 1935, 8; Marshall, "Cathay, Hey-Hey!" 53; Sidney Herschel Small, "Chinatown Guide," *Saturday Evening Post*, July 1, 1939, 15.

8. "The Lure of Chinatown," *Chinese Digest*, July 17, 1936; "Long Fingered Mandarins," *Chinese Digest*, November 22, 1935; Gloria Heyung Chun, *Of Orphans and Warriors: Inventing Chinese American Culture and Identity* (New Brunswick,

NJ: Rutgers University Press, 2000), 35. Chinatown was developed as a tourist destination by the 1910s. Regardless, nationally circulated publications rarely mentioned it as a safe and family-oriented tourist destination until the mid to late 1930s. The district seems to have attracted a largely local clientele before that time.

9. Chun, *Of Orphans and Warriors*, 26–27, 30–31; Robert Dunn, "Does My Future Lie in China or America?" *Chinese Digest*, May 15, 1936; Kaye Hong, "Does My Future Lie in China or America?" *Chinese Digest*, May 22, 1936; Stanford University Chinese Students Club to Robert Dunn, *Chinese Digest*, May 22, 1936; Jane Kwong Lee, "The Future of the Second Generation Chinese Lies in China and America," *Chinese Digest*, June 5, 1936; Robert Dunn to Stanford University Chinese Students Club, *Chinese Digest*, June 12, 1936; George Grace to Editor, *Chinese Digest*, June 19, 1936; Gilbert Woo, "*Li Panlin*" (Lim P. Lee) in *Hujiangnan Wenji* (The collected works of Gilbert Woo), ed. Yuzun Liu, Dehua Zheng, and Larry Lam (Hong Kong: Xiangjiang Publishing Company, 1991), 588; Leo Ou-Fan Lee, *Shanghai Modern: The Flowering of a New Urban Culture in China, 1930–1945* (Cambridge, MA: Harvard University Press, 1999), 320–321; Suisheng Zhao, "Chinese Intellectuals' Quest for National Greatness and Nationalistic Writing in the 1990s," *China Quarterly* 152 (December 1997): 725–26.

10. Karen J. Leong, *The China Mystique: Pearl S. Buck, Anna May Wong, Mayling Soong, and the Transformation of American Orientalism* (Berkeley: University of California Press, 2005), 29; Hauser, "News of the Far East in U.S. Dailies," 653; Harold R. Isaacs, *Scratches on Our Minds: American Images of China and India* (New York: The John Day Company, 1958), 156. White actors, including Sidney Toler and Warner Oland, always played Charlie Chan.

11. "Chinatown Beautification Committee Drafts Program," *Chinese Digest*, March 1938; Louise Edwards, "Policing the Modern Woman in Republican China," *Modern China* 26:2 (April 2000): 130; Antonia Finnane, "What Should Chinese Women Wear? A National Problem," *Modern China* 22:2 (April 1996): 99; "Pep Up the Village," *Chinese Digest*, March–April 1939; Chun, *Of Orphans and Warriors*, 36–37.

12. "Night Playground Not O.K.'D," *Chinese Digest*, May 29, 1936.

13. "The W.P.A. in Chinatown," *Chinese Digest*, January 10, 1936; Albert S. Broussard, *Black San Francisco: The Struggle for Racial Equality in the West, 1900–1954* (Lawrence: University Press of Kansas, 1993), 121; Yung, *Unbound Feet*, 185. Officials elsewhere commonly placed blacks in the most menial WPA jobs; see, for example, Lizabeth Cohen, *Making a New Deal: Industrial Workers in Chicago, 1919–1939* (New York: Cambridge University Press, 1990), 279.

14. Lum, "Chinese During Depression," 10. *Wong gar* (*huangjia* in Mandarin) means "the imperial family."

15. Caseworker Notes, 1935–1936, file 18, box 2, William Hoy Papers, Ethnic Studies Library, University of California, Berkeley; Cohen, *Making a New Deal*, 270–71; Lim P. Lee [Li Panlin/Lee Poonlum], "*Yu chang jian ping yuan you guanzhi renwu*" (Commending Ping Yuen's advocates and builders), *Taipingyang Zhoubao*, October 6,

1951; "Chinatown's Housing Problem Due for Airing," *Chinese Digest*, June 1937; "Chinatown Housing," *Chinese Digest*, August 1937; "Another Housing Problem," *Chinese Digest*, August 1937; "Chinatown Opens Campaign to Get Modernized Housing," *San Francisco News*, June 18, 1937.

16. Lee, "*Yu chang jian ping yuan you guanzhi renwu.*"

17. Robert D. Kohn to Eugene H. Klaber, March 10, 1934, p.1, file 4500.02, box 297, RG 196, NARA; "Forty Per Cent of S.F. Houses Declared Unfit as Residences," *San Francisco Chronicle*, March 15, 1937; Lim P. Lee, "San Francisco Chinatown's Social Problems," *Chinese Digest*, January 1938.

18. Charles A. Christin, "Report on Low Cost Housing in San Francisco," March 6, 1940, p. 2, file 566, ACLU-NC; "Housing Plan Fought by 2 Local Groups," *San Francisco News*, January 24, 1939; "Calvary Cemetery Protest Meeting," *San Francisco Municipal Journal*, July 7, 1939; Alice Griffith, "A Review of the Proceedings of the Housing Authority of San Francisco," ca. September 1943, p. 1, file 77E, box 17, series IV, League of Women Voters San Francisco Records (hereafter, LOWV-SF), North Baker Research Library, San Francisco, CA.

19. "Slums in Chinatown," *San Francisco News*, February 17, 1938; Lee, "*Yu chang jian ping yuan you guanzhi renwu*"; "Housing Program Coming," *Chinese Digest*, November 1938.

20. Ruth M.W. Chue and Lena A. Way, "Comments on Housing Action in Chinatown," May 1940, section IV, p. 1, section III, p. 14, section 1, p. 4, "Chinatown" file, carton 6, Catherine Bauer Wurster papers, Bancroft Library; School of Social Studies, "Living Conditions in Chinatown," p. 18, file "Hogan—Living in Chinatown," box 2, Records Relating to the History of the Agency ("Historical File"), 1934–1948, Records of the Central Office (Records of the Office of the Historian), RG196, NARA.

21. Frederick C. Adams, "The Road to Pearl Harbor: A Reexamination of American Foreign Policy, July 1937–December 1938," *Journal of American History* 58:1 (June 1971): 91–92.

22. George Gallup and Claude Robinson, "American Institute of Public Opinion—Surveys, 1935–1938," *Public Opinion Quarterly* 2:3 (July 1938): 389, 395; "American Institute of Public Opinion—Surveys, 1938–1939," *Public Opinion Quarterly* 3:4 (October 1939): 599.

23. Yong Chen, *Chinese San Francisco: A Trans-Pacific Community* (Stanford, CA: Stanford University Press, 2000), 242; "S.F. Chinatown's 'Bowl of Rice' Pageant," *Chinese Digest*, July 1938; "*Sanfanshi huabu zhi ye xiangqing buzhi*" (San Francisco's Chinatown night: a supplement), *Shaonian Zhongguo Chenbao* (Young China [San Francisco]), June 26, 1938.

24. Brian Masaru Hayashi *"For the Sake of Our Japanese Brethren" Assimilation, Nationalism, and Protestantism Among the Japanese of Los Angeles, 1895–1942* (Stanford, CA: Stanford University Press, 1995), 133; CH-62 interview in Dorothy Swaine Thomas, James Sakoda, and Charles Kikuchi, *Japanese American Evacuation and*

Resettlement, vol. 2, *The Salvage* (Berkeley: University of California Press, 1952), 216; Eiichiro Azuma, *Between Two Empires: Race, History, and Transnationalism in Japanese America* (New York: Oxford University Press, 2005), 165–67; Mae Ngai, *Impossible Subjects: Illegal Aliens and the Making of Modern America* (Princeton, NJ: Princeton University Press, 2004), 200; Yuji Ichioka, "The Meaning of Loyalty: The Case of Kazumaro Buddy Uno," *Amerasia* 23:3 (Winter 1997–1998): 61–62.

25. William Hoy, "The Passing of Chinatown: Fact or Fancy," *Chinese Digest*, January 31, 1936; CH-53 interview in Thomas, Sakoda, and Kikuchi, *The Salvage*, 243; Yung, *Unbound Feet*, 235; Garrett Graham, "Chinatown," *San Francisco Chronicle*, February 25, 1939; Kazumaro Uno, "Let's Face Facts," *Japanese American News* (San Francisco), January 19, 1939. See also, *Shaonian zhongguo chenbao*, "*Meiren fan ri ou*" (Americans, turn against the Japanese), October 4, 1939, 8.

26. School of Social Studies, "Living Conditions in Chinatown," p. 9; Pardee Lowe, "Chinatown's Last Stand," *Survey Graphic* 25:2 (February 1936): 90; *San Francisco's Chinatown*, October 1909, pp. 11–14, Department of Special Collections, Young Research Library, University of California, Los Angeles.

27. Ye Ming, "*Xinke yu huaqiao*" (Newcomers and overseas Chinese), *Jinshan shibao* (Chinese Times [San Francisco]), November 1, 1941.

28. See, for example, Ching-Hwang Yen, "Overseas Chinese Nationalism in Singapore and Malaya, 1877–1912," *Modern Asian Studies* 16:3 (1982): 397–98; Frederic Wakeman, Jr., "Voyages," *American Historical Review* 98:1 (February 1993): 16; John Fitzgerald, "The Misconceived Revolution: State and Society in China's Nationalist Revolution, 1923–1926," *Journal of Asian Studies* 49:2 (May 1990): 329.

29. Prasenjit Duara, "Transnationalism and the Predicament of Sovereignty: China, 1900–1945," *American Historical Review* 102:4 (October 1997): 1049–50, describes this delinkage of territory, nation, and nationalism among Chinese transnationals.

30. Yuan Zhi, "*Yijian youli huaqiao wenhua shiye zhi jianyi*" (A proposal to improve Overseas Chinese cultural initiatives), *Chung Sai Yat Po* (China-Western Daily [San Francisco]), December 19, 1935, alludes to Japanese appropriation of Chinese culture.

31. Tad Uyeno, "Lancer's Column," *Rafu Shimpo*, November 24, 1940; Carey McWilliams, "Once Again the 'Yellow Peril,'" *Nation*, June 26, 1935, 735.

32. California Joint Immigration Committee memo, April 26, 1939, p. 1, file "Calif. Joint-Immigration Committee," box 18, Robert Walker Kenny Correspondence and Papers, Bancroft Library, University of California, Berkeley; Lon Kurashige, *Japanese American Celebration and Conflict: A History of Ethnic Identity and Festival in Los Angeles, 1934–1990* (Berkeley: University of California Press, 2002), 43, 67–71.

33. Housing Authority of the City and County of San Francisco, *Second Annual Report* (San Francisco: SFHA, 1940), 16; Tom Irwin, "Holly Park Project Will Aid Hundreds," *San Francisco Chronicle*, October 9, 1939; School of Social Studies, "Living Conditions in Chinatown," p. 14.

34. "Urge $5 Tax on All Oriental Workers," *Western Worker* (San Francisco), November 20, 1933; Mullins, *The Depression and the Urban West Coast*, 46–47.

272 Notes to Pages 99–101

35. Eleanor Roosevelt, "My Day," July 5, 1939, typescript, file ER Speech and Article File "My Day" July 1–30, 1939, box "ER Speech and Article File 'My Day' June 1939—3075 August 1939—3075 September 1939—3076 December 1939," Franklin D. Roosevelt Presidential Library, Hyde Park, New York.

36. School of Social Studies, "Living Conditions in Chinatown," p. vi. Liberal philosophy professor Alexander Meiklejohn organized the School for Social Studies. Students were adults who studied the condition of the city.

37. "Slums in Chinatown," *San Francisco News*, February 17, 1938; "Chinatown: 'It's an Appalling Slum,'" *San Francisco Chronicle*, July 7, 1939; Arthur Caylor, "Behind the News," *San Francisco News*, July 8, 1939.

38. Gilbert Woo, "*Tan huabu pingminzhuzhai wenti*" (Low-income housing in Chinatown), in *Hu Jiangnan Wenji*, ed. Liu, Zheng, and Lam, 12; Wayne F. Daugherty, *1939 Real Property Survey, San Francisco, California*, vol. 1 (San Francisco: City and County of San Francisco, 1939), 183; "Chinatown Fights Back at Charge It's Largely a Slum," *San Francisco News*, July 8, 1939; Gilbert Woo, editorial, *Taipingyang*, October 20, 1951.

39. "*Xibao jiefa huabu zhuju quedian*" (Western newspapers expose Chinatown housing's shortcomings), *Shaonian zhongguo chenbao*: part 1, July 7, 1939; part 2, July 8, 1939; part 3, July 9, 1939; "*Huabu zhuju jidai gailiang*" (Chinatown housing urgently needs improvement), *Jinshan shibao*, July 7, 1939.

40. Lee, "*Yu chang jian ping yuan you guanzhi renwu*"; Bill Simons, "Districts: Chinese Junior C. of C. Praised," *San Francisco Chronicle*, July 7, 1940. Simons's article contends that the Junior Chamber of Commerce came up with the idea for a Chinatown federal housing project, later seeking the Chinese Junior Chamber's assistance with it. This statement suggests one of two things: either the degree to which political leaders and journalists alike had ignored earlier Chinese American efforts to get a project for the district, or a possible willingness by Chinese Americans themselves to gain support by making the development seem like a white idea.

41. Simons, "Districts: Chinese Junior C. of C. Praised"; San Francisco Junior Chamber of Commerce, "Report of the San Francisco Junior Chamber of Commerce on San Francisco's Chinatown Housing," pp. 4–5, October 1939, file "San Francisco Planning and Housing Association," box 26, Wurster Papers.

42. San Francisco Junior Chamber of Commerce, "Report of the San Francisco Junior Chamber of Commerce on San Francisco's Chinatown Housing," pp. 4–5; "Chinatown's Slum," *San Francisco Chronicle*, November 15, 1939; Laura W. Reed to Eleanor Roosevelt, November 24, 1939, p. 1, file 70 (Straus, Nathan, 1939), box 334, White House Correspondence, 1933–1945, Franklin D. Roosevelt Presidential Library, Hyde Park, New York.

43. T. Y. Chen et al., "Social Service Needs of the Chinese Population of San Francisco" (San Francisco: Emergency Relief Administration, 1935), 9; Chue and Way, "Comments on Housing Action in Chinatown," section I, p.1; Gilbert Woo, "*Poqian an*" (Eviction Case [part 1]), in *Hu Jiangnan Wenji*, ed. Liu, Zheng, and Lam, 74–75.

44. Woo, "*Tan huabu pingminzhuzhai wenti*," 12; George de Carvalho, "Survey of San Francisco's Housing Problem . . . and the Signs of Hope," *San Francisco Chronicle*, January 28, 1940; "Large-Scale Replacement Plan Proposed," *San Francisco Chronicle*, February 9, 1940; Mrs. Charles D. Porter to Nathan Straus, November 30, 1939, p. 1, file 77B, box 17, series IV, LOWV-SF.

45. Reed to Roosevelt, November 24, 1939, p. 1; Gilbert Woo to Eleanor Roosevelt, December 1, 1939, p. 1, file 70 (Straus, Nathan, 1939), box 334, White House Correspondence, 1933–1945, Franklin D. Roosevelt Presidential Library, Hyde Park, NY; Eleanor Roosevelt to Nathan Straus, December 2, 1939, p. 1, file 70 (Straus, Nathan, 1939), box 334, White House Correspondence, 1933–1945, Franklin D. Roosevelt Presidential Library, Hyde Park, NY; Nathan Straus to Eleanor Roosevelt, January 16, 1940, p. 1, file 70 (Straus, Nathan, 1940), box 334, White House Correspondence, 1933–1945, Franklin D. Roosevelt Presidential Library, Hyde Park, NY.

46. "Rice Bowl," *San Francisco Chronicle*, February 9, 1940.

47. Shah, *Contagious Divides*, 227.

48. "S.F.'s New Designs for Living," *San Francisco News*, March 23, 1940.

49. See, for example, Arnold Hirsch, *Making the Second Ghetto: Race and Housing in Chicago, 1940–1960* (Chicago: University of Chicago Press, 1998), 9–10; Thomas J. Sugrue, *The Origins of the Urban Crisis: Race and Inequality in Postwar Detroit* (Princeton, NJ: Princeton University Press, 1996), 9–10; Wendell Pritchett, *Brownsville, Brooklyn: Blacks, Jews, and the Changing Face of the Ghetto* (Chicago: University of Chicago Press, 2002), 64.

50. Loren Miller, statement, *Hearings Before the United States Commission on Civil Rights* (Washington, D.C.: USGPO, 1960), 260.

51. Broussard, *Black San Francisco*, 35–36, 116–19, 133–35.

52. William Issel and Robert W. Cherny, *San Francisco, 1865–1932* (Berkeley: University of California Press, 1986), 66–68; Division of Research and Statistics, Federal Home Loan Bank Board, Area Description San Francisco D-3, ca. 1937, file "San Francisco, California Master File Security Map and Area Descriptions," box 147, RG 195, NARA (hereafter, "Area Description"); Bernard Taper, *San Francisco's Housing* (Washington, D.C: Works Progress Administration, 1941), 21.

53. Charles A. Christin, "Report on Low Cost Housing in San Francisco," p. 2.; Area Description San Francisco C-12, ca. 1937; Larry Tajiri, "Housing," *Japanese American News*, July 13, 1939; Griffith, "A Review of the Proceedings of the Housing Authority of San Francisco," p. 3; Christin, "Report on Low Cost Housing in San Francisco," p. 2.

54. Kenneth T. Jackson, *Crabgrass Frontier: The Suburbanization of the United States* (New York: Oxford University Press, 1985), 196–208, 213, 217. In "Redlining and the Home Owners Loan Corporation," *Journal of Urban History* 29:4 (2003): 394–420, Amy E. Hillier argues that the FHA used different maps and surveys than the HOLC to determine neighborhood soundness. I do not dispute this, but since both agencies drew on local real estate "common sense" in each area, I believe that the

HOLC survey forms and maps still offer a very useful picture of public and private real estate practices in Los Angeles and San Francisco. For this reason, I have combined the surveys with other records of specific FHA decisions to explain the attitude of agency officials towards different neighborhoods and groups.

55. Area Description San Francisco D-4, ca. 1937. As David M. P. Freund, *Colored Property: State Policy and White Racial Politics in Suburban America* (Chicago: University of Chicago Press, 2007), 166–75, has shown, the FHA carried out an extensive campaign to educate homeowners about its programs. And the agency was not reticent about its racial policies: reporters commented on them in contemporary coverage of the FHA, both openly and euphemistically. See, for example, "Quality Factors Cited," *New York Times*, September 17, 1939; "Good Materials Give Home Value," *New York Times*, April 10, 1938; "FHA Urges Jim Crow in Loans," *Los Angeles Sentinel*, August 1, 1940.

56. De Carvalho, "Survey of San Francisco's Housing Problem . . . and the Signs of Hope"; Kevin M. Kruse, *White Flight: Atlanta and the Making of Modern Conservatism* (Princeton, NJ: Princeton University Press, 2005), 60.

57. Albert J. Evers to Langdon Post, January 6, 1942, p. 2, file 581, ACLU-NC; Marshall Dill to San Francisco Board of Supervisors, July 5, 1939, file 77B, box 17, series IV, LOWV-SF.

58. Chue and Way, "Comments on Housing Action in Chinatown," section IV, p. 5.

59. Londa S. Fletcher affidavit, December 19, 1941, p. 1, file 581, ACLU-NC; Western Addition Housing Council circular, January 2, 1942, p. 1, file 581, ACLU-NC; handwritten notes, ca. November 1941, file 566, ACLU-NC.

60. De Carvalho, "Survey of San Francisco's Housing Problem . . . and the Signs of Hope."

61. Western Addition Housing Council circular, p. 1.

62. "Little Japan," *San Francisco Spokesman*, July 6, 1933, "100 Pieces of Silver—and a Navy Ball," *San Francisco Spokesman*, October 26, 1933, 1; Angelo Rossi to W.R. Larsen, September 25, 1936, p. 1, file 4500, box 297, RG 196, NARA; H. T. Sheppard to William Pickens, July 25, 1939, p. 1, in John H. Bracey, Jr., Sharon Harley, and August Meier, eds., *Papers of the NAACP* (microfilm, University Publications of America, 1982), Part 12, Series D, reel 4, frame 109.

63. Western Addition Housing Council circular, p. 1; Western Addition Housing Council to San Francisco Housing Authority, October 22, 1941, p. 1, file 581, ACLU-NC; Londa Fletcher affidavit, p. 1; Evers to Post, January 6, 1942, p. 2; "Application Filed for Fillmore Area Housing Project," *New World-Sun Daily*, October 5, 1940.

64. "To Push Housing Project Plans for Nihonmachi," *New World-Sun Daily*, October 25, 1940; "Local Japanese Urged to Attend Housing Meeting," *New World-Sun Daily*, November 1, 1940.

65. "Local Japanese Urged to Attend Housing Meeting," *New World-Sun Daily*; "Building Under FHA Set," *Japanese American News*, March 3, 1941; "Housing

Council for Uptown Area Sponsors Meeting," *Japanese American News*, March 12, 1941. Like many contemporaries, the *News* reporter confused the FHA and the USHA.

66. Alice Griffith to Mayor Elmer Robinson, January 26, 1950, p. 1, file 566, ACLU-NC; Londa S. Fletcher to Eleanor Sloss, October 6, 1941, p. 1, file 77B, box 17, series IV, LOWV-SF

67. "New Hearing Asked on West Side Courts," *San Francisco News*, March 25, 1941.

68. "Decision Soon on Housing Project Near Nihonmachi," *New World-Sun Daily*, October 21, 1939; "Housing Plan for Lil' Kobe Area Is Seen," *New World-Sun Daily*, September 4, 1939; "New Hearing Asked on West Side Courts," *San Francisco News*

69. "New Hearing Asked on West Side Courts," *San Francisco News*; Area Description San Francisco D-4, ca. 1937.

70. Graham, "Chinatown"; "Chinatown, My Chinatown!" *Business Week*, March 12, 1938, 28; Tad Uyeno, "Lancer's Column," *Rafu Shimpo*, November 24, 1940.

71. CH-53 interview in Thomas, Sakoda, and Kikuchi, *The Salvage*, 242–43.

72. Alexander Saxton, *The Rise and Fall of the White Republic: Class Politics and Mass Culture in Nineteenth-Century America* (New York: Verso, 1990), 300.

CHAPTER FIVE

1. "Housing Project Called Wedge in War with Japan," *Los Angeles News*, August 13, 1940.

2. Yuji Ichioka, *The Issei: The World of the First Generation Japanese Immigrants* (New York: Free Press, 1988), 164–65; Eliot Grinnell Mears, *Resident Orientals on the American Pacific Coast: Their Legal and Economic Status* (Chicago: University of Chicago Press, 1928), 425, 428; David Yoo, *Growing Up Nisei: Race, Generation, and Culture among Japanese Americans of California, 1924–1949* (Urbana: University of Illinois Press, 2000), 4; Bureau of the Census, *Sixteenth Census of the United States: Population* (Washington, D.C.: USGPO, 1942), 567–68, 665.

3. Lon Kurashige, *Japanese American Celebration and Conflict: A History of Ethnic Identity and Festival in Los Angeles, 1934–1990* (Berkeley: University of California Press, 2002), 15, 23, 27; "How Big a Handicap Is My Race?" *Rafu Shimpo*, March 9, 1941.

4. Gail Radford, *Modern Housing for America: Policy Struggles in the New Deal Era* (Chicago: University of Chicago Press, 1996), 192–214; Marc A. Weiss, *The Rise of the Community Builders: The American Real Estate Industry and Urban Land Planning* (New York: Columbia University Press, 1987), 139–40; D. W. Mayborn and T. H. Bowden, "Confidential: Report of a Survey in Metropolitan Los Angeles, California, for the Division of Research and Statistics, Home Owners' Loan Corporation, Washington, D.C.," October 10, 1939, pp. 34–35, file "California," box 74, RG 195, NARA.

5. Joseph R. Ray, B.T. McGraw, and Frank Horne, "A Proposal to Insure the Equitable Participation of Nonwhite Families in the FHA Program," April 1954,

p. 1, file "Policy—Racial Relations," box 748, RG 207, NARA; Kenneth T. Jackson, *Crabgrass Frontier: The Suburbanization of the United States* (New York: Oxford University Press, 1985), 208.

6. Jackson, *Crabgrass Frontier*, 197–219. Regarding the racial views of local real estate agents, see, for example, the following entries in Survey on Segregation, ca. 1927, file "Segregated Housing," box 2, SRRPC: William McMillan, president, Glendale Realty Board; O. D. Jenkins, secretary, Whittier District Realty Board; Sam Ingersoll, secretary, Los Angeles Realty Board; H. H. Henshaw, real estate agent, Laguna Beach, CA; Joseph Schrale, Bell Realty Board; Leslie Taylor, president, Van Nuys Realty Board; E. Spurlock, Compton Realty Board; R. Short, president, Pomona Valley Realty Board; Harrison R. Baker, president, Pasadena Realty Board; E.V. Reed, vice president, San Pedro Realty Board.

7. Division of Research and Statistics, Federal Home Loan Bank Board, "Security Area Map Folder," Vol. II: Security Area Descriptions, October 10, 1939, Area Description Los Angeles C-55; Area Descriptions Los Angeles C-74, C-77, D-13, D-33, D-45, D-52, D-57.

8. Area Descriptions Los Angeles D-7, D-10, D-29, D-30, and D-61.

9. "Louis Blodgett Succeeds Where Others Failed," *California Eagle*, June 27, 1940; Blodgett Tract advertisement, *Los Angeles Sentinel*, July 20, 1939; Andrew Wiese, *Places of Their Own: African American Suburbanization in the Twentieth Century* (Chicago: University of Chicago Press, 2004), 113, 124; Togo Tanaka, "Public Ignorance of Nisei American Standards Laid to Blame for Racial Discrimination against Japanese," *Rafu Shimpo*, June 13, 1940; "Nisei Builds Home Despite F.H.A. Loan Discrimination," *Rafu Shimpo*, July 17, 1940; Mayborn and Bowden, "Confidential: Report of a Survey in Metropolitan Los Angeles," pp. 34–35.

10. "Subdivision of 51-Acre Tract Launched by Pacific Investment Co.," *Rafu Shimpo*, April 21, 1940; "Form 'Equality Committee,'" *Rafu Shimpo*, August 2, 1940; Scott Kurashige, "Transforming Los Angeles: Black and Japanese American Struggles for Race Equality in the 20th Century" (PhD diss., University of California, Los Angeles, 2000), 232; Togo Tanaka, "How to Survive Racism in America's Free Society," lecture, April 3, 1973, in Arthur A. Hansen and Betty E. Mitson, *Voices Long Silent: An Oral Inquiry into the Japanese American Evacuation* (Fullerton: California State University, 1974), 90–91; Radford, *Modern Housing for America*, 193.

11. Kurashige, "Transforming Los Angeles," 232; "Form 'Equality Committee,'" *Rafu Shimpo*; Shuji Fujii, "Big Interests Keep Out Japanese in Jefferson Park," *Doho*, June 15, 1940; Area Descriptions Los Angeles C-112 and C-113.

12. Togo Tanaka, "Public Ignorance of Nisei American Standards Laid to Blame for Racial Discrimination against Japanese"; "Home Owners Make Better Citizens," *Rafu Shimpo*, April 21, 1940.

13. Area Descriptions Los Angeles C-117 and D-50; Josh Sides, *L.A. City Limits: African American Los Angeles from the Great Depression to the Present* (Berkeley:

University of California Press, 2003), 98–99; "Nisei Fight $100,000 to Oust Japanese Family from 'Restricted Area' Lot," *Rafu Shimpo*, July 1, 1940.

14. Kurashige, "Transforming Los Angeles," 232. The FHA and other federal agencies also channeled and controlled the growth of the black population in south central Los Angeles during World War II (this will be discussed in chapter seven).

15. Harold M. Finley, "'Lucky' Baldwin Barony Is Sold for Homesites," *Los Angeles Times*, April 5, 1936; "Site of New Community in Renowned Rancho's Final Tract," *Los Angeles Times*, December 4, 1938; "How Huge Housing Project Will Appear," *Los Angeles Times*, October 8, 1939; Radford, *Modern Housing for America*, 199–200.

16. Shuji Fujii, "Big Interests Keep Out Japanese in Jefferson Park"; "Council Refuses to Approve Plans for Japanese Colony," *Los Angeles Times*, August 17, 1940; "Japanese Tract Wins Approval," *Los Angeles Times*, September 12, 1940; Mike Davis, *City of Quartz: Excavating the Future in Los Angeles* (New York: Vintage Books, 1992), 114–22; Area Description Los Angeles C-117. The FHA also used physical barriers in the area, including railroad tracks and La Ballona Creek, to block nonwhite development from white development.

17. The FHA heavily promoted its programs in the local press, which referred to its racial policies in transparent euphemisms. See, for example, "F.H.A. Attitude Stated Regarding Subdivisions," *Los Angeles Times*, January 27, 1935; "Build a Home with Your Uncle Sam," *Los Angeles Times*, June 9, 1935; "F.H.A. Insurance Fund Explained," *Los Angeles Times*, November 3, 1940. The FHA's own materials, which it offered free to the public, were more direct. "Booklets to Guide Home Building Offered," *Los Angeles Times*, June 28, 1936.

18. Mayborn and Bowden, "Confidential: Report of a Survey in Metropolitan Los Angeles," pp. 34–35.

19. Mr. and Mrs. Maurice L. Young to City Council, August 13, 1940, file 1337, box A731, Council Communications, Los Angeles City Archives; Fujii, "Big Interests Keep Out Japanese in Jefferson Park"; "Nisei Win Victory in Campaign for Equal Rights in Homebuilding as City Council Approves Map," *Rafu Shimpo*, July 15, 1940; "Japanese Tract Wins Approval," *Los Angeles Times*.

20. Shuji Fujii, "Big Interests Keep Out Japanese in Jefferson Park"; Kurashige, "Transforming Los Angeles," 233.

21. Merrill Butler to Lloyd Alrich, June 27, 1940, p. 1, file 1337, box A731, Council Communications, Los Angeles City Archives; Area Descriptions Los Angeles C-110, C-112, C-113; "Housing Project Called Wedge in War with Japan," *Los Angeles Daily News*.

22. Lewis had earned the enmity of the black press as well for his race-baiting. "Democracy in Peril," *Los Angeles Sentinel*, August 15, 1940.

23. Togo Tanaka, "Councilman Lewis in Attack on Nisei Again Over Housing Project," *Rafu Shimpo*, August 12, 1940; Kurashige, "Transforming Los Angeles," 250.

24. Felix Belaire, Jr., "President Offers Alien Control Plan," *New York Times*, May 23, 1940; Fujii, "Big Interests Keep Out Japanese in Jefferson Park"; "Councilman Lewis Shouts 'Yellow Peril' Says Daily in Reporting on Session," *Rafu Shimpo*, July 18, 1940; "Form 'Equality Committee,'" *Rafu Shimpo*.

25. "Nisei Asked to Ignore Exhibitionist Displays by 'Anti' Organization," *Rafu Shimpo*, July 28, 1940.

26. Shuji Fujii, "Jefferson Project Unworthy of Support," *Doho*, August 15, 1940.

27. Fujii, "Jefferson Project Unworthy of Support"; John Modell, *The Economics and Politics of Racial Accommodation: The Japanese of Los Angeles, 1900–1942* (Urbana: University of Illinois Press, 1978), 13–14; Kurashige, "Transforming Los Angeles," 238.

28. "Council Refuses to Approve Plans for Japanese Colony," *Los Angeles Times*; Mark Wild, *Street Meeting: Multiethnic Neighborhoods in Early Twentieth Century Los Angeles* (Berkeley: University of California Press, 2005), 121–22; "Councilmen Rant Against Japanese Home Buyers," *Los Angeles Sentinel*, August 15, 1940. In "Transforming Los Angeles," Scott Kurashige argues that *Sentinel* editors knew about the deed restrictions and simply kept quiet about them. I think it is more likely that they believed Hisatomi rather than lied to their own readers (262).

29. "Democracy in Peril," *Los Angeles Sentinel*; "Blanket Proposal May Affect Japanese Real Estate Holdings in San Gabriel," *New World-Sun Daily* (San Francisco), October 3, 1939; "Two Out of Every Ten," *Rafu Shimpo*, July 21, 1940; Kurashige, "Transforming Los Angeles," 238; "As Primaries Near, Campaign in Climax," *Rafu Shimpo*, August 22, 1940; Modell, *The Economics and Politics of Racial Accommodation*, 14. As Shana B. Bernstein, "Building Bridges at Home in a Time of Global Conflict: Interracial Cooperation and the Fight for Civil Rights in Los Angeles, 1933–54" (PhD diss., Stanford University, 2003), demonstrates, most interracial activism in L.A. dated to the wartime and postwar periods.

30. Modell, *The Economics and Politics of Racial Accommodation*, 168; Kurashige, "Transforming Los Angeles," 240, 246; Togo Tanaka, "Post Script: Our City Council Pulled a Fast One," *Rafu Shimpo*, July 18, 1940. Interestingly, *Rafu Shimpo* devoted more space to the public housing program after the demise of Jefferson Park.

31. Saburo Kido, "Home-Buying Going On 'As Usual' Among Nisei Families," *Rafu Shimpo*, January 12, 1941, 6.

32. "Woman Who Sued Zaima Family for $100,000 But Failed to Get Penny, Voices Her Race Beliefs," *Rafu Shimpo*, August 18, 1940; "Red Paint Smears Houses in Tujunga as 'No Japs' Sign Stirs Mass Meeting," *Rafu Shimpo*, January 9, 1941; "Jefferson Park 'Victory' Recalled in New Project," *Rafu Shimpo*, February 12, 1941.

33. Kido, "Home-Buying Going on 'As Usual' Among Nisei Families"; Tad Uyeno, "Lancer's Column," *Rafu Shimpo*, February 9, 1941; CH-41 interview by Charles Kikuchi, May 2, 1944, transcript, p. 15, folder T1.97, JAERS.

34. CH-34 interview in Dorothy Swaine Thomas, James Sakoda, and Charles Kikuchi, *Japanese American Evacuation and Resettlement*, vol. 2, *The Salvage* (Berkeley:

University of California Press, 1952), 429; CH-26 interview in Thomas, Sakoda, and Kikuchi, *The Salvage*, 463.

35. CH-45 interview in Thomas, Sakoda, and Kikuchi, *The Salvage*, 189; CH-27 interview in Thomas, Sakoda, and Kikuchi, *The Salvage*, 164; Brian Masaru Hayashi, *"For the Sake of Our Japanese Brethren": Assimilation, Nationalism, and Protestantism Among the Japanese of Los Angeles, 1895–1942* (Stanford, CA: Stanford University Press, 1995), 138–39; Tom Sitton, *Los Angeles Transformed: Fletcher Bowron's Urban Reform Revival, 1938–1953* (Albuquerque: University of New Mexico Press, 2005), 63; Warren B. Francis, "Japanese Here Sent Vital Data to Tokyo," *Los Angeles Times*, February 6, 1942; "Radio Seized by Raiders," *Los Angeles Times*, March 30, 1942; "Subversive Acts of Japs Here Related," *Los Angeles Times*, March 25, 1942.

36. See, for example, Kevin M. Kruse, *White Flight: Atlanta and the Making of Modern Conservatism* (Princeton, NJ: Princeton University Press, 2005), 61, 66; Thomas J. Sugrue, *The Origins of the Urban Crisis: Race and Inequality in Postwar Detroit* (Princeton, NJ: Princeton University Press, 1996), 44, 195.

37. Arthur Verge, "Daily Life in Wartime California," in *The Way We Really Were: The Golden State in the Second Great War*, ed. Roger W. Lotchin (Urbana: University of Illinois Press, 2000), 15; John Dower, *War Without Mercy: Race and Power in the Pacific War* (New York: Pantheon, 1986), 103–12; Michi Nishiura Weglyn, *Years of Infamy: The Untold Story of America's Concentration Camps* (Seattle: University of Washington Press, 1996), 36–39; Roger Daniels, *Prisoners Without Trial: Japanese Americans in World War II* (New York: Hill and Wang, 2004), 42–43; CH-64 interview in Thomas, Sakoda, and Kikuchi, *The Salvage*, 550; Earl Warren advertisement, *Rafu Shimpo*, August 25, 1938; Masao Sakada, Kay Hirao, Fred Nomura, et al. to Nisei Voters of Southern California, "Open Letter to All Nisei Citizen Voters of Southern California," *Rafu Shimpo*, August 25, 1938. I use here the common terminology for the Japanese American incarceration. However, in the strictest sense, "internment" refers to the incarceration of enemy aliens, usually prisoners of war, and not to citizens—which two-thirds of the Japanese Americans on the West Coast were.

38. Greg Robinson, *By Order of the President: FDR and the Internment of Japanese Americans* (Cambridge, MA: Harvard University Press, 2001), 93–94, 100–1; President Franklin D. Roosevelt, Executive Order 9066, February 19, 1942; Daniels, *Prisoners Without Trial*, 49–50.

39. War Relocation Authority, *People in Motion: The Postwar Adjustment of the Evacuated Japanese Americans* (Washington, D.C.: USGPO, 1946), 179; CH-34 interview in Thomas, Sakoda, and Kikuchi, *The Salvage*, 434; Weglyn, *Years of Infamy*, 77.

40. Floyd Covington, "Exploratory Survey Racial Tension Areas," December 31, 1942, p. 2, file 27, box 1, Los Angeles Urban League Papers, Special Collections Department, Young Research Library, University of California, Los Angeles; Daniel Widener, "'Perhaps the Japanese Are to Be Thanked?' Asia, Asian Americans, and

the Construction of Black California," *positions: east asia cultures critique* 11:1 (Spring 2003): 165–66; Greg Robinson, "Black Attorney Defended Japanese Americans during World War II," *Nichi Bei Times Weekly*, June 7, 2007, http://www.nichibeitimes. com/articles/stories.php?subaction=showfull&id=1181253732&archive=&start_from= &ucat=2& (accessed January 24, 2008); CH-59 interview in Thomas, Sakoda, and Kikuchi, *The Salvage*, 494; Fusaye Hashimoto interview by Mary Tamura, February 18, 1994, Japanese American National Museum Terminal Island Life History Project, http://content.cdlib.org/xtf/view?docId=kt367n993t&chunk.id=d0e1698&brand= oac&query=Fusaye&set.anchor=4 (accessed September, 25 2006). In "Black and Jewish Responses to Japanese Internment," *Journal of American Ethnic History* 21:4 (Winter 1995): 3–37, Cheryl Greenberg argues that African American organizations supported internment until late in the war.

41. Sue Kunitomi Embrey interview by Arthur A. Hansen, August 24, 1973 and November 15, 1973, Japanese American World War II Evacuation Oral History Project, California State University, Fullerton, http://content.cdlib.org/xtf/view?docId= ft18700334&query=Kunitomi&brand=oac (accessed September 25, 2006); Oak Yip Gee interview, March 21, 1980, transcript, p. 10, file 14, box 25, SCCAOHP; Jackman Hom interview, November 6, 1981, p. 10, file 5, box 18, SCCAOHP.

42. Demaree Bess, "California's Amazing Japanese," *Saturday Evening Post*, April 30, 1955, 68–76; Midori Nishi, "Changing Occupance of the Japanese in Los Angeles County, 1940–1950" (PhD diss., University of Washington, 1955), 79, 84–85.

43. Amy Uno Ishii interview by Betty E. Mitson and Kristin Mitchell, July 9, 1973, and July 20, 1973, Japanese American World War II Evacuation Oral History Project, California State University, Fullerton, http://content.cdlib.org/xtf/ view?docId=ft18700334&doc.view=%20frames&chunk.id=d0e2487& toc.depth=1&toc.id=&brand=oac (accessed September 25, 2006).

44. I have found no mention of Jefferson Park development in *La Opinión*, the major Spanish-language daily in Los Angeles.

45. Dower, *War Without Mercy*, 81.

46. Weglyn, *Years of Infamy*, 111.

CHAPTER SIX

1. Joseph James, "Profiles: San Francisco," *Journal of Educational Sociology* 19:3 (November 1945): 168; R. L. Duffus, "Portrait of a City of All Nations," *New York Times Magazine*, April 15, 1945, 11; Harold R. Isaacs, *Scratches on Our Minds: American Images of China and India* (New York: John Day Co., 1958), 120.

2. David M. P. Freund, *Colored Property: State Policy and White Racial Politics in Suburban America* (Chicago: University of Chicago Press, 2007), 12,18,19.

3. CH-62 interview in Dorothy Swaine Thomas, Charles Kikuchi, and James Sakoda, *Japanese American Evacuation and Resettlement*, vol. 2, *The Salvage* (Berkeley: University of California Press, 1952), 217; Judy Yung, *Unbound Voices: A Documen-*

tary History of Chinese Women in San Francisco (Berkeley: University of California Press, 1999), 441, 482.

4. CH-62 interview, 217; CH-53 interview in Thomas, Sakoda, and Kikuchi, *The Salvage*, 248–49. The federal government closed both the *New World-Sun Daily* and the *Japanese American News*, the two major Japanese American newspapers in San Francisco, but eventually allowed the latter to reopen.

5. "For Your Own Protection," *Chinese Press*, December 12, 1941; photo (courtesy of Priscilla Lee Holmes) in Yung, *Unbound Voices*, 445; Yong Chen, *Chinese San Francisco, 1850–1943: A Trans-Pacific Community* (Stanford, CA: Stanford University Press, 2000), 246; H. K. Wong, "H.K.'s Column," *Chinese Press*, December 19, 1941.

6. CH-31 interview in Thomas, Sakoda, and Kikuchi, *The Salvage*, 273.

7. CH-57 interview by Charles Kikuchi, November 2, 1944, transcript, p. 25, folder T1.986, JAERS; "The Man on the Street," *Chinese Press*, December 12, 1941; "Cities in Darkness," *Chinese Press*, December 12, 1941; H. K. Wong, "H.K.'s Column," *Chinese Press*, May 1, 1942.

8. Yung, *Unbound Voices*, 443–44; K. Scott Wong, *Americans First: Chinese Americans and the Second World War* (Cambridge, MA: Harvard University Press, 2005), 124; *"Kanlai si feishan lei"* (Apparently there are some bad types), *Jinshan shibao* (Chinese Times [San Francisco]), March 3, 1942; "On the Other Hand," *Chinese Press*, March 6, 1942; "For Your Protection" *Chinese Press*, March 6, 1942; Him Mark Lai and Betty Lim, "Gilbert Woo, Chinese American Journalist," in *Hu Jiangnan Wenji* (The collected works of Gilbert Woo), ed. Yuzun Liu, Dehua Zheng, and Larry Lam (Hong Kong: Xiangjiang Publishing Company, 1991), 39.

9. Marie Carey, "Chinese War Workers," *San Francisco Chronicle*, December 3, 1942; "Chinese Girl to Christen Next Ship," *San Francisco Chronicle*, December 3, 1942.

10. Chen, *Chinese San Francisco*, 263; *"Huaqiao huanying hu dashi shengkuang"* (Gala for overseas Chinese to welcome Ambassador Hu), *Jinshan Shibao*, March 5, 1942; editorial, *Chinese Press*, November 22, 1940.

11. "Chinatown Housing," *San Francisco Chronicle*, April 27, 1943; "Rising Steel Prices Postpone Chinatown Housing Project," *Chinese Press*, September 12, 1941; Leon H. Keyserling to Cordell Hull, February 18, 1942, p. 1, Decimal File 1940–1944, 811.502/59, RG 59, NARA; C. F. Palmer to Leon H. Keyserling, February 13, 1942, p. 1, Decimal File 1940–1944, 811.502/59, RG 59, NARA.

12. Robert Dallek, *Franklin D. Roosevelt and American Foreign Policy, 1932–1945* (New York: Oxford University Press, 1995), 329–30, 355–56; A. A. Berle, Jr., to Leon H. Keyserling, February 27, 1942, Decimal File 1940–1944, 811.502/59, RG 59, NARA.

13. *"Huabu jian pingju you kong nan zao cheng"* (Early completion of the China-town housing project once again in doubt), *Jinshan shibao*, March 6, 1942. I have found a handful of cases in Los Angeles and Texas in which Mexican consuls wrote to housing officials or directly to the State Department on behalf of Mexican Americans who either were losing their land to slum clearance or faced segregation within

housing projects. The State Department's interest in such disputes reflected consular involvement. No evidence exists that San Francisco's Chinese Consulate intervened to save Ping Yuen.

14. Lucius Beebe, "San Francisco: Boom Town De Luxe," *American Mercury*, January 1943, 66; Roger Lotchin, *The Bad City in the Good War: San Francisco, Los Angeles, Oakland, and San Diego* (Bloomington: Indiana University Press, 2003), 7–9, 16; Cornelius L. Golightly to John A Davis, March 26, 1944, file "Tension in San Francisco," box 443, RG 228, NARA; Charles S. Johnson, Herman H. Long, and Grace Jones, *The Negro War Worker in San Francisco: A Local Self-Survey* (San Francisco: YWCA, 1944), 2.

15. John Morton Blum, *V Was for Victory: Politics and American Culture During World War II* (New York: Harcourt Brace Jovanovich, 1976), 102–3; Marilynn S. Johnson, *The Second Gold Rush: Oakland and the East Bay in World War II* (Berkeley: University of California Press, 1993), 7–8.

16. "Housing Survey Indicates No S.F. Dwelling Shortage," *San Francisco Chronicle*, November 24, 1940; Franklin D. Roosevelt to Abner H. Ferguson, April 9, 1941, file "Defense Housing, January 21, 1941-May 2, 1941 #2," box 28, RG 196, NARA; Alice Griffith, "A Review of the Proceedings of the Housing Authority of San Francisco," 1943, p. 7, file 77E, box 17, series IV, LOWV-SF.

17. Housing Authority of the City and County of San Francisco, *Road to the Golden Age: A Report on the First Twenty Years of Operations, 1940 to 1960* (San Francisco: Housing Authority of the City and County of San Francisco, 1960), 8–9; "Defense Workers: Influx of 40,000 Here Will Require Additional Housing Facilities," *San Francisco Chronicle*, February 13, 1942, 12; Lotchin, *The Bad City in the Good War*, 128–29. Rent control policies helped keep gouging in check, but landlords divided apartments to skirt regulations.

18. Johnson, Long, and Jones, *The Negro War Worker in San Francisco*, 2.

19. Lotchin, *The Bad City in the Good War*, 128; Johnson, Long, and Jones, *The Negro War Worker in San Francisco*, 24–26; James, "Profiles: San Francisco," 170.

20. James, "Profiles: San Francisco," 166, 171; Albert S. Broussard, *Black San Francisco: The Struggle for Racial Equality in the West, 1900–1954* (Lawrence: University Press of Kansas, 1993), 166–74; Johnson, Long, and Jones, *The Negro War Worker in San Francisco*, 51.

21. "Eviction of Negroes," *San Francisco Chronicle*, June 25, 1943; see also "Housing Cleanup," *San Francisco Chronicle*, June 22, 1943; "Grand Jury Enters the Japtown Muddle," *San Francisco Chronicle*, June 26, 1943.

22. Johnson, Long, and Jones, *The Negro War Worker in San Francisco*, 29.

23. Walter Wright Alley to Eugene Weston, Jr., February 17, 1944, pp. 1–2, file "San Francisco—Racial Relations," box 750, RG 207, NARA; National Housing Agency, "War Housing Programmed for or Occupied by Negro War Workers," July 7, 1944, file "Statistics: War and Defense—Racial Compilations, 1942–1957," box 6, RG 196,

NARA. The FHA performed poorly for minorities throughout the nation, but the San Francisco case stands out. Nationwide, the FHA underwrote fifteen thousand units of private housing for African Americans during the war. Donald W. Wyatt, "Better Homes for Negro Families in the South," *Social Forces* 28:3 (March 1950): 298–99.

24. Western Addition Housing Council memo, January 1, 1942, p. 1, file 581, ACLU-NC; Ernest Besig to Eugene Block, January 16, 1942, p. 1, file 581, ACLU-NC; handwritten notes, January 2, 1942, file 581, ACLU-NC; Alice Griffith to Mayor Elmer Robinson, January 26, 1950, p. 1, file 566, ACLU-NC.

25. Griffith to Robinson, p. 1; Ernest Besig to Roger Baldwin, January 12, 1942, p. 1, file 581, ACLU-NC; Thomas J. Sugrue, *The Origins of the Urban Crisis: Race and Inequality in Postwar Detroit* (Princeton, NJ: Princeton University Press, 1996), 74–75; *San Francisco News* clipping, August 25, 1942, file 567, ACLU-NC.

26. National Housing Agency, "Housing Units Programmed for Negro War Workers," June 30, 1944, file "Statistics: War and Defense—Racial Compilations, 1942–1947," box 6, RG 196, NARA; "PA 671 Projects Region VI," February 28, 1945, p. 1, file "P & P-H Conversions (1943–1947), Defense—War Housing General," box 8, Records of the Intergroup Relations Branch, RG 196, NARA; National Housing Agency, "War Housing Programmed for or Occupied by Negro War Workers," July 7, 1944, "Statistics: War and Defense—Racial Compilations, 1942–1957" file, Box 6, Records of the Intergroup Relations Branch, RG196, NARA.

27. Johnson, *The Second Gold Rush*, 31; Andrew Kersten, *Race, Jobs, and the War: The FEPC in the Midwest, 1941–1946* (Urbana: University of Illinois Press, 2000), 11; Broussard, *Black San Francisco*, 157; Lotchin, *The Bad City in the Good War*, 125; Blum, *V Was for Victory*, 11–12, 196–97.

28. Frank L. Kluckhohn, "50 Billion a Year Is Set by President as Our War Outlay," *New York Times*, December 31, 1941; "Draft Registration June 30 for Youths 18 to 20," *New York Times*, May 23, 1942; "'43 Drafting Put at 3,500,000 Men," *New York Times*, December 28, 1942, 36. Among these soldiers were a million African Americans and fifteen thousand Chinese Americans (Wong, *Americans First*, 58).

29. Lotchin, *The Bad City in the Good War*, 161; Johnson, *The Second Gold Rush*, 38–41; Johnson, Long, and Jones, *The Negro War Worker in San Francisco*, 63. Charles S. Johnson did not break these statistics down by race, so it is impossible to know how many of these workers were Chinese American. However, journalists claimed that some seven thousand Chinese Americans from San Francisco were working in the defense industries by 1943.

30. Hadley Cantril and Mildred Strunk, *Public Opinion, 1935–1946* (Princeton, NJ: Princeton University Press, 1951), 499, 508–20; Johnson, Long, and Jones, *The Negro War Worker in San Francisco*, 64, 66–68.

31. Katherine Archibald, *Wartime Shipyard: A Study in Social Disunity* (Berkeley: University of California Press, 1947), 104; "Chinese in War Work," *San Francisco Chronicle*, December 24, 1942, 6; Carey, "Chinese War Workers"; Demaree Bess,

"The Crane's Eye-View," *San Francisco Chronicle*, December 24, 1942; Yung, *Unbound Voices*, 479; "Chinese Have Excellent Shipyard Safety Record," *Chinese Press*, July 23, 1943.

32. Isaacs, *Scratches on Our Minds*, 64; Cantril and Strunk, *Public Opinion*, 499; Yung, *Unbound Voices*, 479; Johnson, *The Second Gold Rush*, 63.

33. See, for example, Carl Gluck, *Shake Hands with the Dragon* (New York: McGraw-Hill, 1941), 302.

34. Bess, "The Crane's Eye-View." Herbert G. Gutman, "Work, Culture, and Society in Industrializing America, 1815–1919," *American Historical Review* 78(3): 547, discusses immigrants' "work habits" as "alien to the modern factory," yet the Chinese American population fit this characterization far less than the white and black sharecroppers who also worked in the shipyards. Many Chinese immigrants hailed from southern Guangdong Province, then undergoing significant industrialization, and some even invested their American earnings in small factories in China. Some of the shipyards' oldest Chinese American employees probably worked in San Francisco factories in the 1870s and 1880s, while others toiled in Chinatown sweatshops making clothing for Joe Shoong's National Dollar chain in the 1930s. Albert Feuerwerker, "Handicraft and Manufactured Cotton Textiles in China, 1870–1910," *Journal of Economic History* 30:2 (June 1970): 346–47; Y.F. Woon, "An Emigrant Area in the Ssu-Yi Area, Southeastern China, 1885–1949: A Study in Social Change," *Modern Asian Studies* 18:2 (1984): 276–77; Janice E. Stockard, *Daughters of the Canton Delta* (Stanford, CA: Stanford University Press, 1989); Yung, *Unbound Feet*, 210.

35. "From South to West," *Interracial Review*, clipping, ca. 1943, file "Los Angeles," box 442, RG 228, NARA; "Los Angeles, October 1945," October 1945, p. 9, box 442, RG 228, NARA; Archibald, *Wartime Shipyard*, 75, 94.

36. Kevin Starr, *Endangered Dreams: The Great Depression in California* (New York: Oxford University Press, 1996), 229–31; Archibald, *Wartime Shipyard*, 52, 61–65; James N. Gregory, *American Exodus: The Dust Bowl Migration and Okie Culture in California* (New York: Oxford University Press, 1989), 168–69.

37. Robert W. O'Brien, "Status of Chinese in the Mississippi Delta," *Social Forces* 19:3 (1941): 386–90. James W. Loewen, *The Mississippi Chinese: Between Black and White*, 2nd ed. (Prospect Heights, IL: Waveland Press, 1988), 73–101, portrays the 1930s and 1940s as an era of transition for Chinese Americans in the South.

38. Bess, "The Crane's Eye-View."

39. George H. Roeder, Jr., *The Censored War: American Visual Experience During World War Two* (New Haven, CT: Yale University Press, 1993), 57; Isaacs, *Scratches on Our Minds*, 174–76; Gregory, *American Exodus*, 166–69; Archibald, *Wartime Shipyard*, 104; Cantril and Strunk, *Public Opinion*, 477.

40. Theodore White, "Far Eastern News in the Press," *Far Eastern Survey* 15:12 (June 1946): 181–82; "How to Tell Your Friends from the Japs," *Time*, December 22, 1941, 33; "How to Tell the Japs from the Chinese," *Life*, December 22, 1941, 81; Carl Crow, "Our Allies, the Chinese," *Ladies' Home Journal*, January 1944, 5; Milton

Caniff, *Terry and the Pirates* series, Chicago Tribune Syndicate; *Flying Tigers*, DVD, directed by David Miller (1942; Santa Monica, CA: Lions Gate Home Entertainment, 2000); *The Lady from Chungking*, DVD, directed by William Nigh (1943; Alpha Video Distributors, 2005); "The Battle of China" *(Why We Fight, vol. 6)*, directed by Frank Capra (U.S. Dept. of War, 1944); Dallek, *Franklin D. Roosevelt and American Foreign Policy*, 329, 391.

41. *Regan v. King*, 49 F. Supp. 222 (1942); "We Want No Citizen-Japs, Webb Says," *San Francisco Chronicle*, June 27, 1942; Lawrence E. Davies, "Upholds Japanese in Citizens' Right," *New York Times*, February 21, 1943.

42. "We Want No Citizen-Japs," *San Francisco Chronicle*; Davies, "Upholds Japanese in Citizens' Right"; *Regan v. King*, 319 U.S. 753 (1943).

43. Frederick Warren Riggs, *Pressures on Congress: A Study of the Repeal of Chinese Exclusion* (New York: King's Crown Press, 1950), 35; Barbara Tuchman, *Stilwell and the American Experience in China, 1911–1945* (New York: Grove Press, 2001), 353.

44. "Hail Mme. Chiang in San Francisco," *New York Times*, March 26, 1943; Lawrence E. Davies, "Mme. Chiang Puts War to Workers," *New York Times*, March 30, 1943.

45. Gilbert Woo, *"Lun Zhongzuqishi"* (A discussion of racial discrimination) in *Hu Jiangnan Wenji*, 20.

46. U.S. Department of the Treasury, "For Freedom's Sake Buy War Bonds," 1943, Northwestern University Library World War II online poster archive, http://www.library.northwestern.edu/govinfo/collections/wwii-posters/img/ww1647-24.jpg (accessed December 15, 2006); U.S. War Manpower Commission, "United We Win," 1943, Northwestern University Library World War II online poster archive, http://www.library.northwestern.edu/govinfo/collections/wwii-posters/img/ww1645-41.jpg (accessed December 15, 2006); U.S. Office of War Information, "No Loyal Citizen," 1943, Northwestern University Library World War II online poster archive, http://www.library.northwestern.edu/govinfo/collections/wwii-posters/img/ww1645-49.jpg (accessed December 15, 2006).

47. Blum, *V Was for Victory*, 184, 209; John Dower, *War Without Mercy: Race and Power in the Pacific War* (New York: Pantheon, 1986), 173; Jennifer Brooks, *Defining the Peace: World War Two Veterans, Race, and the Remaking of Southern Political Tradition* (Chapel Hill: University of North Carolina Press, 2004), 42; John Hope Franklin, "A Round Table: The Living and Reliving of World War II," *Journal of American History* 77:2 (September 1990): 578; Brenda Gayle Plummer, *Rising Wind: Black Americans and U.S. Foreign Affairs, 1935–1960* (Chapel Hill: University of North Carolina Press, 1996), 74–77, 84–86.

48. "Job Discrimination Laid to Officials," *New York Times*, August 24, 1942; William Issel, "Humanity Is One Great Family: Jews and Catholics in the San Francisco Civil Rights Campaign, 1940–1960"; http://bss.sfsu.edu/issel/jews%20catholics.htm (accessed October 27, 2006); Broussard, *Black San Francisco*, 194;

Ralph G. Wadsworth to Charles Leong, August 29, 1942, p. 1, file 19, carton 3, Charles Leong Papers, Ethnic Studies Library, University of California, Berkeley.

49. Dower, *War Without Mercy*, 5, 166–67, 210–11, 285–90; Mark Eykholt, "Aggression, Victimization, and Chinese Historiography of the Nanjing Massacre," in *The Nanjing Massacre in History and Historiography*, ed. Joshua Fogel (Berkeley: University of California Press, 2000), 58.

50. Riggs, *Pressures on Congress*, 48–64, 83–84.

51. Lawrence E. Davies, "House Vote on Chinese Pleases Many on Coast," *New York Times*, October 31, 1943; Riggs, *Pressures on Congress*, 83–86.

52. Riggs, *Pressures on Congress*, 113.

53. Broussard, *Black San Francisco*, 198–200; "Defense Homes Are Possible," *Chinese Press*, August 21, 1942.

54. "Sam Young Seated on Republican County Committee," *Chinese Press*, January 8, 1943; Earl C. Behrens, "Chinese to Join District Attorney Staff," *San Francisco Chronicle*, December 10, 1943; Minutes of the Mayor's Civic Unity Committee, San Francisco Public Library, San Francisco, CA; "Albert Chow, Chinatown's 'Mayor,' Dies," *San Francisco Chronicle*, October 18, 1957.

55. James, "Profiles: San Francisco," 167, 172–73. For voter advertisements, see, for example, *Jinshan Shibao*, October 26, 1941, Chinese and English advertisements for Supervisor Adolph Uhl, Municipal Judge Melvyn Cronin, Supervisor John F. McGown, Supervisor Adolph E. Schmidt, and Supervisor James. B. McSheehy. Typical ads addressed the politicians' "Chinese friends" or described the candidate as a "friend of the Chinese."

56. Thomas C. Fleming, "Reflections on Black History: Sargent Johnson and the Bohemian Life," *San Francisco Sun-Reporter*, February 4, 1999; Isaacs, *Scratches on Our Minds*, 87; December 12, 1945 Minutes of the Mayor's Civic Unity Committee, San Francisco Public Library, San Francisco; Bai Hong, "*Mantan qishi*" (A discussion about discrimination), *Jinshan shibao*, December 5, 1944; Chen, *Chinese San Francisco*, 146, 199; Arnold Shankman, "Black on Yellow: Afro-Americans View Chinese Americans, 1850–1935," *Phylon* 39:1 (1st Quarter 1978): 14. Shankman also notes the prevalence in the African American press of stories of Chinese American business discrimination against blacks.

57. Isaacs, *Scratches on Our Minds*, 87; Thelma Thurston Gorham, "Negroes and Japanese Evacuees," *The Crisis*, November 1945, 330.

58. Gilbert Woo, "*Poqian an 1*" (Eviction case, part 1), in *Hu Jiangnan Wenji*, 75.

59. Preamble, Charter of the United Nations, June 26, 1945; Woo, "*Poqian an 1*," 74.

60. Isaacs, *Scratches on Our Minds*, 120; Bill Simons, "My Chinatown," *Chinese Press*, February 13, 1942.

61. "Chinatown Wants Nothing Special in Homes," *San Francisco Housing Authority News*, September–October 1946, 4.

62. Freund, *Colored Property*, 19; Johnson, *The Second Gold Rush*, 103.

63. Davis McEntire, "The Problem of Segregation," p. 2, n.d., file 581, ACLU-NC; Gilbert Woo, "*Poqian an 2*" (Eviction case, part 2), in *Hu Jiangnan Wenji*, 76–77.

64. Woo, "*Poqian an 2*," 76–77.

CHAPTER SEVEN

1. Brian Masaru Hayashi, *Democratizing the Enemy: The Japanese American Internment* (Princeton, NJ: Princeton University Press, 2004), 189; Kevin Allen Leonard, *The Battle for Los Angeles: Racial Ideology and World War II* (Albuquerque: University of New Mexico Press, 2006), 201–2, 228, 243; "We Shan't Pretend to Like It," *Los Angeles Times*, December 19, 1944. Prior to this time, the WRA and the military had allowed a few Japanese Americans, mostly the wives of white men, to come back to the Bay Area and Los Angeles.

2. Most of these committees dealt with anti-Semitism as well as anti-black racism and included Jews among their members.

3. Minutes of the Mayor's Civic Unity Committee, November 9, 1944, p. 4, San Francisco Public Library. An interesting study of housing project activism is Henry Kraus, *In the City Was a Garden: A Housing Project Chronicle* (New York: Renaissance Press, 1951), which deals with a project in San Pedro, the port area of Los Angeles.

4. Mark Brilliant, "Color Lines: Civil Rights Struggles on America's 'Racial Frontier,' 1945–1975" (PhD diss., Stanford University, 2002), 73–91, 128–50; Josh Sides, *L.A. City Limits: African American Los Angeles from the Great Depression to the Present* (Berkeley: University of California Press, 2003), 142–45; Gracia Booth to Galen Fisher, August 9, 1945, pp. 1–3, file 2, box 7, Records of the Pacific Coast Committee on American Principles and Fair Play (hereafter, Fair Play Committee), Bancroft Library, University of California, Berkeley; John M. Yamazaki, "Report of Survey on West Coast," May 1945, p. 7, file 13, carton 2, Fair Play Committee.

5. Shana B. Bernstein, "Building Bridges at Home in a Time of Global Conflict: Interracial Cooperation and the Fight for Civil Rights in Los Angeles, 1933–54" (PhD diss., Stanford University, 2003), 204–32.

6. Lon Kurashige, *Japanese American Celebration and Conflict: A History of Ethnic Identity and Festival in Los Angeles, 1934–1990* (Berkeley: University of California Press, 2001), 110; Bureau of the Census, *Special Census of Los Angeles, California* (USGPO: Washington, D.C., 1946), 1. The city itself gained about three hundred thousand new residents, but the county also grew tremendously during this period.

7. See, for example, tracts 227, 248, 249, 250, 251, 253, and 254 in Bureau of the Census, *Special Census of Los Angeles, California*; Earl Hanson and Paul Beckett, *Los Angeles: Its People and Its Homes* (Los Angeles: Haynes Foundation, 1944), 39; Minutes, Los Angeles Coordinating Committee for Resettlement, October 8, 1945, file 1, carton 3, Fair Play Committee.

8. Kango Kunitsugu interview by Dave Biniasz, November 28, 1973, p. 6, Japanese American Project, California State University Fullerton Oral History Collection http://content.cdlib.org/dynaxml/servlet/dynaXML?docId=ft9z09p2bp&doc.view= entire_text, (accessed March 23, 2007); Arthur F. Miley to John Anson Ford, August 10, 1943, p. 3, file BIV5idd(9), box 75, John Anson Ford papers (hereafter, Ford papers), Huntington Library, San Marino, California.

9. Edward J. Escobar, *Race, Police, and the Making of a Political Identity: Mexican Americans and the Los Angeles Police Department, 1900–1945* (Berkeley: University of California Press, 1999), 11, 237, 247.

10. Miley to Ford, p. 2; May Goldman, Hollywood Women's Council, to Los Angeles City Council, November 29, 1943, file 16287, box A837, Council Communications, Los Angeles City Archives; Preston L. Wright to J. Bion Philipson, June 19, 1945, p. 1, "Los Angeles, California correspondence #3" file, box 9, Records of the National Housing Agency, RG 207, NARA; M. H. Jim Driggers to John E. McGovern, District Director, FHA, January 17, 1945, pp. 1–2, "Los Angeles, California correspondence #3" file, box 9, Records of the National Housing Agency, RG 207, NARA; "Los Angeles Negro Housing," ca. February 1945, p. 2, "Los Angeles, California correspondence #3" file, box 9, Records of the National Housing Agency, RG 207, NARA.

11. Charles Bratt, "Profiles: Los Angeles," *Journal of Educational Sociology* 19:3 (November 1945): 182, 183; National Housing Agency, "War Housing Programmed for or Occupied by Negro War Workers," July 7, 1944, file "Statistics: War and Defense—Racial Compilations, 1942–1957," box 6, RG 196, NARA; George Gleason, "The Housing Crisis in Los Angeles County," April 1, 1945, p. 2, "Los Angeles, California correspondence #3" file, box 9, RG 207, NARA; Roger Lotchin, *The Bad City in the Good War: San Francisco, Los Angeles, Oakland, and San Diego* (Bloomington: Indiana University Press, 2003), 215.

12. Dillon S. Myer to Harvey M. Coverley, January 23, 1945, p. 1, file "Personal Correspondence, 1945," box 2, Dillon Myer Papers, Truman Library Institute, Independence, MO; Booth to Fisher, p. 2; Dillon Myer to Ben Kuroki, October 5, 1945, p. 1, file "Personal Correspondence, 1945," box 2, Dillon Myer Papers; Myer to Mike Masaoka, December 21, 1944, p. 2, file "Personal Correspondence, 1943–1944," Dillon Myer Papers.

13. Several thousand Nisei soldiers also served in the Pacific theater, mostly as interpreters and in other intelligence work. The military kept their service a secret until very late in the war.

14. Gracia Booth to Galen Fisher, August 9, 1945, p. 2, file 2, box 7, Fair Play Committee; "20 Nisei Win Bronze Stars," *New York Times*, January 3, 1945; "7 Nisei Win the DSC for Bravery in Italy," *New York Times*, January 12, 1945; Milton Bracker, "Nisei Troops Take Mountain in Italy," *New York Times*, April 9, 1945; *Press Digest*, August 15, 1944, pp. 57–58, file "OWI Alpha #2," box 18, Phileo Nash papers (hereafter, Nash papers), Truman Library Institute, Independence, MO; *Press*

Digest, September 14, 1944, p. 26, file "OWI Alpha #1," box 18, Nash papers; "Hood River Legion Stirs Ire at Front," *New York Times*, December 31, 1944; "Private Hachiya, American," *New York Times*, February 17, 1945; Myer to Masaoka, p. 2; War Agency Liquidation Unit (WALU), *People in Motion: The Postwar Adjustment of the Evacuated Japanese Americans* (Washington, D.C.: USGPO, 1948), 18; Earl C. Behrens, "Stimson Calls Nisei Critics Undemocratic," *San Francisco Chronicle*, December 14, 1944; "Housewife" correspondent, December 28, 1944, p. 3, file "OWI-Race Tension #1," box 25, Nash papers.

15. "West Coast Incidents Involving Persons of Japanese Ancestry," 1945, file 591, ACLU-NC.

16. "Housewife" report, January 27, 1945, p. 6, file "Correspondents' Reports," file "OWI-Race Tensions #1," Nash papers; Robert Kenny to John Anson Ford, February 14, 1945, p. 1, file BIV5ibb(8), box 74, Ford papers; Behrens, "Stimson Calls Nisei Critics Undemocratic"; "Anti-Nisei Terror," *San Francisco Chronicle*, June 4, 1945; A. A. Liveright to Phileo Nash, March 15, 1945, pp. 1–3, file "Minority #3," box 46, Nash papers; "West Coast Incidents Involving Persons of Japanese Ancestry," 1945, file 591, ACLU-NC; "Bus Workers Protest Hiring of Nisei," *San Francisco Chronicle*, August 28, 1945; Tom Sitton, *Los Angeles Transformed: Fletcher Bowron's Urban Reform Revival, 1938–1953* (Albuquerque: University of New Mexico Press, 2005), 65–66; WALU, *People in Motion*, 91; Dillon S. Myer to Harvey M. Coverley, September 21, 1945, p. 2, file "Personal Correspondence, 1945," box 2, Myer Collection.

17. See, for example, Mary T. MacNair, "Report on Democracy in Action," ca. early 1945, pp. 1–2, file 2, box 41, Anderson Papers, Japanese American Research Project Collection of Material about Japanese in the United States, 1893–1985 (hereafter, JARP), Young Research Library, University of California, Los Angeles.

18. WRA, Monthly Report, Los Angeles District Office, June 1945, p. 6, file F3.671, reel 65, JAERS; Arthur F. Miley to John Anson Ford, June 1, 1945, p. 1, file BIV5ibb(8), box 74, Ford papers; "West Coast Incidents Involving Persons of Japanese Ancestry," 1945, file 591, ACLU-NC. The only internment camp not closed was Tule Lake, the so-called disloyal camp for Japanese Americans who opted to repatriate to Japan or give up their American citizenship. Some Japanese Americans in Tule Lake refused to be moved to another camp when the WRA designated Tule Lake for "disloyals."

19. Dillon S. Myer to Ben Kuroki, February 10, 1945, p. 1, file "Personal Correspondence 1945," box 2, Myer papers; Myer to John C. Baker, March 30, 1945, p. 1, file "Personal Correspondence 1945," box 2, Myer papers; Myer to Baker, July 2, 1945, pp. 1–2, file "Personal Correspondence 1945," box 2, Myer papers; Chief Clerk to Dillon S. Myer and Harold Ickes, October 1, 1945, p. 1, file "Personal Correspondence 1945," box 2, Myer papers; Arthur F. Miley to John Anson Ford, September 25, 1945, p. 1, file BIV5ibb(8), box 74, Ford papers; Homer Crotty to Arthur C. McGiffert, July 13, 1945, p. 2, file 2, box 7, Fair Play Committee; Liveright to Nash, p. 2; Lotchin, *The Bad City in the Good War*, 214–15; WALU, *People in Motion*, 173–74.

20. The WRA was one of the most racially liberal federal agencies. In contrast to the FPHA, WRA officials viewed the integration of Japanese Americans into mainstream American life (and white neighborhoods) as one of their main goals.

21. "Conference notes re: Japanese housing," March 21, 1946, p. 1; Los Angeles County Committee on Human Relations, Report on Winona Avenue F.P.H.A Project, May 28, 1946, p. 1; Melvin H. Harter to Dillon Meyer [*sic*], April 4, 1946, pp. 1–2; and Dillon S. Myer to L.A. County Board of Supervisors, May 29, 1946, pp. 1–8, all in folder BIV5ibb(9), box 45, Ford papers; Estelle Ishigo handwritten note ca. 1946, file 12, box 78, JARP.

22. Estelle Ishigo notes, June 22, 1948, p. 1, file 8, JARP; T. Sasaki, "The Present Japanese Communities in Los Angeles," draft typescript, August 30, 1946, p. 14, file F3.67, reel 65, JAERS. For more on resettlement, see Charlotte Brooks, "In the Twilight Zone between Black and White: Japanese American Resettlement and Community in Chicago, 1942–1945," *Journal of American History* 86:4 (March 2000): 1655–87.

23. Los Angeles County Committee on Human Relations, "Report on Winona Avenue F.P.H.A. Project," pp. 1–3; Estelle Ishigo notes, June 22, 1948, p. 1; Eiji Tanabe, Seido Ogawa, and Frank Chuman to Myer Simon, June 10, 1948, p. 2, file 8, box 78, JARP; Leonard J. Roach, "Statement Regarding Japanese Relief Load in Los Angeles County," January 22, 1946, p. 1, file BIV5ibb(9), box 74, Ford Papers; Estelle Ishigo to Tai, ca. May 1948, file 12, box 78, JARP. In more anti-Japanese American counties such as Placer and Imperial, county supervisors and welfare boards illegally attempted to keep Japanese Americans from using assistance.

24. Estelle Ishigo to Mr. Eaton, ca. 1948, JARP. Estelle Ishigo was a white artist married to an older Nisei, Arthur Ishigo. She voluntarily went into an internment camp in order to stay with her husband, a choice a handful of other non-Japanese American spouses also made.

25. WALU, *People in Motion*, 179–83.

26. Sasaki, "The Present Japanese Communities in Los Angeles," pp. 8–9, 15–16. Leonard Bloom and Ruth Riemer, *Removal and Return: The Socio-Economic Effects of the War on Japanese Americans* (Berkeley: University of California Press, 1949), 65, contends that Japanese American hotel owners, not whites or African Americans, were responsible for most of the exploitation that occurred.

27. Yamazaki, "Report on Survey of West Coast," p. 6; Midori Nishi, "Changing Occupance of the Japanese in Los Angeles County, 1940–1950" (PhD thesis, University of Washington, 1955), 79–93.

28. Sasaki, "The Present Japanese Communities in Los Angeles," p. 4; WALU, *People in Motion*, 84–86, 101, 103, 112.

29. Nishi, "Changing Occupance," 132–35; Yamazaki, "Report of Survey on West Coast," p. 6. For a more detailed discussion of Japanese American gardeners, see Ronald Tadao Tsukashima, "Politics of Maintenance Gardening and the Formation of the Southern California Gardeners' Federation," in *Greenmakers: Japanese American*

Gardeners in Southern California, ed. Naomi Hirahira (Los Angeles: Southern California Gardeners' Federation, 2000), 67–93.

30. Bloom and Reimer, *Removal and Return*, 119, 123; Tsukashima, "Politics of Maintenance Gardening," 79; Yamazaki, "Report of Survey on West Coast," p. 6; Nishi, "Changing Occupance," 133; Dorothy Swaine Thomas, James Sakoda, and Charles Kikuchi, *Japanese American Evacuation and Resettlement*, vol. 2, *The Salvage* (Berkeley: University of California Press, 1952), 610–11.

31. Nishi, "Changing Occupance," 84–86, 104; Sasaki, "The Present Japanese Communities in Los Angeles," p. 15. A new problem, smog, also pushed farms farther out.

32. "The Race War That Flopped," *Ebony*, July 1946, 3; Samuel Ishikawa, "Common Ground," September 10, 1945, p. 1, file BIV5ibb(8), box 74, Ford papers; "Evict Negroes to Make Way for Japs," *Los Angeles Herald-Express*, December 30, 1944.

33. Cheryl Greenberg, "Black and Jewish Responses to Japanese American Internment," *Journal of American Ethnic History* 14:2 (Winter 1995); "Minorities Have Responsibilities," *Now*, November 1944, 9; Thelma Thurston Gorham, "Negroes and Japanese Evacuees," *The Crisis*, November 1945, 315; "Reconversion," *Spotlight*, ca. 1945, file BIV5iee(9), box 76, Ford Papers.

34. Joseph James, "Profiles: San Francisco," *Journal of Educational Sociology* 19:3 (November 1945): 167, 172; "Housewife" correspondent, January 27, 1945, p. 6, file "OWI-Race Tension #1," Box 25, Nash papers; "Highlights of Conference on Interracial Cooperation," January 11, 1945, file 2, box 41, JARP. Flippin served on the Mayor's Civic Unity Committee. Shelley was head of the San Francisco Labor Council, the AFL umbrella group whose members included some of the most nativist locals on the West Coast. However, Shelley was a racial liberal and sponsored civil rights legislation after the war. Participants in both fair play and civic unity activities included Edward Howden, Harry Kingman, Ruth Kingman, Monroe E. Deutsch, G. Raymond Booth, and Gracia D. Booth.

35. Gorham, "Negroes and Japanese Evacuees," 316; Fred Ross, San Francisco District Report, p. 1, November 1, 1945, file F10211, JAERS; Joseph James, "Annual Report," December 8, 1945, in John H. Bracey, Jr., Sharon Harley, and August Meier, eds., *Papers of the NAACP* (microfilm, University Publications of America, 1982), Part 26, Series D, reel 3, file "Geographical: San Francisco, CA, 1946-," p. 8–9; "The Race War That Flopped," 4.

36. Lloyd H. Fisher, "The Problem of Violence: Observations on Race Conflict in Los Angeles," pp. 11–12, file 4, box 5, California CIO Council Union Research and Information Services Records, Southern California Library for Social Studies and Research, Los Angeles, CA.

37. Sasaki, "The Present Japanese Communities in Los Angeles," p. 7; Sides, *L.A. City Limits*, 45, 53; "The Race War That Flopped," 5; Memorandum, September 27, 1945, p. 1, file BIV5iee(7), box 76, Ford papers.

38. "The Race War That Flopped," 3; "Evict Negroes to Make Way for Japs," *Los Angeles Herald-Express*; John S. Meaney to Edwin Ferguson, September 15, 1945, p. 2, file F3.65, reel 65, JAERS; Meaney to Ferguson, October 12, 1945, p. 3, September 15, 1945, p. 2, file F3.65, reel 65, JAERS; Rev. Art Takemoto interview by James Gatewood, May 19, 1998, p. 403, REgenerations Oral History Program, http://content.cdlib.org/xtf/view?docId=ft358003z1&doc.view=frames&chunk.id=doe& 1909&toc.depth=1&toc.id=doe19091&brand=calisphere (accessed March 26, 2007).

39. Lawrence Brooks deGraaf, "Negro Migration to Los Angeles, 1930 to 1950" (PhD diss., University of California, Los Angeles, 1962), 203; Sasaki, "The Present Japanese Communities," 21; Takemoto interview, p. 403; WALU, *People in Motion*, 225; "The Race War That Flopped," 3.

40. Takemoto interview, p. 403; Sasaki, "The Present Japanese Communities," pp. 6, 7, 9; T. Sasaki, final draft, typescript, December 18, 1946, pp. 6–7, file F3.67, reel 65, JAERS.

41. Sasaki, "The Present Japanese Communities," p. 6; Katsumi (Hirooka) Kunitsugu interview by Leslie Ito, April 22, 1998, p. 259, REgenerations Oral History Project, http://content.cdlib.org/xtf/view?docId=ft358003z1&doc.view=frames&chunk.id=doe10902&toc.depth=1&toc.id=doe10902&brand=calisphere (accessed March 26, 2007); Harry K. Honda interview by Leslie Ito, April 1, 1998, pp. 12–13, REgenerations Oral History Project, http://content.cdlib.org/xtf/view?docId=ft358003z1&doc.view=frames&chunk.id=doe1017&toc.depth=1&toc.id=doe1017&brand=calisphere (accessed March 26, 2007).

42. Eichiro Azuma, *Between Two Empires: Race, History, and Transnationalism in Japanese America* (New York: Oxford University Press, 2005), 188, 206–7; Kurashige, *Japanese American Celebration and Conflict*, 30–39; John Modell, *The Economics and Politics of Racial Accommodation: The Japanese of Los Angeles, 1900–1942* (Urbana: University of Illinois Press, 1977), 13–14.

43. Mike Masaoka to Walter White, June 24, 1942, p. 1, Papers of the NAACP, reel 23, part 18B.

44. Eiji Tanabe, Seido Ogawa, and Frank Chuman to Myer Simon, June 10, 1948, p. 2, file 8, box 78, JARP; "San Francisco JACL Declares Slum Project Does Not Protect Race Minorities," *Pacific Citizen*, July 3, 1948; "Quick Settlement of Housing Issue over Racial Occupancy Urged by Civic Unity Group," *Pacific Citizen*, December 17, 1949.

45. Kurashige, *Japanese American Celebration and Conflict*, 115.

46. Editorial, *Crossroads*, May 28, 1948, Bancroft Library, University of California, Berkeley; Bernstein, "Building Bridges at Home in a Time of Global Conflict," 234, 240.

47. "CPS" to "Posten," November 25, 1944, file "Racial Tension #1," box 25, Nash papers; Ernest Besig to A.A. Heist, August 30, 1946, file 605, ACLU-NC; Besig to Joe Grant Masaoka, August 8, 1946, file 605, ACLU-NC.

48. A. A. Heist to Ernest Besig, October 4, 1946, p. 1, file 567, ACLU-NC; Ruth W. Kingman to Members and Friends of the California Council for Civic Unity, September 16, 1946, pp. 1–2, file 567, ACLU-NC; Ernest Besig speech to the Commonwealth Club of California, August 7, 1946, file 605, ACLU-NC; "Nisei Union Man Swings CIO Resolution," *Progressive News* (formerly *Hokubei Mainchi* [San Francisco]), October 15, 1946, file 567, ACLU-NC; "NC District JACL to Launch Drive to Defeat Proposition 15," *Progressive News*, October 4, 1946; "Measure Hits Korean Minority, Editor Points Out," *Progressive News*, October 25, 1946; "Defeat Proposition 15," *Los Angeles Sentinel*, October 31, 1946; "Foreign Papers Aid in Campaign Against Prop. 15," *Rafu Shimpo*, October 26, 1946; "Nisei Troops Get Truman Citation," *New York Times*, July 16, 1946; Leonard, *The Battle for Los Angeles*, 279–80; WALU, *People in Motion*, 26.

49. California Secretary of State, *Statement of the Vote of California, 1932–1946* (Sacramento: Secretary of State, 1947), 35. The 1946 election was definitely not a complete victory for civil rights in California. Proposition 11, an attempt to create a permanent state FEPC, failed by a large margin.

50. Fisher, *The Problem of Violence*, 9; Andrew Wiese, *Places of Their Own: African American Suburbanization in the Twentieth Century* (Chicago: University of Chicago Press, 2005), 129–30.

51. "Los Angeles Paper Exposes Drive to Oust Non-Caucasians from San Fernando Valley," *Pacific Citizen*, July 5, 1947; "Tale of Two Cities," *Pacific Citizen*, January 4, 1947; "Race Friction on Peninsula," *San Francisco Chronicle*, July 12, 1947.

52. Xiaojian Zhao, *Remaking Chinese America: Immigration, Family, and Community, 1940–1965* (New Brunswick, NJ: Rutgers University Press, 2002), 79–80; "Judge Upholds Race Restriction on Nob Hill," *San Francisco Chronicle*, June 29, 1946, file 567, ACLU-NC; Gilbert Woo, *"Poqian an 2"* (Eviction case, part 2), in *Hu Jiangnan Wenji* (The collected works of Gilbert Woo), ed. Yuzun Liu, Dehua Zheng, and Larry Lam (Hong Kong: Xiangjiang Publishing Company, 1991), 77.

53. Carey McWilliams, "Critical Summary," *Journal of Educational Sociology* 19:3 (November 1945): 196. McWilliams asserts that more African Americans filed lawsuits questioning the validity of covenants in Los Angeles than anywhere else in the nation. I suspect, however, that his numbers actually reflected lawsuits initially brought against African Americans.

54. Sides, *L.A. City Limits*, 98–99; Grace Simons, "56th Street Whites Fight Chinese, Too," *Los Angeles Sentinel*, May 30, 1946.

55. "Chinese Americans Win Case in Opposing Restrictive Covenants," *Progressive News*, March 17, 1948, file 567, ACLU-NC; "Covenanteers Lose," *Progressive News*, ca. 1947, file 567, ACLU-NC; "L.A. Judge Again Rules Restrictive Covenants Violate Constitution," *Progressive News*, November 1, 1947, file 567, ACLU-NC; Sides, *L.A. City Limits*, 99; "No Mexican Race," *Los Angeles Times*, February 16, 1945; "Nisei Homeowner Wins Case on Race Restrictive Covenant," *Pacific Citizen*, June 28, 1947.

56. "Court to Rule on Racial Restrictions," *San Francisco Chronicle*, February 25, 1946.

57. Bernard Taper, *San Francisco's Housing* (Washington, D.C: Works Progress Administration, 1941), 25; Division of Research and Statistics, Federal Home Loan Bank Board, Area Description San Francisco D-16, ca. 1937, file "San Francisco, California Master File Security Map and Area Descriptions," box 147, RG 195, NARA; "Council Fights Move to Bar Non-Caucasians," *Pacific Citizen*, October 25, 1947; "Restrictive Covenants," *Progressive News*, December 12, 1947, file 567, ACLU-NC.

58. "Non-Caucasians Form Group to Fight Housing Restrictions," *Pacific Citizen*, November 15, 1947; Wen-Hui Chung Chen, "Changing Socio-Cultural Patterns of the Chinese Community in Los Angeles" (PhD thesis, University of Southern California, 1952), 64. In this dissertation, Kim is "anonymously" described as "Dr. K, a Korean-American." Dr. K's district is exactly the same as Dr. Kim's, and the organization he joined has the exact same number of members and racial composition. Dr. K also lives on the same block as Dr. Kim. Given the tiny number of Korean Americans in California at the time, the identity of the real "Dr. K." is hardly in question.

59. "Form Los Angeles Committee to Support Campaign Against Restrictive Housing Covenants," *Pacific Citizen*, September 27, 1947.

60. August Meier and John H. Bracey, Jr., "The NAACP as a Reform Movement, 1909–1965: 'To Reach the Conscience of America,'" *Journal of Southern History* 59: 1 (February 1993): 15; Simons, "56th Street Whites Fight Chinese, Too." Miller was the local counsel for the NAACP; Wirin worked for the Southern California branch of the ACLU.

61. Clifford Forster to Thurgood Marshall, December 31, 1947, p. 2, file "California, 1947–1950," *Papers of the NAACP*, part 5, reel 20.

62. The California State Legislature changed the Alien Land Act in 1945 in part to ensure that the lack of a binding treaty between the United States and Japan definitely denied Issei property ownership rights. The California Supreme Court finally found in favor of Issei rights in *Palermo v. Stockton Theatres, Inc.*, 32 Cal. 2d 53; 195 P.2d 1 (1948) but had to overturn a lower court ruling to do so.

63. "New Unit to Prevent Land Law Evasion by Japanese," *San Francisco Chronicle*, August 12, 1943; Galen M. Fisher, "Resettling the Evacuees," *Far Eastern Survey* 14:19 (September 26, 1945): 267; Earl C. Behrens, "Jap Property Title Search Proposed," *San Francisco Chronicle*, December 12, 1944. "Escheat" is a legal term that in these cases equaled state confiscation of Japanese American–owned land.

64. "Ex-Sgt. Akira Iwamura Is Puzzled," *Los Angeles Times*, file F3640: 3675, Earl Warren Papers, California State Archives, Sacramento; Heist to Besig, p. 1. Years later, in an interview for the Regional Oral History Project at UC Berkeley, Kenny ducked questions about the escheatment drive and claimed to have forgotten much about the period immediately following the war.

65. "Report Mattoon Refuses Bid to Withhold Cases," *Pacific Citizen*, June 21, 1947. California law allowed candidates to cross-file, so Earl Warren's name appeared on both parties' ballots in the June 1946 primary.

66. "13 Escheat Suits May Be Filed Against Nisei in Sonoma," *Pacific Citizen*, March 1, 1947; Everett Mattoon to Robert Kenny, handwritten, ca. 1946, p. 1, file "Mattoon, Everett," box 41, Robert W. Kenny Papers, Bancroft Library, University of California, Berkeley; "Report New California Official Bars Compromise Settlement," *Pacific Citizen*, February 8, 1947; Fisher, "Resettling the Evacuees," 267; "The Alien Land Laws," *Pacific Citizen*, April 12, 1947.

67. The court also considered the status of land held for another Nisei, June Kushino.

68. *Porterfield v. Webb*, 2 63 U.S. 225; 44 S. Ct. 21 (November 1923); Edward H. Schafer, Jr., Ephraim Rosen, Dale R. Cunningham, Norman D. Lee, Leonard U. Riave, and Anne Riave to editor, *Oakland Tribune*, August 10, 1946, file 605, ACLU-NC; *People v. Oyama*, 29 Cal. 2d 164; 173 P.2d 794 (1946).

69. *People v. Oyama*; "Nisei Seeks to Regain Property Escheated Under Alien Land Act," *Pacific Citizen*, August 9, 1947; "Coast Magazine Notes Nisei Have Man-Sized Task in Reestablishing Selves on Coast," *Pacific Citizen*, August 2, 1947.

70. "Los Angeles Housing Meeting Calls for Protection of Nisei Right in Land Law," *Pacific Citizen*, January 25, 1947; Greg Robinson and Toni Robinson, "Korematsu and Beyond: Japanese Americans and the Origins of Strict Scrutiny," *Law and Contemporary Problems* 29 (Spring 2005): 34; "Acheson Challenges Validity of California Alien Land Act," *Pacific Citizen*, October 25, 1947, 1; *Oyama v. California* 332 U.S. 633; "New California Budget Contains No Provision for Funds to Enforce State's Alien Land Law," *Pacific Citizen*, March 20, 1948. The JACL submitted amicus briefs both in the *Kim* and *Amer* cases and in the *Hurd v. Hodge* case dealing with Washington, D.C. The Supreme Court ruled on the *Shelley v. Kraemer* covenant case and *Hurd* on May 3, 1948.

71. Mary Dudziak, *Cold War Civil Rights: Race and the Image of American Democracy* (Princeton, NJ: Princeton University Press, 2002), 91; *Shelley v. Kraemer* 334 U.S. 1 (1948).

72. *Shelley v. Kraemer*; Tosuke Yamasaki, "Supreme Tribunal Says Courts Cannot Be Used to Enforce Discrimination in Housing," *Pacific Citizen*, May 8, 1948. Wirin and Okrand, the civil rights law firm associated with the Southern California ACLU, represented Kim and Amer.

73. *Amer v. Superior Court of California, in and for the County of Los Angeles* (1948); and *Kim v. Superior Court of California, in and for the County of Los Angeles*, 334 U.S. 813 (1948). White residents later tried to use the loopholes in the 1948 cases, contending that they could still sue white homeowners who sold to nonwhites for the depreciation of property values. The Court rejected this approach in *Barrows v. Jackson*, 346 U.S. 249; 73 S. Ct. 1031 (1953).

74. The initial JACL push began in Oregon. In fact, a host of other western states had Alien Land Acts modeled on California's. Charles Fairman, "Finis to Fujii," *American Journal of International Law* 46:3 (July 1952): 685, discusses the progression from the Oregon case to the unusual reasoning of the California court, which in 1952 considered the applicability of the United Nations Charter to the Alien Land Act cases.

75. The Fujii plot was in East Los Angeles; the Masaoka house was in Pasadena.

76. Fairman, "Finis to Fujii," 685; *Fujii v. California*, 38 Cal. 2d 718; 242 P.2d 617 (1952); *Masaoka v. People*, 39 Cal. 2d 883; 245 P.2d 1062 (1952).

77. Arnold R. Hirsch, "With or Without Jim Crow: Black Residential Segregation in the United States," in *Urban Policy in Twentieth-Century America*, ed. Arnold R. Hirsch and Raymond A. Mohl (New Brunswick, NJ: Rutgers University Press, 1993), 84–90; David M.P. Freund, *Colored Property: State Policy and White Racial Politics in Suburban America* (Chicago: University of Chicago Press, 2007), 207–13; Kenneth T. Jackson, *Crabgrass Frontier: The Suburbanization of the United States* (New York: Oxford University Press, 1985), 206, 208, 213–15; Sides, *L.A. City Limits*, 107. Matt Garcia, *A World of Its Own: Race, Labor, and Citrus in the Making of Greater Los Angeles, 1900–1970* (Chapel Hill: University of North Carolina Press, 2001), 223–55, discusses the experience of Southern California Mexican Americans with postwar housing.

78. Li Panlin (Lim P. Lee), "*Daliyuan yu xianju qiyue*" (The Supreme Court and restrictive covenants), *Taipingyang Zhoubao* (Chinese-Pacific Weekly [San Francisco]), May 22, 1948.

79. "Bayshore City Negro Family Threatened," *San Francisco Chronicle*, October 26, 1949; "Occupants Escape in Night," *Los Angeles Sentinel*, September 16, 1948; "Mysterious Fire Razes Home for Rent to Nisei Family," *Pacific Citizen*, July 30, 1949; "Councilman Discloses Housing Prejudice in Los Angeles," *Pacific Citizen*, September 10, 1949. Jews also continued to face some housing discrimination, although far less than nonwhite Californians.

80. Bill Burkhardt, "Chinese Modern," *San Francisco News*, October 24, 1950.

81. Bureau of the Census, *Seventeenth Census of the United States, 1950: Census of Population, Census Tract Statistics: Los Angeles, California and Adjacent Area* (Washington, D.C.: USGPO, 1952), 19–29; Thomas Sugrue, *The Origins of the Urban Crisis: Race and Inequality in Postwar Detroit* (Princeton, NJ: Princeton University Press, 1996), 183, 233; Arnold R. Hirsch, *Making the Second Ghetto: Race and Housing in Chicago, 1940–1960* (Chicago: University of Chicago Press, 1997), 41; Becky M. Nicolaides, *My Blue Heaven: Life and Politics in the Working-Class Suburbs of Los Angeles, 1920–1965* (Chicago: University of Chicago Press, 2002), 210–12; Sides, *L.A. City Limits*, 101–15; George H. Dunne, "And Who Is My Neighbor?" *Commonweal*, October 6, 1950, 624; Report on Meeting of the Normandie Avenue Protective Association, March 17, 1950, p. 1, file BIV5iee(15), box 76, Ford papers; "Hoodlums Threaten Family," *California Eagle*, November 23, 1950.

82. Charles Chinn interview by Rick Louie, ca. 1976, p. 126, file "Chinn, Charles," Asian American Oral History Composite, Bancroft Library, University of California, Berkeley.

83. Harold Isaacs, *Scratches on Our Minds: American Images of China and India* (New York: The John Day Company, 1958), 123; Katherine Archibald, *Wartime Shipyard: A Study in Social Disunity* (Berkeley: University of California Press, 1947), 74–75.

84. Weiss, *Places of Their Own*, 98; Chen, "Changing Socio-Cultural Patterns of the Chinese Community in Los Angeles," 72; "The Sheng Story: Scientific Study Shows Property Loses No Value When Races Mix," *San Francisco Chronicle*, February 21, 1952. See, for example, 1950 census tracts Los Angeles 127-A, 158, 162, 168, 197-A; 1960 census tracts Los Angeles 2042, 2065, 2181, 2184, 2198, 2199; 1950 and 1960 census tracts San Francisco J12, J13, J15, J16, J17, J20, L5, O9.

85. Michael S. Sherry, *In the Shadow of War: The United States Since the 1930s* (New Haven, CT: Yale University Press, 1995), 123; Stephen J. Whitfield, *The Culture of the Cold War* (Baltimore: The Johns Hopkins University Press, 1996), 19, 21; Edward L. Barrett, Jr., *The Tenney Committee: Legislative Investigation of Subversive Activities in California* (Ithaca, NY: Cornell University Press, 1951), 170; Kenneth C. Burt, "The Battle for Standard Coil: The United Electrical Workers, the Community Service Organization, and the Catholic Church in Latino East Los Angeles," in *American Labor and the Cold War: Grassroots Politics and Postwar Culture*, ed. Robert W. Cherny, William Issel, and Kieran Walsh Taylor (New Brunswick, NJ: Rutgers University Press, 2004), 124; Sides, *L.A. City Limits*, 147.

86. Bernstein, "Building Bridges at Home in a Time of Global Conflict," 267; "Councilman Discloses Housing Prejudice in Los Angeles," *Pacific Citizen*. See, for example, "Acid Thrown on Home of Couple Threatened by White Neighbors," *California Eagle*, April 11, 1946; "Area Hoodlums Try Again," *California Eagle*, October 19, 1950; "Hoodlums Threaten Family," *California Eagle*, November 23, 1950; "6 Held for Arson in Redwood City Blaze," *Los Angeles Sentinel*, March 6, 1947; "Hateful Sign Plastered on 'King' Cole's $85,000 Palace," *Los Angeles Sentinel*, August 12, 1948; "Owners Find Slurs Painted on House," *Los Angeles Sentinel*, September 2, 1948.

87. Josh Sides, *L.A. City Limits*, 118; Don Parson, *Making a Better World: Public Housing, the Red Scare, and the Direction of Modern Los Angeles* (Minneapolis: University of Minnesota Press, 2005), 65, 102–3; Sugrue, *The Origins of the Urban Crisis*, 81; Hirsch, *Making the Second Ghetto*, 224; "Segregation and S.F. Housing," *San Francisco Chronicle*, January 15, 1950.

88. "Chinatown Housing," *San Francisco Chronicle*, January 4, 1946; "Chinatown Project First of Six Local Housing Developments," *San Francisco Chronicle*, July 3, 1949; "New Face for S.F. Chinatown," *San Francisco Chronicle*, October 21, 1951.

89. "*Bairen bingzhu qishi an zhi yuyin*" (The reverberations of a white landlord's discriminatory suit), *Chung Sai Yat Po* (Chinese-Western Daily [San Francisco]),

March 3, 1948; "Housing Group Criticized on Segregation Issue," *San Francisco Chronicle*, December 12, 1949; "Housing Board Bows to Ruling," *San Francisco Chronicle*, May 25, 1954; "The Neighborhood Pattern," *Pacific Citizen*, September 6, 1952; "S.F. Supervisors Approve Housing Non-Segregation," *Chinese Press*, November 11, 1949; "Your Man for Mayor" (English-headlined, Chinese-language advertisement for John Sullivan), *Taipingyang Zhoubao*, October 27, 1951; "Segregation Ban in New S.F. Housing," *San Francisco Chronicle*, November 9, 1949; "Recommendations," *Chinese Press*, November 2, 1951.

90. "Chinatown Housing History Marks Milestone October 21st," *Chinese Press*, October 19, 1951.

91. Dr. Thomas Wu testimony, "San Francisco Citizens Committee for Equal Employment Summary of Findings and Conclusions," May 14, 1951, p. 5, file "San Francisco Citizens Committee for Equal Employment," carton 45, National Association for the Advancement of Colored People, Region 1 records, Bancroft Library, University of California, Berkeley (hereafter, NAACP-R1).

92. Victor G. Nee and Brett de Bary Nee, *Longtime Californ': A Documentary Study of an American Chinatown* (Stanford, CA: Stanford University Press, 1986), 166.

93. Gilbert Woo, *"Heiren Yi Nei Ping Yuan"* (Blacks moving into Ping Yuen), in *Hu Jingnan Wenji*, 540.

94. "Racial Distribution of Public Housing Units Operated by the Housing Authority of the City and County of San Francisco," June 30, 1952, file "Programs—Housing—Public Housing Administration, September–December 1952," carton 39, NAACP-WC; Norman V. Petersen, Administrative Officer, SFHA, to San Francisco Council for Civic Unity, March 31, 1954, p. 1, file "Programs—Housing—Banks v. San Francisco Housing Authority, 1952 #2," carton 39, NAACP-R1C; Loren Miller, statement, *Hearings Before the United States Commission on Civil Rights* (Washington, D.C.: USGPO, 1960), 260.

CHAPTER EIGHT

1. "State's Leaders Deplore Ban on Chinese Family," *Oakland Tribune*, February 20, 1952, Richard Sheng collection (hereafter, Sheng collection; in possession of author). Portions of this chapter first appeared in Charlotte Brooks, "Sing Sheng vs. Southwood: Residential Integration in Cold War California," *Pacific Historical Review* 73:3 (August 2004).

2. Barbara W. Tuchman, *Stilwell and the American Experience in China, 1911–1945* (New York: Grove Press, 2001), 530; Thomas J. Christensen, *Useful Adversaries: Grand Strategy, Domestic Mobilization, and Sino-American Conflict, 1947–1958* (Princeton, NJ: Princeton University Press, 1996), 61; Warren I. Cohen, *America's Response to China: A History* (New York: Columbia University Press, 2000), 164–66.

3. Cohen, *America's Response to China*, 165; Blair Bolles, "Asia Policy and the Election," *Far Eastern Survey* 19:21 (December 6, 1950): 221–22.

4. Stephen J. Whitfield, *The Culture of the Cold War* (Baltimore: The Johns Hopkins University Press, 1996), 9; Xiaojian Zhao, *Remaking Chinese America: Immigration, Family, and Community, 1940–1965* (New Brunswick, NJ: Rutgers University Press, 2002), 124; Renqiu Yu, *To Save China, To Save Ourselves: The Chinese Hand Laundry Alliance of New York* (Philadelphia: Temple University Press, 1992), 184–85.

5. Gary Gerstle, *American Crucible: Race and Nation in the Twentieth Century* (Princeton, NJ: Princeton University Press, 2001), 252.

6. See, for example, Andrew J. Grad, "Land Reform in Japan," *Pacific Affairs* 21:2 (June 1948): 135; Kazuo Kawai, "Japanese Views on National Security," *Pacific Affairs* 23:2 (June 1950): 117.

7. Thomas Borstelmann, *The Cold War and the Color Line: American Race Relations in the Global Arena* (Cambridge, MA: Harvard University Press, 2001), 2; Penny M. Von Eschen, *Race Against Empire: Black Americans and Anti-Colonialism, 1937–1957* (Ithaca, NY: Cornell University Press, 1997), 124; Mary Dudziak, *Cold War Civil Rights: Race and the Image of American Democracy* (Princeton, NJ: Princeton University Press, 2000), 12, 28–29.

8. Christina Klein, *Cold War Orientalism: Asia in the Middlebrow Imagination, 1945–1961* (Berkeley: University of California Press, 2003), 28, 39–41.

9. Lizabeth Cohen, *A Consumers' Republic: The Politics of Mass Consumption in Postwar America* (New York: Vintage Books, 2003), 8; Elaine Tyler May, *Homeward Bound: American Families in the Cold War Era* (New York: Basic Books, 1988), 17–18.

10. Andrew Wiese, *Places of Their Own: African American Suburbanization in the Twentieth Century* (Chicago: University of Chicago Press, 2005), 172; John T. McGreevey, *Parish Boundaries: The Catholic Encounter with Race in the Twentieth Century Urban North* (Chicago: University of Chicago Press, 1996), 103–7.

11. Victor G. and Brett de Bary Nee, *Longtime Californ': A Documentary Study of an American Chinatown* (Stanford, CA: Stanford University Press, 1972), 219–20; Zhao, *Remaking Chinese America*, 117–19; Larry Tajiri, "Fear Along Grant Avenue," *Pacific Citizen*, December 9, 1950, 4. Nationalists on the mainland often referred to the Communists as "bandits."

12. Lon Kurashige, *Japanese American Celebration and Conflict: A History of Ethnic Identity and Festival in Los Angeles, 1934–1990* (Berkeley: University of California Press, 2002), 122–23; Japanese American Citizens League, "Blueprint for Tomorrow: Program of the 11th Biennial Convention of the JACL," 1950, p. 77, file "White House File—Minorities-Japanese Jap.-American Citizens League-Mike Masaoka, 1947–1950," box 51, Nash papers; "California's Gov. Warren Assures Chinese-Americans," *Chinese Press*, December 8, 1950; "Nixon Meets the Press," *Chinese Press*, November 10. 1950.

13. Mae Ngai, *Impossible Subjects: Illegal Aliens and the Making of Modern America* (Princeton, NJ: Princeton University Press, 2004), 213; Him Mark Lai, "A Historical Survey of Organizations of the Left Among the Chinese in America," *Bulletin of Concerned Asia Scholars* 4:3 (Fall 1972): 16; Him Mark Lai and Betty Lim, "Gilbert Woo, Chinese American Journalist," in *Hu Jiangnan Wenji* (The collected works of Gilbert Woo), ed. Yuzun Liu, Dehua Zheng, and Larry Lam (Hong Kong: Xiangjiang Publishing Company, 1991), 42–44.

14. Gilbert Woo, "*Nimen de quanli bing bu bi women da*" (Our rights are equal to yours), in *Hu Jiangnan Wenji*, 527.

15. Larry Tajiri, "The Chinese Americans," *Pacific Citizen*, January 18, 1951; Zhao, *Remaking Chinese America*, 104; Nee and Nee, *Longtime Californ'*, 207.

16. Chiou-Ling Yeh, "'In the Traditions of China and in the Freedom of America': The Making of San Francisco's Chinese New Year Festivals," *American Quarterly* 56:2 (2004): 401–4; "Blueprint for Business," July 6, 1953, file 25, carton 2, Charles Leong papers, Ethnic Studies Library, University of California, Berkeley; Judy Tzu-Chun Wu, "'Loveliest Daughter of Our Ancient Cathay!': Representations of Ethnic and Gender Identity in the Miss Chinatown U.S.A. Beauty Pageant," *Journal of Social History* (Fall 1997): 10.

17. Zhao, *Remaking Chinese America*, 170; Gilbert Woo, "*Li Panlin*" (Lim P. Lee), in *Hu Jiangnan Wenji*, 588–89; George Chu, "Chinatown," *San Francisco Magazine*, June 1969, 25; Woo, "*Nimen de quanli bing bu bi women da*," 527.

18. "Fact-Sheet #1: America Plus," January 21, 1952, pp. 1–4, "Housing" file, carton 1, California Federation for Civic Unity Papers (hereafter, CFCU), Bancroft Library, University of California, Berkeley; Earl C. Behrens, "'America Plus' Urges Haste on Petitions," *San Francisco Chronicle*, December 10, 1951; Franklin H. Williams to Walter White, Roy Wilkins, Thurgood Marshall, Gloster Currant, Henry Lee Moon, and Clarence Mitchell, December 3, 1951, file "American [*sic*] Plus, 1951–1953," carton 43, NAACP-R1.

19. Bernard Taper, "South S.F. City Council Deplores Exclusion Vote," *San Francisco Chronicle*, February 19. 1952; "New Action on 'Test of Democracy,'" *San Francisco Chronicle*, February 22, 1952, Sheng collection.

20. "Southwood Residents Strike Back at Critics," *San Francisco Examiner*, February 22, 1952, Sheng collection.

21. Thomas Sugrue, *The Origins of the Urban Crisis: Race and Inequality in Postwar Detroit* (Princeton: Princeton University Press, 1996), 216–17.

22. Becky M. Nicolaides, *My Blue Heaven: Life and Politics in the Working-Class Suburbs of Los Angeles, 1950—1965* (Chicago: University of Chicago Press, 2002), 5.

23. May, *Homeward Bound*, 10.

24. "Backers Turn Against Free Choice Bill," *Los Angeles Times*, March 22, 1953; Notes, ca. February 1952, "Housing" file, carton 1, CFCU.

25. Gilbert Woo, "*Sheng An de Zhongzhong*" (Straight talk on the Sheng case), *Taipingyang Zhoubao*, February 23, 1952; Franklin H. Williams, "Our Unfinished

Task," speech to the Los Angeles County Community on Human Relations, October 11, 1952, p. 4, file "Los Angeles County Conference on Community Relations, December 1950–ca. 1953, folder 2," carton 44, NAACP-R1; California State Assembly, House Resolution 33, March 19, 1952; "Bombing Probes on as Protests Mount," *Los Angeles Times*, March 18, 1952. The Los Angeles City Council passed a resolution condemning the bombings in an acrimonious, politically charged meeting. Rather than the bombing itself, the FBI actually investigated phone calls the city received from people protesting the bombing, and Mayor Bowron tried to cast such protestors as Communists.

26. See, for example, Luigi Laurenti, *Property Values and Race: Studies in Seven Cities* (Berkeley: University of California Press, 1961), 18; Catherine Bauer Wurster, *Housing and the Future of Cities in the San Francisco Bay Area* (Berkeley: University of California Press, 1963), 13; "The Sheng Story: Scientific Study Shows Property Loses No Value When Races Mix," *San Francisco Chronicle*, February 21, 1951; Davis McEntire, "A Study of Racial Attitudes in Neighborhoods Infiltrated by Nonwhites: San Francisco, Oakland, and Berkeley," 1955, pp. 127–29, "Bay Area Real Estate Reporter" file, carton 43, NAACP-R1; Lawrence E. Davies, "Case of the Sing Shengs Has Aroused West Coast," *New York Times*, February 24, 1952, Sheng collection.

27. Robert Lee, "Community Exclusion: A Case Study," *Phylon*, 15:2 (Second Quarter 1954): 204–5.

28. "The Sing Shengs and Democracy," *Pacific Citizen*, February 23, 1952.

29. Isaacs, *Scratches on Our Minds*, 228, 233, 237; Roger W. Lotchin, *Fortress California, 1910–1961: From Warfare to Welfare* (New York: Oxford University Press, 1992), 206–7, 231–59; Lisa McGirr, *Suburban Warriors: The Origins of the New American Right* (Princeton, NJ: Princeton University Press, 2001), 8–9; Evelyn Nakano Glenn, *Issei, Nisei, Warbride: Three Generations of Japanese American Women in Domestic Service* (Philadelphia: Temple University Press, 1986), 8; Ji-Yeon Yuh, *Beyond the Shadow of Camptown: Korean Military Brides in America* (New York: New York University Press, 2002), 1; Yen Le Espiritu, *Filipino American Lives* (Philadelphia: Temple University Press, 1995), 18; U.S. Bureau of the Census, "Supplementary Report: Veterans in the United States, 1960" (Washington, D.C., USGPO, December 14, 1962), 5; "Trade with Asia, Business Urged," *New York Times*, October 5 1957; Russell Porter, "More Trade with Asia Urged," *New York Times*, September 25, 1958; "Harbors' Trade Boosted by Mission from L.A.," *Los Angeles Times*, May 26, 1957; "Far East Firms Show High Interest in Trade," *Los Angeles Times*, May 14, 1954; McGirr, *Suburban Warriors*, 291n131; Naoko Shibusawa, *America's Geisha Ally: Reimagining the Japanese Enemy* (Cambridge, MA: Harvard University Press, 2006), 5; Yukiko Koshiro, *Trans-Pacific Racisms and the U.S. Occupation of Japan* (New York: Columbia University Press, 1999), 81; Dana Adams Schmidt, "Initiative in Asia Is Urged on West," *New York Times*, October 30, 1955; James Reston, "The U.S. and Taiwan," *New York Times*, May 29, 1957. Asian American soldiers brought

wives from Asia to the United States, but this practice drew far less interest than interracial marriage.

30. "24 Against Nisei As Neighbor," *San Jose Mercury*, October 9, 1952; "Neighbors Welcome Yoshihara," *San Jose Mercury*, October 10, 1952.

31. "Case of Sam Yoshihara," *Pacific Citizen*, October 17, 1952; "24 Against Nisei As Neighbor," *San Jose Mercury*; "Neighbors Welcome Yoshihara," *San Jose Mercury*.

32. "Young Chinese Family Target of Note," *Watsonville Register-Pajoranian*, July 16, 1953; "Oh, CAN'T It Happen?" *Watsonville Register-Pajoranian*, July 16, 1953; "Public Pours Forth Its Support, Congratulations for Lee Family," *Daily Palo Alto Times*, June 26, 1954; "Anti-Chinese Attitude Not Popular Here," *Daily Palo Alto Times*, June 28, 1954; "Neighbors Say They Want Japanese Dentist," *San Francisco Chronicle*, March 18, 1955.

33. Mr. and Mrs. Earl Goon, letter to the editor, *Watsonville Register-Pajoranian*, July 16, 1953; "Pressure Causes Chinese Not to Buy Home in P.A.," *Palo Alto Times*, June 25, 1954; "Death Threat in Home Sale," *Oakland Tribune*, March 17, 1955.

34. "Thornton Way Drops Fight Against Nisei," October 10, 1952; "Oh, CAN'T It Happen?," *Watsonville Register-Pajoranian*; "Anti-Chinese Attitude Not Popular Here," *Daily Palo Alto Times*; "Offers Stream in for Nisei Family Denied Home by Death Threat," *Oakland Tribune*, March 18, 1955.

35. Josephine Duvenack, "San Leandro Field Service Visit," September 16, 1948, p. 1, file "Discrimination," carton 1, CFCU; C. Wilson Record, *Minority Groups and Intergroup Relations in the San Francisco Bay Area* (Berkeley: Institute of Governmental Studies, 1963), 22–23; Haruo Ishimaru, "Scene from the Golden Gate," *Pacific Citizen*, July 15, 1955.

36. Klein, *Cold War Orientalism*, 36; "Sad Story Has Happy Ending," *San Francisco News*, January 11, 1954, Sheng collection; "Nisei Family Victim of Neighborhood 'Fears,'" *Civic Unity Reporter*, May 1955, p. 3, file CFCU, box 3, NAACP-R1. The 1956 Palo Alto City Directory listed the Lees' new home as 991 N. California in Palo Alto, the only remaining John Mackay house in the area today. My thanks to John Fyten for his assistance in locating "Sunshine Glen," the Mackay tract where the Lees tried to buy initially.

37. "Neighbors Welcome Yoshihara," *San Jose Mercury*; "Public Pours Forth Its Support, Congratulations for Lee Family," *Palo Alto Times*; "Neighbors Say They Want Japanese Dentist," *San Francisco Chronicle*.

38. South San Francisco City Council Resolution 1743, February 18, 1952; "Neighbors Welcome Nisei Veteran," *San Francisco Chronicle*, October 11, 1952; "Realty Board Won't Act on Race Bias," *San Francisco Chronicle*, March 29, 1955.

39. Gladwin Hill, "Japanese in U.S. Gaining Equality," *New York Times*, August 12, 1956; Statement of Frank Chuman, January 1959, *Hearings before the United States Commission on Civil Rights* (Washington, D.C.: USGPO, 1960), 110–11; "Nisei Navy Ensign Refused Sale of FHA-Insured Tract Home in L.A.," *Pacific Citizen*, April 10,

1953; "Prudential Reconsiders, OKs Nisei Purchase of New Home," *Pacific Citizen,* April 17, 1953; "East Los Angeles Couple Fight Anti-Japanese Housing Sentiments," *Pacific Citizen,* August 14, 1953. Similarly, in *The First Suburban Chinatown: The Remaking of Monterey Park, California* (Philadelphia: Temple University Press, 1994), 22, Timothy Fong refers to a meeting between real estate developers Edgar and Daniel Cohen and a group of Japanese Americans who wanted to buy homes in Monterey Park but would not do so if it would "cause a racial problem." It is quite likely that this group included JACL leaders or members.

40. Dudziak, *Cold War Civil Rights,* 12, 14.

41. Harold Isaacs, "World Affairs and U.S. Race Relations: A Note on Little Rock," *Public Opinion Quarterly* 223 (Autumn 1958): 364; Von Eschen, *Race Against Empire,* 124.

42. Dudziak, *Cold War Civil Rights,* 12; Borstelmann, *The Cold War and the Color Line,* 3.

43. Franklin Williams to Walter White, March 19, 1952, pp. 1–2, file "Legal: Gary, Wilbur, March 1952, Folder 1," carton 40, NAACP-R1; "Neighbors Object to Negro Family," *San Francisco Chronicle,* December 11, 1953; "Negroes' New Benicia Homes Defaced," *San Francisco Chronicle,* October 6, 1954; "Charge of Unethical Realty Practice in MP Area Probed," *Daily Palo Alto Times,* August 4, 1955; Elaine D. Johnson, "Survey of Peninsula Realtors," November 6, 1957, p. 1, file "Survey of Peninsula Realtors," carton 45, NAACP-R1.

44. "Residents Rap Critics," *San Francisco Examiner,* February 22, 1952; Franklin Williams to Douglas Stout, March 21, 1952, p. 2, file "Legal: Gary, Wilbur, March 1952, Folder 1," carton 40, NAACP-R1; "Neighbors Object to Negro Family," *San Francisco Chronicle.*

45. Trudy Baum, "Opinion Survey," 1953, p. 7, file "Marin City—Redevelopment, 1953–1954," carton 45, NAACP-R1; Constance L. Jensen, John Lindberg, and George L. Smith, "The Minority Group Housing Market in San Francisco with Special Reference to Real Estate Broker and Mortgage Financing Practices" (master's thesis, University of California, Berkeley, School of Social Welfare, 1955), 43–44, 48; Statement of Frank Quinn, January 1959, *Hearings before the United States Commission on Civil Rights,* 551.

46. Jensen, Lindberg, and Smith, "The Minority Group Housing Market in San Francisco," 40, 43–44, 48; Harry Kitano, "Housing of Japanese-Americans in the San Francisco Bay Area," in *Studies in Housing and Minority Groups,* ed. Nathan Glazer and Davis McEntire (Berkeley: University of California Press, 1960), 188–89, 192–93; Trevor Thomas, *A Civil Rights Inventory of San Francisco: Part II, Housing: San Francisco's Housing Market—Open or Closed?* (San Francisco: Council for Civic Unity of San Francisco, 1958), 32.

47. "Pressure Causes Chinese Not to Buy Home in P.A.," *Daily Palo Alto Times*; Jensen, Lindberg, and Smith, "The Minority Group Housing Market," 25; Johnson, "Survey of Peninsula Realtors," p. 13; Lin Yupu, "*Sun Zonglingshi ni gou zhuzhai bei*

qishi zhi hanshi" (Consul-General Sun's attempted home purchase made a matter of regret by discrimination), *Jinshan Shibao* (Chinese Times [San Francisco]), February 16, 1960.

48. Bureau of the Census, *U.S. Censuses of Population and Housing, 1960: San Jose, Calif., Standard Metropolitan Statistical Area* (Washington, D.C.: USGPO, 1961), 17 (Tract A-21 and O-110); idem., *U.S. Censuses of Population And Housing, 1960. Census Tracts. San Francisco-Oakland, Calif., Standard Metropolitan Statistical Area* (Washington, D.C.: USGPO, 1961), 29 (Tract SL-34). The tract in which Sammy Lee, whom I discuss later in the chapter, tried to buy, Garden Grove's H-83, shows the same shift. Idem., *U.S. Census of Population and Housing, 1960. Census Tracts. Los Angeles-Long Beach, Calif. Standard Metropolitan Statistical Area* (Washington, D.C.: USGPO, 1961), 140. The only real exception to this was Southwood itself; however, many of the other tracts in South San Francisco showed the same kind of change by 1960. Even in 1970, no discernable racial transition had occurred in these tracts. The only tract with a significantly larger black population in 1970 was the Palo Alto tract, but this occurred because a group of white integrationists actually purchased and developed land for interracial housing there. Idem., *U.S. Census of Population and Housing, 1970. Census Tracts: San Jose, Calif., Standard Metropolitan Statistical Area* (Washington, D.C.: USGPO, 1972), 3, 6; idem., *U.S. Census of Population and Housing, 1970. Census Tracts: San Francisco-Oakland, Calif., Standard Metropolitan Statistical Area* (Washington, D.C.: USGPO, 1972), 3, 21; idem., *U.S. Census of Population and Housing, 1970. Census Tracts: Anaheim-Santa Ana-Garden Grove, Calif., Standard Metropolitan Statistical Area* (Washington, D.C.: USGPO, 1972), 37.

49. Tats Kushida, "The Sou'Wester: You Can't Live Here," *Pacific Citizen*, August 28, 1955.

50. Glenn, *Issei, Nisei, Warbride*, 80–81; Bureau of the Census, *U.S. Census of Population: 1950—Los Angeles Census Tracts* (Washington, D.C.: USGPO, 1952), 143–89. Several California Assembly members introduced bills in the late 1950s to grant old age assistance to longtime residents previously ineligible for U.S. citizenship.

51. Glenn, *Issei, Nisei, Warbride*, 88–89; Leonard Bloom, "Transitional Adjustments of Japanese-American Families to Relocation," *American Sociological Review* 12:2 (April 1947): 209.

52. Wiese, *Places of Their Own*, 156; Josh Sides, *L.A. City Limits: African American Los Angeles from the Great Depression to the Present* (Berkeley: University of California Press, 2003), 124; Eric Avila, *Popular Culture in the Age of White Flight: Fear and Fantasy in Suburban Los Angeles* (Berkeley: University of California Press, 2004), 199, 206–9.

53. Sides, *L.A. City Limits*, 111; Tracts 2201 and 2362, *U.S. Censuses of Population And Housing, 1960. Census Tracts. Los Angeles-Long Beach, Calif. Standard Metropolitan Statistical Area*, 63, 65; George Jiro Abe interview by Marsha Bode, February 20, 1984, p. 33, Honorable Stephen K. Tamura Orange County Japanese Ameri-

can Oral History Project, http://content.cdlib.org/ark:/13030/ft0g5002b8/?query=
george%20abe&brand=calisphere (accessed February 7, 2007).

54. Bureau of the Census, *U.S. Censuses of Population And Housing, 1960.
Census Tracts. Los Angeles-Long Beach, Calif. Standard Metropolitan Statistical
Area,* 62, 63, 67, 68; idem., *U.S. Censuses of Population And Housing, 1970. Census
Tracts. Los Angeles-Long Beach, Calif. Standard Metropolitan Statistical Area,* 66,
71; Kazuo Inouye interview by Los Angeles Project Team, p. 197, REgenerations Oral History Project, http://content.cdlib.org/xtf/view?docId=ft358003z1&doc.
view=frames&chunk.id=d0e8311&toc.depth=1&toc.id=d0e8239&brand=calisphere
(accessed February 7, 2007); Katsumi (Hirooka) Kunitsugu interview by Leslie Ito,
April 22, 1998, p. 260, REgenerations Oral History Project, http://content.cdlib.org/
xtf/view?docId=ft358003z1&doc.view=frames&chunk.id=d0e10902&toc.depth=1&
toc.id=d0e10902&brand=calisphere (accessed March 26, 2007).

55. Fred E. Case and James H. Kirk, "The Housing Status of Minority Families,
Los Angeles, 1956" (Los Angeles: UCLA Real Estate Research Program and Los
Angeles Urban League, 1956), 20–21; Marion (Funakoshi) Manaka interview by Leslie
Ito, November 2, 1997, pp. 284–85, REgenerations Oral History Project, http://
content.cdlib.org/xtf/view?docId=ft358003z1&doc.view=frames&chunk.id=
d0e11972&toc.depth=1&toc.id=d0e11972&brand=calisphere (accessed April 10,
2007); Scott Kurashige, "The Many Facets of Brown: Integration in a Multiracial
Society," *The Journal of American History* 91:1 (June 2004).

56. Midori Nishi, "Changing Occupance of the Japanese in Los Angeles County,
1940–1950" (PhD diss., University of Washington, 1955), 84.

57. Greg Hise, *Magnetic Los Angeles: Planning the Twentieth-Century Metropolis* (Baltimore: The Johns Hopkins University Press, 1997), 195–215; Sides, *L.A.
City Limits,* 176; Aiko Tanamachi Endo interview by Marsha Bode, November 15,
1983, p. 41, Honorable Stephen K. Tamura Orange County Japanese American
Oral History Project, http://content.cdlib.org/ark:/13030/ft938nb4z1/?brand=jarda
(accessed February 7, 2007).

58. Gladwin Hill, "Coast 'Poker City' Draws Polls Test," *New York Times,* April 4,
1954; Demaree Bess, "California's Amazing Japanese," *Saturday Evening Post,* April
30, 1955, 76; "Gardena: A 'Success Story' of Thousands," *Scene,* June 1954, 15–16.

59. Spencer C. Olin, "Globalization and the Politics of Locality: Orange County,
California, in the Cold War Era," *Western Historical Quarterly* 22:2 (May 1991): 150–
51; McGirr, *Suburban Warriors,* 29–35, 43; Larry Tajiri, "Vagaries," *Pacific Citizen,*
August 26, 1955; Inouye interview by Los Angeles Project Team, p. 191.

60. "Don't Sell, Farmers, Don't," *Pacific Citizen,* November 18, 1955.

61. "Olympic Star Refused County Homes," *Santa Ana Register,* August 19, 1955.

62. "2 Realty Dealers Bar Olympic Star," *New York Times,* August 20, 1955;
"Olympic Star Refused County Homes," *Santa Ana Register;* "Lee Lane's Residents
'Up in Arms' Over Discrimination Claims against Sammy Lee," *Santa Ana Register,*

August 22, 1955; Robert Lee, "The Case of Sammy Lee," *The New Leader*, September 5, 1955, 15; Tajiri, "Vagaries."

63. Tajiri, "Vagaries"; Sammy Lee interview by Margaret Costa (Los Angeles: Amateur Athletic Association of Los Angeles, 1999), 22–23, http://www.aafla. org/6oic/OralHistory/OHlee.indd.pdf (accessed February 7, 2007); "Not a Story to Hide," *San Francisco Chronicle*, August 19, 1955.

64. McGirr, *Suburban Warriors*, 109; "Prejudice Can Only Lead to Injury," *Santa Ana Register*, August 21, 1955; Totton J. Anderson, "The 1958 Election in California," *Western Political Quarterly* 12:1, part 2 (March 1959): 289; "2 Realty Dealers Bar Olympic Star," *New York Times*, August 20, 1955.

65. McGirr, *Suburban Warriors*, 76–78, 183; "The Case of Sammy Lee," *New York Times*, August 24, 1955; "2 Realty Dealers Bar Olympic Star," *New York Times*; Michael Harris, "Diving Champ Gets Bias-Case Support," *New York Times*, August 20, 1955; "Offers of Aid Pour in for Swimming Star," *Santa Ana Register*, August 22, 1955.

66. Stephen J. Whitfield, *A Death in the Delta: The Story of Emmett Till* (Baltimore: The Johns Hopkins University Press, 2001), 28–31; Dudziak, *Cold War Civil Rights*, 113.

67. Nancy K. MacLean, *Freedom Is Not Enough: The Opening of the American Workplace* (Cambridge, MA: Harvard University Press and the Russell Sage Foundation, 2006), 50; Bureau of the Census, *U.S. Censuses of Population and Housing, 1960. Census Tracts. Los Angeles-Long Beach, Calif. Standard Metropolitan Statistical Area*, 139; Robert Bland, "Report on Garden Grove," ca. 1957, pp. 1–3, file 6, box 30, ACLU–Southern California Branch Collection, Young Research Library, University of California, Los Angeles; "Dr. Sammy Lee Strikes at Assailants' Charges," *Los Angeles Times*, January 16, 1957.

68. Shibusawa, *America's Geisha Ally*, 3, 7–9; Kurashige, *Japanese American Celebration and Conflict*, 120.

69. Thomas, *A Civil Rights Inventory of San Francisco: Part II*, 22; Statement of Mayor George Christopher, January 1959, *Hearings before the United States Commission on Civil Rights*, 478.

70. Kenneth T. Jackson, *Crabgrass Frontier: The Suburbanization of the United States* (New York: Oxford University Press, 1985), 244, 289–90; Jerry Hulse, "Chinatown Changing as Suburbs Call Residents," *Los Angeles Times*, October 26, 1959; statement of William H. Parker, January 1959, *Hearings before the United States Commission on Civil Rights*, 323–24; statement of Thomas J. Cahill, January 1959, *Hearings before the United States Commission on Civil Rights*, 774–76. Ellen Dionne Wu, "Race and Asian American Citizenship from World War Two to the Movement" (PhD diss., University of Chicago, 2006), 222–36, explores this issue in the context of outsiders' perceptions of Chinese Americans' supposed lack of juvenile delinquency.

71. Sugrue, *The Origins of the Urban Crisis*, 81; Sides, *L.A. City Limits*, 118; "Little Tokyo Tenants Will Ask for New City Housing Project," *Pacific Citizen*, April 23,

1949; Horace Sutton, "China 'Cross the Bay," *Saturday Review*, August 10, 1957, 26; "Our Amazing Chinese Kids," *Coronet*, December 1955, 34.

72. Irene Dalrymple to editor, *Saturday Evening Post*, June 11, 1955, 6; "West Coast, Too, Has Its Race Problems," *U.S. News and World Report*, June 29, 1956, 43; Statement of William Hogan, January 1959, *Hearings before the United States Commission on Civil Rights*, 506.

73. C. Wilson Record, *Minority Groups and Intergroup Relations in the San Francisco Bay Area* (Berkeley: Institute of Governmental Studies, 1963), 33–34. See also Albert S. Broussard, *Black San Francisco: The Struggle for Racial Equality in the West, 1900–1954* (Lawrence: University Press of Kansas, 1993), 233, for more on the sometimes tense relationship between blacks and Chinese Americans in the postwar period.

74. Jensen, Lindberg, and Smith, "The Minority Group Housing Market in San Francisco," 25–26. This comment certainly referred to Asian Americans, since this study dealt mainly with "Negroes" and "Orientals."

75. *Housing Authority of the City and County of San Francisco v. Mattie Banks, et al.*, 347 U.S. 974 (1954); *Mattie Banks et al. v. Housing Authority of the City and County of San Francisco*, 120 Cal. App. 2d 1; 260 P.2d 668 (1953); Hu Jingnan (Gilbert Woo), "*Heiren Yi Nei Ping Yuan*" (Blacks Moving into Ping Yuen), in *Hu Jingnan Wenji*, 540; "PHA Low-Rent Projects Under Management Which Are Completely Integrated," September 30, 1955, file "Statistics, Trends, Studies (Open Occupancy in Housing Programs of PHA)" box 3, Records of the Intergroup Relations Branch, RG 196, NARA; "Integrated and 'No Pattern' Projects," March 1957, file, "Statistics—All Programs, Integrated Projects, Lists 1949–1957," box 6, NARA; Minutes, Commission of the Housing Authority of the City and County of San Francisco, May 2, 1963, pp. 2–3, San Francisco Public Library.

76. Statement of Franklin Williams, January 1959, *Hearings before the United States Commission on Civil Rights*, 482; Statement of William T. Hogan, *Hearings before the United States Commission on Civil Rights*, 506; Minutes, Commission of the Housing Authority, p. 2; "Housing Body in Heated Meeting," *San Francisco Sun-Reporter*, June 15, 1963.

77. Bureau of the Census, *U.S. Censuses of Population and Housing, 1960. Census Tracts. San Francisco-Oakland, Calif., Standard Metropolitan Statistical Area*, 268–69; Chu, "Chinatown," 22–23; Nong, "*Heiren fan geli yundong yu ping yuan*" (The black campaign in opposition to segregation, and Ping Yuen), *Jinshan shibao*, June 10, 1963. The census statistics for Chinatown and its surrounding areas starkly illustrate the class gap that existed. In tracts A-14, A-15, and A-16, the average annual income was about $2,200, compared to about $6,000 in the nearby Nob Hill tracts; the median school years completed in A-14 and A-15 was 0.9 years, compared to more than 12 years in Nob Hill.

78. "Housing Body in Heated Meeting," *San Francisco Sun-Reporter*, June 15, 1963; Alison Isenberg, *Downtown America: A History of the Place and the People Who*

Made It (Chicago: University of Chicago Press, 2004), 188–92; Cohen, *A Consumers' Republic*, 212–13.

79. Yeh, "'In the Traditions of China and in the Freedom of America,'"405; Gilbert Woo, *"Gongping Juzhu Ti An"* (Fair Housing Ordinance) in *Hu Jingnan Wenji*, 572. See, for example, Gilbert Woo, *"Heiren Yi Nei Ping Yuan,"* 540; *"Gongping Juzhu Ti An,"* 572–73; *"Heiren de Douzheng"* (The black struggle), in *Hu Jingnan Wenji*, 580–81; Nong, *"Heiren fan geli yundong yu ping yuan,"* 2. See also Philip A. Lum, "The Creation and Demise of San Francisco Chinatown Freedom Schools: One Response to Desegregation," *Amerasia* 5:1 (1978): 62.

80. Testimony of Judge Harry W. Low and Rev. Larry Jack Wong, May 1967, *Hearing Before the United States Commission on Civil Rights* (Washington, D.C.: USGPO, 1967), 200–1; California Fair Employment Practices Commission, *Californians of Japanese, Chinese, and Filipino Ancestry* (San Francisco: Fair Employment Practices Commission, 1965), 12–13; Bureau of the Census, *1960 Census of Population: Population Characteristics of Selected Ethnic Groups in Five Southwestern States* (Washington, D.C.: USGPO, 1968), 16, 24.

81. Bureau of the Census, *1950 Census of Population: Census Tract Statistics, Los Angeles, California and Adjacent Area* (Washington, D.C.: USGPO, 1952), 9–53; idem., *1960 Census of Population: Census Tract Statistics, Los Angeles-Long Beach SMSA* (Washington, D.C.: USGPO, 1962), 576–602; Minnesota Population Center, *National Historical Geographic Information System: Pre-release Version 0.1* (Minneapolis, MN: University of Minnesota 2004); Avila, "Popular Culture in the Age of White Flight," 52; Bureau of the Census, *1960 Census of Population: Population Characteristics of Selected Ethnic Groups in Five Southwestern States*, 24. The census in 1940 and 1950 did not separate Mexican Americans or the "White Population with Spanish Surname." However, both censuses included counts of foreign-born Mexicans, and the 1950 census profiled tracts with more than 250 "Spanish surname" whites. I have used these numbers, estimates of the Mexican American population in 1940, and the published total for the "Spanish surname" population in Los Angeles County in 1950 to calculate estimated dissimilarity and isolation rates for Mexican Americans in 1940 and 1950. To calculate home ownership rates between 1940 and 1960, I have compared statistics for heavily Asian American and heavily African American neighborhoods. The census in 1960 lists homeownership and renter statistics for the "Spanish surname" population.

82. Bureau of the Census, *1960 Census of Population: Population Characteristics of Selected Ethnic Groups in Five Southwestern States*, 24; Sides, *L.A. City Limits*, 176; Robert O. Self, *American Babylon: Race and the Struggle for Postwar Oakland* (Princeton, NJ: Princeton University Press, 2003), 171–72.

83. Bureau of the Census, *1970 Census of Population, Subject Report: Japanese, Chinese, and Filipinos in the United States* (Washington, D.C.: USGPO, 1973), 15, 31, 74, 87, 90; idem., *1970 Census of Population, Subject Report: Negro Population* (Washington, D.C.: USGPO, 1973), 33, 92; idem., *1970 Census of Population, Subject*

Report: Persons of Spanish Surname (Washington, D.C.: USGPO, 1973), 52. Chinese American incomes in California were far below Japanese American incomes in 1970, but the difference was much smaller when overall, rather than just urban, Chinese American incomes were considered. This suggests a marked divide between poorer, often immigrant Chinese Americans living in older urban Chinatowns and wealthier Chinese Americans, many of them professionals, who lived in suburban areas. By 1970, Japanese American and Chinese American average incomes statewide had surpassed black incomes. Japanese American average incomes had also now surpassed Mexican American incomes, while Chinese American average incomes were about equal to Mexican American ones. Japanese Americans in particular had begun to move out of traditional ethnic economic niches, a shift apparent among Chinese Americans in certain age groups as well.

84. Raymond E. Wolfinger and Fred I. Greenstein, "The Repeal of Fair Housing in California: An Analysis of Referendum Voting," *American Political Science Review* 62:3 (September 1968): 759; Bureau of the Census, *1960 Census of Population: Population Characteristics of Selected Ethnic Groups in Five Southwestern States*, 28. Chinese Americans earned less than both Japanese Americans and Hispanics. California Fair Employment Practices Commission, *Californians of Japanese, Chinese, and Filipino Ancestry*, 14, 17; Sides, *L.A. City Limits*, 130.

85. Timothy P. Fong, *The First Suburban Chinatown: The Remaking of Monterey Park, California* (Philadelphia: Temple University Press, 1994), 20–25; Monthly Report, July 15-August 14, 1963, p. 6, file 55, carton 58, NAACP-R1. The report refers to the Southwest Village tract in Torrance tract 6505, where no Asian Americans lived. Still, more than one thousand Asian Americans but fewer than thirty blacks lived in Torrance. By 1970, a number of Asian Americans lived in Southwest Village as well, while the black population of the tract and Torrance as a whole had barely changed.

86. Bureau of the Census, *U.S. Censuses of Population and Housing, 1960. Census Tracts. Los Angeles-Long Beach, Calif. Standard Metropolitan Statistical Area*, 93–95, 101; Sides, *L.A. City Limits*, 101–2; Bureau of the Census, *U.S. Censuses of Population and Housing, 1960. Census Tracts. San Francisco-Oakland, Calif., Standard Metropolitan Statistical Area*, 26–30, 37–39, 58, 60; Council for Civic Unity of San Francisco, "Among These Rights," January–February 1961, p. 1, file 23, carton 75, NAACP-R1; Gilbert Woo, "*Gongping Juzhu Ti An*," 572.

87. Augustus F. Hawkins interview by Clyde Woods, November 18, 1992, pp. 70–72, University of California, Los Angeles Oral History Program, http://content.cdlib.org/xtf/view?docId=hb858011v4&doc.view=frames&chunk.id=div00020&toc.depth=1&toc.id=&brand=oac (accessed May 4, 2007); Wallace Turner, "Rightists in West Fight Housing Act," *New York Times*, May 10, 1964; Sides, *L.A. City Limits*, 168–73; McGirr, *Suburban Warriors*, 185; Nicolaides, *My Blue Heaven*, 308–15.

88. Allen J. Matsuow, *The Unraveling of America: A History of Liberalism in the 1960s* (New York: Harper, 1984), 361–2.

89. Sides, *L.A. City Limits*, 192–93; Bureau of the Census, "Technical Studies: Special Census Survey of the South and East Los Angeles Areas: November 1965," March 23, 1966, 4–5, 14. The census measured population change between 1960 and November 1965, a period of tremendous flux in the area. Even before the riots, white residents were leaving neighboring areas in large numbers, while the factories that provided jobs to residents began to move to outlying parts of the county as well. Some of the working-class Japanese American gardeners and nurserymen who lived in the multiracial neighborhoods of southwestern Los Angeles likely followed their customers out of the city before the riots. But the special census also looked at areas of heavily Mexican American East Los Angeles, where blue-collar Japanese Americans lived in large numbers. There, no comparable population exodus took place; indeed, Asian Americans left East Los Angeles at a much slower pace than either Anglos and blacks.

90. Woo, *"Heiren de Douzheng,"* 580; William Wei, *The Asian American Movement* (Philadelphia: Temple University Press, 1993), 2, 41.

91. Wei, *The Asian American Movement*, 4, 15–28.

EPILOGUE

1. William Pettersen, "Success Story, Japanese American Style," *New York Times Magazine*, January 9, 1966, 21; "Success Story of One Minority Group in U.S.," *U.S. News and World Report*, December 26, 1966, 73; Nancy K. MacLean, *Freedom Is Not Enough: The Opening of the American Workplace* (Cambridge, MA: Harvard University Press/Russell Sage Foundation, 2006), 258–59.

2. Frank H. Wu, *Yellow: Race in America Beyond Black and White* (New York: Basic Books, 2002), 62; Robert G. Lee, *Orientals: Asian Americans in Popular Culture* (Philadelphia: Temple University Press, 1999), 149–50; Sucheng Chan, *Asian Americans: An Interpretive History* (New York: Twayne Publishers, 1991), 167.

3. Raymond E. Wolfinger and Fred I. Greenstein, "The Repeal of Fair Housing in California: An Analysis of Referendum Voting," *American Political Science Review* 62:3 (September 1968): 759.

4. Harold Isaacs, "World Affairs and U. S. Race Relations: A Note on Little Rock," *Public Opinion Quarterly* 22:3 (Autumn 1958): 366.

INDEX

California (*cont.*)
    racial geography, 161, 176, 184–87,
    213; war veterans in, 205; as "white
    man's country," 21, 41, 50, 56, 68,
    112, 130–32
Calvary Hill Cemetery (San Francisco),
    105, 107
Cal-Vet program, 212
Caniff, Milton, 148
Cannon, William, 117–19, 131
Canoga Park, CA, 47
Capra, Frank, 148
Carey, Marie, 138
Carr, Robert K., 83
Carskadon, Harry, 177
Castro Valley, CA, 229
Catholics, 19, 48, 50, 60, 62, 257n29
CCBA. *See* Chinese Consolidated
    Benevolent Association
CCRCE. *See* Citizens Committee to
    Repeal Chinese Exclusion
Central Avenue district (Los Angeles),
    60–61, 63, 161, 166
Central Manufacturing District
    (Los Angeles), 41
Central Pacific Railroad, 17
Chandler, Harry, 39, 43, 119–20
Chandler, Norman, 119–20
Charlie Chan films, 91, 269n10
CHC. *See* Citizens' Housing Council
Chen, Wen-Hui Chung, 187, 261n68,
    294n58
Chen, Yong, 23, 154
Chiang Kai-shek, 140, 148, 149, 194–95,
    198, 222
Chicago, IL, 189, 197; Black Belt,
    245n10
China City (Los Angeles), 80–82
China Weekly, 199
China, 17, 35, 36–37, 90, 91, 97; Amer-
    ican public opinion of, 86, 95, 102–
    4, 113, 147–49, 195; Communist-
    Nationalist civil war, 195, 299n11;

1911 Revolution, 91; and overseas
    Chinese, 97; war with Japan, 6, 86,
    90, 94–96, 98, 104, 112, 126; World
    War II alliance with U.S., 135, 140,
    147, 149, 153, 156–57, 197. *See also*
    People's Republic of China; Repub-
    lic of China
Chinatown (Los Angeles), 74–76, 80–82
Chinatown (San Francisco), 74, 244n8;
    average incomes in, 307n77; Chinese
    American merchants in, 31–33, 89,
    96, 111, 137–38; community lead-
    ers, 88, 189, 198, 200–1, 225, 236;
    community organizations, 24, 31,
    88, 197–201; early history, 11, 21–22;
    housing activism in, 92–94, 98, 100,
    101–2; Japanese American businesses
    in, 86, 88, 96–98, 112–13, 136, 137–
    38, 198, 200; living conditions, 15,
    23, 25, 34, 99, 102, 222; as nation's
    first segregated neighborhood, 5,
    11–13, 221, 222; nightclubs in, 88–
    89, 138; post-1948 movement from,
    185, 225–26; and public health, 23,
    244n8; responses to anti-Chinese
    movement, 20–21; restaurants in, 33,
    89, 138, 154; sex ratio in, 24; spread
    of, 101; symbolism of, 36–37; 68, 97,
    156, 192, 221, 225–27; tourism in, 15,
    31–38, 86, 87–91, 95, 113, 156, 191,
    200, 226, 268n8; white attempts to
    remove, 18, 23–24, 97, 112, 155; white
    property owners, 24, 25, 252n70
Chinatown Beautification Committee,
    91
Chinese American Citizens Alliance
    (CACA), 91, 190–91, 198
Chinese Americans: American-born,
    24–25, 37, 90; average incomes,
    308n83; changing ideas about, 100,
    102–3, 112, 147, 155–56, 192–93; cold
    war repression of, 195, 198–201, 239;
    compared to Japanese Americans,

Japanese Americans (*cont.*)
internment of, 85, 128–30, 132, 135,
136, 137–38, 150, 159, 161, 165, 168,
174, 195, 198–99, 216, 239, 279n37;
and interracial activism, 159; isolation rate of, 245n9, 250n54; loyalty
to U.S., 114, 121–22, 126, 131, 239;
migration to Southern California,
43; military service of, 150, 163–64,
181, 185, 288n13; as neighborhood
"pioneers," 214–15; in nursery business, 129–30, 168–69, 216–17, 227;
and politics, 115, 142, 174–75; population in Los Angeles, 82, 114–15, 161;
postwar property rights of, 183–84;
and public housing, 72, 75, 82–83,
108, 109–10, 123, 124–25, 165, 174;
relationship with African Americans,
108, 111, 173; responses to residential segregation, 56–58, 59; return
from internment camps, 159–74, 180,
214, 290n23; rights of Nisei, 68–69,
85, 98, 114, 125, 127, 131–32, 183–84;
in San Francisco Chinatown, 86,
88, 96–98, 112–13, 136, 137–38, 198;
school segregation, 27, 68, 263n84;
social networks of, 215–16; and social welfare programs, 82–83; and
Southwood-style incidents, 206, 213;
stereotypes of, 169, 239; sympathy
for Japan, 96–98; and urban homes,
3, 5–6, 128–29, 166, 181–84; World
War II resettlement of, 166
Japanese Association of Los Angeles,
56–57
Japanese immigrants, 27, 125, 166; education of, 261n65; ineligibility of
for citizenship, 45–46, 63, 68, 83;
postwar difficulties of, 180, 214; sentiment against, 26, 40; women, 46, 114–
15
Jefferson Park housing development,
114–27, 131–32, 221, 277n16

Jefferson Square area (San Francisco),
105, 110
Jenkins, Percy, 50, 257n34
Jews, 19, 59, 60, 63, 64, 73, 78, 82, 120,
129, 172, 175, 178, 184, 287n3
John Birch Society, 219–20
Johnson, Charles S., 143, 283n29
Johnson, Marilynn, 146
Johnston, David, 218
Jones, Lillian, 78
Judd, Walter, 152

Kaiser Shipyards, 145, 146
Kanno, George, 218, 219
Kashu Realty, 217
Kawai, Kazuo, 64
Kazal, Russell, 20
Kearney, Dennis, 18
Kenney, Clinton, 202
Kenny, Robert, 171, 180–81, 294n64
Keyserling, Leon, 139–40
Kibei, 169
Kido, Saburo, 125–26
Kim, Yin, 179–80, 182–83, 294n58,
295n70, 295n72
King, Cameron, 148
King, Martin Luther, Jr., 220, 225
Kingman, Harry, 291n34
Kingman, Ruth, 291n34
Klein, Christina, 196, 208
Knight, Goodwin, 220
Knowland, William F., 194, 205
Kohn, Robert, 75
Korean Americans, 4, 160, 179–80, 218–
21
Korean War, 195, 196, 198, 199, 200,
203, 211, 239
Kraus, Henry, 287n3
Kropp, Phoebe, 36, 267n31
Kunitsugu, Kango, 162
Kunitsugu, Katsumi, 173, 215
Kuomintang (Chinese Nationalist
Party), 90, 194–95, 198, 199

race science, 45, 132
racial definitions, 241n.2
racial uplift ideology, 57, 259n58
racially restrictive covenants, 6, 26,
30, 55, 60–61, 76, 101, 106, 142–43,
149, 155, 157, 159, 161, 176–83, 184,
187, 188, 190, 238, 248n38, 249n45,
293n53
Radford, Gail, 71–72, 117
Rafu Shimpo (Los Angeles), 83, 114, 118,
124, 278n30
Ramona Gardens public housing project
(Los Angeles), 77, 78, 82–83, 123
Rancho 57 housing development (Los
Angeles), 126
real estate industry, 3, 53–55, 106, 116,
127, 162, 184, 185, 201, 212–13, 217–18,
224, 229
Record, Cy Wilson, 224
Red China. *See* People's Republic of
China
Red Turban Uprising, 17
Red-baiting, 160, 188, 195–96, 201,
214
Reed, Laura, 101, 102
Regan, John, 148–49
rent control, 282n17
Republic of China, 155, 194–95, 196,
199–200, 222
Republican Party, 18, 153, 188
Rhee, Dolly, 219
Richmond, CA, 165
Richmond District (San Francisco), 27,
31, 93, 157; as "second Chinatown,"
229
Riemer, Ruth, 169
Riis, Jacob, 15
Roediger, David, 16
Rollingwood tract (San Pablo), 211
Roosevelt, Eleanor, 98–100, 101–2, 104,
107, 113, 127
Roosevelt, Franklin, 71, 77, 95, 116, 127,
140, 141, 144, 152

Roosevelt, Theodore, 27
Roosevelt, Theodore, Jr., 95
Rose Hill (Los Angeles), 48, 50–51, 52;
description, 257n36
Rose Hill Civic Improvement Associa-
tion, 50–51
Rossi, Angelo, 93–94, 100, 106, 141, 149,
151
Roughing It (Twain), 22
Rowell, Chester, 29
Roybal, Edward R., 185, 188
Ruff, Oscar, 54
Rumford, William Byron, 229
Rumford Fair Housing Act, 229
Russian Hill (San Francisco), 29
Russo-Japanese War (1905), 27, 45

Saiki v Hammock, 260n61
Saint Mary's Park (San Francisco), 89
Salinas, CA, 164
San Bruno, CA, 229
San Diego, CA, 41
San Fernando, CA, 47
San Fernando Valley (Los Angeles), 177,
216, 218
San Francisco Apartment House
Owners' and Managers' Association
28, 57, 110
San Francisco Bay Area: anti-
communism in, 208–9; housing
discrimination, 157, 204; housing
shortages, 141; labor shortages, 144–
45; nonwhite employment, 145; population, 140–41; public housing, 171;
racial geography of, 193, 204, 213,
227–28, 230–31; racial transformation of, 211–13, 227–28; World War II
racial tensions, 146–47
San Francisco Board of Supervisors, 13,
24, 25, 27, 92, 103, 109, 110–11, 139,
152, 189, 244n8
San Francisco Central Council of Civic
Clubs, 30, 110

San Francisco Central Labor Council,
149
San Francisco Chamber of Commerce,
35, 141, 152
San Francisco Chronicle, 34, 101, 112,
142, 152, 153, 187, 191, 219–20
San Francisco Community Chest, 86, 99
San Francisco Council for Civic Unity,
151, 153, 154, 178–79, 189–91, 212
San Francisco Examiner, 170
San Francisco Housing Authority, 93–
94, 98, 104, 139, 141; neighborhood
opposition to projects, 93–94, 105,
107, 110; segregation and "neighbor-
hood pattern," 106–11, 113, 143–44,
154, 189–93, 224–27
San Francisco Housing Commission,
94, 98, 99, 106, 225–27
San Francisco Junior Chamber of
Commerce (Jaycees), 100–2, 113,
272n40
San Francisco Municipal Railway, 165
San Francisco News, 99
San Francisco peninsula, 177
San Francisco Real Estate Board, 28, 57,
224
San Francisco Reporter, 154
San Francisco Spokesman, 108
San Francisco: anti-Nisei activity, 164–
65; Depression in, 77, 86; earthquake
of 1906, 18, 24, 28–29, 33, 253n1;
European immigrants in, 19, 29;
labor movement in, 5, 15, 18–19,
27, 30, 45, 47, 77, 108, 145, 149;
1939 World's Fair, 91; population
changes, 154; racial geography and
housing patterns of, 21, 29–31, 105,
107, 108, 110–11, 135, 141–43, 154, 161,
171, 178–79, 184, 191, 204, 221, 229,
245n9
San Gabriel (Los Angeles), 124
San Gabriel Wash (Los Angeles), 116
San Jose, CA, 164, 206, 207

San Jose Mercury, 207
San Jose News, 206
San Leandro, CA, 207, 208, 213, 229
San Marino, CA, 167
San Mateo, CA, 213
Sanders, Sue, 25
Santa Ana Register, 219
Sasaki, Tom, 173
Sato, J., 59
Schmitz, Eugene, 21
School of Social Studies (San Francisco),
99–100, 272n36
school segregation, 26, 28, 160
second Ku Klux Klan, 60
Sei Fujii v. California, 183
SERA. *See* State Emergency Relief
Administration
SFHA. *See* San Francisco Housing
Authority
Shah, Nayan, 20, 89, 103, 244n8
Shankman, Arnold, 154, 286n56
Shaw, Frank, 71, 72, 75
Shelley v. Kraemer, 161, 182–83, 184–85,
201, 295n70
Shelley, Jack, 171, 291n34
Sheng, Sing, 194, 201–3, 204, 208, 211
Sherry, Michael S., 188
Shibusawa, Naoko, 221
Shigekuni, Tsueno, 179–80
shipbuilding, 138, 144–46
Shoong, Joe, 284n34
Shortridge, Samuel, 48
Sides, Josh, 44, 228–29
Silver Terrace (San Francisco), 178–79
Simons, Bill, 156
slavery, 16
slum clearance programs, 71–75
Small, Sidney Herschel, 89
Social Security Act of 1935, 84; Asian
immigrant ineligibility for programs,
214
social welfare state, 2–3; racially discrim-
inatory nature of, 3, 70, 76, 83–85,